Other Minds

Is there a problem about other minds? If so, what is it? Exploration of this problem raises many questions that lie at the intersection of the philosophy of the mind, epistemology and metaphysics.

Other Minds is a compelling investigation of the issues surrounding this problem. Anita Avramides clarifies the nature of the problem and situates the responses given by major philosophers in relation to their general philosophy. Part One looks at how questions concerning our knowledge of the mind of another may be considered as having their origins in the history of philosophy. The views of the Ancient Sceptics through to Descartes are explored, as well as those of post-Cartesian philosophers such as Malebranche, Locke and Berkeley. Part Two continues this historical overview by looking at the work of two philosophers – Reid and Wittgenstein – who raise questions concerning other minds which arise from within the Cartesian philosophy. In Part Three, an alternative to the Cartesian way of thinking about the mind is proposed and defended – with reference to the work of contemporary philosophers such as P. F. Strawson and Donald Davidson. Challenges to this proposal from Thomas Nagel, John Searle and Galen Strawson are considered and rejected. Key features of this book include its rejection of the idea that the problem of other minds is an epistemological one, and its detailed discussion of the work of Malebranche and Reid, whose influence on this problem has not been thoroughly explored until now.

Other Minds provides a clear and accessible introduction to one of the most important problems in philosophy. It will prove invaluable to students of philosophy at all levels.

Anita Avramides is The Southover Manor Trust Fellow in Philosophy at St Hilda's College, University of Oxford. She is the author of *Meaning and Mind* (1989) and the editor of *Women of Ideas* (1995).

The Problems of Philosophy

Editors: Tim Crane and Jonathan Wolff, *University College London*

This series addresses the central problems of philosophy. Each book gives a fresh account of a particular philosophical theme by offering two perspectives on the subject: the historical context and the author's own distinctive and original contribution. The books are written to be accessible to students of philosophy and related disciplines, while taking the debate to a new level.

Recently published:

Other Minds

Anita Avramides

London and New York

First published 2001
by Routledge
2 Park Square, Milton Park, Abingdon, Oxon, OX14 4RN

Simultaneously published in the USA and Canada
by Routledge
270 Madison Ave, New York NY 10016

Routledge is an imprint of the Taylor & Francis Group

Transferred to Digital Printing 2005

Typeset in Times by M Rules

British Library Cataloguing in Publication Data
A catalogue record for this book is available from the British
Library

Library of Congress Cataloging in Publication Data
Avramides, Anita
Other Minds / Anita Avramides.
p. cm. – (Problems of philosophy)
Includes bibliographical references and index.
1. Other minds (Theory of knowledge) I. Title. II. Problems of
philosophy (Routledge (Firm))
BD213. A97 2000
121'.2–dc21   00-055314

ISBN 0–415–03336–5 (hbk)
ISBN 0–415–24193–6 (pbk)

*For Anne
and Aidan*

Contents

Preface

When, over a decade ago, Routledge asked me to contribute to a new series on the problems of philosophy, I looked at the list of the topics proposed, but did not really want to write on any of them. Instead I asked if I could write a book about other minds, a topic I happened to be thinking about at the time. My earliest philosophical interests had lain in the relationship between mind and meaning, but I soon found myself wondering if the key to understanding this was to be found in understanding the relationship of one mind to another. My interest in writing on this topic deepened when I began to search for the history of the problem – something I had to do if I was to contribute a book to this series. I began by asking the question: who first raised the 'problem of other minds' as a problem? My expectation that Descartes' work would be a rich source was confounded; the topic is virtually ignored in his work. I then turned to the Greeks, considering that, as the problem of other minds is often taken to be an epistemo-logical one, I would find what I was looking for in the work of the ancient Greek sceptics. Again I was surprised; there was no mention in their work of any problem about the mind of another. As I began to read around the topic, I was further struck by the fact that some philosophers considered the problem of other minds to be one of the utmost importance, while others looked on it as one of secondary or indeed negligible interest. I wanted to understand why this was so, and to see what a philosopher's attitude to the problem could reveal about his general philosophical position. So I am very grateful that my proposal to contribute a book on other minds to this series was accepted.

Over the years that I have been working on this book, I have alter-nated between feeling embarrassed to be working on this topic, because it was so unfashionable, and feeling excited by what I was finding. As I began to get further into my work, I found myself drawn to a way of thinking about the problem of other minds that is at odds with what has come, in some circles at least, to be the dominant way of thinking about the mind. Indeed, I began to believe that a failure to take the problem seriously was a hallmark of a misguided approach to thinking about the mind. Whether or not one agrees with this, I hope I have provided – especially for the student of philosophy – a discussion that helps to clarify both the nature of the problem of other minds and where the answers philosophers have given to it stand in relation to their general philosophical position.

My approach is largely historical. But, as the history of this topic is so elusive, what I have produced has necessarily to be taken as one particular interpretation of its history. I attempt to carry through my interpretation from ancient times until today. I would like to think that what I have done may have some merit both from a scholarly and from a philosophical perspective, but I am painfully aware of my lack of expertise in the many areas of scholarship that I have broached. It is my hope that my work on the early history of the problem will prove of interest to historians of philosophy, who may be stimulated by what I say to investigate the work of these earlier philosophers on this issue further.

I should also say at the outset that I have looked at this problem from the perspective of standard analytic philosophy. To many this will be a serious shortcoming, as there is much interesting writing on this topic in the work of philosophers working outside analytic philosophy. I did at one point believe I could include the work of philosophers such as Husserl, Max Scheler, Heidegger, and Merleau-Ponty, but I soon realized that I could not do their work justice within the scope of a book such as this. For the same reason I have chosen in the historical sections of the book to concentrate on the work of a few, as I saw them representative, philosophers, rather than make cursory mention of every philosopher who has *something* to say on the topic.

Acknowledgements

Apart from the readers of the manuscript for the press, no one has read the manuscript in its entirety. But there are many people I need to thank for reading various chapters of this book, discussing the issues involved and pointing out some of my errors.

First of all, I want to thank Myles Burnyeat whose work it was that guided me in my thinking about the ancient Greek sceptics. In particular, his important paper 'Idealism and Greek philosophy: what Descartes saw and Berkeley missed' gave me the germ of the idea for the entire book. Myles read a very early paper that I wrote on this topic, and his interest in the project at an early stage helped me to believe it was possible. The chapter on Descartes was first read by Katherine Morris. I was encouraged by her reaction, as I admire her own work on Descartes for its freshness and boldness. Michael Ayers also read this chapter at an early stage and caught a few errors. I would also like to thank John Cottingham for his comments on a version of this chapter read as a paper at the University of Reading some years ago. John was critical of my work, and I found his criticism illuminating. Michael Frede and Christopher Kirwan both read my brief comments on St Augustine. As it is particularly daunting to try to extract a single point from the work of so complex a thinker, I am most grateful to both of them for looking over what I have written here. I would also like to thank Michael Frede for providing me with his own translation of a passage from Augustine. In the light of his other commitments, it was very kind of Ralph Walker to find time to read and comment on the chapter on Malebranche. I am grateful to him for this. Plinio Smith read several of the early chapters, and I thank him for many stimulating discussions – especially on the work of Malebranche and Arnaud.

I found the chapter on Locke particularly difficult to write. Even when I thought I had understood what Locke has to say on this topic,

I found that I had made many errors. I am most grateful to Michael
Ayers for pointing out so many of them. Tom Stoneham also read this
chapter. I must thank him for stimulating discussions of both this
chapter and the chapter on Berkeley. Tom's knowledge of the history
of philosophy, in combination with his wide range of interests across
philosophical topics, make discussions with him a real pleasure. I
must also thank Paul Snowdon for reading the chapter on Berkeley
and for an interesting and helpful discussion of its topics. Roger
Teichmann also read this chapter – as well as the one on
Wittgenstein – and we had some interesting discussions based on
them. The chapter on Reid was read by Dan Robinson, whose enthu-
siasm for and knowledge of Reid's work made him the perfect person
to read it. I thank him for discussing the chapter with me, and for
pointing up my errors. I also thank him for his enthusiastic support of
my work. Dan Isaacson read and commented upon the brief section on
the work of Carnap and Schlick. I am convinced from my discussion
with him, as well as from my own study, that there is much more work
to be done here exploring the way this topic developed around this
time. Galen Strawson and I have discussed the topic from time to
time, but remain firmly opposed in our outlooks. Many people discussed the topic with me in a general way, among them Brian Klug
and Mark Rowe.

The chapter on Wittgenstein proved the most daunting of all.
Clearly his work must have an important place in any discussion of
this topic, yet the complexity of his thinking, combined with the
immense influence it has had, makes the task of presenting it seem
impossibly difficult. I read widely, both in his work and among the
secondary texts. In the end the person whose work proved most helpful was that of Marie McGinn. Marie's guide to Wittgenstein's
Philosophical Investigations proved invaluable. Furthermore, her own
work on Wittgenstein on the topic of other minds is a most subtle and
sensitive reading of the text. It is hard to read her work and not be persuaded that she has truly understood this work. My own chapter on
Wittgenstein is profoundly influenced by Marie's reading of his work,
as well as by conversations with her. I thank her for her understanding,
and for her friendship and support over the many years that this book
was written.

The last chapters of the book have had audiences, rather than readers. Over the years I have read them at various stages of their
development in many places, including the Universities of Liverpool,
York, Sheffield, Sussex, Kent, Hertfordshire and Glasgow, St
Andrew's University, the University of Lund and my own university.

I would also like to thank Tim Crane for advice and comments on much of the manuscript, and Adrian Moore for discussions on all aspects of the work over the many years of its writing. I must also acknowledge the help of Jo Cartmell, for her care and attention to the final manuscript.

Finally, I must also express my gratitude to the AHRB for a sabbatical term, matched by sabbatical terms from the University of Oxford and St Hilda's College. Without this sustained research time I would not have been able to complete the book. I would like to thank the fellowship of St Hilda's for providing such a supportive College environment for research. I would also like to thank Oxford University Press Inc. for their kind permission to reprint from *The View From Nowhere*, by Thomas Nagel, © 1986 Thomas Nagel.

Overview

PHILOSOPHY AND THE PROBLEM OF OTHER MINDS

What sort of problem is the problem of other minds? One very general response to this question is the following: The problem of other minds is a distinctively *philosophical* problem. This is not to deny that non-philosophers occasionally find themselves faced with a problem about other minds. For the non-philosopher the problem can take the form, How do I know if a computer or other complex machine has a mind?; or, How do we know whether non-human animals have minds?; or even, perhaps, How do we know if a new-born baby has a mind? Sometimes the problem can take the form of wondering whether or not, assuming that another does have a mind, we can know just *what* the other is thinking. So, for example, can I know how you feel when you are depressed, or can I know that you see the same colour that I do when you look at the sky on a sunny day? All of these are questions asked by the philosopher and non-philosopher alike; but to these questions the philosopher adds another: How do I know if there are *any* minds besides my own? This is a distinctively *philosophical* question. That we live in the world and with other people is not something we ordinarily question. But the philosopher is perplexed even by what even he himself takes for granted in his life away from his desk (or armchair). Where the non-philosopher assumes a community of minds who share a common world and then is struck by the question whether this community extends beyond the human sphere, the philosopher is struck by the possibility that even this human community is an illusion.

The philosopher's question is often taken by the non-philosopher to amount to either an oddity or an absurdity. A certain impatience is often voiced when the philosopher tries to raise this question or questions like it. Dr Johnson is reported to have shown just such impatience when faced with a philosophical scepticism about the existence of the external world. It is claimed that in response to Bishop Berkeley's idealism Dr Johnson kicked a stone and said, 'I refute it [Berkeley's idealism] thus!' A similar response to a scepticism about other minds can be envisaged. The analogue to Dr Johnson's act of kicking a stone might be the act of speaking to another person, or reaching out to help him when he is injured. Yet, as we have seen, even the non-philosopher can be struck by questions about machines, non-human animals, and new-borns. Even the non-philosopher can see the point of wondering if your depression is really like mine, or if you and I have the same colour experience when we look at the sky. And from these questions it can appear not to be such a big step to the philosopher's question: Why do I take it that another experiences anything at all?

At this point it may seem as though we can give a more specific response to my opening question. That response would be: the problem of other minds is a problem about how we know things, or how we can justify certain of our beliefs; that is to say, it is an *epistemological* problem. Thus, one person might claim to believe that her cat feels a certain way or believes certain things, and another might question how she knows this. Or one person might be quite sure that machines do not have a mind while another may disagree; how can we know which is right? If we do say that the problem is an epistemological one, then it looks as if no firm line can be drawn between philosophical and non-philosophical questions here. The connection would be this: The person who is asked to justify her belief that her cat has a mind will very soon find herself asking how she knows that other *human beings* have minds. And, similarly, the person who denies minds to computers may soon find herself wondering why she is so sure there are *any* other minds. We soon find ourselves faced with the philosophical question, How do I know that there are any minds other than my own? In this way the non-philosopher can be drawn into asking the philosopher's question. Yet, despite the seeming naturalness of it, there is an oddity about the philosopher's question.

There is another, more philosophical, way of arriving at this quite general question concerning other minds. Philosophers will often begin by reflecting upon how things are from their own, first-person, perspective. From this perspective there is an assurance about one's own mind that makes the attribution of minds apart from this perspective hard to justify. In other words, given the way I know that I have a mind it can seem to be a real problem how I can know there are any minds that are not mine. Philosophers have characterized this feature of our mental lives in various ways. It is sometimes said that the content of one's own mental life is *immediate* or *transparent* to one in the way the content of another's mental life is not. Connected with this it is sometimes said that I have a certain *privileged access* to my own mental life or that I have a certain *authority* with respect to what I am thinking or feeling, and that this privileged access or authority does not extend to the mental life of anyone else. The danger with beginning to think about the mind by reflecting on one's own mind is that one may end up unable to justify any move beyond this to any other mind. Reflection on the special nature of the first-person perspective may be thought to approach a position that philosophers refer to as 'solipsism'. Solipsism in its most radical form is a position that rejects all but what is present to the consciousness of an individual. One of the things ruled out by solipsism is the existence of other minds (the other things that are ruled out are other, non-mental, things and other, non-present, times). Solipsism is a distinctively philosophical position, but, as we have seen, there may be non-philosophical as well as philosophical ways of finding oneself in this position. I take it that solipsism is a position to be avoided. The question is whether one is in a position to avoid it if one insists on beginning to think about the mind from the first-person perspective.

I shall have a great deal to say about what I have called the philosophical way of thinking about the mind. I shall suggest that there are deep mistakes involved in taking reflection on one's own mind as one's starting point for thinking about the mind more generally. Because of these mistakes, the problem one encounters about other minds may look to be insoluble. One can twist and turn – make this philosophical move or that – but the possibility of one's aloneness in the universe remains. At this point the non-philosopher may once again grow impatient: of course there are minds other than my own; my relationships with others are living proof of this. But the philosopher may press his point: if a mind is such that I can be in doubt whether some non-human animals or machines have one, how can you be so sure that other human beings have one? Notice that the philosopher has now turned us away from our original epistemological question and is asking us to consider what a mind is. Perhaps the question we ought to be asking is not, How do I know whether others (other human animals, non-human animals or machines) have minds?, but rather, What is a mind such that we can understand that others as well as myself can be said to have a mind?

The method of approaching the problem of other minds from this perspective, and of focusing on the question, What is a mind?, will evoke approval from many who will otherwise disapprove of what I will have to say. One way of crystallizing differences here is this: in the approach I shall be pursuing, the recognition of one mind by another will play an essential role in the characterization of what a mind is; according to my opponent's approach we need first to establish what a mind is before we consider whether or not there are any other minds. On the approach I shall be recommending, the way we understand what a mind is leaves no room for sceptical questions about whether or not other minds exist; that they exist is part of the starting point. On my opponent's approach, I can understand what a mind is without reference to the existence of any mind other than my own; once I understand in this way what a mind is, I must then set about giving my reasons for thinking that there are *other* minds. My opponent takes it to be a relatively straightforward matter to say why we think that there are other minds. One fairly standard proposal here is to argue from analogy to the existence of other minds.[1]

To both my opponent and me, then, the problem about other minds – identified as an epistemological problem – receives a fairly simple reply. However for me the reply is, as it were, built into our conception of mind at the outset, while for my opponent other minds are an addition – something that could have been left out of the picture.

This leads me to consider once again the question with which I began, What is the problem of other minds? Although I do not want to deny that there is a problem about our knowledge of the mind of another, I do not believe that the problem is *au fond* an epistemological one. This is implicit in the way I have introduced the issue. Although we may begin with what looks like an epistemological problem about our knowledge of the existence of other minds, we end up with a question about what the mind is. This latter question, I shall argue, is the more fundamental; the epistemological question is not the fundamental one. Indeed, I shall suggest that the epistemological problem needs to be seen in context, and its motivation properly understood. We need to ask *why* our knowledge here strikes us as problematic in the first place. To this end I shall look at the way in which the epistemological issue may be thought to have arisen in the history of philosophy. I shall argue that when we look at the problem historically we can see that the epistemological problem of other minds has its roots in certain more basic issues.

THE HISTORY OF THE PROBLEM

Philosophers are all familiar with the problem of other minds. The history of the problem, however, is not well researched. There appears to have been an 'explosion' of interest in the problem around the middle of the twentieth century, but it is not at all obvious what gave rise to this interest. Unlike many philosophical issues, this is not one for which it is easy to find a clear historical line. One paper from this period which finds its way without fail on to undergraduate reading lists for this topic is Norman Malcolm's 'Knowledge of other minds'.[2] Malcolm's paper begins with an excerpt from J. S. Mill's *An Examination of Sir William Hamilton's Philosophy*. In this work Mill raises the question, How do I know that others are sentient, have sensations and thoughts – in brief, have minds? According to Malcolm, the answer Mill gives to this question is that we conclude that there are other minds by following a line of reasoning that has come to be known as the argument from analogy. Mill writes,

> I conclude that other human beings have feelings like me, because, first, they have bodies like me, which I know, in my own case, to be the antecedent condition of feelings; and because, secondly, they exhibit the acts, and other outward signs, which in my own case I know by experience to be caused by feelings.[3]

Mill's statement in response to this epistemological problem of other minds is often taken to be the *locus classicus* for the argument from analogy. It bears all the important hallmarks we have come to associate with that argument: (a) an assurance that I have a mind; (b) the observation that there is a connection between my mind and the behaviour I exhibit; and (c) the observation of a similar sort of behaviour (the 'outward signs') in others. From these observations Mill concludes that the others we observe must also have a series of thoughts and feelings that we call 'mind'.[4] Most discussions of the problem do not look any further back than Mill. Yet Mill must have been responding to some issue in offering this argument. In fact Mill was responding to the work of the eighteenth century philosopher Thomas Reid.[5] Reid's work contains an attack on a philosophical tradition that, as he see it, begins with the philosophy of René Descartes and culminates in the idealism of Bishop Berkeley and the scepticism of David Hume. The underlying problem Reid finds in this tradition is the scepticism it threatens – scepticism about other intelligent beings as well as about the world of bodies.

As Reid sees it, the problem is that these philosophers begin by taking the arguments of the sceptic altogether too seriously. In order to reply to the sceptic they then attempt to re-build our knowledge on the slender foundation of a consciousness of a single existence. From this foundation we are meant to show that we can have reason to believe in, among other things, the existence of a world of bodies existing independent of us and other intelligent beings. What worries Reid is that this foundation is altogether *too* slender, and that the reasons we offer for believing in the existence of things and minds outside ourselves may not prove strong enough to repel the sceptic. Reid's greatest concern is the asymmetry which philosophers introduce between the assurance I have with respect to my own mind and the insecurity that follows from this with respect to our knowledge of an independent world of bodies and other intelligent beings. Contrary to this tradition in philosophy, Reid insists that there is a symmetry in our knowledge here. We can avoid scepticism, according to Reid, if we take the deliverances of consciousness to be on a par with the deliverances of perception.

In many respects, Mill's own work can be seen to be part of the philosophical tradition that Reid rejects. Like Berkeley and Hume before him, Mill attempts to explain our belief in the existence of both matter and our own mind on the basis of experience. In the place of Berkeley's God, Mill relies on the mind's capacity for association and expectation. Mill rightly sees Reid as opposed to any such philosophical project. Mill quotes Reid as arguing that,

> If . . . my mind is a series of feelings, or, as it has been called, a thread of consciousness . . . what evidence have I (it is asked) of the existence of my fellow creatures? . . .
> Dr. Reid unhesitatingly answers, None. If the doctrine is true, I am alone in the universe.

Mill then continues and replies:

> I hold this to be one of Reid's most palpable mistakes. Whatever evidence . . . there is on the ordinary theory [for my fellow creatures], exactly that same evidence is there on this. . . . There is nothing in that doctrine to prevent my conceiving, and believing, that there are other successions of feelings besides those of which I am conscious, and that these are as real as my own.[6]

Indeed, Mill goes so far as to claim that 'I do not believe that the real externality to us of anything, *except other minds*, is capable of proof' (my emphasis).[7]

Mill's *is* an interesting text to read in connection with the issue of other minds. However, most of this interest is dissipated when that work is taken out of context. Mill's work here is important largely because it is written in reaction to Reid's. And, in my opinion, Reid's work is important because it is the first recognition that there might be a deep and difficult problem in connection with other minds. It is Reid who looks at an entire tradition in philosophy – one that he takes to begin with Descartes and to culminate in Berkeley and Hume – and argues that the weaknesses in that tradition are manifest in the conclusions that have to be drawn concerning our knowledge of, *inter alia*, the existence of our fellow beings. Reid takes this problem to be most manifest in the system of Bishop Berkeley. According to Reid, Berkeley is unable to avoid solipsism; in Berkeley's system ordinary human relations and interactions contract to nothing. About Berkeley's system Reid writes:

> There is one uncomfortable consequence of his [Berkeley's] system which he seems not to have attended to, and from which it will be found difficult, if at all possible, to guard it.
>
> The consequence I mean is this, that, although it leaves us sufficient evidence of a supreme intelligent Mind, it seems to take away all the evidence we have of other intelligent beings like ourselves. What I call a father, a brother, or a friend, is only a parcel of my own mind; . . . I am left alone, as the only creature of God in the universe, in that forlorn state of *Egoism* into which it is said some of the disciples of Descartes were brought by his philosophy.[8]

Contrary to this Reid espouses a system that accepts as one of its first principles that 'there is life and intelligence in our fellow-men with whom we converse'.[9] What is important here is that Reid does not say that we reason to the conclusion that there are other intelligent beings because we converse with them; rather, it is a natural conviction that there are other intelligent beings and we converse with them. It is the starting point to which Reid believes we must pay attention. It is only if we get this right that we can avoid the kind of problems concerning others that Reid takes Berkeley to have encountered.

It is the starting point that philosophers operating in the Cartesian tradition get wrong. And when we start in the wrong place, the defect in our system is most evident when we consider that system's conclusions concerning our fellow men. I shall suggest that Reid is the first philosopher to notice this. In Part One I shall, like Reid, trace the problem back to its roots in Descartes' philosophy. I shall argue that Descartes put in place a philosophical framework that nurtures a deep and difficult problem about other intelligent beings. This problem, however, remains largely unrecognized in the history of philosophy. Unrecognized, that is, until Reid. But it is not at all clear that – for all that he clearly identified a problem here – Reid succeeded in correctly locating the source of that problem. I shall argue that Reid failed to locate the source of that problem deep enough in the Cartesian tradition.

What Reid failed to notice is that the problem of other minds is not, at its root, an epistemological one. The epistemological question can be seen to presuppose a certain, quite general, conception of mind. But it is a real question whether we can be said to have such a general conception of mind. Mill writes in one place that 'there is nothing in [my] doctrine to prevent my conceiving . . . that there are other successions of feelings besides those of which I am conscious'.[10] It is here that Mill is in error, or so I shall argue. Mill, like many before and after him, takes it that I come by my concept of mind from reflection on, or experience of, my own mind. From this starting point, however, it is not at all clear that it *is* possible to conceive of others like myself. The argument from analogy (or any other form of argument to the existence of another mind) begins with a steadfast assurance that I have a mind, and then reasons from there to the conclusion that there exist minds in others. But in order to raise the question about other minds to which this argument purports to give an answer, we must assume that we do have a quite general conception of mind: a conception that applies to others as well as myself. It is not at all clear that philosophers working in the Cartesian tradition are entitled to assume that we do have such a conception of mind. This question is particularly pressing if, like so many working within this tradition, one takes it that I come by my conception of mind by reflecting on my own mind. Of course our conception of mind *is* entirely general; the question we need to consider is how we are to understand the generality that our concept undoubtedly has. Insofar as philosophers whose work I examine in Part One have paid attention to this question, it is hard to see that they can give an adequate answer to it.

On our conception of mind there is nothing in Reid's work. Indeed, as the philosophical waters closed over Reid's work, the idea of there being any deep and difficult problem about other minds was lost. For some decades philosophers wrote, once again, as though other minds presented a challenge to philosophy that could be met by some form of reasoning – whether that be by analogy or some other (similar) form.[11] I want to suggest that the second figure in the history of analytic philosophy to find the issue of other minds problematic in a

deep and perplexing way is Ludwig Wittgenstein.[12] It could be said
that, like Reid, Wittgenstein found the problem he identified here to be
symptomatic of an error in a certain way of doing philosophy. Solving
the problem would not be a matter of making a new move in an
already established framework. The problem forces us to make a fundamental reassessment of the framework.[13] While both Reid and
Wittgenstein are united in their belief that there is a problem in the
Cartesian tradition that threatens difficulties over other minds,
Wittgenstein goes further than Reid in his diagnosis of the problem.
Indeed, while Reid is explicit that the problem is endemic to Cartesian
philosophy, Wittgenstein takes the problem to be endemic to a certain
way of thinking about the mind – a way of thinking to which we are
all susceptible. What Wittgenstein asks us to consider is our very conception of mind. It is not just that we have a natural commitment
both to our own and other minds (on this Wittgenstein and Reid would
agree); rather, Wittgenstein asks us to re-assess our conception of that
to which we have this natural commitment. It is in doing this that
Wittgenstein's work turns us away from epistemological questions, to
conceptual ones.

That Descartes' work gives rise to a problem about other minds
will not excite much disagreement. But it is not often considered just
what the problem is that his work gives rise to here. Indeed, philosophers are not even agreed whether there is a problem at all. It is not
uncommon to find philosophers writing of the 'so-called problem' of
other minds, indicating that they do not agree that there is any deep or
difficult problem that needs to be addressed. However, philosophers
who may agree that there is no deep or difficult problem, may differ
radically in their reasons for saying this. Let me now explain two
very different reasons that philosophers may have for saying that
there is no real problem. I shall begin by considering those philosophers whose work can be said to lie within what I have been calling
the 'Cartesian tradition' – I take this to include not only Descartes and
those who follow his work quite closely, but also those who reject
much of that work but continue to accept the conception of a subject
in relation to her world that Descartes set in place. (For a detailed
explanation of what is involved in this framework see Chapters I and
II.) I shall take it that the work of the philosophers that I consider in
Chapters II–V – that is, Descartes, Malebranche, Arnaud, Locke and
Berkeley – all lies squarely in this tradition. It is an interesting fact
that there is no evidence in the work of any of these philosophers to
indicate that they find anything particularly problematic about other
minds. Each of these philosophers acknowledges that I know my own

mind immediately and can have the highest degree (or most secure form) of knowledge only of my own mind. In most cases, it is also explicitly acknowledged that I cannot know any other mind in this immediate way and that my knowledge of another mind cannot be as secure as that of my own mind. This, then, leaves us with the question, how do I come by my knowledge of *another* mind? It is clear that Descartes' own work leaves us with this question, but it is interesting to note that Descartes himself does not make much of this issue.[14] Moreover, it is not entirely clear how, had Descartes paid more attention to this issue, he would have answered this question – although in Chapter II I do offer an interpretation of certain passages in his work that may be thought to indicate how he might have answered the question. It is only when we turn to the work of Nicolas Malebranche that we find a philosopher who explicitly acknowledges the need to say how I come by my knowledge of another mind. While Descartes concentrates on the question of our knowledge of the external world, Malebranche breaks up our knowledge into four different kinds and explains each in turn: our knowledge of God, of our own mind, of bodies, and of other men's minds. Furthermore, Malebranche clearly differentiates questions about our knowledge of the existence of another mind from those relating to our knowledge of what this other mind is thinking and feeling. Because of his attention to the many questions that arise here, Malebranche's work deserves attention in any study of this kind.

Also worthy of attention is what John Locke has to say on these matters. Locke is a philosopher well known to the student of philosophy, although what he has to say about other minds is much less well known. Locke is clear about our reasons for believing in the existence of minds in creatures other than human beings, in beings who have been separated from bodies (e.g. angels), and in other men. Locke is also clear that our reason in each of these cases does not provide us with knowledge of the existence of other minds; of other minds we must rest content with what Locke calls *opinion* (see Chapter IV for a discussion of Locke's distinction between knowledge and opinion). The final philosopher whose work I consider in some depth in Part One is Bishop Berkeley. It is arguable that, although Malebranche and Locke have something to say about our knowledge of other minds, this issue is not central to their concerns. The same cannot be argued of Berkeley's work. The question of our knowledge of another mind or spirit is central to Berkeley's concern. The reason for this is that, as Berkeley denies the existence of material substance, the cause of my ideas is held to be spirit; and, as my ideas are not entirely within my control, their cause is taken by Berkeley to be some *other* mind or spirit. In the case of my ideas of the movements of another body, the cause is held to be another finite spirit like myself. As we have already seen, however, not all philosophers have been convinced that Berkeley has given adequate reason to believe in the existence of other finite spirits. Whether or not his argument is successful, what is interesting to note at this point is that Berkeley – like Locke and Malebranche (and to some extent Descartes) before him – thinks that any questions that may be thought to arise in his system concerning our knowledge of (or opinion concerning) the mind of another can receive an adequate response. None of these philosophers sees anything particularly problematic about the questions raised within their system of philosophy concerning the minds of others. Even more notable is the fact that each of these philosophers is clear that the only questions that do arise with respect to other minds have to do with our *knowledge* (or opinion) – questions about our knowledge of the existence of minds in other men, other animals, and incorporeal beings, as well as questions concerning our capacity to know just what another mind is thinking and feeling. So there is an acknowledgement that there are certain epistemological issues that must be addressed, and each of these philosophers addresses these issues in his own way, as I show below in Part One. What these philosophers – and any philosopher whose work follows that of these philosophers – would reject is the suggestion that there is anything particularly problematic about other minds. At best they would accept that there is a problem in the sense that there is an issue concerning other minds that their system needs to address. What these philosophers would most strenuously deny is that there is an *outstanding* problem about others – a problem that their system cannot adequately address. A rejection of any outstanding or difficult problem about other minds is not confined to philosophers working in the seventeenth and eighteenth centuries. There are many philosophers working today who hold that there is nothing particularly problematic here; the only issue is the (relatively easily) addressed one of explaining how it is that we know that others have minds. When these philosophers consider the arguments of their opponents, they are likely to refer to the 'so-called problem' of other minds in order to distance themselves from it – to indicate that, as far as they are concerned, there is no serious problem here.

Let me now turn to philosophers who give a very different reason for dismissing the problem. I shall label these philosophers 'anti-Cartesians' because they all reject the philosophical framework that Descartes put in place. I have already mentioned two philosophers who, for somewhat different reasons, can be taken to be anti-Cartesians: Reid and Wittgenstein. In Part Three, I shall introduce some others. These anti-Cartesian philosophers are also liable to write of the 'so-called problem' of other minds, or to reject the idea that there really is anything particularly problematic here. This is because these philosophers hold that, if one rejects the Cartesian framework, it is possible to put in its place a philosophical system (or approach) within which no such problem or issue arises. Furthermore, anti-Cartesians hold that one *must* reject this Cartesian framework if one is to avoid a serious problem concerning the mind of another. They argue that Cartesians run into insuperable difficulties when they attempt to show how we in fact come by our knowledge of other minds. Mill's proof – as well as other (similarly-styled) proofs – are argued to be deeply flawed. If, however, one abandons the Cartesian framework and adopts an alternative philosophical approach, one can avoid these problems. On the alternative approach other minds are part of the starting point in much the way my mind is the starting point of the Cartesian way of thinking.[15]

Thus we can see that philosophers can have very different reasons for agreeing that there is no real problem of other minds. Looked at in one way, we might say that *no* philosopher is doubtful about the exis-tence of other minds, and no philosopher believes that his philosophical system harbours a deep or difficult problem in this area. The clearest case of a reference to a real problem (or where philoso-phers are content to drop the inverted commas around the word 'problem' when discussing things here) is when the anti-Cartesian refers to those working in the Cartesian tradition. From the anti-Cartesian's point of view, the Cartesian most definitely has a problem – a deep and difficult problem – about other minds. Although Cartesians may believe that they can accommodate others in their philosophical system in a fairly straightforward manner, the anti-Cartesian argues that the real problem has been overlooked. Roughly speaking, insofar as Cartesians insist on taking the issue to be an epistemological one, they will not see where the real problem lies. Strictly speaking, then, a problem over other minds (no inverted commas) is only something which the anti-Cartesian accuses the Cartesian framework of harbouring.

It is because of this division between those who refuse to acknowl-edge any real problem in their system and those who find a deep and difficult problem in a certain approach to philosophical issues that I have chosen to break up my discussion of the history of topic into two parts: Chapter I aside, Part One is largely concerned with the various proposals about how we come to know about the existence of other minds that one finds in the work of philosophers operating within a Cartesian framework; Part Two looks at two somewhat different criticisms of that framework and two alternative ways of approaching philosophical issues. Chapters II–V of Part One focus on the work of four philosophers: Descartes, Malebranche, Locke and Berkeley (with brief interludes on two others: Augustine and Arnaud). The work of each of these philosophers is covered in some depth so the reader may come away with an understanding of the place of this issue in the overall system of each philosopher. It should be clear that, although the work covered in Part One is fairly representative of the thinking during this period regarding issues relating to other minds, it is not intended to be comprehensive. In accordance with my discussion above, I hold that during this period there is no recognition of a particular *problem* of other minds. There are issues that arise – issues concerning our knowledge of the existence of another mind and our knowledge of what another mind thinks and feels – but these are issues that these philosophers aim to address in their work. It is only when we get to Part Two that there is any recognition of a real problem of other minds. It should now be clear that this is not an absolute recognition of a problem here. By this I mean that the philosophers whose work I discuss in Part Two – Reid and Wittgenstein – both hold that there is a deep and difficult problem about other minds *if* one approaches philosophical issues in a certain way. Reid and Wittgengstein also agree that those philosophers whose work I consider in Part One do approach matters in such a way as to run into the problem, but each identifies in a somewhat different manner what it is in the Cartesian way of proceeding that gives rise to the problem. The work of Reid and Wittgenstein is interesting both for its recognition of a real problem of other minds (endemic in a certain way of approaching philosophical issues) and for the proposals each makes in an attempt to avoid the problems. I shall conclude Part Two by suggesting that it is Wittgenstein, rather than Reid, who offers the better diagnosis of the problem here.

AND MORE HISTORY

In my discussion so far I have traced the history of the problem of other minds as far back as Descartes, and I have explained that Reid finds a problem about other minds in the Cartesian philosophical tradition. However, Reid does not limit his historical observations to the work of Descartes. He compares and contrasts the philosophy of

Descartes and his followers with that of the ancient Greeks. This is a most illuminating comparison. In Chapter I, I shall argue that it is by looking at the scepticism of the ancient Greeks – and in particular Pyrrhonian scepticism – that we can see that the problem of other minds is first and foremost a conceptual one. In doing so I am developing ideas originally put forward by Myles Burnyeat in his paper 'Idealism and Greek philosophy: what Descartes saw and Berkeley missed'.[16] In Burnyeat's view Berkeley's idealism is a philosophy profoundly unsuited to the Greek way of thinking. Building on this, I shall argue that, if Burnyeat is right here, we can explain why it is that the Greeks did not have a problem about other minds.

The sceptic is a well-known – if not notorious – figure in philosophy. Broadly speaking, the philosophic sceptic questions our entitlement to knowledge. Thus, we find the philosophical sceptic asking, given the assurance with which we can know the contents of our own mind, what entitles (or justifies) us in believing in the existence of a world that extends outside our mind? This is the sceptic about the external world who provoked Dr Johnson's impatience. The sceptic about other minds simply turns his attention to minds: given the assurance with which we can know the existence of our own mind, what entitles us in believing in the existence of *another* mind? These are questions with which any first year philosophy student is familiar. Now it is a well-known fact that scepticism is an ancient doctrine. Pyrrhonian scepticism, for example, takes its name from Pyrrho of Elis who lived c. 365 until c. 270 BCE. Sceptics held a central place in Greek philosophy, yet it is hard to find a reference in these writings to any scepticism concerning the mind of another. This should strike the philosopher of modern times as an oddity worthy of some attention. It was, in fact, this observation that led to my sustained interest in the topic of other minds. After all, to the tyro the problem of other minds is simply an epistemological one; it is a sceptical problem concerning our entitlement to knowledge. If this view were correct, it would be odd not to find mention of the problem among those ancient philosophers concerned with sceptical issues. Yet the ancient sceptics are largely silent on this issue. It is this that has led me to ask: (a) what is it about the scepticism of the ancients that makes it the case that a scepticism about other minds is not forthcoming?; and (b) is there some reason to believe that the problem of other minds is not an epistemological one? I have come to believe that the answer to question (a) should lead one to answer question (b) in the affirmative. In Chapter I, I examine the scepticism of the ancient Greeks, and I contrast it with the scepticism of Descartes more familiar to contemporary philosophers. In order fully to understand Cartesian scepticism it is necessary to appreciate how it differs from the scepticism of Descartes' predecessors. Descartes himself was very conscious of the tradition with which he was, in many essential respects, breaking. It may be that by looking to the older tradition we may better be able to locate the error in Descartes' way of thinking. This is indeed what I shall be suggesting.

THE PROBLEM TODAY

As I remarked earlier, there was an intense interest in the problem of other minds around the middle decades of the twentieth century. Since that time, however, various preoccupations of philosophers have conspired to make this problem one to which philosophers have given very little attention. The extent to which consideration of the problem has fallen out of favour is reflected in this comment by Jerry Fodor:

When I was a boy in graduate school, the philosophy of mind had two main divisions: the mind/body problem and the problem of other minds. . . .
   Philosophical fashions change. It's gotten hard to believe that there is a *special* problem about the knowledge of other minds (as opposed to knowledge of anything elses).[17]

Fodor is certainly correct to say that it is no longer part of philosophical fashion to give much attention to the problem of other minds.[18] It is not at all clear why this is so, and I do not endeavour to give any explanation here. It is notable, however, that Fodor, who espouses a position that he recently described as 'neo-Cartesian', should say that there is nothing especially problematic about other minds.[19] As I explained above, it is those philosophers from an earlier period – who can be said to be working within a Cartesian framework – who would deny that there is anything problematic about our knowledge of another mind. It is hardly surprising, then, that, as Fodor is content to work within that framework himself, he too finds nothing problematic about our knowledge of other minds. Fodor correctly recognizes that it is only the *anti*-Cartesians who identify a problem about other minds.[20] But it is not clear that Fodor recognizes just what it is that these anti-Cartesians find problematic about other minds. In particular, it is not clear that Fodor appreciates that what anti-Cartesians find problematic is something that they take to be endemic to the Cartesian framework that he, Fodor, is happy to accept.

As I explained above, the anti-Cartesian would say that, if one approaches one's philosophy correctly, there is *no* problem about other minds; his point is that Cartesians do not approach matters correctly and so do encounter a problem. According to Fodor, as with Cartesians of an earlier time, the only issue here is an epistemological one: to say how other minds come to be known. Fodor puts forward a straightforward answer here: the existence of other minds is the best explanation we have of another's behaviour. In this context it is instructive that in a very early work Fodor not only accepts that minds explain behaviour, but he also appreciates that accepting this requires that one also accept a certain amount of scepticism about other minds.[21] In other words, the way Fodor (and other Cartesians) responds to the question of how we know that there are minds other than our own leaves us with some degree of uncertainty over the existence of the mind of another and opens up the possibility (no matter how slight) of solipsism. To do better we must reject the Cartesian framework; we must understand the conceptual assumptions that shape and give rise to our epistemological questions. Unless we do this, we are left (*pace* Fodor) with a problem about other minds.

I begin Part Three with an attempt to clarify the anti-Cartesian view of the Cartesian problem of other minds. The problem, I suggest, is conceptual in nature and I attempt to explain why this is so. The problem is connected with the generality of our mental concepts. The problem isn't that our mental concepts are not general; of course they are. The problem lies in understanding how these concepts can be general given a certain philosophical starting point. I shall suggest that, if we eschew this philosophical starting point, it is possible to provide an understanding of our concepts here such that no problem can be thought to arise about the mind of another. In this I take my lead from the work of P. F. Strawson (influenced in its turn by the work of Wittgenstein).[22] This is philosophical work that Strawson once called 'descriptive metaphysics'. It attempts to describe our concept of mind in such a way that its generality will not be seen to be problematic. I shall argue that – despite superficial differences – Strawson's work here can be seen to have profound affinities with the work of Donald Davidson. What we learn when we put the work of Strawson together with that of Davidson is the centrality in our system of concepts of the concept of action. Our concepts of mind and action are intimately related. For this reason there will be no correct account of mind that fails to give proper place to behaviour – the problem with the work of the Cartesians is that it fails correctly to understand the way mind is to be understood through action. The work of both of these philosophers also teaches that, if one goes about one's philosophical business correctly, there will be no room for the traditional sceptic's questions. This fits in nicely with the inclination of many philosophers to respond to the sceptic not by answering his questions, but by showing that his questions have no place. And what all this teaches us, as far as the problem of other minds is concerned, is that conceptual considerations precede epistemological ones.

Once the centrality of our concept of action is established, I turn to consider some recent work that runs counter to this conclusion and holds that behaviour has nothing to do with mind. Thomas Nagel, John Searle and Galen Strawson are examples of philosophers who, for roughly similar reasons, either play down or ignore altogether the importance of behaviour in the understanding of mind. What all three of these philosophers insist upon is the importance of the subjectivity of the mental, and they associate this subjectivity with (as Nagel has so memorably put it) 'what it is like' when one has a mind.[23] These three philosophers – each in his own way – take it that the result of a proper emphasis on the first-person aspect of mind is to pull the mind apart from any but the most contingent connection to behaviour. For this reason they claim that behaviour plays no part in the understanding of mind. This is clearly an extreme reaction to what some philosophers would label the 'behaviourism' of the middle part of the twentieth century.[24] Such a sweeping aside of behaviour leaves us, however, in an uncomfortable position over the mind of another. Nagel, adopting a realist position not dissimilar from that of John Locke's, is content (like Fodor) to live with a certain scepticism here. As far as Nagel is concerned, radical Cartesian-style scepticism is a natural concomitant of realism. However, Nagel appreciates the importance of what I have called the conceptual problem of other minds. Nagel's solution to this problem is underdeveloped, but what is clear is that Nagel wishes to avoid reference to behaviour in his response to this problem. I argue that by attempting to respond to the conceptual problem in the way that he does Nagel misunderstands that problem. When one turns from Nagel's work to that of Searle and Galen Strawson, one can find no acknowledgement of the conceptual problem of other minds. Galen Strawson suggests that it is too much attention to concepts that has led philosophers astray when thinking about mind. (Here Strawson is in agreement with Fodor.) I shall argue that, unless philosophers recognize and address the conceptual issue, they are in danger of running into a serious problem about the minds of others. Recent philosophy is littered with discussions which either misunderstand or altogether ignore the conceptual problem. It is perhaps not surprising that many philosophers today take the issue to be a relatively simple epistemo-logical one. It is interesting to note that the period when philosophers showed the greatest interest in the problem of other minds (roughly speaking the middle part of the twentieth century) coincides with the time when Wittgenstein identified what he saw as a deep and difficult conceptual problem. Leaving to one side pre-Cartesian philosophy, one could say that, in the period before this (running back to Descartes) as well as in the period since, philosophers have tended to treat this issue as somewhat marginal to their concerns. But for a short time in the history of philosophy the problem of other minds was cor-rectly understood as a deep and difficult issue that, when understood correctly, can help us to approach many philosophical issues – both conceptual and epistemological – aright.

Part One

Knowledge of other minds

CHAPTER I

Ancient and modern scepticism and the problem of other minds

INTRODUCTION

The sceptic is a familiar figure in philosophy. His questions have dominated the subject since ancient times. The sceptic challenges, among other things, our claims to know about – or to be justified in our beliefs about – the world around us. The sceptic also raises questions about our knowledge of other minds. Most contemporary discussions of scepticism take their lead from the writings of Descartes, and in particular his *Meditations on First Philosophy*. While Descartes does not explicitly discuss questions concerning the mind of another, it is true to say that his philosophical work bequeaths this problem to us.[1] And it is notable that the problem is directed specifically at the mind of others, of our own mind there can be no doubt. Starting from the secure point of knowing my own mind the question is raised: How do I come to know that another has a mind?

If we were to think that the sceptic has a *standard* repertoire, then we would expect sceptics of all times to raise this question about other minds. It would come as something of a surprise, then, to learn that, on the whole, the sceptics of ancient times did not raise this question. The sceptic does not have a standard repertoire. I propose to try to understand *how* the question of other minds arises for Cartesian scepticism by comparing and contrasting this scepticism with that proposed by ancient philosophers. I shall suggest that what such a study reveals is that the problem of other minds is not, *au fond*, an epistemological problem.

THE ANCIENT SCEPTICS: A BRIEF INTRODUCTION

As with so many philosophical problems, the problem of scepticism concerning our knowledge of the world has its roots in the writing of the ancient Greek sceptics. There were, in ancient times, two main schools of sceptical thought: the Academic and the Pyrrhonian. Both were primarily concerned to reject the views of the Dogmatists, and chief among these, the Stoics. There are two aspects of Stoic philosophy that it is important to note for our purposes. The first is that it has a clear practical dimension: the concern is to attain happiness and peace of the soul in the conduct of everyday life. To this end the Stoics turn to science and the pursuit of scientific knowledge. Following from this, the second aspect of Stoic philosophy to be noted is this: the Stoics are optimistic about the achievement of knowledge through a science founded on the unarguable truth of certain perceptions. On the Stoic view, some perceptions are such that they simply grab you and drag you to the truth. A perception which is both clear and compelling – and for which there is no countervailing reason – is one from which the soul cannot withhold assent. The Stoics believe that it is upon such perceptions that science is founded.

This belief in the positive knowledge that is to be gained from science is the target of sceptical attack. Academic scepticism is usually identified as the first school of sceptical thought. It developed within Plato's Academy under the leadership of Archesilaus in the early part of the third century BCE, and was revitalized in the second century BCE by the dialectician Carneades. The Academic sceptics urge their opponents to set out their views and then systematically oppose them. In this way they aim to provide a demonstration of opposing argument.[2] This method is designed to undermine the Stoic's claim that knowledge is attainable. The Academic sceptics also argue that the clear and compelling perceptions of the Stoics are liable to be illusions, hallucinations or the product of a dream. Contrary to the dogmatism of the Stoics, the Academic sceptics aim to show that there is no criterion for determining truth. The end result of the sceptic's line of thought is that the (Stoic) Sage should suspend judgement about, or withhold assent from, all propositions. Should the Sage do this, however, a certain problem is thought to arise: if he does withhold assent, how is the Sage to act? It should be noted that the Academic sceptic shares with the Stoic a similar practical dimension to his philosophy: the motivation is to attain peace and happiness in the conduct of life. The question is, if the sceptic is right to conclude that the Sage must withhold assent, how is he to attain this happiness? At this point the Academic sceptic introduces the idea of the reasonable or the plausible: despite his refusal to submit to dogma, the Sage will act in accordance with that which he takes to be the more reasonable or plausible.[3]

There is another school of sceptical philosophy in ancient times which also opposes the dogmatism of the Stoics, but which formulates its scepticism differently from the Academics. This is Pyrrhonism.[4] Pyrrhonism could be said to be both older and younger than Academic scepticism: older because its founder, Pyrrho of Elis, pre-dates the Academic sceptics by about fifty years; younger because its theoretical formulations are due to Aenesidemus who lived and wrote some two hundred years after the early Academic sceptics. Pyrrhonists are the more thoroughgoing of the ancient sceptics: they make no concession to the reasonable or the plausible; they accept the conclusion of the sceptical argument and aim to accommodate it in their daily life. In this they claimed to follow Pyrrho who, it is alleged, was a living example of a complete doubter, a man who would commit himself to nothing beyond what seemed to be the case.

There are several stories reported concerning Pyrrho which illustrate both the aim and the inherent difficulties of Pyrrhonism. Here is one: It is reported that Pyrrho was once standing on the deck of a ship caught up in a raging storm. Also on board was a pig, who continued to eat his supper despite the panic and frantic activity of the passengers all around him. Pyrrho is said to have pointed to the pig, unperturbed by the storm, as an example of what they should all be like. Another story points up the difficulties in this advocated way of life. It is reported that Pyrrho was once frightened by a vicious dog. When charged with failing to practise what he preached – that is, not to commit oneself to the belief in the danger posed by the dog which in turn brings about one's fear – Pyrrho is said to have replied that it is regrettable that it is so difficult to divest oneself of one's humanity.[5] What one learns from the example of Pyrrho's life is the extent of the Pyrrhonist's commitment to live his scepticism. It is not just that such a sceptic renounces knowledge (for that may be consistent with the retention of belief), but he renounces the very beliefs by which we ordinarily live. Or rather, he renounces a commitment to the truth or falsity of these beliefs. It is in reaction to this that Hume wrote in his *Enquiry Concerning Human Understanding* that 'a Pyrrhonian cannot expect, that his philosophy will have any constant influence on the mind: . . . On the contrary, he must acknowledge, if he will acknowledge anything, that all human life must perish, were his principles universally and steadily to prevail. All discourse, all action would immediately cease; and men remain in a total lethargy, till the necessities of nature, unsatisfied, put an end to their miserable existence.'[6]

It is not altogether clear, however, that Hume is right in his condemnation of the Pyrrhonist. Without further argument, it looks as if Hume simply overlooks the fact that the Pyrrhonist does not reject action, just commitment to the truth of one's beliefs. It is important to remember that the Pyrrhonist does not formulate his scepticism in a void. Like the Academic sceptics and the Dogmatists, he is motivated by the question, How should we live our lives so that we might achieve happiness or tranquillity (*ataraxia*)? Tranquillity, according to the Pyrrhonist, will descend upon us once we suspend judgement in the face of opposing argument; it comes when we stop chasing it. A comparison is some-times drawn with the painter Apelles who strove to achieve the effect on canvas of the horse's foam, but only achieved it when he finally gave up and flung his sponge at the canvas.[7] There is no tranquillity in life when one spends one's time arguing for this or that opinion – that way lie frustration and anxiety. Better to accept the teachings of the sceptics. Do not seek a criterion of truth. Furthermore, action in accordance with what is more reasonable or plausible is not a solution. Better to settle for suspension of judgement (or *epoche*). *Epoche* is the prelude to *ataraxia*.

There does, however, appear to be a tension between the achieve-ment of tranquillity and the Pyrrhonian sceptic's concern with propounding a way of living. If we do abandon the dogma of the Stoics, and if we do reject what is more reasonable or plausible, how are we to act? It looks as if we have to conclude with Hume that Pyrrhonism is incompatible with living. But this is to overlook the fact that the Pyrrhonian advocates a life in accordance with appearance. To this end he proposes the following fourfold scheme of life:

(i)   Be guided by nature as you perceive it.
(ii) Yield to the constraints of bodily drives such as hunger and thirst.
(iii) Keep to the laws and customs of the society.
(iv) Take instruction in the arts.

At first sight the recommended life looks no different from the ordi-nary one. The difference is that in the ordinary case we believe that the opinions that guide our actions are true or matter, whereas in the rec-ommended life we manage to suspend belief or judgement as to the truth of our opinions. The important thing to notice is that action is not discouraged – only commitment. We are to act as one who has no reason to act one way or another; we may as well flip a coin. Allowing ourselves to live in accordance with the fourfold scheme of life would seem to serve the same purpose as the toss of a coin.[8]

While Pyrrho allegedly provided his followers with an example of a way of life, he wrote nothing. It was Aenesidemus and his followers who provided the theoretical formulations of the sceptical doctrine. Following on from the Academics, these sceptics developed arguments, or tropes, which were designed to lead us to a life devoid of commitment. A record of these arguments is available in the writings of Sextus Empiricus, a Pyrrhonian sceptic who lived around 200 CE. Sextus' *Outlines of Pyrrhonism* is a compendium of Pyrrhonist thought dating back to Aenesidemus, and includes the Ten Modes of Aenesidemus as well as a further Five Modes usually attributed to Agrippa.[9] In his Ten Modes Aenesidemus sets out the modes or ways in which things give rise to belief and then shows how each of these modes produces conflicting beliefs of equal persuasiveness. The conclusion he wishes us to draw from all this is that these modes should not be relied on to put us in touch with the truth.

Of the Ten Modes, the first five are particularly interesting for our purposes. Sextus characterizes the first four modes as 'arguments from the subject judging'. The First Mode presents the argument from differences in animals. One form of this argument begins by noting the way that sense impressions differ when the organ of sense is altered in a man (say, because he is suffering from jaundice), and concludes from this that the very different sense organs of non-human animals must produce sense impressions in them that are different from those in us. So, for example, the sense of touch is different in fleshy animals than in hard-shelled or thorny ones, and different again in feathered or scaled animals. The question is then pressed, What reason is there for taking the perceptions of one kind of creature to be revealing of the way things really are? The Second Mode presents the argument from differences in humans. This argument is designed either to supplement or to replace the argument of the First Mode. It may replace that argument if one were to believe, for whatever reason, that the perceptions of man are superior to those of all other animals. The Second Mode restricts its observations to men. Even when we do this, what we find is that there are differences in the bodies of men that result in the same object affecting different men differently. This is clear from the fact that each man takes his pleasures – as well as his displeasures – in different things. Again the question is pressed: What reason is there for taking the perceptions of one man to be revealing of the way things are in reality? In the Third Mode the argument from different senses is invoked. It is pointed out, for example, that honey can appear pleasant to the tongue but unpleasant to the eyes, that perfume can be pleasant to the smell but disgusting to the taste, and so on. Here the question is pressed: Why take the perceptions of one sense to be more revealing about how things are in themselves than those of another? Finally, in the Fourth Mode attention is drawn to the various states of the body and the way perceptions are affected by these states. Thus, it is pointed out that things appear different to a joyous man and a grief stricken one, to a drunk and a sober man, to an old and a young man, to one awake and one asleep, and the like. Again it is asked: Why trust the judgements of a man in one state rather than another? The Fifth Mode is one of several that Sextus characterizes as combining elements from arguments from the subject judging with elements from arguments that he characterizes as 'arguments from the object judged'. This mode draws attention to the fact that the same object can appear differently due to differences in its position, distance and place. Thus, for example, the same tower may appear round from afar and square close up, and the light of a lamp will appear dim in sunlight but bright in the dark. Such observations make it impossible to give one sense-impression preference over another.

The point of making such observations and pressing these questions is to encourage us to suspend our judgement. The study of these arguments is meant to banish dogma. It is only by avoiding dogma that the Pyrrhonist believes that we can achieve tranquillity in our everyday lives.

ANCIENT GREEK SCEPTICISM AND THE PROBLEM OF OTHER MINDS

Let us now look a little more closely at the scepticism bequeathed to us by the Pyrrhonists. What these sceptics challenge is our ability to come up with a criterion of truth which is independent and which can be used to determine what an object is *really* like. Very roughly, we could say that the sceptics of ancient times bequeathed to us a scepticism *about the world*. We must be very careful how we understand this.

In the writings of the ancient sceptics we find arguments not dissimilar to those familiar from any contemporary textbook on epistemology. There is reference to the jaundiced eye, the square tower viewed from a distance and to dreams. Less familiar to us today, but no less powerful once we consider them, are the arguments from different animals and differences among different humans. The challenge is to the Dogmatist's claim to have found a criterion of truth. The Sceptic's arguments are designed to raise what is sometimes called the 'problem of the criterion'. On the one hand, there is a world and, on the other hand, there are the experiences of different human and non-human animals. The problem is to determine *which* of these experiences – if any – are true to reality. The sceptical arguments are designed to point out our inability to go beyond experience and to know the truth about the world we are acting in. But notice that these sceptics appear to preface their work on an assumption that there are experiencing subjects who act in a world. Their concern is focused on the question of how we can know the truth about the world that we act upon and live in with others. The distinction between appearance and reality is accepted and used to question whether our appearances are true to reality. What the sceptic of ancient times despaired of finding is a criterion of truth. Of the ancient sceptics Myles Burnyeat writes:

All these philosophers, however radical their scrutiny of ordinary belief, leave untouched – indeed they rely upon – the notion that we are deceived or ignorant about *something*. There is a reality of some sort confronting us; we are in touch with something, even if this something, reality, is not at all what we think it to be. Greek philosophy does not know the problem of proving in a general way the existence of an external world.

It is for this reason, Burnyeat concludes, that idealism would have been 'repellent to Greek thought'.[10] Following the work of, *inter alia*, Bernard Williams, Burnyeat claims that 'Idealism is one of the few philosophical positions which did not receive its first formulation in antiquity.'[11] The idealism being referred to here is the doctrine, familiar from the writing of Bishop Berkeley in the eighteenth century, according to which *esse ist percipi* (to be is to be perceived). Berkeley's idealism is a rejection of material substance in favour of the immaterial or spiritual. According to Berkeley, only spiritual substance and ideas exist. What Berkeley rejects is the symmetrical balance between subject and object that is, in the opinion of Burnyeat, Williams and others, so characteristic of Greek thought.[12]

If the conclusion of Burnyeat, Williams and others that idealism has no place in Greek philosophy is correct, it may help us to understand something else. It may help us to explain why it is that there is virtually no mention of any problem concerning the mind of others in the writings of the ancient Greek sceptics. At least, there is no mention of this problem in the writings of Pyrrhonians or the Academic sceptics. However, Sextus does report on the epistemological doctrines of a group of lesser-known sceptics, the Cyrenaics, and what he writes about them may be thought to raise a problem about the minds of others. In his work *Against the Professors*, in a section in which he discusses the criterion of truth, Sextus reports the Cyrenaics as making the following observation:

> For all people call something white or sweet in common, but they do not have something common that is white or sweet. For each person is aware of his own private *pathos*, but whether this *pathos* occurs in him and his neighbour from a white object neither can he himself tell, since he is not submitting to the *pathos* of . . . the other person.[13]

The Cyrenaic sceptic observes the infallible awareness we have of our own experiences, and as a result questions our knowledge of another's experiences.

In order to evaluate this passage, it is important that we distinguish two problems here. If we refer back to the scepticism raised by Pyrrhonians concerning the world around us, what we see is that it is possible to distinguish a weak and a strong form of this scepticism: on the one hand we can ask what grounds we have for taking the world to be truly one way or another; on the other hand we ask what grounds we have for taking there to be any world at all beyond our appearances. It is the latter sort of question – the *radical* sceptical question – that leads to the idealism of Berkeley, while the former sort of question – the *weak* sceptical question – leads to the Pyrrhonian position of belief without commitment. A similar sort of distinction – between a radical and weak sceptical question – can be drawn when the sceptic raises a question about the mind of another. On the one hand, the sceptic may ask what grounds we have for taking there to be any mind in addition to our own (a radical sceptical question about the mind of another); on the other hand, the sceptic may question our grounds for taking another's mind to be in a condition similar to our own as opposed to some other condition (a weak sceptical question about the mind of another). The former sort of question may draw us to a belief in solipsism (the belief that no mind exists beyond one's own), while the latter may lead us only to reserve judgement on the precise state of this other mind. Just as Burnyeat and Williams conclude that idealism has no place in Greek philosophy, it is possible to add that solipsism has no place in Greek philosophy either.

Burnyeat has argued at some length that the scepticism of the ancients not only does not question, but is prefaced on the assumption, that there is a world beyond our appearances. It is only if this is so, he argues, that it can be asked why we take it that the world is this way rather than some other. When we run our eyes back over the arguments of the ancient sceptics we find that, not only does this sceptic preface his questions on an assumption that there is a world of which we have experience, he assumes as well that experience exists *across individuals*. It is precisely this that leads Aenesidemus to the first four of his tropes – the arguments from the subject judging. These arguments call upon the experience of others – be it human or non-human experience – and question the superiority of one over another. It seems that the very scepticism formulated by the Pyrrhonist *relies* on the existence of other minds. Solipsism cannot here be formulated. The differences that Sextus invokes are not designed to urge us to suspend belief in the truth of the propositions concerning the existence of another's mind. Rather, the first quartet of tropes is designed to do what all ten tropes are designed to do: to draw our attention to the variation in different individuals' perceptions of the world around them. This variation is such that we must, according to Sextus and the Pyrrhonians, suspend belief in the truth of propositions concerning the world around us; propositions about the states of mind of those around us are not similarly brought into question.

While there is no mention in the Ten Modes – or in any of the other Modes – of any scepticism concerning the mind of another, we find, as we can see from the quotation above, that there is some scepticism raised by the Cyrenaics. The question we need to ask is this: Are the Cyrenaics here raising a radical or a weak sceptical question concerning the mind of another? In her extensive work on this topic, Voula Tsouna comes to the conclusion that 'ancient denials that we can have access to the *pathē* [experiences] or thoughts of our neighbours, are weaker than similar claims occurring in modern discussions about other minds'.[14] Tsouna's argument here is based on an interpretation of the Cyrenaic concept of *pathē* and of thoughts which takes them to cut across the mind–body divide. Concerning experiences, she writes: 'Although the Cyrenaics emphasised the subjective aspects of the *pathē* and studied them primarily as experiences, they still conceived of them as ontologically derivative internal states that can be described both in mental and in physical terms.'[15] Tsouna concludes that the Cyrenaics ask only a weak sceptical question about the mind of another (she calls this form of scepticism 'local scepticism'). Like Pyrrhonian scepticism concerning the world, weak Cyrenaic scepticism concerning the minds of others would appear to be prefaced on the assumption that other minds exist.

In a footnote Burnyeat writes, 'It is of the essence of skepticism . . . as practiced throughout the skeptic literature, to set one person's impressions against those of another. Questions could be raised about the skeptic's entitlement to talk of other people's impressions, and suitable answers could have been devised. But on the whole such questions are not raised.'[16] Burnyeat does not use this observation as evidence that the ancient sceptics did not have a problem about other minds, but it is clear that he could have. Burnyeat's conclusion that idealism is not available to Greek thought needs to be extended: it would seem that solipsism is equally unavailable to Greek thought.

Several philosophers have touched on the point. Thus we find, for example, Stephen Everson writing: 'the ancients were not impelled to the sort of subjective understanding of the mind that lays the ground for solipsism'.[17] The solipsism Everson has in mind here – following the work of Burnyeat – is one that divorces the subject from the world of objects; the solipsism that divorces the subject's mind from other minds is not noted by Everson and needs to be made explicit. Gisela Striker makes an observation about other people in the course of her commentary on a passage from Sextus. She writes: '[the Pyrrhonists] do not intend to deny *that* we see; they suspend judgement, however, as to *how* it is that we see. . . . So one might be tempted to say that they accepted it as a fact that there are people, trees, and houses around them.'[18] This, however, is all that Striker says, and the implications for the problem of other minds are not highlighted. Richard Sorabji notes an absence of a problem of other minds in the work of Aristotle. Sorabji observes: 'It never occurs to Aristotle to raise doubts about other minds.'[19] The problem does not arise, according to Sorabji, because of Aristotle's view of the relationship between body and soul. Sorabji's observations about Aristotle's work fit in with my conclusions concerning the work of the ancient sceptics.

In the section that follows I shall suggest that there is an important relationship between the fact that the ancients formulated their scepticism in the way that they did and the fact that no radical problem about other minds can be found in their writing. That there is such a relationship can be seen when we compare and contrast the scepticism of the ancient with that of modern philosophers.

ANCIENT AND MODERN SCEPTICISM

According to Pierre Bayle, the late-seventeenth century sceptic, it is the rediscovery of the works of Sextus in the sixteenth century that can be seen to mark the beginning of what is called 'modern philosophy'. Descartes is a great modern philosopher and modern sceptic. The work of Sextus and the Pyrrhonists was well-known to Descartes, and he developed his scepticism against the background of Sextus' text. The scepticism that Descartes was to develop, however, is notably different from the one he inherited. Most importantly, Descartes' motivation for his scepticism is different from that of the ancients, and this can be seen reflected in the scepticism he formulated.

Descartes, unlike his Pyrrhonian predecessors, does not hold that we have to live with scepticism. Rather, he aims to conquer scepticism and to show how knowledge is possible. Descartes adopts the sceptical stance only in order to refute it. The paradox of his position is that it is generally acknowledged that Descartes' reply to the sceptic fails, leaving him, in the words of Richard Popkin, 'sceptic *malgré lui*'.[20] Insofar as this is true, so is the claim that the Cartesian sceptic leaves us in a far more radical state of doubt than does his Pyrrhonian predecessors. Why this is so is something we shall see in a moment.

Another way in which Descartes differs from his Pyrrhonian predecessors is that he is not primarily interested in the question, How should I live my life? That is to say, the ultimate motivation for Descartes' scepticism is not the desire to attain happiness or tranquillity in everyday life. Descartes' doubt is not practical. He wants an answer to the question, How is knowledge possible?, and to this end he separates off the conduct of ordinary life.[21] Descartes writes in one place, 'We must note the distinction which I have insisted on in several passages, between the actions of life and the investigation of the truth.'[22] And in another place he writes, 'the task now in hand does not involve action, but merely the acquisition of knowledge'.[23]

Motivated by a desire for truth and knowledge, Descartes rises to the sceptic's challenge. Quite rightly, he sees the sceptic as an enemy of knowledge, and so sets out to show where the sceptic makes his mistake. Let us call the conviction that the sceptic can be shown to be mistaken 'Cartesian optimism'. The sceptics of ancient times did not share this optimism. They could see no way of responding to the sceptical challenge and concluded that some form of life incorporating scepticism is necessary. Descartes, on the other hand, believed he could reply to the sceptic's challenge. For this reason he could put action to one side; he could, for the time of his meditations, abstract himself from the activities of life. Famously Descartes sat in his armchair by the fire. Bernard Williams refers to the stance of someone who is committed only to the pursuit of knowledge – of someone willing to abstract themselves from the concerns of ordinary life – as the stance of the 'Pure Enquirer'.[24]

I said a moment ago that according to Popkin, insofar as Descartes' reply to the sceptic fails, he is a sceptic in spite of himself. What

Popkin does not point out is this: if we accept that Descartes' optimism in the face of the sceptic is misplaced, then we philosophers are left in our armchairs searching for knowledge; we are left in a state of perpetual reflection, abstracted from the concerns of everyday life. Actually, the situation is far worse even than this. Descartes did not just bequeath to us the philosopher sitting in his armchair meditating on the possibility of knowledge; he left us in a position of being unable to prove the very existence of the chair or the fire. This is because Cartesian scepticism introduces a divide between the world of the meditating mind and everything else. This is the real Cartesian legacy. Let us now see how this came to be.

In his first *Meditation* Descartes briefly considers some reasons for doubting many of the propositions that he has hitherto taken to be true. He considers first that his senses have sometimes deceived him (the argument from illusion). But immediately he writes, 'Yet although the senses occasionally deceive us with respect to objects which are very small or in the distance, there are many other beliefs about which doubt is quite impossible, even though they are derived from the senses.'[25] He gives as an example of something that he cannot doubt the fact that he is sitting in his armchair by the fire, in his dressing gown, with a piece of paper in his hand.

Descartes' rejection of the argument from illusion is interesting and revealing. What it reveals is that Descartes wants a form of scepticism that will encompass as much as possible. What the argument from illusion shows is that, for any given perception, we can doubt that it is veridical. What such an argument does not do is allow us to doubt all our perceptions at once. The difference is neatly summarized thus: the argument from illusion gives us the universal possibility of doubt, it does not allow for the possibility of universal doubt. Interestingly, it is the latter sort of doubt that Descartes is seeking.

In an attempt to widen the doubt Descartes moves swiftly on to consider the possibility that he is dreaming. The dreaming argument is more all encompassing than the argument from illusion. With this argument Descartes can doubt even that he is sitting by the fire, in his dressing gown. Nevertheless, Descartes is not content to rest his doubt on the dreaming argument. About this argument he writes: 'it must surely be admitted that the visions which come in sleep are like paintings, which must have been fashioned in the likeness of things that are real'.[26] Descartes uses as an analogy here the painter who, while he may draw all manner of exotic creatures, makes only a medley of the parts of different animals drawn from his experience. In a similar fashion, our imagination, although fertile, draws upon simple objects that are 'real'. Once again Descartes finds that his scepticism is limited. The possibility of universal doubt eludes him.

The argument from dreaming, like the argument from illusion, is not new to Descartes. These are arguments that are familiar from the writings of the ancient Greek sceptics. However, as we have seen, the sceptic of ancient times uses such arguments only to illustrate the universal possibility of doubt. Arguments such as these are designed to challenge us to find a criterion of truth, to find a way of knowing how the world really is. Descartes considers these arguments and the scepticism they produce, and he acknowledges their limitation. He then introduces another argument into the sceptic's repertoire. This argument is designed to push the doubt further, to move us from the universal possibility of doubt to the possibility of universal doubt.[27]

The argument which provides Descartes with the doubt he is looking for comes at the end of the first *Meditation*. There he considers the possibility that there may be 'some malicious demon of the utmost power and cunning [who] has employed all his energies in order to deceive me'. With such a supposition Descartes is able to consider that 'the sky, the air, the earth, colours, shapes, sounds, and all external things are merely the delusions of dreams which [this demon] has devised to ensnare my judgement'.[28] According to Popkin, with this supposition Descartes presents us with 'a basis for doubting apparently never dreamed of before'.[29] Descartes himself admits that he is here presenting a doubt additional 'to the customary difficulties of the Sceptics'.[30]

This move is deeply significant. Once the possibility of a malicious demon is raised we are in a position to question, not just this belief or that, but all our beliefs at once. Illusions make sense against a background of veridical experience, dreams derive their general content from waking experience, but once we consider the possibility of a malicious demon the world may drop away as unnecessary. The idea of the demon does not presuppose reality, it pre-empts it. Instead of the content of our thoughts deriving from contact with an independent reality, content may simply be the result of the demon's doings. The demon might be the source of our experiences instead of reality. With the introduction of this device, Descartes believed he had circumvented the problem of earlier arguments; the sceptic is now in a position to present us with the possibility of universal doubt.

Notice that for universal doubt to be possible the evidence as a whole must be divorceable from that for which it is evidence. It is here that we can observe another move which is said to be new to Descartes' philosophy. Once the malicious demon is introduced the evidence of our senses is no longer evidence for some state or other of the world. The subject may exist, with all her experiences intact, and the objective world may not exist.[31] The possibility of a radical divide – or divorce – of the subject from the objective world has now been introduced into philosophy. A corollary of this radical divorce is that an appearance may simply be an appearance to a subject. According to Burnyeat, such a radical divorce of the subject from the world did not exist in the writings of the ancient Greek sceptics. For these earlier sceptics, appearances – no matter how distorted they may be – are not just appearances *to* a subject but they are also considered to be appearances *of* an objective world.

According to Burnyeat, 'It was Descartes who put subjective knowledge at the centre of epistemology.'[32] Burnyeat puts forward the following explanation of how the shift from the concept of a subject dependent upon its objects to a subject divorceable from its objects occurred in philosophy. As we have seen, what the sceptics of ancient times despaired of finding is a criterion of truth. What Descartes claims to have discovered is that there is at least one truth that does not need a criterion. The *cogito* is such a truth.[33] What Descartes noticed is that the *cogito* is a truth that is self-guaranteeing and as such does not need a criterion. It is only truths that go outside the subject that need to be guaranteed – these truths are not self-guaranteeing. Once we see this, we can see also that a gap opens up between those truths that are self-guaranteeing and those that need to be guaranteed. On the one side of the gap we find one kind of truth: subjective truths; on the other side of this gap we find another kind of truth: objective truths. What Descartes' sceptic does is exploit the existence of this gap to question our belief in the very existence of an objective world. Thus Descartes is able to escape the Pyrrhonist's dilemma by coming up with a truth which he takes to be unassailable and for which no criterion is required. But in doing this he introduces the idea of a truth that can be obtained without going beyond personal experience. The Pyrrhonist could not find a way of securing any truth; Descartes gained security in *some* truths (subjective truths), but at the risk of losing the world altogether. This is because once subjective truths are in place we can ask whether we have any reason to advance beyond these truths to objective reality. Appearance is no longer set off in contradistinction to reality; appearance has now become the veil that cuts us off from reality. John McDowell writes of 'the characteristic Cartesian willingness to face up to losing the world, with the inner for consolation'.[34] And Bernard Williams writes that 'to Greek thought the distinction between appearances and reality was so basic, and knowledge so associated with reality, that knowledge which was of *subjective appearances* perhaps did not count as genuine knowledge at all'.[35] The concept of an appearance has shifted with the work of Descartes. The idea of an appearance is now assumed to be such that it can be understood without reference to any reality beyond itself.

Once such a radical divide is introduced between appearance and reality, it becomes conceivable that one side of the divide drop away as unnecessary. The sceptic who asks us to accept such a divide is not simply questioning our knowledge of the world; he is questioning the very existence of the world. This is the *radical* scepticism that Descartes was looking for. It should be remembered that Descartes does not embrace such a scepticism, but sets it up in order to refute it. It is also important to understand, however, that the scepticism that Descartes sets out to refute is one that is prefaced on a radical conceptual divide between the world and the knowing subject. Knowledge, on this Cartesian conception of things, comes to be a subject's way of bridging this divide, or reaching across this gap. Not only is this perilous as regards the subject's knowledge of the world around her, but it is also perilous as regards the subject's knowledge of other subjects. This radical divide between the subject and her world not only leads to a radical scepticism concerning our knowledge of the world, but it also leads to a radical scepticism about knowledge of other subjects. In other words, this radical divide threatens us with solipsism.

Descartes' sceptic manages to cut off the subject from its object and, thereby, from all other subjects. The one divorce precipitates the other. The reason for this is that the doubt that allows us to question all our beliefs at once extends to the body of the doubter. As Burnyeat puts it in one place, 'in the modern [i.e. Cartesian] formulation "external" means external to the mind'.[36] This move cuts two ways: on the one hand, it divorces the subject from his own body; on the other hand, it ensures that observation of another's body is nothing but that: observation of a body. Another body may be a mere body, as the subject that is myself could be a mere subject involving no body and no world. Burnyeat continues, 'but in Sextus it ["external"] means simply external to oneself, the cognitive subject, i.e. a man'.[37] The problem starts when the subject is prised apart from the world that contains his body.[38] McDowell summarizes the nature of the problem nicely when he writes: 'In the fully Cartesian picture, the inner life takes place in an autonomous realm, transparent to the introspective awareness of its subject; the access of subjectivity to the rest of the world becomes correspondingly problematic.'[39] And we must remember that the 'rest of the world' includes the body of the subject as well as other subjects. What McDowell's way of making the point emphasizes is the autonomy of the subject *vis-à-vis* the rest of the world. What this helps us to see is the conception of a subject that emerges in Descartes' philosophy.

Descartes acknowledges that this conception of a subject cuts her off from the world; he acknowledges as well that this conception of a subject also cuts her off from other subjects. In the *Principles of Philosophy* he writes:

> From the mere fact that each of us understands himself to be a thinking thing and is capable, in thought, of excluding from himself every other substance, whether thinking or extended, it is certain that each of us, regarded in this way, is really distinct from every other thinking substance and from every corporeal substance.[40]

It is because of this essential distinctness that, in the second *Meditation*, Descartes can look from his window and wonder whether the people he sees moving along the streets are men or automatic machines.[41] It is clear that we here have a conception of mind that gives rise to a question about our knowledge of other minds.[42]

OTHER MINDS: AN EPISTEMOLOGICAL PROBLEM?

Insofar as Descartes' philosophy introduces a conception of a subject that gives rise to a question about our knowledge of the minds of others, it is relevant to ask whether this conception can be avoided. The sceptic asks a string of questions, the end result of which is to raise a doubt about the existence of the world and the mind of another. It looks as if the sceptic's question forces us to accept a certain conception of mind such that a certain problem about the mind of another is unavoidable. And just as Descartes' scepticism concerning the external world is radical, so this scepticism concerning the mind of another is radical: the Cartesian sceptic does not just question how we know that another's mind is one way rather than another; he questions the very existence of any mind other than his own. It might be thought that one way to avoid this radical sceptical problem – and the conception of a subject that is associated with it – would be to deny the sceptic the right to ask his questions. In particular, one could simply draw a line before the introduction of the evil demon. But this looks like a blatant refusal to entertain the problems to which the sceptic's questions give rise. It could be argued that a certain epistemological challenge leads us to certain conclusions concerning our concept of mind. This would be an acknowledgement that epistemological issues are primary, conceptual ones secondary. An insistence on placing conceptual issues first may appear to be a sort of cowardice, a refusal to ask questions that manifestly can be asked.

This attitude towards the relationship between matters epistemological and conceptual may come unstuck, however, when one takes into account Burnyeat's assessment of the ancient Greek sceptics. When one compares the scepticism of ancient times with that proposed by Descartes, one begins to see that epistemological matters may themselves be driven by certain conceptual assumptions. Let us now look a little more closely at the differences between ancient Greek and Cartesian scepticism.

When one first encounters the scepticism of the ancients one cannot help wondering *why* they did not raise the radical sceptical doubt, why they did not ask the questions that would lead to the possibility of universal doubt. The possibility seemed to be staring them in the face, so to speak, and yet the further step which would take them to the possibility of universal doubt is not taken. A plausible reply here may be thought to emerge from consideration of the motivation behind Greek scepticism.[43] As we have seen, the sceptics of ancient times (and no less the Dogmatists) are motivated by a practical concern. Their aim is to achieve happiness in the ordinary activities of everyday life. Thus, the emphasis in their work is on activity in the world and with others. The external world and other people are the starting point from which the ancient sceptic aims to show that one person's beliefs about the world have no more to be said for them than any other's. We could say that the sceptic's starting point is a collective practice with the aim of achieving happiness.

This motivation contrasts starkly with that which informs Descartes' scepticism. As we have seen, Descartes' ultimate concern is with knowledge, not action. He moves from a practical to a theoretical doubt. Consistent with this he abandons the collective practice in favour of a radically first-person stance. Descartes is engaged in a *solo* enterprise. Unlike the sceptics before him, Descartes is careful to formulate all his sceptical arguments without reference to any mind other than his own. Nowhere in Descartes' work is there any reference to the argument from different animals, or the argument from differences in different men. Descartes' question is not, How can we (collectively) know about the world? It is, rather, How can I know about the world? On this solo enterprise anything – and this includes any*one* – that is not me (not my mind) is open to doubt.

The question, Why did the Greek sceptics not raise the radical sceptical challenge?, now looks to have a coherent reply. We could say that it is their conception of a subject and her relationship to her world – and to others – that conditions and informs the way their epistemological questions are formulated. Philosophers have become accustomed to the sceptic, and some take the sceptic's questioning for granted as part of the philosophical repertoire. It is enlightening to learn that the sceptics of ancient times had a particular motivation for their scepticism: to achieve happiness in the ordinary activities of everyday life. The obstacle to happiness, in their opinion, is the pursuit of knowledge. The solution of the Pyrrhonian is to act, while at the same time to accept that it is mere opinion that informs one's actions. The Pyrrhonian, then, starts from a position that accords action precedence over knowledge. Notice that Burnyeat's assessment of the ancient's view of the subject–object relationship is clearly in keeping with this emphasis on action: action is the business of a body. If one begins with a conception of the subject living in the world with others, then any epistemological problems that arise will be tempered by this conception.

McDowell writes, 'Ancient scepticism did not call our possession of the world into question; its upshot was, less dramatically, to drive a wedge between living in the world and (what is meant to seem dispensable) knowing about it.'[44] We could say that for the sceptics of ancient times action is the primary thing. McDowell links this observation of ancient scepticism with a disjunctive account of experience. Since the time of Descartes, philosophers have been inclined to take the fact that our senses may be deceived as a reason to retreat from a position whereby our appearances are of a world to a position whereby our appearances are to a subject. McDowell believes that such a position is not necessary and that we can accommodate the possibility of illusion within a disjunctive account of experience: sometimes experience gives us access to the world, and sometimes it gives us only apparent access to the world. Which is the case is not something we are in a position to know just by reflection on our appearances (the point the ancient sceptics make so much of). McDowell insists that the fact that we are sometimes mistaken need not lead us to conclude that experience is not object involving. What follows from this is a scepticism only of the ancient variety. What we cannot get, once this conception of experience is in place, is a scepticism of the Cartesian variety. A disjunctive theory of experience allows us to retain an emphasis on living in the world.

Descartes' motivation for his scepticism is radically different from that of his predecessors. It should not be surprising, then, that he is led to a more radical sceptical challenge. For Descartes, the ordinary conduct of life is temporarily suspended so that he can establish, once and for all, that knowledge is possible. Descartes' optimism allows us to say that ultimately his conception of a subject is both as a knower and as an agent living in the world with others. But his willingness to suspend action, to retreat from the ordinary business of life in order to re-engage with it on the firm foundation offered by knowledge, reveals that Descartes' conception of the subject is not *primarily* as an agent who lives in the world and with others. This shift away from the subject as an agent living in the world is later reinforced by the mind–body divide to which Cartesian scepticism leads. The relationship between these ideas is all important. The move from practical doubt to pure enquiry is not the innocuous move it may at first appear when we read of it in the *Meditations*. The repercussions of this move are far reaching.

The idea that Descartes' epistemological concerns do not operate in a void is a familiar one from the writings of several philosophers. Various different assumptions have been identified in Descartes' work. Let us look at some of the suggestions. Michael Williams writes that 'Descartes' doubts are much less natural, much less metaphysically committal than they are made to seem.'[45] By 'less natural' Williams intends a contrast with the scepticism of the ancient Greek sceptics who, he argues, propose a scepticism that is as an extension of common sense. In contrast to this, Descartes presents us with a scepticism that is 'a theoretical problem in philosophy'.[46] Central to this theoretical epistemology is an unargued for assumption of a foundational structure to knowledge. Williams points to the second paragraph of the first *Meditation* where Descartes claims that the examination of each of his beliefs would be an 'endless task' and that in its place he proposes 'to go straight for the basic principles on which all [his] former beliefs rested'.[47] It is the foundations of our knowledge that Descartes proposes to attack, and this metaphor brings with it, argues Williams, a particular conception of justification. Williams claims that the progressive development of Descartes' doubt insinuates, without ever arguing for, a foundational conception of knowledge. According to Williams, this foundational conception of knowledge is part of Descartes' theoretical epistemology, and not commonsense scepticism.

While Williams concentrates on Descartes' conception of knowledge, Stephen Everson draws our attention to the Cartesian conception of mind. Everson examines the idea that what Descartes is proposing is an 'unadulterated epistemology' which is undertaken in advance of any commitment to a view of the nature of the world or of the mind.[48] Everson claims that the purity of the Cartesian project is illusory. According to Everson, Descartes' epistemological project begins with certain presuppositions about the mind. In particular, there is a presupposition that it is possible to be in a state of subjective certainty with regard to one's beliefs while remaining doubtful about the existence of the world around one. The preconceptions that Everson finds in Descartes' work tie in with those that Williams finds: a foundational conception of knowledge rests on a conception of mind which allows for subjective certainty in the face of objective doubt.

Other philosophers have pointed out yet other preconceptions at work in Descartes' epistemology. Marie McGinn agrees with Everson that Descartes' 'discovery' of a subjective realm is not just the outcome of a more vigorous application of doubt, but is a consequence of Descartes already having divided off the experiences of the subject from the natural world of bodies. Nevertheless, McGinn does not agree that it is Descartes' conception of the subject that is the primary motivating factor in the work. She argues, rather, that it is his conception of *reality* that is the primary motivating factor here. McGinn sees Descartes' work as contributing to an essentially Democritean conception of reality by showing how sensible or phenomenal properties can be moved to a realm all of their own – the subjective realm.[49] It is Descartes' conception of the world that drives his conception of the subject, and that lies behind and informs his epistemology. John McDowell, like McGinn, also takes the Cartesian conception of a subject to be the result of Descartes' conception of the objective world. However, McDowell takes things one step further and locates the Cartesian conception of the world in a picture of the natural sciences which is beginning to emerge in the seventeenth century. Looking back, McDowell believes we can see in Descartes an 'aspiration to accommodate psychology within a pattern of explanation characteristic of the natural sciences'.[50] This requires not only that phenomenological properties be extruded from the objective world, but also that they follow a certain pattern of explanation: these properties are the result of the causal impact of the world, and they, in turn, have a causal impact on the world. What McDowell wants is an explanation of why it is that we find the Cartesian way of thinking about the mind as gripping as we do. In effect, his explanation is that this conception of the mind is as gripping as the conception of reality that has been part of the natural sciences since the seventeenth century.

The last philosopher whose work I want to consider in this connection is Bernard Williams. Williams, like McDowell, takes the conceptual presuppositions of Descartes' work to be in line with those of science. As Williams sees it, there is at the heart of Descartes' work a scientific conception of reality and of knowledge. Descartes' project of pure enquiry – the project of 'setting aside all externalities or contingent limitations on the pursuit of truth' – is, according to Williams, motivated by 'the implicit presence of the absolute conception [of reality]'.[51] According to the absolute conception of reality, knowledge is of what is *there anyway* – independent of that knowledge. Williams takes it that Descartes adopts the stance of the pure enquirer in order to ground such a conception of reality. The idea is this: by setting aside all externalities and contingent limitations, the pure enquirer is in a position to reach beyond the occasional error introduced by our outlook on the world; he is in a position to undercut, not just ordinary occasional error, but every *conceivable* error. Thus the project of pure enquiry is linked to a particular conception – the absolute conception – of reality.

Bernard Williams – like McDowell, McGinn, Everson and Michael Williams – has drawn our attention to considerations that should make us suspicious of the idea that Descartes is presenting us with an epistemological project that we must accept at face value. However, each of these philosophers concentrates on one part of the picture to the exclusion of the whole. We need to put together all these suggestions in order fully to understand what motivates the Cartesian epistemological project. What one gets when one does put all these suggestions together can be summed up in my suggestion that in Descartes' work what one finds is a conceptual priority of knowledge over action. Let me now elaborate.

On the Cartesian picture of things we find a subject abstracted from ordinary intercourse with the world – including the world of other subjects. This is the (albeit temporary) rejection of action which is part and parcel of the pure enquirer's stance. Descartes begins his intellectual quest as an isolated subject. From this position he asks a series of questions which, at their most extreme, lead him to doubt the very existence of the world and other subjects. The conception of knowledge that is then introduced is that of an individual, temporarily isolated subject, who reaches out to a world that exists beyond him and all his experiences. Knowledge is seen as that which helps the subject to bridge the gap between himself and the world. Without this knowledge of the world, the subject must rest content with just so many subjective truths. The knower and the world are taken to be isolable units; and any individual subject's knowledge of the world is conceptually isolable from the existence of other subjects. Scepticism is forever threatening; the possibility of radical doubt about the existence of the world and other subjects is built into this picture. This is a philosophy of atoms: mental and physical atoms. It is an important part of such a philosophy that its conception of a subject is as someone isolated from other subjects. Knowledge, then, is a faculty possessed by an individual and designed to put him in touch with the world and with other subjects. Thus, Descartes can sit alone in his study and contemplate his knowledge of the world. True, he claims to be engaging in this exercise for the sake of mankind, but the rest of mankind is as much a figment of his imagination as the rest of the world until such time as he can show how we can have such knowledge.

When our concept of knowledge is tempered by that of action, the relationship between a subject, her world, and other subjects is dramatically altered. The world and other subjects can no longer be taken – even in the first instance – to be standing over and away from the subject. Knowledge cannot be thought of as an isolated subject's way of reaching out to the world and other subjects; and knowledge that is merely of subjective appearances does not count as genuine knowledge at all. On this picture of things, knowledge of the world and other subjects is bound up with our conception of the subject and her engagement with the world. One's conception of the world and of subjects comes together in the very idea of action. And in our questioning of our capacity to know the way the world is, the existence of other subjects and the world is presupposed. Which questions we then choose to ask is conditioned by these presuppositions. On this picture the radical sceptical possibility is not raised.

It is in this way that conceptual considerations drive epistemological projects. This is the lesson to be learned from the comparison of Descartes' scepticism with ancient scepticism. If one considers only Descartes' work, it would appear that epistemological considerations drive conceptual ones. That is, it looks as if the evil demon argument is just one more step that the sceptic can take, and one that the ancient sceptic simply overlooked. The result of taking this step would be a conception of the subject and his relationship to the world along Cartesian lines. But this view of the relationship leaves epistemological questions hanging in a void. The questions that Descartes' sceptic raises have lost their original motivation. They have become instead questions asked for their own sake, which we can refuse to take seriously only by appearing to miss the point. By contrast, in the scepticism of ancient times the motivation was clear: to achieve happiness in the ordinary activities of everyday life. Such happiness eludes us if we try to argue for the truth of this or that proposition. Better to live the life of the sceptic. When we look at Cartesian scepticism, we find the motivation has altered. Descartes is not primarily interested in action, nor in the happiness which may result from it. He is primarily concerned with knowledge, and to this end pursues a solo enterprise.

If one is impressed by the radical scepticism which the conception of the subject primarily as a knower threatens, it is tempting simply to reject this starting point and avoid the problem. One can justify one's rejection here by pointing back beyond Descartes to the sceptics of ancient times. Yet it is very difficult to overlook Descartes' work. Once Descartes pushes knowledge on to centre stage and shows us the radical sceptical possibility that results, it is not so easy to restrict oneself to the kind of questions raised by the sceptics of earlier times. Or so it seems. The *possibility* of pushing the doubt, of shifting our conceptual focus, seems undeniable. Once we are brought to question whether other bodies contain minds, the question remains nagging. Even once we acknowledge that conceptual issues drive epistemological ones, the Cartesian picture can look quite tempting. It may be that the philosophers of ancient times did not have a problem of other minds, but how can we return to their way of looking at the world? It can become very difficult to see just how we can return to such a state of innocence – for that is precisely how the ancient's position can look to philosophers today. Theirs is a philosophical innocence that assumes the existence of a world and other minds. Once we see the possibility of raising issues in another way, we may also see that perhaps we do need to say something about how we can know that the world and other minds exist. McDowell writes in another context of a 'postlapsarian or knowing counterpart of Aristotle's innocence'.[52] I want to borrow this phrase and suggest that what we need here is a postlapsarian or knowing counterpart of the ancient sceptic's innocence. What I mean is that we need to understand just how we can, in the light of Descartes' considerations, continue to affirm a realism about the world and about other minds – a realism that does not allow for the possibility of solipsism. We can begin to see how this can be done if we continue to emphasize the concept of action and keep it in balance with that of knowledge. It is in the concept of action that the world of objects and of other subjects is to be found. This is because the concept of action involves the concept of a behaving subject, and it is in a certain understanding of behaviour that we find reference must be made to a subject in interaction with other subjects.

In the remaining chapters of Part One, I want to look in some detail at the work of philosophers who accept this radical conceptual divide between the subject and her world. I shall hereafter refer to this radical conceptual divide as the *Cartesian framework*. It is important to note that this Cartesian framework is to be found embedded in the philosophical system of many a philosopher who would reject much else to do with Descartes' system. Thus, philosophers of what is called the classical empiricist school – i.e. John Locke and Bishop Berkeley – are committed to this Cartesian framework as much as heterodox rationalists such as Nicolas Malebranche. Furthermore, as we saw towards the end of the previous chapter, this Cartesian framework can also be seen to be in place in the work of many modern-day philosophers who would insist that their work must be understood to exist at some distance from the substantial dualism that Descartes introduced into philosophy. I shall be looking at the work of some of these philosophers in Part Three. So long as this Cartesian framework is in place, our knowledge of the mind of another remains open to question. In Part One I shall be looking at how philosophers working within this framework propose to answer that question. In Part Two I shall look at the work of two philosophers who find these proposed answers inadequate, and who suggest an anti-Cartesian alternative to them. Building on the anti-Cartesian foundations of these philosophers, I shall suggest in Part Three that the real problem of other minds is a conceptual one. If one begins with a conception of the subject acting in the world with other subjects, the epistemological questions that one encounters are of a limited kind. So long as philosophers insist on understanding the problem of other minds to be the epistemological one of saying how an individual with a mind can know the existence of any other mind, they will fail to see the real problem of other minds that arises within the Cartesian framework.

CHAPTER II

Descartes and knowledge of other minds

INTRODUCTION

The epistemological problem of other minds is, as I explained in Chapter I, a legacy of Cartesian philosophy. By this I mean that Descartes put in place a conceptual framework which can be understood to give rise to a radical scepticism about the mind of another. Once the mind is radically divorced from the body, then even if we can show that there can be knowledge of body there remains the further question, How do we know whether there is a mind connected with any given body that we may encounter? One standard response to this question – and a very natural one – has come to be known as the argument from analogy. According to this argument, I come to know that another has a mind in the following manner: I begin by assuming the existence of my own mind and noting a correlation between my having a mind and my behaviour. I then observe similar sorts of behaviour in another, and conclude *by analogy* that the other also has a mind. Thus I reason from what I know with certainty to what I have reason to think is the case. Notice that there is a certain insecurity involved in such a form of reasoning; the conclusions of such an argument are no more than probable: given what I do know with security (the existence of my own mind), it is probable to some degree or other that there are other minds. The important point to note is that, as things stand, I am not in a position to do more than observe the external trappings of your mind; the mind of another is not the sort thing I can observe. Hence, if we are to have even probable knowledge that another mind exists, it must be based on some form of reasoning from what can be observed. Philosophers have been quick to find the argument from analogy in the work of philosophers from Descartes onwards. One question I shall be asking in Chapters II–V is whether we really can find this argument in the work of the philosophers I shall be presenting. I shall begin in this chapter by asking whether there is any reason to think that that argument – or anything resembling it – can be discerned in the work of Descartes himself. Before I turn to Descartes, however, I want to pause and take a very brief look at a passage that we can find in the writings of St Augustine which very much resembles the argument from analogy that I have just outlined.

BRIEF INTERLUDE: ST AUGUSTINE

St Augustine lived at the turn from the fourth to the fifth century CE. He is generally taken to have anticipated Descartes' *cogito ergo sum* (I think therefore I am) with his *si fallor sum* (if I am mistaken, I am). In the light of this, the question of just how far Augustine may be taken to have prefigured Descartes is an interesting one. In particular, it is interesting to ask whether Augustine used the observation that one cannot be in any doubt about one's own mind to raise a radical sceptical doubt about the world of bodies. Descartes, himself, was of the opinion that he and Augustine differed in an important way. In a letter to Colvius Descartes writes:

> I am obliged to you for drawing my attention to the passage of St Augustine relevant to my *I am thinking, therefore I exist*. I went today to the library of this town to read it, and I do indeed find that he does use it to prove the certainty of our existence. He goes on to show that there is a certain likeness of the Trinity in us, in that we exist, we know that we exist. . . . I, on the other hand, use the argument to show that this *I* which is thinking is *an immaterial substance* with no bodily element. These are two different things. In itself it is such a simple and natural thing to infer that one exists from the fact that one is doubting that it could have occurred to any writer.[1]

More recent commentators agree with Descartes. Copleston sums up Augustine's work on epistemology thus:

> In fine, Augustine may have anticipated Descartes with his '*Si fallor sum*', but he was not occupied with the question whether the external world really exists or not. That it exists, he felt no doubt, though he saw clearly enough that we sometimes make erroneous judgements about it and that testimony is not always

reliable, whether it be testimony of our own sense or that of other people.[2]

If this is correct, then we can say that Augustine did not take the step that would divorce appearance from reality and thus lead to a radical scepticism about the world and, consequently, to a radical scepticism about the mind of another. Indeed, we find in Augustine's writings passages that indicate that he holds that it is, in part, by reliance on other persons that we come by what knowledge we do have. Thus in *De Trinitate* Augustine points out that it would be 'absurd' to deny that we know what we have learned from the testimony of others. From this we must acknowledge that 'not only the senses of our bodies, but those of the bodies of others, too have added very much to our knowledge'.[3] And in the *Confessions* Augustine points out that it is necessary for the practical life that we must believe, among other things, the testimony of others (including what another tells us about his mental states). He writes: 'Unless we believed what we are told, we would do nothing at all in this life.'[4]

If it is correct that Augustine did not question the existence of other minds, it is unclear how we are to understand the following passage from *De Trinitate*:

> For we recognize the movements of bodies also, by which we perceive that others live besides ourselves, from the resemblance of ourselves; since we also so move our body in living as we observe those bodies to be moved. For even when a living body is moved, there is no way opened to our eyes to see the mind, a thing which cannot be seen by the eyes; but we perceive something to be contained in that bulk, such as is contained in ourselves, so as to move in a like manner our own bulk, which is the life and the soul. . . . Therefore we . . . know the mind of any one from our own, and believe also from our own of him whom we do not know. For not only do we perceive that there is a mind, but we can also know what a mind is, by reflecting upon our own: for we have a mind.[5]

Prima facie it looks as if Augustine is proposing an argument from analogy for our knowledge of the existence of another mind. This, however, would be in tension with the suggestion that Augustine never questioned the existence of another mind. Some commentators have suggested another, very interesting, interpretation of this passage.[6] This alternative interpretation emphasizes what Augustine writes towards the end of the above-quoted passage: 'we . . . believe also from our own of him whom we do not know'. We do not know that another has a mind, but we believe he does.

Augustine is quite clear about what it is that stands in the way of knowledge here. He writes:

> 'Know thyself' is not said to the mind as 'Know the cherubim and seraphim'; for they are absent, and we believe concerning them, according to that belief they are declared to be certain celestial powers. Nor again as it is said, 'Know the will of that man', for it is not within our reach to perceive at all, either by sense or understanding, unless by corporeal signs set forth; and this in such a way that we rather believe than understand.[7]

The problem, then, is that we cannot perceive another's will. Augustine is also clear that the case of another is very different from one's own. About one's own case, he writes:

> But when it is said to the mind, 'Know thyself'; then it knows itself by the very act by which it understands the word 'thyself'; and this for no reason than that it is present to itself.[8]

From this Augustine concludes that we can know ourselves, but not another. Yet we do believe in the existence of others. At this point Augustine raises a very important question: How are we to understand this belief? Given that we know the mind by reflection on our own mind, what needs to be accounted for is our belief that there are *other* minds. It is to this end that, according to Matthews and McNulty, Augustine introduces an argument from analogy: we understand what it is for another to have a mind by analogy with what we know in our own case. Matthews suggests that the passage in question has to do, not with the limits of what one can *know*, but rather with the limits of what one can *think about*.[9] He writes: 'The problem for Augustine is how to understand the word "soul" (or "mind") as a general term. But equally it is how to conceive, as a general thing, what a soul or mind is.'[10] Matthews' interpretation finds support in *De Trinitate* 8, 6, 9, just before the passage where he introduces this so-called argument from analogy. Augustine writes:

> And we say, indeed, not unfitly, that we therefore know what a mind is, because we too have a mind. For neither did we ever see it with our eyes, and gather a special or general notion from

the resemblance of more minds than one, which we had seen; but rather, as I have said before, because we too have it. For what is known so intimately, and so perceives itself to be itself, as that by which also all other things are perceived, that is, the mind itself?

Augustine then proceeds to set out a so-called argument from analogy.

The problem with which Augustine can here be taken to be grappling is the conceptual problem of other minds. We need an understanding of how it is that we so much as think that there are other minds, given that my knowledge of mind comes from reflection on my own case. Without such an understanding we are in danger of succumbing to conceptual solipsism. The conceptual solipsist challenges us so much as to make sense of the attribution of mind to another. His point is that, if I come to think about mind in the first place from reflection on my own mind, it is a real question how I extend this concept to include the mind of another. As Augustine does hold that we come to think of the mind by reflection on our own case, he must say something to avoid conceptual solipsism. If Matthews and McNulty are right, Augustine understands the need to give some account of this belief.[11] The account that Augustine offers draws on the argument from analogy: I get my concept of mind by reflection on my own case and I extend it from there by analogy.

Augustine is surely right to think that, given the way he thinks I come to know mind, the generality of that concept needs some account; what is not so clear is that the argument from analogy gives us that account. In Part Three I shall raise some problems for this way of understanding our belief in another mind. For the moment the important thing is not so much the question whether the argument from analogy succeeds in providing us with a general concept of mind, but the recognition that some argument or account of the generality of our concept of mind is required. The problem for Augustine is to say how generality can be achieved for a concept that I come to have from reflection on my own case. Without such an account I appear to be left with a concept that applies in my own case, but whose extension to others is problematic. Without some workable account here it is hard to see how we so much as come by our *belief* that another has a mind. This problem precedes and is quite distinct from the question how we know that another mind exists.

When one looks at the work of philosophers of the modern period – philosophers from Descartes to, roughly, Berkeley – one finds no recognition of this problem. As far as these philosophers are concerned, the only issue that is raised concerning others is how I know of their existence. Yet all of these philosophers begin where Augustine begins, by insisting that I know what mind is by reflection on my own mind. And insofar as they do start here, it would appear that there *is* a conceptual question to be raised. Nevertheless, there is no recognition of this question in the work of philosophers throughout this period. For this reason, I shall put the conceptual question to one side for the moment and concentrate on what these philosophers do have to say – which concerns the question of our knowledge of the existence of another mind. I shall, however, from time to time draw attention to the conceptual problem and indicate the way in which it might be thought to arise in the work of these philosophers. On the whole, however, I shall not say much about the conceptual problem again until Part Three. I want to begin by looking at Descartes' work. Interestingly, it would appear that Descartes does not recognize either the conceptual or the epistemological problem of other minds.

DESCARTES AND THE PROBLEM OF OTHER MINDS

Despite the fact that Descartes can be credited with having put in place a philosophical framework that gives rise to an epistemological problem about the mind of another, there is little acknowledgement of this problem in his work. Towards the end of Chapter I, I quoted a passage from the *Principles of Philosophy* where Descartes notes the separation of every thinking thing from every other thinking thing and from corporeal substance. Removed from context this passage looks set to introduce a problem about other minds. However, the passage in fact is part of a discussion of substance; it sheds no light at all on the problem of other minds. Descartes touches upon the issue in *The Search for Truth*, where he writes,

> Thus I shall be uncertain not only about whether you are in the world and whether there is an earth or a sun; but also about whether I have eyes, ears, a body, and even whether I am speaking to you and you are speaking to me. In short, I shall doubt everything.[12]

However, having raised a doubt about those with whom he converses, Descartes does not return specifically to explain how it is that I can have knowledge that I do indeed converse with others. Descartes concentrates on showing how we have knowledge of bodies; our knowledge of other minds is left unattended. There is, nonetheless, a temptation to assume that Descartes does address at least the episte-mological problem of other minds, and that he responds to it by offering an argument from analogy.[13] The passages most often cited in this connection come from the end of the second *Meditation* and Part V of the *Discourse on Method*. I shall argue below that, contrary to what is widely believed, close reading of these passages reveals that Descartes could not have been thinking along the lines of the argu-ment from analogy. Despite the fact that Descartes does hold that I can know my own mind with certainty, there is evidence in these passages that he does not employ this as a premise in *any* argument or form of reasoning to the existence of mind in another. Indeed, I shall argue that some of what Descartes does say would be incompatible with such a form of argument. One must, of course, be careful not to base too much on so little. Nevertheless, given that Descartes' work can be argued to have bequeathed to philosophy a certain problem about the mind of another, it is hardly surprising that we should try to see what Descartes might have had to say on the subject. As for the conceptual question introduced by Augustine, it is evident that Descartes did not think he needed to address this question. Although Descartes could agree (up to a point) with Augustine that we get our idea of mind by reflection on our mind, he appears to hold that the idea I come to have is a completely general one.[14] For the moment I shall assume that there is no difficulty with Descartes' conceptual position here, although I shall return to question it in Part Three, Chapter IX. For the rest of this chapter I shall concentrate on the question whether Descartes uses the argument from analogy to address the epistemo-logical question about other minds.

DESCARTES AND THE ARGUMENT FROM ANALOGY

As we have seen, the argument from analogy to the conclusion that other minds exist proceeds in two stages: first there is the observation that another body moves in a way similar to the way I move; and second there is the observation that the other must have a mind by analogy with what I know to be the case in myself. The argument can be seen to involve two quite separate observations and two quite sep-arate judgements. These two observations, or judgements, are in keeping with the metaphysics of the Cartesian framework: there is, on the one hand, mind and, on the other, body; the judgement that there is another mind is additional to the judgement that there is a body of a certain sort. Although it would have been open to Descartes to argue in this way, there is no evidence that he did. Indeed, Descartes appears to hold that there is one single judgement involved in the observation of another mind. I take this to be evidence that he did not employ any argument from analogy.

Let us begin by looking at a passage from Descartes' second *Meditation*:

> But then if I look out of a window and see men crossing the square, as I just happen to have done, I normally say that I see the men themselves . . . Yet do I see more than hats and coats which could conceal automatic machines? I *judge* that they are men.[15]

In this passage Descartes introduces a contrast between men who have minds and automatic machines that do not. It is tempting to read this passage as revealing of Descartes' view on the question of how we come to know about the existence of minds in others. If we look at the passage in context, however, we find that his passage is supplementary to the discussion of a quite different issue. Let me briefly set out Descartes' discussion at this point.

At the beginning of the second *Meditation* Descartes finds that, although he can doubt whether the things he sees really do exist, what he cannot doubt is that it seems to him that he sees certain things – of himself as a thinking thing he can have no doubt. From this he concludes that mind is better known than body. Descartes is quick to acknowledge that this conclusion may appear counterintuitive: it certainly seems to be that case that corporeal objects that one can sense are better known than mind. In order to prove that things are other than they seem, Descartes asks us to consider a piece of wax. He asks us to note the qualities of the wax – its colour, figure, size, etc. – and also to note how all these qualities change when the wax is placed in fire. Despite all the changes, we would say that we have before us the same piece of wax. Descartes then asks how we come to this conclusion given that all the information that the senses yield has undergone alteration in the fire. In answer to this question Descartes draws a distinction between the work of the senses or imagination and the work of the understanding. According to Descartes, the imagination is limited to what is presented to the senses. The imagination cannot comprehend what the wax is; it cannot comprehend the infinitude of possible changes that the wax may undergo. That the wax remains the same is something 'perceived by the mind alone'; it is something we understand or judge.[16] This intuition is part of our human perception of the wax. Descartes draws a firm line between the perception of human and non-human animals. The sensible modes of a body are perceived by both, but it is only human animals that perceive the true nature of body. Descartes concludes that,

> without any effort I have now finally got back to where I wanted. I now know that even bodies are not strictly perceived by the senses or the faculty of imagination but by the intellect alone, and that this perception derives not from their being touched or seen but from their being understood; in view of this I know plainly that I can achieve an easier and more evident perception of my own mind than of anything else.[17]

Descartes does, however, note that, although this should be clear when we reflect upon it, we are apt to fall into error on this point. He suggests that an erroneous way of thinking here is aided and abetted by the terms of ordinary language. We are, he writes,

> almost tricked by ordinary ways of talking. We say that we see the wax itself, if it is there before us, and not that we simply judge it to be there from its colour or shape; and this might lead me to conclude without more ado that knowledge of the wax comes from what the eyes see, and not from scrutiny of the mind alone. But then if I look out of a window and see men crossing the square, as I just happen to have done, I normally say that I see the men themselves, just as I say that I see the wax. Yet do I see more than hats and coats which could conceal automatons? I *judge* that they are men.[18]

In this passage, language, which would appear to lead *away* from Descartes' conclusion concerning the role of understanding in human perception, is shown to be deceptive. Descartes compares the case of the wax to that of seeing men from the window. We say that we see men, when all we really see are hats and coats. This example is used by Descartes to reveal the lie which language tells. The point is that, on the basis of what we do see – in this case hats and coats – we judge that there are men in the street. In similar fashion we see the outward forms and judge that we are seeing a piece of wax. Descartes writes,

> But when I distinguish the wax from its outward forms – take the clothes off, as it were, and consider it naked – then although my judgement may still contain errors, at least my perception now requires a human mind.[19]

As well as to show how language misleads us, Descartes appears also to use the comparison with the case of men to provide an appropriate metaphor for human perception. Just as men can be considered apart from their literal clothing, the piece of wax can be considered apart from its metaphorical clothing. The qualities that we see serve as clothes which obscure from us the true nature of the object. At this point, however, the comparison may look somewhat strained. Surely, in the case of men further metaphorical clothing lies beneath the literal clothing. Yet to mention this would spoil the simplicity of Descartes' point. What Descartes is after here is a use of language concerning perception that is clearly deceptive.[20]

Descartes' concern in this passage is clearly not with the problem of other minds. His comments about men and automatons are incidental to his discussion of the piece of wax. What Descartes wants to show in this passage is how language misleads us, and he offers two examples. The point about how language works in the case of the wax is well taken, but surely had Descartes been considering the perception of men in its own right he would not have wanted to suggest that we judge on the basis of the literal clothing worn by the figures that what we have before us are men. Clearly, when we see men without their hats and coats we are seeing them 'naked' in a most superficial sense. Like the piece of wax, the men have outward forms that can change while they, the men, remain the same. Despite the fact that Descartes only introduces the case of men as an analogy for the case wax, we do find upon closer examination that Descartes is rather careful with his chosen example. The contrast he draws between men and automatons is in keeping with his thinking elsewhere in his writings, and, given this, it may be possible to glean something of his views concerning other men and our perception of them from this passage. Let us explore this idea and see what happens if we pursue the analogy between seeing the wax and seeing men.

If we substitute the word 'man' for 'wax' in the above-quoted passage we discover something interesting. Thus:

> But when I distinguish the man from his outward forms – take his clothes off, as it were, and consider him naked – then although my judgement may still contain errors, at least my perception now requires a human mind.

The question that is thrown up by consideration of this passage so transposed is this: Are the outward forms here under consideration those of a human being without a mind or those of a human being with a mind? These two questions fall apart quite naturally once one accepts the Cartesian framework. Where there is a logical separation of mind from body, it would seem natural for two distinct questions to be raised: first, concerning the body of the other and second, concerning the mind of the other. It would appear from the passage under consideration, however, that Descartes does not raise two questions. He does not say that we look at the individual before us and perceive it first as a body of a certain sort – say, the body of a human being – and then perceive that this body has a mind. Descartes raises only one question: is the individual before me a man or not? So the question naturally arises whether, when he speaks of 'man', Descartes means to refer to a human being only, or to an individual with a mind?

I shall suggest an answer to this question below. Before I do this, however, I want first to answer another question that may arise in connection with the contrast that Descartes draws between men and automatons in the second *Meditation*. The question is this: Why is it that Descartes contrasts men only with automatons? Why does he not mention the possibility that what lurks beneath the hats and coats is a monkey or a dog walking on its hind legs? It is to this question that I turn in the next section.

MEN VERSUS AUTOMATONS

In the passage from the second *Meditation* under consideration Descartes contrasts men with automatons: we judge that the figures we see from our windows are men and not automatons. It may seem curious that Descartes should have chosen this contrast. Why does he not consider the possibility that there are non-human animals beneath the hats and coats? That Descartes draws the contrast in the way he does is related to the fact that he accepts the following two theses:

(I)   There is a distinction in kind between men and all other living creatures; and
(II) There is no distinction in kind between living creatures and mere mechanisms.

As a result of holding these two theses, Descartes concludes that all non-human animals are *bêtes*-machines. Once this is understood, we can see that when Descartes contrasts men with automatons he is, in effect, contrasting men with all non-human animals.

Gareth Matthews has written that in holding these two theses Descartes is making an important – and conscious – break with the past.[21] Descartes makes evident his commitment to Thesis I when he writes the following in reply to an objection from Gassendi:

> Thus, primitive man probably did not distinguish between, on the one hand, the principle by which we are nourished and grow and accomplish without any thought all the operations which we have in common with the brutes, and, on the other hand, the principle in virtue of which we think. He therefore used the single term 'soul' to apply to both; and when he subsequently noticed that thought was distinct from nutrition, he called the element which thinks 'mind', and believed it to be the principle part of the soul. I, by contrast, realizing that the principle by which we are nourished is wholly different – different in kind – from that in virtue of which we think, have said that the term 'soul', when it is used to refer to both these principles, is ambiguous. . . . For I consider the mind not as a part of the soul but as the thinking soul in its entirety.[22]

Descartes here makes it clear that he wishes to introduce a firm distinction between those functions which man shares with the lower animals, such as growth and nourishment, and that which is distinctively human. He wants to restrict the term 'mind' to cover the thinking part of man; the mind is 'the thinking soul in its entirety'. There is to be no more equivocation: mind is soul. As a result, the lower animals who grow, are nourished and move in various ways are considered by Descartes to have no mind, no soul. Despite the fact that Descartes does not think that they have a mind or soul, he allows that these lower animals are alive. Bodies are alive, and this is a fact independent of the possession of a mind or soul. That some bodies are in possession of a mind is something extra – something divinely ordered. Matthews writes that with this demarcation of the soul Descartes seeks to break the conceptual connection between being conscious and being alive which was upheld by earlier philosophers.[23]

Once the soul is divorced in this way from the living body, the way is clear to think of the body as a machine. This is Descartes' view of *all* bodies – including the human body – viewed as devoid of a mind. Thus we find Descartes writing in his *Treatise on Man*:

> I should like you to consider . . . all the functions I have ascribed to this machine – such as the digestion of food, the beating of the heart and arteries, the nourishment and growth of the limbs,

respiration, waking and sleeping, the reception by the external sense organs of light, sounds, smells, tastes, heat and other such qualities . . . I should like you to consider that these functions follow from the mere arrangement of the machine's organs every bit as naturally as the movements of a clock or other automaton follow from the arrangement of its counter-weights and wheels.[24]

Here Descartes makes it clear that some machines are living things. This coincidence between mechanism and living thing is, once again, something that philosophers of earlier times would have rejected.[25] Just as philosophers before Descartes would have claimed a connection between consciousness and being alive, so they would have claimed a separation between living things and mechanisms. The break for pre-Cartesian philosophers is between living things which possess souls and mechanisms, while the break for Descartes is between those creatures that God has endowed with a mind or soul and those that He did not so endow. Drawing on the passage from Descartes' *Treatise* just quoted, we can extract the following definition of an automaton:

(A)   An automaton is a body whose functions – no matter how sophisticated – can be seen to follow from the arrangement of its parts.

All animal bodies are, by this definition, automatons. What distinguishes human animals from non-human animals is the fact that the former have been endowed by God with minds. Devoid of a mind, non-human animals are subsumed under the category of automatons; they are *bêtes*-machines.[26] When Descartes contrasts men with automatic machines in the second *Meditation*, he is, in effect, contrasting a body to which God has conjoined a mind with a mindless body. Monkeys and dogs on hind legs are among the automatons which he rules out when he judges that there are indeed men beneath the hats and coats that he sees from his window. This follows from the fact that, for Descartes, a soul-less living body is an automaton.

In a letter written to Reneri for Pollot, Descartes considers a certain opposition to his conclusion concerning non-human animals. In this letter he acknowledges that many of the actions of non-human animals resemble ours, and that, as a result, we are liable to judge that these animals have a mind or soul. Descartes even admits that 'all of us are deeply imbued with this opinion by nature'.[27] So strong is this belief that it is hard to deny it, says Descartes, without exposing oneself to ridicule. In order to uphold his thesis concerning non-human animals in the face of this belief, Descartes asks us to consider the following: Imagine a man who has been brought up his entire life without ever having encountered non-human animals. And imagine that such a man is devoted to mechanics, and is able to construct automatons in the shape of men. And say that such a man sometimes finds it extremely difficult to tell the difference between these automatons and real men, but learns from experience that there are, in fact, two tests for telling them apart: a real man uses language and he is capable of highly adaptable behaviour.[28] Finally, let us say that this man acknowledges that God possesses a superior skill in constructing things. Now consider that such a man is presented for the first time with non-human animals that are clearly of God's making. Descartes claims that this man would notice that, despite the high quality of design in these creatures, the tests that he found to separate real men from his own constructed men would be applicable in connection with God's created non-human animals. Descartes concludes: 'There is no doubt that [this man] would not come to the conclusion that there was any real feeling or emotion in [these animals], but would think they were automatons.'[29]

Thus, Descartes gazes from his window into the street and judges that the figures that he sees are men and not *bêtes*-machines. But what about the possibility that these figures are *hommes*-machines? According to definition (A), an automaton may be a mindless living human body. Should a human body be devoid of a mind, would this body not then fall into the category of automaton, and, as such, must it not be distinguished from a real man? If it is possible for there to be mindless human bodies, then when Descartes looks from his window he must judge that the figures he sees are neither *bêtes*-machines nor *hommes*-machines. Furthermore, it may be thought that he must also judge that the figures that walk in the street below his window are men produced by God and not mindless robots produced in the workshops of men.

It is clear from the text that Descartes does not intend the term 'automaton' to cover so many possibilities. If we first consider the difference between a soul-less machine produced in God's workshop and one produced in the workshop of men, we find Descartes believes there is a discernible difference here: God's machines are 'incomparably better ordered' and possess movements which are 'more wonderful' than any machine that can be devised by man.[30] So long as the figures seen from the window are of the more admirably arranged kind, we can ignore the possibility that they were produced in the workshop of a man. What, though, of the possibility of a God-produced *homme*-machine? That God could produce such machines, there seems little doubt. That God in fact produced such machines, Descartes appears not to believe.[31] I shall cite the textual evidence for this in the following section.

The conclusion of this section is that, when Descartes considers the judgement that the figures beneath the hats and coats are men and not automatons, he is here subsuming the contrast between men and non-human animals. The distinction Descartes draws between men and automatons can be seen to be a distinction between those bodies with which God has chosen to unite a mind and those bodies – living or otherwise – which He has not. In effect the distinction Descartes is drawing is between human animals and everything else.

ALL AND (OF CORPOREAL BEINGS) ONLY HUMAN ANIMALS HAVE MINDS

Towards the end of the previous section I suggested that Descartes does not believe that God has produced any *hommes*-machines; he believes that all human animals have minds. Descartes also believes that, if one restricts consideration to corporeal beings, only human animals have minds. All non-human animals – along with other automatons – are mindless or soul-less. I shall present the evidence for each of these claims in turn.

If we first consider the claim that human animals are unique and different from all other animals by their possession of a mind, we find that this claim was brought under attack even in Descartes' own time. Philosophers challenged Descartes' claim that human animals alone exhibit behaviour of a particularly sophisticated kind.[32] But such criticism overlooks the fact that Descartes never denies that some animals exhibit extreme dexterity of behaviour in certain situations. What Descartes claims is that the observation of animal dexterity is offset by another: non-human animals can be observed to manifest no dexterity in certain other situations. If these animals were possessed of genuine intelligence, there would not be such an asymmetry in their behaviour. Descartes here concludes:

> It is nature which acts in them according to the disposition of their organs. In the same way a clock, consisting only of wheels and springs, can count the hours and measure the time more accurately than we can with all our wisdom.[33]

Further to this Descartes writes in a letter to the Marquess of Newcastle:

> If they thought as we do, [non-human animals] would have an immortal soul like us. This is unlikely, because there is no reason to believe it of some animals without believing it of all, and many of them such as oysters and sponges are too imperfect for this to be credible.[34]

It would appear from this passage that Descartes was driven by theological and moral considerations to deny souls or minds to all non-human animals. This is reinforced by the following passage from the *Discourse on Method*:

> For after the error of those who deny God . . . there is none that leads weak minds further from the straight path of virtue than that of imagining that the souls of the beasts are of the same nature as ours, and hence that after this present life we have nothing to fear or to hope for, any more than flies and ants.[35]

Descartes is openly dismissive of the idea of non-human animal immortality in a letter that he writes to More:

> It is more probable that worms, flies, caterpillars and other animals move like machines than that they all have immortal souls.[36]

Leaving aside, for the moment, his reasons for the claim, it is quite clear that Descartes believes that, of corporeal beings, only human animals have been endowed by God with minds.

There is equally clear evidence from the texts that Descartes believes that God has endowed all human animals with minds. God's workshop has produced no *hommes*-machines. To see this it is important to understand the connection, as Descartes sees it, between having a mind and having a language. In the *Discourse on Method* Descartes suggests two 'means of recognizing' whether an individual is a cleverly constructed machine or a real man. The first is that a real man uses language, and the second is that the actions of a real man manifest a high degree of a dexterity and adaptability.[37] Descartes then considers the possibility that a machine may be so constituted as to utter words – even to utter words in response to certain stimuli. About such a possibility he writes,

But it is not conceivable that such a machine should produce different arrangements of words so as to give an appropriately meaningful answer to whatever is said in its presence, as the dullest man can do.[38]

Further to this, in the same letter to the Marquess of Newcastle quoted from earlier, Descartes writes,

There is no human being so imperfect as not to . . . invent special signs to express their thoughts.[39]

And in the letter to More quoted from above, Descartes writes,

Such speech is the only certain sign of thought hidden in a body. All human beings use it, however stupid and insane they may be, even though they may have no tongue and organs of voice; but no animals do.[40]

Finally, returning to the *Discourse on Method* we find Descartes writing,

For it is quite remarkable that there are no men so dull-witted and stupid – and this includes even madmen – that they are incapable of arranging various words together and forming an utterance from them in order to make their thoughts understood.[41]

Descartes does recognize that animals such as magpies and parrots utter words, much as we do, but he concludes that they 'cannot speak as we do: that is, they cannot show that they are thinking what they are saying'.[42]

It is clear that Descartes believes that it is the use of language that marks off those individuals that are endowed with a mind from those that are not. All and (of corporeal beings) only human animals have minds. Descartes does not believe that God has produced any *hommes*-machines.[43]

When Descartes looks from his window on to the figures in the street below he judges that they are men and not automatons. We can now understand that this distinction between men and automatons is designed to encompass all the distinctions that Descartes thinks there are. He does not need to consider separately the possibility that the figures in the street are non-human animals, because he takes this possibility to be subsumed by the possibility that they are automatons. Nor does he need to consider the possibility that the figures are mere *hommes*-machines since he does not believe that God created any such individuals.

THE TEST OF A REAL MAN[44]

I pointed out earlier that Descartes makes these comments about our judgement concerning the figures in the street as an incidental part of a passage which is designed to illustrate the sometimes deceptive nature of language. There is no evidence that he intends these comments to be part of any discussion about other minds. Nevertheless, we have seen that Descartes is careful here to illustrate the operation of judgement in a manner which reflects his thinking about minded and non-minded individuals. Despite the incidental nature of these remarks, then, they may be taken to be revealing of Descartes' thoughts about our judgement concerning other men. With this in mind, I want now to return to the passage in the second *Meditation* where Descartes makes these comments about our judgement and pursue the analogy between our perception of the piece of wax and our perception of the men in the street.

Concerning our judgement of the piece of wax, Descartes writes that the human mind is not just capable of perceiving the sensible or outward forms of the wax, but can consider the wax apart from its 'clothes'. It is in this way that the human mind is able to appreciate the true nature of the wax. I suggested earlier that we might consider the perception of the figure of a man to work in a similar way. Thus, the human mind is not just capable of perceiving the sensible or outward forms of a man, but can consider him apart from his 'clothes'. It is in this way that the human mind is able to appreciate the true nature of a man. In the passage under consideration Descartes writes of the hats and coats which the man wears, and I suggested earlier that these literal clothes could not be what Descartes had in mind as the sensible or outward forms of a man. When, however, we do ask the question, What are the outward forms of a man?, we run up against a certain ambiguity: are the outward forms under consideration those of a human being without a mind or those of a minded human being?

When we consider a piece of wax what we find is that it is the colour, the shape and the like that constitute its outward forms. It is these that are transformed when the wax is placed near the fire. If we now turn to consider the case of the man, a parallel would suggest that the outward forms here are the man's shape, colour and the like. If these are what Descartes takes the outward forms of a man to be, it would follow that by the term 'man' Descartes is referring to a human being – an animal considered apart from his mind. There is evidence, however, that Descartes does not intend us to understand the outward forms of a man in this way.

The question before us is this: In the case of Descartes' man, what is it that we perceive when we judge that what is before us is a man and not an automaton? I want to suggest that we find an answer to this question in the *Discourse on Method*, Part V. Here we find Descartes recounting something he had written elsewhere, regarding the possibility of producing automata of some sophistication. Descartes writes,

> Here I made special efforts to show that if any such machines had the organs and outward shape of a monkey or of some other animal that lacks reason, we should have no means of knowing that they did not possess entirely the same nature as these animals; whereas if any such machines bore a resemblance to our bodies and imitated our actions as closely as possible for all practical purposes, we should still have two very certain means of recognizing [tests] that they were not real men.[45]

The first test is that a real man uses language. As we have already seen, Descartes considers that a machine may be so constructed as to emit verbal responses in reaction to things said to it, but is quick to point out that such a machine would be unable to respond to everything that was said to it. The second test that Descartes mentions is that a real man is able to respond and adapt to many different situations, while a machine would have to have its organs especially adapted for every occasion. Thus we find that, although a machine may be immeasurably better than we are in some respects, it will fall well short of our ability in others. True reason allows for adaptability and flexibility.

Descartes ends Part V of the *Discourse* by remarking that the rational soul 'cannot be derived in any way from the potentiality of matter, but must be specially created'. Furthermore, it must be closely united with the body 'to constitute a real man'.[46] Descartes' man has a mind. This is in keeping with the two proposed tests of a real man: a real man uses language and is able to adapt his actions to suit the circumstance. It is by reference to language and adaptability that men are to be distinguished from mere automata. It is quite plausible that Descartes regarded language and adaptable behaviour as the (metaphorical) clothes – the outward forms – of a man. What we observe when we encounter a man is not just his hat and coat but his actions and his use of language. On this basis the human mind perceives – understands – that what is before it is a man and not an automaton.[47]

According to Descartes, when we judge that the figure before us is a man we are judging that he is a human being with a mind. In doing this we have distinguished this figure from all non-human animals and other automata. And it would appear that we make this distinction with a single judgement. Descartes does not suggest that we first judge that the figure before us is a human being and then make a further judgement to the effect that this human being has a mind. Rather, we observe the outward forms – the use of language – and judge that the figure is a man.

DESCARTES' OPTIMISM

I want now to turn to the question of knowledge. To see how the question of knowledge arises here, let us return to the passage towards the end of the second *Meditation* where Descartes writes of the outward forms of the wax. Recall that Descartes here writes: 'when I distinguish the wax from its outward forms . . . then although my judgement may still contain errors, at least my perception now requires a human mind'.[48] When Descartes writes here of 'errors' what does he have in mind? The errors that Descartes has in mind here are those that he outlines in the first *Meditation*. He is referring back to the sceptic who challenges us to say how we know that our judgement may not be in error about the absolute existence of what we judge to be the case. That is, the sceptic asks how we know that we are not being deceived by a malicious demon with the result that the wax that I judge to be before me, and the figures in the street that I judge to be men, may not all be a product of this demon. It is only if we are in a position to reply to the sceptic that, according to Descartes, we can be said to have knowledge.

Descartes thinks he can show that the situation with which the sceptic faces us is not our true situation. Thus he ends his *Principles of Philosophy* by writing:

> Besides, there are some matters, even in relation to the things in nature, which we regard as absolutely, and more than just morally, certain. <Absolute certainty arises when we believe that it is wholly impossible that something should be otherwise than we judge it to be.> This certainty is based on a metaphysical

foundation, namely that God is supremely good and in no way a deceiver, and hence that the faculty which he gave us for distinguishing truth from falsehood cannot lead us into error, so long as we are using it properly and are thereby perceiving something distinctly. Mathematical demonstrations have this kind of certainty, as does the knowledge that material things exist; and the same goes for all evident reasoning about material things.[49]

Descartes holds that we advance from moral certainty (certainty which he describes as 'sufficient . . . for application to ordinary life'[50]) to absolute certainty (certainty whereby it is 'wholly impossible that something should be otherwise than we judge it to be') once we prove the existence of a non-deceiving God. Descartes takes it that he has given this proof in the third and sixth *Meditations*. Once we do have a proof of the existence of a non-deceiving God, we can rest assured that the faculty He has given us for distinguishing truth from falsehood will not lead us astray – provided, that is, we use it properly. Descartes writes of God's non-deceiving nature in the sixth *Meditation*, thus:

> For God has given me no faculty at all for recognizing any [alternative] source for these ideas; on the contrary, he has given me a great propensity to believe that they are produced by corporeal things. So I do not see how God could be understood to be anything but a deceiver if the ideas were transmitted from a source other than corporeal things.[51]

For all his interest in showing that knowledge is possible, it is notable that Descartes nowhere explicitly mentions our knowledge that other minds exist. It is not implausible, however, that Descartes, had he considered it, would have extended his argument concerning our knowledge of the external world to cover the case of other minds.[52] Let us again consider the case of the piece of wax. According to Descartes, I observe the external forms and I judge that this is wax – I understand its nature. I also have a very great inclination to believe that the piece of wax is an object distinct from my idea of it. Once I take care to ascertain that I am not being tricked by the light, or some such, if I continue to believe that the wax exists, I may take this belief to be true. This follows once we have proof of a non-deceiving God. We may then say the same thing about the figure of a man: I observe the outward forms and I judge that this is a man – I understand his nature. And the outward forms that I observe are his use of language and the quality of his behaviour more generally. Now I also have an overwhelming inclination to believe that this man exists. If I take care in coming to have this belief, I may take it to be true. Our knowledge that there are other minds – like our knowledge of all things external to us – is the result of God's beneficence.

Thus we can find in Descartes material that, when put together, reveals the direction of his thinking about other minds and our knowledge of them. And it is a notable feature of Descartes' thinking here that there is no room for an argument by analogy. Two essential elements of that argument are lacking in the way that Descartes appears to think about other men. First of all, where the argument from analogy proceeds from the premise that I can have knowledge of mind from my own case, there is no indication that Descartes uses the very certain knowledge I have of my own mind as part of any argument to the conclusion that there are other minds. Second, where the argument from analogy involves two separate judgements, there is evidence (as I have shown) that Descartes takes there to be one single judgement here. To fit the argument from analogy into Descartes' picture we would have to proceed as follows: first I judge that there is a human body, and then I come to know that this body exists; next I judge that this body has a mind (and I do this by noticing that my mind animates my body, and conclude by analogy that this other body is animated by a mind like mine), and then I come to know that this mind exists. The argument from analogy thus requires that I make two quite separate judgements. Such a two-step judgement would acknowledge the possibility that the figure before me may be a mere human being – that is, a human animal without a mind. But as we have seen, in what he says about the operation of the judgement in the second *Meditation*, Descartes does not recognize this possibility.

Of course Descartes does recognize the possibility that God might not have endowed other human beings with minds, just as he recognizes the possibility that God might have chosen to endow non-human animals with minds. Both possibilities would be consistent with the logical separation of mind and body that Descartes introduces into philosophy. That Descartes does acknowledge the latter possibility seems evident in a letter to More, when he writes:

> But though I regard it as established that we cannot prove there is any thought in animals, I do not think it can be proved there is none, since the human mind does not reach into their hearts.[53]

Descartes' point is only that we have no reason to think that there is thought in non-human animals. In order to be certain that there is no thought in these animals our minds would need to 'reach into their heart' – and this we cannot do. When Descartes writes of the absence of thought in animal and non-animal machines, he writes only of the 'moral impossibility' – or the impossibility for practical purposes – of thought here.[54] For a machine to act in all circumstances just like a man is, according to Descartes, morally impossible. Descartes never asserts that such a thing would be logically impossible. It is this moral impossibility that is reflected in Descartes' considerations concerning how we come to judge that the figures in the street are men.[55]

In Descartes' philosophy we advance moral certainty to 'absolute certainty' once we have a proof of the existence of a non-deceiving God. And this is, I have suggested, just as true for our belief in the existence of other minds as it is for our belief in the existence of an external world of bodies. Of course, this is 'absolute certainty' that exists in the face of the existence of a logical gap between the mind and the body. Whatever degree of certainty we are able to achieve, it is a certainty that reaches across this logical divide. In Descartes' system, we are able to reach across this divide because of the bridge provided by a non-deceiving God. Insofar as we are capable of reaching across the double divide that exists between my mind and the mind of another, this too must be thanks to the existence of a non-deceiving God.

I have suggested that it is because Descartes holds that, of corporeal beings, all and only men have minds that he is able to suggest that my judgement that there is a man before me (a minded individual) proceeds in a single step. If, however, Descartes were to acknowledge as a real possibility that God should have endowed non-human animals with minds, then presumably he would have to say that the judgement involved in saying that there is a man before me proceeds in two steps. Once a double judgement is recognized to operate here, it becomes possible to introduce the argument from analogy. I shall suggest in the next chapter that philosophy moves closer to the argument from analogy with the work of Nicolas Malebranche.

CHAPTER III

Malebranche and knowledge
of other men's souls

INTRODUCTION

Nicolas Malebranche was born in 1638, twelve years before Descartes' death. He lived roughly contemporaneously with John Locke and died in 1715. His work, until relatively recently, has been largely neglected in the English speaking world.[1] My reason for focusing on Malebranche's work in this chapter is that, unlike in the work of Descartes before him, one finds in it an explicit acknowledgement of an issue concerning our knowledge of the mind of another. Malebranche understands that the philosophical system that Descartes puts in place gives rise as much to a question about our knowledge of other men's minds or souls as it does to our knowledge of bodies. Furthermore, what Malebranche has to say about our knowledge of other minds brings out, albeit unclearly, the fact that there are two questions to be raised: one concerning our knowledge of the existence of another's mind and another concerning our knowledge of what the other thinks and feels. It is tempting to say that Malebranche's work gives us an early statement of the argument from analogy to the existence of another mind. Indeed, several commentators do claim to find such an argument in Malebranche's work.[2] On the contrary, I shall suggest that there is little evidence of this form of argument in Malebranche's work. Finally, it should be noted that, despite his acknowledgement of issues relating to other minds, one question that Malebranche does *not* raise is Augustine's question: why do I so much as think that there is a mind other than my own? On this matter we can find nothing in Malebranche's work.

Malebranche is a follower, if a somewhat unorthodox one, of Descartes' work. The subtitle that Malebranche gave to his most important work – *The Search After Truth: Wherein Are Treated the Nature of Man's Mind and the Use He Must Make of It to Avoid Error in the Sciences* – indicates the overlap between his work and that of his predecessor. In Book I of *The Search* Malebranche is explicit about his debt to Descartes for his teaching concerning the difference between sense perception and the operation of the pure intellect. Following Descartes, Malebranche holds that it is only if we reason upon clear and evident ideas that we can establish a firm foundation for the sciences. If we ignore this teaching and judge things by the senses, we are bound to fall into error. The senses may 'dazzle' and 'seduce' but do not yield to knowledge.[3]

Malebranche distinguishes two faculties of the mind: the understanding, or the passive reception of ideas, and the will. Concerning the understanding he writes: 'It is the understanding that perceives or that knows, since it only receives ideas of objects; for it is the same thing to the soul to perceive an object as to receive the idea that represents the object.'[4] Malebranche then explains that the soul has two different kinds of perception: the first he calls pure perceptions and the second sensible perceptions. Pure perceptions neither make an impression on the soul nor modify it; sensible perceptions (such as pain and pleasure, light, taste and odour) do make an impression on the soul and can be considered 'nothing but modes of mind'.[5] Malebranche calls the second sort of perception 'feeling' or 'sentiment'. Sensible perception informs us of objects in our environment, and its purpose is the preservation of the body.[6] If we wish to have knowledge of the essence or nature of things, we must turn away from sensible perception and towards pure perception or pure intellection.

Corresponding to these two kinds of perception are two sorts of thing that the soul perceives: things that are outside the soul and things that are in it. Concerning our perception of things that are in the soul, Malebranche writes,

> Our soul has no need of ideas in order to perceive these things in the way that it does, because these things are in the soul, or rather because they are but the soul itself existing in this or that way.[7]

It is because these things are in the soul that Malebranche takes them to be modifications of it. He also writes that it is not possible for these things to be in the soul and the soul not be aware of them through inner sensation. When we consider the perception of things that are outside the soul, we find that things are very different. In order to perceive these, outer, things, the mind has need of ideas.

How are we to understand these ideas that are essential to the pure perception of things outside the soul? About ideas Malebranche writes,

> I think everyone will agree that we do not perceive objects external to us by themselves. We see the sun, the stars, and an infinity of objects external to us; and it is not likely that the soul should leave the body to stroll about the heavens, as it were, in order to behold these objects. Thus, it does not see them by themselves, and our mind's immediate object when it sees the sun, for example, is not the sun, but something that is intimately joined to our soul, and this is what I call *idea*. Thus, by the word *idea*, I mean here nothing other than the immediate object, or the object closest to the mind, when it perceives something.[8]

Malebranche goes on to note that when a mind perceives an object, it is 'absolutely necessary for the idea of that object to be actually presented to [the mind]'.[9] We see objects through the ideas that represent them.

An idea, then, is what is before the mind when it perceives an object outside itself. The question then arises how we come by our ideas (or, how we come by our knowledge of objects). It is in reply to this question that Malebranche makes an important move away from Cartesian philosophy. According to Descartes ideas are in the mind. Malebranche considers this, and asks how it is that ideas can come to be in the mind. He considers several possibilities: (i) ideas come from the bodies themselves; (ii) our soul has the power to produce ideas; or (iii) God has placed ideas in us. And if God produces our ideas he may choose to do this in one of two ways: (a) by placing all ideas in our mind at the moment of its creation, or (b) by providing us with ideas occasion by occasion. Malebranche considers and rejects each of these suggestions in turn. The Cartesian doctrine that ideas are in our mind is, concludes Malebranche, inconsistent with our position of complete dependence upon God. According to Malebranche God has all ideas within Himself, and we see all things because of the union of our mind with His.[10] It is through this union that Malebranche thinks we come to know God Himself, objects external to us, and other minds.

Malebranche's doctrine that we know all things in God was heavily criticized in his lifetime by Antoine Arnaud. Arnaud upheld the Cartesian view that ideas are in the mind, and his *Of True and False Ideas* sparked a debate with Malebranche which lasted from the time of its publication in 1683 until Arnaud's death in 1694.[11] Another critic of Malebranche's central doctrine was John Locke, who wrote his *Examination of P. Malebranche's Opinion of seeing all Things in God* but declined to allow its publication during his – Locke's – lifetime. The attack was published posthumously in 1706. Despite heavy criticism, Malebranche's work continued to have a profound effect on the work of several philosophers whose work is much more widely read today. Hume, for example, is known to have urged his friend Michael Ramsey to read Malebranche's *Search After Truth* in preparation for reading Hume's own *Treatise Concerning Human Understanding*.[12] And, although Berkeley insists that his work is *not* to be compared with that of Malebranche, we find Thomas Reid writing that one has only to remove a 'few peculiarities' from the work of Malebranche to get the work of Berkeley.[13] It is not hard to see what Reid means. Both Malebranche and Berkeley emphasize our total dependence on God. However, while Malebranche asserts our dependence on God and the powerlessness of external, material, bodies he does allow that material bodies exist; Berkeley, on the other hand, insists that talk of material substance is a 'nonsense'. The world of external bodies is left to do no work in Malebranche's philosophy, so it can drop away in Berkeley's.[14]

Once Malebranche has made it clear that we know all things because of our union with God, he proceeds to explain the very different ways we have of knowing things. He clearly separates out four ways. They are these:

(i) To know things by themselves. Malebranche holds God is the only thing we can know in this way.
(ii) To know things through their ideas – that is, through something different from the things themselves. This is how Malebranche thinks we know bodies.
(iii) To know things through consciousness or inner sensation. This, according to Malebranche, is how we know our own minds.
(iv) To know things by conjecture. According to Malebranche, this is how we know other men's souls or minds.

For our purposes we can set aside knowledge of God, or knowledge of things by themselves. This, according to Malebranche, is a unique kind of knowledge, and studying it will not shed any light on any of the others. It is the fourth kind of knowledge – by conjecture – that is most relevant to this study. As a preliminary to understanding this kind of knowledge I shall briefly run through the way we come by our knowledge of our own minds and of bodies. It is by contrast with these kinds that we can better understand how it is that Malebranche thinks we come by our knowledge of another mind.

KNOWLEDGE OF ONE'S OWN MIND

According to Malebranche, knowledge of one's own mind is through consciousness. He writes,

> Of all our knowledge, the first is of the existence of our soul; all our thoughts are incontestable demonstrations of this, since there is nothing more obvious than that what actually thinks, is actually something.[15]

Knowledge of the existence of one's own mind is first knowledge, and it is incontestable. Here Malebranche is a faithful follower of Descartes. When, however, Malebranche turns from a consideration of one's knowledge of the existence of one's mind to a consideration of the essence or nature of mind, we find Malebranche in radical disagreement with his predecessor. Malebranche writes, 'If it is easy to know the existence of our soul, it is not so easy to know its essence and nature.'[16]

As we have seen, Malebranche agrees with Descartes that knowledge of bodies is derived not from the senses, but from the working of the pure intellect. Malebranche sees this teaching as Descartes' supreme contribution to science. It is in the second *Meditation* that Descartes considers the contribution of the intellect to knowledge. Descartes concludes that, because the senses are not involved in the understanding of one's mind, the nature of mind is better known than the nature of any other thing (*vide supra*, Chapter II). Malebranche vigorously disagrees. In opposition to Descartes, Malebranche asks:

> If the nature of the soul is better known than the nature of any other things, if the ideas we have of it are as clear as the idea we have of the body, then I ask only this: how is it that there are so many people who confuse the two?[17]

Malebranche goes on to point out that people do not confuse other clear ideas, for example the idea of a circle and that of a square. He also points out that there is no agreement – even among Cartesians – over what we should believe about the soul and its modifications. Malebranche reminds us that there are those people who think that pain and heat – and especially colour – do not belong to the soul. And this he thinks is hardly surprising, as it is no easy matter to conclude that these are modifications of the soul. He writes:

> One cannot discover through simple perception whether these qualities belong to the soul. One imagines that pain is in the body that occasions it, and that colour is spread out on the surface of objects, although these objects are distinct from our soul.[18]

Malebranche claims that in order to determine that these are in fact modes of mind, Cartesians themselves do not consult an idea of mind. Rather, they reason thus: pain, heat and colour cannot be modifications of extension, there are only two kinds of thing, so they must be modifications of mind.

Malebranche asks, 'Where, then, is the clear idea of the soul so that the Cartesians might consult it, and so that they might all agree on the question as to where colours, tastes, and odours are to be found?'[19] And he concludes that there is none. Indeed he concludes that, not only do we not have a clear idea of soul, but we have no idea of soul at all. This is in contrast to bodies: we do have ideas of bodies. Earlier we saw that Malebranche introduces the term 'idea' in Book III of *The Search* to be 'nothing other than the immediate object, or object closest to the mind, when it perceives something'. In Elucidation 11, however, he admits that his use of the term is equivocal. Sometimes he takes it in the quite general way that he introduced in Book III, but he also understands it in a 'most precise and restricted sense' thus: 'as anything that represents things to the mind in a way so clear that we can discover by a simple perception whether such and such modifications belong to them'.[20] According to his more restricted sense of the term, to have an idea of something would enable us to deduce all its modifications. We would be able to know not only what actually belongs to that thing, but also what can belong to it. This, according to Malebranche, we can do in the case of body, but not of mind. As he writes in one place: 'If we had never sensed pain, heat, light and such, we would be unable to know whether the soul was capable of sensing these things, because we do not know it through ideas.'[21]

If we wish to learn of the modifications of bodies, we consult our ideas of them. We do not deduce what a modification of body is by deciding first that it cannot be a modification of mind. We consult our idea of body directly. Malebranche writes,

But who does not see that there is quite a difference between knowing through a clear idea and knowing through *consciousness*?[22]

What we know when we know our mind through consciousness is the mind's modifications. By this Malebranche understands 'all those things that cannot be in the soul without the soul being aware of them through the inner sensation it has of itself – such as its sensations, imaginings, pure intellections, or simple conceptions, as well as its passions and natural inclinations'.[23] Because we have no idea of mind we cannot know all that it is capable of; nevertheless, we are able to know everything that actually is in the soul: 'our soul has no need of ideas in order to perceive these things in the way it does, because these things are in the soul, or rather because they are but the soul itself existing in this way or that'.[24]

Malebranche draws our attention to several further differences between ideas and sensations. In Book III of *The Search After Truth* he notes that, while ideas resemble what they represent, sensations do not resemble anything. In the place of representation, we find that a sensation may signify. For example, a pain in no way resembles the open wound in the arm, but it may signal that bodily state to the mind.[25] Another difference between ideas and sensations is this: sensations are modes of mind, while ideas are abstracted from any sensuous element. The reality of ideas is, for Malebranche 'immutable, necessary, eternal, common to all intellects, and does not consist in modifications of the intellect's own being'.[26] Finally, Malebranche holds that knowledge which is gained, not through ideas, but through sensation is limited. It is limited to the sensations experienced. We cannot have knowledge of the nature of sensation. In *Dialogues on Metaphysics and Religion*, Malebranche writes,

> The internal sensation which I have of myself teaches me that I am, that I think, that I will, that I sense, that I suffer, etc.; but it does not reveal to me what I am, the nature of my thought, of my will, of my sensations, of my passions, of my pain, nor of the relations which all these things have to one another. . . . All this follows . . . because . . . I am not a light unto myself, because my substance and my modalities are a total darkness, and because for many reasons God has not found it fitting to disclose to me the idea or archetype which represents the nature of spiritual being.[27]

Thus, according to Malebranche, while we know *that* we are, we cannot know *what* we are. We are capable of understanding the true nature of bodies, but God has chosen to leave us in the dark when it comes to the understanding of the nature of mind.

Although God has not given us an idea of mind, we sometimes mistakenly attempt to form an idea of the mind. We try to represent the mind by an idea, as we would represent a body. But this, according to Malebranche, is to misunderstand the source of our knowledge of mind. Mind is not represented by an idea and, thus, is not knowable through ideas. Malebranche writes,

> There are some things, such as our soul with all its modifications, that, not being corporeal, cannot be represented to the mind by corporeal images. When, therefore, our soul wishes to represent to itself its own nature and its own sensations, it tries to form a corporeal image of them. . . . Thus, bent on being located among bodies and on fancying its own modifications as modifications of bodies, the soul should cause no wonder if it loses its bearings and altogether misunderstands itself.[28]

Malebranche assures us that, if we avoid the mistake of attempting to represent the mind by an idea, then our knowledge, although imperfect, is not false. He writes, 'To a certain extent, then, when we see colours or have a certain sensation, we know what we immediately perceive';[29] our consciousness of mind 'does not involve us in error'.[30] According to Malebranche, it is because our sensations are not false that we do not need an idea of mind. We do, however, need an idea of body, as our sensations of these can be in error. We need an idea of body in order to able to correct our sometimes false sensations of it.

Although Malebranche is quite clear that we have no – and need have no – idea of mind, he allows that an idea of mind does exist. God has an idea of mind, but he has chosen not to give this idea to us.[31] Malebranche writes at one point that if we did have an idea of soul like the idea we have of body, that idea would have inclined us too much to view our soul as separated from the body, thus diminishing our understanding of the union between the soul and the body.[32] Whatever the reason, Malebranche believes we know enough concerning the soul to demonstrate its immortality, its spirituality and its freedom.

Thus, Malebranche holds that we know our own minds through consciousness or inner sensation, and that this form of knowledge is to be distinguished from knowledge of bodies which is through ideas. Where Descartes holds that self-knowledge is a form of knowledge superior to our knowledge of bodies, Malebranche holds that our knowledge of mind is different from – not superior to – our knowledge of bodies. According to Malebranche we are unable to know the essence or nature of mind, and this follows from the fact that we have no idea of mind. It is through the contemplation of ideas that we come by our knowledge of the nature of things. As God has chosen to withhold the idea of mind from us, we are unable to know its nature.

KNOWLEDGE OF BODIES

Malebranche clearly demarcates knowledge of bodies and knowledge of our own mind: the latter is through sensation while the former is through ideas. Malebranche also distinguishes (i) our knowledge of the nature of things and (ii) our knowledge of the existence of things. As we have just seen, when it comes to our own mind Malebranche holds that we can know for certain *that* our mind exists but we cannot know *what* the mind is (we cannot know the nature or essence of mind). In the case of bodies, Malebranche holds that we can know *what* bodies are (we can know their nature) but we cannot know *that* they are without faith.

The reason we can understand the nature or essence of body is that we have an idea of body (and from this can deduce the modifications of body). That we have ideas of bodies, and that we perceive these ideas directly and bodies indirectly, are two doctrines that Malebranche shares with Descartes. That the ideas we have of bodies are independent existences and not modes of mind is, as we have seen, one important difference in the views of these philosophers. Following on from this difference is another. According to Descartes, ideas are implanted in our souls by nature. Opposing this, Malebranche argues that the origin of ideas is not nature but God, and that the pure intellect perceives these ideas in God's mind. Here we arrive at one of the central doctrines of Malebranche's philosophy: we see all things in God. It follows from this that our soul is intimately united to God; it is through this union that we come to have knowledge of the nature of bodies. The doctrine that we see all things in God is central to Malebranche's philosophy, and he gives several arguments to support it. There is no need to review them here.[33] I shall, however, mention one reason that Malebranche gives for rejecting the Cartesian thesis that ideas are implanted in our minds by nature and for favouring the doctrine that we see all things in God. In *The Search After Truth* Malebranche writes:

> God can have no other special end for His actions than Himself. . . . Therefore, not only must our natural love . . . tend

76

toward Him but also the knowledge and light He gives it must reveal to us something in Him, for everything coming from God can be only for God. If God had made a mind and had given the sun to it as an idea, or immediate object of knowledge, it seems to me God would have made this mind and its ideas for the sun and not Himself.[34]

Malebranche takes it that the end of our knowledge should be God – not bodies. To this end ideas are in the mind of God, and we know objects through our knowledge of God. One commentator writes,

According to Malebranche the notion that there are powers or faculties in bodies which produce the ostensible effects of bodies is the most dangerous error in the philosophy of antiquity. Believing that bodies have the power of affecting us, we come to love and fear *them* rather than the true cause of our well-being. And in philosophy we remain ignorant of the true principles of change in bodies: the movement of their parts in accordance with laws of motion established and administered by God.[35]

It should be noted that, despite the fact that it is ideas of bodies in God's mind that we perceive, bodies do also exist. Malebranche is not yet an immaterialist.[36]

So, we come to know the true nature of body when we reason concerning the clear ideas which we perceive in God's mind. The senses are not the source of this knowledge. According to Malebranche, the senses *cannot* be the source of our knowledge of bodies, because the senses may deceive us. Indeed Malebranche holds that every sensation of an external body includes some false judgement. The reason is this: our soul sees things as outside the body, while what we actually see are 'the perfections of God that correspond to these [things]' and represent them.[37]

According to Malebranche, ideas are the representatives of bodies. He writes in one place:

Our souls do not leave the body to measure the heavens, and as a result, they can see bodies outside only through the ideas representing them. In this everyone must agree.[38]

Reid notes an important consequence of Malebranche's commitment to representative ideas. Reid writes,

It is obvious that the system of Malebranche leaves no evidence of the existence of a material world, from what we perceive by our senses; for the Divine ideas, which are the objects immediately perceived, were the same before the world was created. Malebranche was too acute not to discern this consequence of his system, and too candid not to acknowledge it.[39]

Malebranche acknowledges this consequence of his system in several places. For example, in Elucidation VI he writes,

> Why should we conclude then, merely on the testimony of the senses that deceive us on all sides, that there really are external bodies, and even that those bodies are like those we see, i.e. like those that are the soul's immediate object, when we look at them with the eyes of the body. Whatever is to be said of this view, it certainly is not without difficulties.[40]

Malebranche is also clear about why these difficulties arise. They arise because there is 'no necessary connection between the presence of an idea to a man's mind and the existence of the thing the idea represents'.[41] Unlike Descartes, Malebranche does not dwell on the various sceptical arguments that lead us to acknowledge this distinction. He does, however, mention in passing that experiences in sleep and delirium are sufficient to prove the distinction.

The question then arises, how we know of the existence of bodies. Descartes, you will recall, holds that such knowledge is possible with the help of a non-deceiving God, if we take care to think clearly and distinctly. This non-deceiving God is the guarantor of our ideas. Where we have an overwhelming inclination to believe, and no power to correct any error, these beliefs God guarantees to be true. Malebranche acknowledges that Descartes has given 'the strongest proofs that reason alone can muster' for the existence of bodies. Nevertheless, he concludes that the matter is not yet 'perfectly demonstrated'.[42] According to Malebranche, the only evidence we can have of the real existence of bodies further to our ideas of them is through faith. In the *Dialogues on Metaphysics and Religion* he writes:

> In order to see the material world – or rather to judge that this world exists, as it is invisible in itself – God must of necessity reveal this to us. . . .
> Now, God reveals the existence of His creatures in two ways, through the Authority of the Holy Scripture and by means of the

senses. Granting the first authority – and we cannot reject it – the existence of bodies can be rigorously demonstrated. . . . Special revelation can never lead to error since God cannot will to deceive us.[43]

Revelation through the Scriptures, then, is the only way we can come to have knowledge of the existence of the material world of bodies. Once we have faith, then we can trust the evidence. Where Descartes relies on argument to prove the existence of bodies, Malebranche holds that faith is a precondition of argument.

Thus far we have seen that Malebranche delineates two different kinds of knowledge: knowledge of our own mind and knowledge of bodies. He distinguishes, as well, between knowledge of existence and knowledge of the nature or essence of things. He holds that, while we can have knowledge of the existence of our own mind, we can have no knowledge of the essence of mind; and though we can have knowledge of the essence of body, we are not in a position to have knowledge of the existence of bodies without Divine Revelation. He now introduces a third kind of knowledge: knowledge of other minds.

KNOWLEDGE OF OTHER MEN'S MINDS

Of all the objects of our knowledge, only the souls of other men and pure intelligences remain; and clearly we know them only through conjecture. At present we do not know them either in themselves or through their ideas, and as they are different from ourselves, we cannot know them through consciousness.[44]

In order to appreciate the importance of Malebranche's contribution to our understanding of this form of knowledge it is not necessary to accept his doctrine of our vision in God. The important point to understand is that Malebranche clearly recognizes that knowledge of other minds is different from all other kinds of knowledge. It is different from our knowledge of bodies, as we do not have an idea of another mind. It is also different from our knowledge of our own mind, as it cannot be through consciousness. And finally, it is different from our knowledge of God, as another mind is not known by itself. With his explicit recognition that knowledge of another own mind is different from knowledge of one's own mind Malebranche is acknowledging that the former kind of knowledge is not direct. Furthermore, Malebranche recognizes that, although our knowledge of another mind is indirect, it is not through the intermediary of an idea as is our indirect knowledge of bodies. Malebranche's suggestion is that our knowledge of other minds is indirect through being *by conjecture*.[45]

When Malebranche writes of our knowledge of other men's minds or souls in Book III, Part ii, chapter 7 of *The Search After Truth*, he is quite clear that this is *not* through ideas. Nevertheless, only a few chapters earlier, in chapter 1, he writes that we know all things that are outside the soul – be they material or spiritual – through ideas. It is quite clear from the context that by 'spiritual thing' Malebranche is here referring to another soul or mind. In chapter 1 Malebranche also makes the point that, although we can only know spiritual things through ideas, it is not 'absolutely necessary' that they be known in this way. Spiritual things can be known immediately, or 'through themselves'. In this connection he writes:

> For though experience teaches us that we cannot communicate our thoughts to one another immediately and by ourselves, but only through speech or some other sensible sign to which we have attached our ideas, still it might be said that God has established this state of affairs only for the duration of this life in order to prevent the disorder that would now prevail if men could communicate as they pleased.[46]

Malebranche follows this with a paragraph in which he clarifies his reason for thinking that spiritual things are not, for the duration of this life at least, known to us immediately. He writes,

> We are and shall be unintelligible to each other until we see each other in God, and until he presents us with the perfectly intelligible idea He has of our being contained in His being.[47]

It would appear that Malebranche rejects the thought that in this life we may know of minds other than our own immediately, or without the intervention of ideas, because this would be inconsistent with our position of complete dependence on God.

How are we to reconcile what Malebranche writes in chapters 1 and 7 of Book III, Part ii of *The Search*? How can it be that, on the one hand, he writes that our knowledge of spiritual things is through ideas, while, on the other, he writes just a few chapters later that our knowledge here is not through ideas but by conjecture? The difficulty might appear to be resolved if we recall that Malebranche, by his own admission, uses the term 'idea' in two quite different senses. As I explained above, sometimes he uses the term to refer to what is before the mind when it perceives a thing, and sometimes he uses the same term to refer to a clear representation that reveals to us all the modifications that belong to each object. When Malebranche introduces the second of the two uses of the term, he points out that it is because there are these two uses that sometimes he can write that we have an idea of the soul while at other times he can deny this.[48] Does Malebranche mean us to understand that when we have knowledge of another mind or soul there is a representative idea before our mind, only not an idea that reveals the nature or essence of that mind? But how can this be? Is it that some ideas are representative without being revealing of essence, while others are both representative and revealing of essence? But if this is so, why does Malebranche not consider that I have such an idea of my own mind? I want now to suggest a way around these difficulties.

We must begin by recognizing that the mind of another cannot be known through consciousness. Now, the alternative to knowing through consciousness is knowing through ideas. Given this, we must have an idea of another mind. But if we do have an idea of another mind why is it that we are unable to know the essence of mind? We perhaps avoid the dilemma if we remember that Malebranche writes that we do not have knowledge of other minds through *their* ideas. (See the quotation cited above from Book III, Part ii, chapter 7, V. What Malebranche writes here is consistent with what he writes earlier in Book I, chapter 13, IV: 'our soul . . . not being corporeal, cannot be represented to the mind by corporeal images'.) It would appear that there are ideas involved in our knowledge of another mind, but the ideas are not representative of those minds. Recall that in Book III, Part ii, chapter 1, I, Malebranche writes that we reveal ourselves 'only through speech or some other sensible sign to which we have attached our ideas'. We can conclude from this that Malebranche thinks that the ideas that reveal my soul or mind to another are words or, presumably, actions (the 'other' sensible sign to which he refers). There *are* ideas involved in the knowledge of another mind, but those ideas are only representative of the other's body. Notice that Malebranche suggests that the ideas that represent another's body are at the same time a 'sign' of another mind. Unfortunately, Malebranche neither elaborates nor explains how it is that an idea of body can be a sign of a mind. The point he wants to make is that the idea that is involved here is not an idea *of another mind*. It is for this reason that reflection on the idea cannot give us knowledge of the nature of mind. In Elucidation 11 Malebranche writes that where we have a clear idea of a thing, and hence knowledge of its nature, we can compare that thing with another. And he continues: 'But we cannot compare our mind with other minds in order to discover clearly some relation between them'. Thus Malebranche thinks that if we did have knowledge of the nature of mind, then we would be in a position to know just what another is thinking and feeling. But we are not able to do this, and he takes this to show that we do not have an idea of mind. Malebranche concludes that we do not know the mind of another through its idea. But if we cannot know another mind through its idea, how can we know it? It would appear to be in answer to this that Malebranche writes: 'we conjecture that the souls of other men are of the same sort as our own'.

When Malebranche writes of our conjecture concerning other men's souls, he differentiates between two aspects of this knowledge: on the one hand there is our knowledge that another man has sensations such as we have, and on the other there is our knowledge that another man knows such truths as that twice two is four and that it is better to be just than rich.[49] The difference between these two aspects of our knowledge of the mind of another results from the fact that, while the body plays a part in the experience of sensations, it plays no part in the knowledge of truths. Where the body does play a part, Malebranche holds that 'I am almost always mistaken in judging others by myself'.[50] Things are otherwise where the body is not involved; in these cases we can know that others think as we do.

Consider first our conjecture that others experience things as we do. In the case of our knowledge of our own sensations we know immediately what we perceive – e.g. that we see colours or have a certain sensation. Now it is very natural to believe that other people have the same sensations when confronted with the same objects: you and I both see the green of the meadow and the blue of the sky and we both suffer pains when pricked by sharp objects. Despite the naturalness of this belief, Malebranche holds that we are mistaken when we think that everyone has the same sensations when confronted with the same objects. In fact, if we were to be correct in our beliefs about another's sensations, Malebranche believes that it would only be 'through the most remarkable luck in the world'.[51] The reason is this: if we recognize that there is a difference between a sensation and the cause of a sensation (something Malebranche takes himself to have established), then we must also recognize that 'it can happen that similar motions in the interior fibers of the optic nerve do not produce the same sensation for different people, i.e. do not make them see the same colors; and it might happen that motion that will cause the sensation of blue in one person will cause that of green or grey in another, or even a novel sensation that no one has ever had'.[52] This said, Malebranche goes on to acknowledge that it is very likely that God has arranged things so that the same ideas are joined to similar motions in the brain. So it looks as if we have, after all, a reason to believe that all men do have the same sensation when they look at the same object. But we must change our opinion when we realize that the relation of sensation to brain motions is not the only thing that we must take into consideration; we must consider, as well, the objects that produce these motions in the brain. Now it is here that Malebranche thinks that we will find variations. He writes: 'it cannot be doubted that there is a great deal of diversity in different people's organs of sight as well as of hearing and taste, for there is no reason to suppose a perfect resemblance in the optic nerve of all men since there is an infinite variety found in nature's works and especially in material things'.[53] So, even if God has established discoverable laws linking sensations and the motions of our brain, the differences in men's sense organs will make it likely that different men experience different sensations even when confronted with the same objects. It is for this reason that it is 'by the most remarkable luck in the world' that we are not mistaken when we think that another mind experiences the world in the same way that we do. Malebranche takes it that this variation in sensation explains the fact that different people take pleasure in different things. Men take pleasure, or its opposite, in a thing depending upon how that thing strikes them. As things strike different people differently, so we find different people embracing and rejecting different things.

Malebranche differentiates between our knowledge of another's sensations and our knowledge of another's thoughts. The body plays no part in the latter, and for this reason, Malebranche holds that our conjectures concerning another's thoughts are more certain than our conjectures concerning their sensations. He writes,

> I love pleasure and good, I abhor pain and evil, I want to be happy, and I am not mistaken in believing that all men, the angels, and even demons have these same inclinations. I even know that God will never make a mind that does not desire to be happy. . . . I know this with evidence and certainty because it is God who teaches it to me.[54]

Malebranche ends his discussion of our knowledge of other men's souls thus: 'since all men have the same nature, we all have the same ideas, because we all need to know the same things'.[55]

Thus we employ conjecture to know things that we cannot know through their ideas; we conjecture that the mind of another is like our own mind.[56] There is reason to think that such conjecture will not lead us astray when we consider the thoughts of the other, but that we will be led into error if we conjecture in this way about another's sensations. On the interpretation I have offered, Malebranche's talk of conjecture is confined to how we know the nature of another's mind, what he is thinking and feeling; it is not involved in our knowledge of the existence of another mind. Malebranche does not clearly separate out for this kind of knowledge questions concerning existence from questions concerning essence or nature, as he does with all other kinds of knowledge. Nonetheless, these questions can be separated. If we employ conjecture to know the nature of another mind, this still leaves us with the question of our knowledge of the existence of another mind. It may be that certain 'sensible signs' lead me to think that there are other minds, but what gives me the assurance that this is true? It is notable that Malebranche does not explicitly mention other minds when he writes of Revelation and faith in connection with our knowledge of the existence of material bodies (*vide supra*). Nevertheless, it is reasonable to assume that Malebranche would have included the existence of other minds or souls among the things that we can know once we have faith. McCracken suggests that there is some evidence that Malebranche was not content with this conclusion. Many years after writing *The Search After Truth* Malebranche explains to Dortous de Morain that there is an important difference between our knowledge of the existence of bodies and of other minds. The difference is that, while it may be possible to deny the existence of bodies, it is not possible to deny the existence of minds. Malebranche suggests that this is because in the case of other minds or souls I am assured that they exist from consideration of the 'whole moral order of the world'.[57]

The argument from analogy to the conclusion that another mind exists is nowhere employed by Malebranche. I suspect that philosophers have been inclined to attribute that argument to him because of a misunderstanding of his claim that we know other minds by conjecture. Because of more recent preoccupations with the question of our knowledge of the existence of other minds and the argument from analogy as a response, it is tempting to interpret Malebranche's reference to conjecture along the lines of that argument. But, as I have explained, Malebranche does not argue in this way. At best we might say that we find in Malebranche an argument from analogy to the nature of another mind. But even this is not quite right. Nowhere does

Malebranche spell out exactly how this conjecture is supposed to work, and there is no evidence that he would understand it to follow the lines of what we today understand as an argument from analogy.

We get some idea of how we might further understand this conjecture if we turn to consider the work of Antoine Arnaud. Arnaud considers, among other things, Malebranche's suggestion that we know other men's minds by conjecture, and suggests a very particular understanding of this conjecture. Let us now turn to a very brief look at Arnaud on Malebranche on our knowledge of other minds.

BRIEF INTERLUDE:
ARNAUD ON MALEBRANCHE ON
KNOWLEDGE OF OTHER MINDS

Antoine Arnaud (1612–1694) devoted his *On True and False Ideas* to a critique of Malebranche's doctrine that we know all things in God. Arnaud, like Descartes, holds that ideas are modes of mind. Furthermore, Arnaud follows Descartes in holding that *all* knowledge is through ideas.[58] Towards the end of his work, Arnaud considers Malebranche's suggestion that we know other souls not through ideas but by conjecture, and against this suggestion Arnaud makes two observations.

First of all Arnaud insists that we can and do have ideas of mind. He can see no reason why God should have exempted our soul from being known through ideas. Furthermore, even if we were to grant Malebranche his position that we know our own minds through consciousness rather than through ideas, Arnaud still sees no reason to deny that we know *other* minds through ideas. He writes, 'if we are unable to see the souls of other men by consciousness, as each sees his own, then it would be even more contrary to the uniformity of God's conduct not to reveal to us the soul of others in the same way in which . . . He gets us to see material things'.[59]

Arnaud has a second reason for thinking that we perceive other men's souls in the same way that we see bodies, that is, by clear ideas. He writes,

If we can perceive by clear ideas individual things like the sun, fire, water, a horse, a tree, I do not understand why we cannot see in the same way the souls of other men by clear ideas. For I do not see the substance of the sun in a single glance, but by judgements that I make on the reports of my senses, which make me perceive something very high in the sky, very bright and very hot. I judge in the same way from the report of my senses that bodies like mine approach me, and this leads me to believe that they are human bodies. However, when I speak to them and they reply to me, and when I see them perform a large number of actions which are infallible signs of mind and reason, I conclude from this very much more clearly that these bodies which are like mine are animated by souls similar to mine, i.e. by intelligible substances really distinct from these bodies, than I conclude that there is a sun and what the sun is.[60]

Thus, Arnaud, like Descartes, holds that we judge on the basis of what the senses report that the object we see is the sun, and similarly we judge on the basis of what the senses report that what approaches me is a human body animated by a soul. But notice that, despite Arnaud's agreement with Descartes about the role of judgement here, Arnaud separates out two judgements in the case of other men where Descartes speaks only of one (*vide supra*, Chapter II). Arnaud writes of our judgement that the individual approaching is a human being, and *another* judgement that the human body is animated by a soul. He cites as a basis for this second judgement the fact that the approaching figures use language and perform a large number of actions. Here Arnaud again follows Descartes' two 'tests of a real man', but Arnaud is clear – where Descartes is not – that these are 'tests' of a minded individual.[61] Arnaud is also clear that another man's mind or soul is not known '*at a single glance*', but is a matter of 'reasoning'.[62] I reason from my observation of a body that speaks and acts that this body is animated by a soul.

Arnaud concludes his discussion of Malebranche here by writing that he has no objection to Malebranche's claim that we know other minds through conjecture *if* we understand by this that we know them through a form of reasoning as opposed to at a single glance. As far as Arnaud is concerned, the important thing is that we recognize that we know other men's minds through ideas, and this can be so despite the fact that we do not know them at a single glance but by reasoning. In this way we can acknowledge that knowledge of other minds is, like all knowledge, through ideas. Arnaud thus gives us an understanding of knowledge by conjecture that does make it look more like a standard argument by analogy. First of all, Arnaud concentrates on our judgement that other minds exist. And furthermore, he separates out two judgements, and makes it clear that we judge on the basis of the behaviour of this body which is like mine that this body is animated by a soul which is similar to mine. This really is beginning to look like a standard argument from analogy.

If we return to Malebranche, it is hard to know how to take Arnaud's criticism. First of all, Arnaud does not differentiate questions of our knowledge of the existence of another mind from knowledge of its nature. It would appear that he understands Malebranche as holding that we know by conjecture that there exist souls in other men, but, as I argued above, this does not appear to be what Malebranche holds. Furthermore, Arnaud appears to concentrate on what Malebranche writes in Book III, Part ii, Chapter 7 and overlooks entirely what he writes in Book III, Part ii, Chapter 1. In this way Arnaud does not see that Malebranche *does* allow that we know other men's souls through ideas. Malebranche's point is that the ideas we have are of the other's body, not their mind. However, Malebranche does not make it clear how we get from the ideas which represent another's body to the thought that there is another mind or soul. Arnaud clarifies things when he writes that we *reason* from the idea of this body to the conclusion that these bodies have minds like our own. It could be said that, while Arnaud makes clear the reasoning involved in my coming to judge that there are other minds, Malebranche recognizes more clearly that the idea involved here is not an idea *of another mind*. This is why Malebranche says that we do not know other minds through *their* ideas.

The debate between Malebranche and Arnaud can be seen to connect directly with my interpretation of Descartes on our knowledge of other minds. In Chapter II I argued that, because he believed that, of corporeal beings, all and only men have minds, Descartes allows that we know another mind in a single glance, or by the exercise of a single judgement. Arnaud's recognition that two judgements are required, and that we know another mind as the result of a form of reasoning, highlights more clearly the logical separation of mind and body that characterizes the Cartesian philosophy. The epistemological problem of other minds has begun to come into focus more clearly, and a clear response to it is beginning to emerge in the form of an argument from analogy.

CHAPTER IV

John Locke and knowledge
of other spirits

INTRODUCTION

John Locke lived and worked roughly contemporaneously with Malebranche (1632–1704). Locke, however, is an empiricist who opposed the innatist doctrines of Descartes as well as Malebranche's doctrine that we see all things in God. Locke rejects that Cartesian doctrine which Malebranche took to be Descartes' supreme contribution to science: that knowledge of body is to be derived from the working of the pure intellect. In its place Locke holds that our knowledge of the world comes from an examination of that world; knowledge arises from experience. According to Locke the mind is an 'empty cabinet', furnished with ideas by the senses.[1] All human knowledge is based on ideas, and all ideas come to us either from sensation of the world around us or by reflection on the mind's own operation.

Locke states that his purpose in writing his *Essay concerning Human Understanding* is to 'enquire into the Original, Certainty, and Extent of humane Knowledge'.[2] In the *Essay* Locke clarifies the limitations in our capacity to know about the world around us. In his journal Locke writes: 'we are [on this earth] in a state of mediocritie, finite creatures, furnished with powers and facultys very well fited to some purposes, but very disproportionate to the vast and unlimited extent of things'.[3] Locke, thus, insists that there are some things that we are not suited to know. Despite this limitation, he believes that God has fitted us with powers and faculties which are suited to our purposes in this life. Clarifying the extent and limits of our knowledge, then, is Locke's purpose in writing his *Essay*. Locke is also clear about the method he is to employ. He calls it 'the plain Method' whereby one simply considers those faculties we have and the objects they are employed about. Locke intends that the end result of such an inquiry should be that mankind learn when to 'be more cautious in meddling with things exceeding its Comprehension; to stop, when it is at the utmost Extent of its Tether; and to sit down in a quiet Ignorance of those Things, which, upon Examination, are found to be beyond the reach of our Capacities'.[4]

Our ignorance of things extends not just to the material but also to the intellectual world, and this, too, we must accept with all due humility. Thus Locke writes,

> But how much these few and narrow Inlets [i.e. sensation and reflection] are disproportionate to the vast whole Extent of all Beings, will not be hard to persuade those, who are not so foolish, as to think their span the measure of all Things. What other simple *Ideas* 'tis possible the Creatures in other parts of the Universe may have, by the Assistance of the Senses and Faculties more perfect, than we have, or different from ours, 'tis not for us to determine. But to say, or think there are no such, because we conceive nothing of them, is no better an argument, than if a blind Man should be positive in it, that there was no such thing as Sight and Colours, because he had no manner of *Idea*, of any such thing, nor could by any means frame to himself any Notions about Seeing. . . . Only this, I think, I may confidently say of [our ignorance], that the intellectual and sensible World, are in this perfectly alike; That part, which we see of either of them, holds no proportion with what we see not; And whatsoever we can reach with our Eyes, or our Thoughts of either of them, is but a point, almost nothing, in comparison with the rest.[5]

Here Locke is emphasizing our ignorance with respect to what another creature may be experiencing, while insisting that we should not conclude from this ignorance that these other creatures do not have experiences. This is what I shall refer to as Locke's robust – or as I shall call it 'hard' – realism about other minds. That is to say, Locke believes that other minds or spirits exist and that this is something we cannot deny. And Locke holds this despite also holding that it is not possible for us to know what things are like for these other minds.[6]

Locke admits that we cannot know that other minds or spirits exist, but he believes that we are of the opinion that they do, and that this opinion is based on reasons that make it probable that our opinion is true. Locke defines opinion, or faith, thus: 'whereby I mean that

Assent, which we give to any Proposition as true, of whose Truth yet we have no certain Knowledge'.[7] Opinion is, thus, differentiated from knowledge. Locke makes it clear from the outset that it is also his aim in the *Essay* to 'search out the *Bounds* between Opinion and Knowledge; and examine by what Measures, in things, whereof we have no certain Knowledge, we ought to regulate our Assent, and moderate our Perswasions'.[8]

Locke's distinction between knowledge and opinion raises some interesting issues about the minds of others, not all of which he addresses in his *Essay*. First of all it focuses attention on an interesting difference between our epistemic relations to the world of bodies and to other minds: of the former we may have knowledge; of the latter we may have only opinion. Second, once opinion is differentiated from knowledge we can see that we entertain a range of opinions about the minds of others. Locke outlines several different reasons, each of which leads us to think that there are minds in very different sorts of beings. Thus Locke entertains the possibility that there are minds not just in men, but in bodies very different from those of men; and he considers as well the ideas that exist in these other minds. This is a departure from the way Descartes and Malebranche think of other minds. Descartes, as we have seen, allows that, at least of corporeal beings, all and only men have minds. And Malebranche only considers the existence and nature of other *men's* minds. In Locke's work, however, we find consideration of other minds far and wide – in one place he even considers the existence of 'intelligent Inhabitants in the Planets, and other Mansions of the vast Universe'.[9] Here we see a consequence of Locke's robust realism: there are many different minds.

Locke's comments on the minds of others are brief and scattered throughout the *Essay*. In order to understand these comments it is necessary to have a working knowledge of many different aspects of that work. In particular, we need to understand how ideas come to be in the mind, and the knowledge that is based on them. Furthermore, we need to understand the distinction that Locke draws between knowledge and opinion. Only then will we be in a position to understand what Locke says about our opinion that others have minds.

OUR IDEA OF MIND

Locke devotes Book I of his *Essay* to an attack on the doctrine of innate ideas. He begins Book II ready to explain the true origin of our ideas. The work of Book II is a necessary preliminary to that of Book IV where Locke turns finally to the question of knowledge. According to Locke there can be no knowledge where there are no ideas; ideas form the foundation of knowledge. Locke differentiates several degrees of knowledge, but each degree is founded on ideas. Here Locke is in disagreement with Malebranche. In his critique of Malebranche's work, Locke makes it clear that there is no knowledge by conjecture which is not through ideas. Locke writes,

> 'The 4th way of knowing, [Malebranche] tells us, is by conjecture, and thus only we know the souls of other men and other pure intelligences', i.e. we know them not at all; but more probably think there are such beings really existing in 'rerum naturâ'. But this looks to me to be besides the author's business here, which seems to me to examine what ideas we have, and how we come by them. So that the thing here considered should in my opinion be, not whether there were any souls of men or pure intelligences any-where existing, but what ideas we have of them, and how we come by them.[10]

Where Malebranche differentiates kinds of knowledge – that based on ideas, that which is immediate, and that which is by conjecture – Locke takes all knowledge to be founded in ideas and differentiates between, on the one hand, degrees of knowledge and, on the other, knowledge and opinion. If conjecture is not based on ideas, then it cannot yield knowledge. Conjecture is, for Locke, a form of opinion, not knowledge. So the real question, as far as Locke is concerned, is where we come by our idea of other minds or spirits. It is only by engaging in such an inquiry that we can determine whether there can be knowledge of another spirit.[11]

Let us begin where Locke begins, with the following understanding of the term *idea*:

> Before I proceed on to what I have thought on the Subject, I must here in the Entrance beg pardon of my Reader, for the frequent use of the Word *Idea*, which he will find in the following Treatise. It being a Term, which, I think, serves to stand for whatsoever is the Object of the Understanding when a Man thinks, I have used it to express whatever is meant by *Phantasm*, *Notion*, *Species*, or whatever it is, which the Mind can be employed about in thinking.[12]

Locke's use of the term is not Malebranche's. Malebranche, as we have seen in the previous chapter, may agree with Locke that ideas are what are before the mind when a man thinks, but Malebranche also uses the term in another sense. For Malebranche, to have an idea of something would enable us to know its nature or essence. Locke does not restrict his understanding of ideas in this way.

Locke asks, When does a man first come to have ideas? His answer is unequivocal. In Book II Locke writes,

> To ask, *at what time a Man has first any* Ideas, is to ask, when he begins to perceive; having *Ideas*, and Perception being the same thing.[13]

At the same time that Locke here puts forward a positive thesis, he also advances a negative one: to say that men begin to have ideas when they begin to perceive is, as far as Locke is concerned, to deny the Cartesian doctrine that the soul always thinks. Consulting our experience we find that we sometimes think, and from this we conclude that there is something in us that has the power to think. If we wish to know if that substance always thinks, we must again consult experience. And experience informs us that it is not the case that the soul always thinks: consider a man in a dreamless sleep. According to Locke, the child comes into the world with a mind empty of ideas and comes, by degrees, to be furnished with them.[14] Now the most obvious – and indeed the first – way that the child comes to have ideas is through sensation, through the operation of its five senses. But if the source of ideas were limited only to sensation, our knowledge would indeed be most impoverished. We would have no ideas – and hence no knowledge – of the operations of mind such as willing, knowing, perceiving, reasoning, believing, doubting, thinking and the like. It is not sensation, but reflection, that yields up such ideas. We come by our idea of bodies from sensation, and of the operations of mind from reflection. Locke writes,

> As I call the other *Sensation*, so I call this REFLECTION, the *Ideas* it affords being such only, as the Mind gets by reflecting on its own Operations within it self.[15]

There are, then, two 'fountains of knowledge': sensation and reflection. It is only through reflection that we come to have an idea of the mind's operations. Some simple ideas are received from both sources at once; thus, according to Locke, we come to have the ideas of pain and pleasure and the attendant passions: love, hate, sorrow, fear, anger, envy, and the like.[16]

Locke considers the way our mind comes to be furnished with ideas from infancy through to old age. He claims that in its early years the child's attention is taken up with the colourful and changing world outside it, and comes, on the whole, to have ideas only of sensation. As the child grows, it can turn its attention away from the world and point it inwards to contemplate the operations of its own mind. By this sort of reflection the child's mind comes to be furnished with another set of ideas, those of the mind's own operations. To remind us that reflection operates much in the way that sensation does, Locke refers to reflection as 'internal sense'.[17] Potentially, the mind and its operations are there to be contemplated from the earliest years, but reflection is difficult and children tend to come to it later in life. Locke remarks that even some grown men never come to have clear ideas of the mind's operations because they never pay them much attention. Reflection is the more difficult of the two routes to the having of ideas, and some do this better than others.

It is this capacity to perceive, and hence to have ideas, that, according to Locke, *'puts the distinction betwixt the animal Kingdom, and the inferior parts of Nature'*.[18] According to Locke *all* animals are provided by nature for the 'reception of sensation', while the motions of plants are all mechanical. It follows that even the lower orders of animal can have *some* ideas. But there is a great difference in the quality of perception depending upon the animal. Locke notes: 'we may, I think, from the Make of an *Oyster*, or *Cockle*, reasonably conclude, that it has not so many, nor so quick Senses, as a Man, or several other Animals'.[19] All animals may have more or less acute powers of perception, but this is the only difference between them. Locke, then, does not follow Descartes in holding that non-human animals are mere mechanisms. Indeed, Locke considers at one point the human being in what he calls 'decrepid old age' who has little memory of the past, in whom many ideas have been wiped out, and whose senses are largely stopped up, and he asks: 'How far such an one . . . is in his Knowledge, and intellectual Faculties, above the Condition of the Cockle, or an Oyster. . . .' And he continues: 'If a Man had passed Sixty Years in such a State, as 'tis possible he might, as well as three Days, I wonder what difference there would have been, in any intellectual Perfections, between him, and the lowest degree of Animals.'[20] The lower animals, although they may have ideas (insofar as they have perceptions), are unlikely to have ideas of the operations of mind. It is through sense perception that all animals have ideas, but it is through reflection that some animals come to have ideas concerning the operations of mind.

'[IMMATERIAL] SUBSTANCE, WHICH WE CALL SPIRIT'[21]

Sensation and reflection furnish the mind with simple ideas. The mind has the capacity to combine and compound simple ideas, to abstract from them to form general ones, and to bring them together in order to survey them and find relations among them. Simple ideas are the material out of which the mind fashions further, complex, ideas. In the having of simple ideas the mind is passive; in the having of complex ideas the mind is active. For all its activity, the mind is confined to act upon the material with which it is passively furnished through external and internal perception. Locke groups the endless number of complex ideas that we entertain under the following three headings: (i) modes; (ii) relations; or (iii) substances. Modes are complex ideas which cannot subsist by themselves but are dependent upon substances. Locke gives as examples of modes ideas signified by the words 'triangle', 'gratitude', and 'murder'. Relations are ideas that arise from the consideration and comparison of one idea with another. For example, when the mind considers a man to be a husband or a father, it is carried to consider that person in relation to another, a wife or a child. Substances are such collections of ideas 'as are taken to represent distinct particular things subsisting by themselves'.[22] Locke gives the example of putting together the simple ideas of 'a certain sort of Figure with powers of Motion, Thought, and Reasoning, joined to Substance, [to] make the ordinary *Idea* of *a Man*'.[23] Of these three kinds of complex ideas, the one most relevant to our concerns is that of substance. Let us turn to a brief consideration of the complex idea of substance. For the purposes of this discussion I shall pass over what Locke has to say about our idea of substratum or the notion of pure substance in general, and shall concentrate only on his discussion of particular sorts of substances.[24]

According to Locke the mind forms complex ideas of particular sorts of substance by combining certain simple ideas. The mind experiences these simple ideas as existing together, and so presumes that they belong to one thing. Thus, says Locke, we come to have the idea of a man, a horse, gold, water and the like. These ideas bring together simple and clear ideas such as relate to the substance's figure, weight, colour and the like, as well as a much less clear idea of some support or substance in general. Another idea that forms part of our complex idea of particular sorts of substance is that of power. And this idea of power, says Locke, forms the greater part of our complex ideas of substances. Locke describes the idea of power that forms an important part of our complex ideas of bodies as 'the power of *communication of Motion by impulse*'; while he describes the idea of power that forms an important part of our complex ideas of spirit as 'the power of *exciting Motion by Thought*'.[25] These ideas of power are, says Locke, evident to us from our daily experience. Nevertheless, Locke believes that we are entirely at a loss when it comes to saying exactly how these powers operate. Important as this idea of power is to our complex ideas of particular sorts of substance, it is beyond our comprehension how it works – and this is true both for the power we see operating in bodies and for the power we see operating in spirits.

This is one of the many places where Locke finds a limitation on human understanding. We are unable to comprehend how bodies communicate motion by impulse or how spirits communicate motion by thought. Locke considers this limitation in connection with bodies and suggests that, had our senses been more acute and able to discern the minute particles of bodies, we would be able to comprehend the 'real Constitution [of things] on which their sensible Qualities depend'.[26] Our actual senses are not so acute; we are limited in what we can know. This limited knowledge is, however, sufficient for our purposes. Locke suggests that, had we the capacity to know the real inner constitution of things, this knowledge would prove inconsistent with our well-being in the part of the universe that we inhabit. As Locke sees it, God created us with senses, faculties and organs that are 'suited to the conveniences of Life, and the Business we have to do here'.[27]

At this point Locke interrupts the flow of his argument to introduce what he calls his 'extravagant conjecture'. This conjecture concerns other spirits. Locke writes:

> That since we have Reason (if there be any credit to be given to the report of things, that our Philosophy cannot account for), to imagine, that Spirits can assume to themselves Bodies of different Bulk, Figure, and Conformation of Parts. Whether one great advantage some of them have over us, may not lie in this, that they can so frame, and shape to themselves Organs of Sensation or Perception, as to suit them to their present Design, and the Circumstances of the Object they would consider.[28]

This is a most interesting conjecture. Here Locke is considering other kinds of finite spirit – those that have bodies or sense organs different from men.

Notice that Locke's extravagant conjecture is not that such spirits exist – he assumes that they do – but that they experience the world in a manner different from men. Different sense organs and different bodies experience the world differently. Recall that Locke does not take our knowledge to be the measure of all things. That the universe contains things that we are not in a position to know is, according to Locke, undeniable. In connection with this, Locke now conjectures that other creatures may be in a position to know things that we are not capable of knowing. As he writes in Book IV: 'The Ignorance, and Darkness that is in us, no more hinders, nor confines the Knowledge, that is in others, than the blindness of a Mole is an Argument against the quick-sightedness of an Eagle.'[29] Locke even allows that the sense organs of some other spirit may be capable of penetrating to the inner constitution of things. Locke introduces his extravagant conjecture immediately after explaining that *our* senses are suited to the business of *our* life. He points out that, as other creatures have a different business in this life than we do, their faculties and the ideas to which they give rise most likely differ accordingly.

Despite this extravagant conjecture, Locke is careful to point out that we can have no idea of the ideas that these other spirits may have. It is because we lack ideas here that we need to resort to conjecture. Thus Locke writes,

> And though we cannot but allow, that the infinite Power and Wisdom of God, may frame Creatures with a thousand other Faculties, and ways of perceiving things without them, than what we have: Yet our Thoughts can go no farther than our own, so impossible it is for us to enlarge our very Guesses, beyond the *Ideas* received from our own Sensation and Reflection.[30]

This is a most important point. Although we may conjecture that other kinds of creature have ideas of a different sort, we are not capable of comprehending these different ideas. We cannot know what goes on in these other minds. The reason why our knowledge is limited here is that knowledge is founded on ideas, and our ideas are limited to what our senses and our reflection reveal to us. It is important to note that, just as our ideas of bodies are limited by what our senses reveal to us, so our ideas of mind are limited by what reflection on our own mind reveals. Locke repeats the point:

The simple *Ideas* we receive from Sensation and Reflection, are the Boundaries of our Thoughts; beyond which, the Mind, whatever efforts it would make, is not able to advance one jot.[31]

The greater part of *Essay* II.xxiii is taken up with explaining how our knowledge is limited in what it can know about the real inner constitution of things. Because of this limitation, we are unable to understand the powers whereby bodies produce motion by impulse or spirit produces motion by thought. However in II.xxiii.13 Locke also considers our ignorance concerning the very ideas that other creatures may have. Furthermore, Locke is explicit about the cause of our ignorance here: our thoughts can go no further than our own. So different are the experiences of different kinds of creature that they do not fall within the sphere of what we can comprehend. Locke remarks that, where we refuse to accept our limitations and attempt to extend our knowledge, we 'fall presently into Darkness and Obscurity, Perplexedness and Difficulties; and can discover nothing but our own Blindness and Ignorance'.[32] When Locke says this he is considering our attempts to comprehend the substance of body and of spirit, but he would no doubt say the same thing about our attempts to extend our conjectures and hazard guesses about the ideas had by other kinds of spirit. Despite our ignorance, however, Locke insists that what we do experience convinces us that there are both extended substances and many different sorts of thinking ones.

Let us look a little more closely at how the mind forms its complex ideas of particular sorts of immaterial substance or spirit. In II.xxiii.15, Locke suggests that we form our complex idea of spirit in a fashion that parallels our idea of body. Thus he writes,

Besides the complex *Ideas* we have of material sensible Substances . . . by the simple *Ideas* we have taken of those Operations of our own Minds, which we experiment daily in our selves, as Thinking, Understanding, Willing, Knowing, and Power of beginning Motion, *etc.* co-existing in some Substance, we are able to frame *the complex* Idea *of an immaterial Spirit*. . . . For whilst I know, by seeing or hearing, *etc.* that there is some Corporeal Being without me, the Object of that sensation, I do more certainly know, that there is some Spiritual Being within me, that sees and hears.[33]

Locke here parallels our knowledge of sensible bodies and of spiritual being. But there is an important asymmetry in the two kinds of knowledge that he does not remark upon. In the case of bodies, I see and hear many different bodies; in the case of spiritual being I see and hear only one, myself. It is by reflection on my own mind that I come to have the idea of spirit. How is it, then, that I come to have my idea of *another* spirit? Locke does not address this question. In II.xxiii he simply offers the conjecture that the ideas that other kinds of spirit have are different from our own. As I said above, Locke does not conjecture *that* there are spirits, he simply assumes that there are. His interest here is not so much in why we think there are any other spirits besides myself, as in why we have reason to believe that the experiences of other kinds of spirit are very different from our own – so different as to be incomprehensible to us. I shall return to this point in the final section of this chapter. For the moment I shall stay with Locke and consider what else he has to say about other kinds of spirit.

Towards the end of *Essay* II.xxiii Locke considers our ideas of God and what he calls 'separate spirits'. By 'separate' Locke apparently means 'separate from matter or sensible body'. Locke takes it that we come by our complex ideas of God and of separate spirits in the same way that we come by our complex ideas of all spirits. That is, we reflect on our own mind and come to have the simple ideas of existence, duration, knowledge, power, pleasure, happiness and the like, and then – in the case of our complex idea of God – we enlarge these ideas and add to them the idea of infinity. Locke then writes: 'there is no *Idea* we attribute to God, bating Infinity, which is not also a part of our complex *Idea* of other Spirits'.[34] I want to put to one side our idea of God, and concentrate on our idea of what Locke calls separate spirits.

In his discussion of separate spirits Locke points out another limitation to what we can know. In the case of these spirits what we are unable to comprehend is how they communicate. The problem is that, as these spirits lack a body, they clearly cannot communicate in the same manner that we do. It is in his discussion of the communication of separate spirits that Locke makes it clear how he thinks *we* communicate. Men, says Locke, are 'fain to make use of corporeal Signs, and particularly Sounds'. And he continues,

> But of immediate Communication, having no Experiment in our selves, and consequently, no Notion of it at all, we have no *Idea*, how Spirits, which use not Words, can with quickness; or much less, how Spirits that have no Bodies, can be Masters of their own Thoughts, and communicate or conceal them at Pleasure, though we cannot but necessarily suppose they have such a Power.[35]

Locke is here making a comparative point: we communicate our thoughts through the use of words, but words require a body and a body is what separate spirits are separated from. So how do incorporeal spirits manage to communicate? It is of this that Locke thinks we can have no idea. We must believe that such spirits do communicate their thoughts, but we are at a loss to say how they do this. Once again we run up against the limits of what we can know concerning particular immaterial substances that we call 'spirit'. It is worth noting the reason that Locke cites for our ignorance at this point. It is a reason that Locke has mentioned before for our ignorance:

> Because being capable of no other simple *Ideas*, belonging to any thing but Body, but those which by Reflection we receive from the Operations of our own Minds, we can attribute to Spirits no other, but what we receive from thence: And all the difference we can put between them in our Contemplation of Spirits, is only in the several Extents and Degrees of their Knowledge, Power, Duration, Happiness, etc.[36]

Thus we find that Locke discusses a whole range of spirits: the one supreme spirit that is God, other separate spirits, and other kinds of spirit that inhabit bodies very different from ours. In the case of each of these spirits we encounter a limitation in our knowledge. We cannot know how different kinds of embodied spirit experience the world, and we cannot know how more perfect incorporeal spirits communicate their thoughts. But for a brief comment about how we, human spirits, communicate, Locke says nothing in *Essay* II.xxiii about other spirits like ourselves. Indeed, Locke says very little altogether about our belief that other men have minds. I consider what little he does say in the next section.

OTHER MEN'S MINDS

It is not until Book IV that we find Locke commenting directly on how it is that we come to think that there are other finite spirits like ourselves. In Book II Locke confines himself to conjectures about the experiences of other kinds of spirit and the communication of separate spirits. In Book IV he writes:

> That there are Minds, and thinking Beings in other Men as well as himself, every Man has reason, from their Words and Actions, to be satisfied.[37]

Here Locke states our reason for the belief that other men have minds. Notice that our reason for this belief is confined to the body of these other men. We have no direct experience of another mind. This is as true for other men's minds as it is for minds in other kinds of body. In all these cases the ideas we have of mind are from reflection on our own mind. Nevertheless, as we have reason to suppose that there are other kinds of mind (in creatures with different bodies and sense organs), so we have reason to believe that other men (creatures with bodies like us) have minds.

If we compare what Locke says here in Book IV with what he says earlier in Book II when he considers the communication of men in contrast with that of incorporeal or separate spirits, we find that the communication of men is a sort of second-best thing. It is true that we cannot comprehend just what first-best is like, but we must suppose that beings that are more perfect than we are do have a more perfect means of communication. We get some idea of what this more perfect way of communicating is in II.xxxii, when Locke considers whether, given a different structure in their eyes, the idea produced in one man's mind by a violet might not be the same as that produced in another man's mind by a marigold. The question is whether the difference here could ever be known, and Locke points out that it could not be 'because one Man's Mind could not pass into another Man's Body, to perceive, what Appearances were produced by those Organs'.[38] We could take from this discussion that a more perfect way for one man to know the thoughts and feelings of another would be to pass into that other man's body. This, of course, is no straightforward matter, for the first man must perceive the appearances in the second man's body *while remaining the first man*. In other words, the first man must perceive those appearances as those of the second man. Perhaps it is because of this sort of difficulty that Locke concludes that we cannot comprehend how more perfect beings achieve this sort of communication.

Locke also touches on the limitation encountered when one man tries to know the ideas of another in Book III. Here Locke considers man's use of language, and he writes:

> Man, though he have great variety of Thoughts, and such, which from others, as well as himself, might receive Profit and Delight; yet they are all within his own Breast, invisible, and hidden from others, nor can by themselves be made to appear. The Comfort and Advantage of Society, not being to be had without Communication of Thoughts, it was necessary, that Man should find out some

external sensible Signs, whereby those invisible *Ideas*, which his thoughts are made up of, might be known to others.[39]

Again we find that Locke recognizes the invisibility of a man's thoughts or ideas. It is in order to receive the benefits that communication of thoughts can bring that a man must find a way to make his thoughts known to another. Language is the conventional device man developed for this purpose. Locke writes: 'Thus we may conceive how *Words*, which were by Nature so well adapted to that purpose, come to be made use of by Men, as *the Signs of* their *Ideas*; not by any natural connection . . . but by a voluntary Imposition.'[40] Thus, one man hears another's words and this gives him a reason to be satisfied that there are 'Minds, and thinking Beings in other men as well as himself'. The ideas in men's minds may be 'invisible', yet a man is able to make his ideas available to another by the use of language. Locke does not appear to think that the invisibility of another man's ideas is particularly problematic; there is simply a difference in the way that more perfect beings communicate and the way we, in this life, must communicate.

When, in the *Essay* Book IV, Locke explains our reason for thinking that there are minds in other men, it is in the context of a discussion about the extent of human knowledge. In the course of his consideration of all that we can know concerning what he calls the 'intellectual World', Locke reminds us that there is much that lies beyond what we are able to know. We must acknowledge the existence of an 'infinite number of *Spirits*', despite our inability to know their ideas. Here Locke appears to be making reference to his discussion of other kinds of spirit and separate spirits in Book II. However, when he discusses other kinds of spirit, Locke concentrates not on their existence but on the different ideas they may have; while when he discusses other men's minds he concentrates only on our reason for thinking that such minds exist. A man's words and actions give us our reason for believing that other men have minds. We may well ask why Locke does not raise the further question, whether we can have any idea of the ideas that are in another man's mind.

This question may seem pressing when we remember that Locke understands that 'one Man's Mind could not pass into another Man's Body, to perceive, what Appearances were produced by those Organs'. But notice that when Locke makes this observation, he prefaces it by saying that he is here considering ideas that would be produced if our sense organs had had a different structure.[41] But, although Locke does not consider it, does the point not hold even in the situation that *does* obtain between men? In other words, is it not possible that, even as things are, different men may have different ideas? Locke certainly does allow that, when men communicate through the use of words, it is possible that the speaker and hearer have different ideas in mind. This appears to be part of what is meant by saying that communication between men is imperfect. Thus, he writes:

> *Words* by long and familiar use, . . . come to excite in Men certain *Ideas*, so constantly and readily, that they are apt to suppose a natural connexion between them. But that they *signify* only Men's peculiar *Ideas*, and that *by a perfectly arbitrary Imposition*, is evident, in that they often fail to excite in others (even that use the same Language) the same *Ideas*, we take them to be Signs of.[42]

Locke, however, draws a distinction between the differences there may be in the minds of a speaker and a hearer when they use words in connection with the various complex ideas, and when they use words as the names of simple ideas. He writes: 'the *Names of simple* Ideas *are*, of all others the *least liable to Mistakes*'.[43] In this connection Locke explains that we are less liable to error in our use of names for simple ideas because (i) these ideas are the result of a single perception, and because (ii) these ideas 'are never referr'd to any other Essence, but barely that Perception they immediately signify'.[44] To illustrate the point Locke says that a man seldom makes a mistake and applies the word 'red' to the idea of green, or the word 'sweet' to the idea bitter.[45] However, it is not yet entirely clear why Locke is so sure that, because our ideas are simple, the names we use to communicate about them are the same in the speaker as in the hearer.

Part of the answer is to be found in II.xxxii when Locke considers the question of whether our ideas of things are true. Locke explains that he is not interested in what he calls the 'metaphysical Sense of Truth'.[46] That is, he is not interested in the question whether things really do exist in conformity with our ideas of them. Rather what interests Locke is whether our ideas are true or false 'in the more ordinary Acceptation of those Words'.[47] In this sense, the mind supposes that the idea it has conforms to some real existence. Now about the truth of our simple ideas Locke writes:

> Our simple *Ideas*, being barely such Perceptions, as God has fitted us to receive, and given Power to external Objects to produce in us by established Laws, and Ways, suitable to his Wisdom and Goodness, though incomprehensible to us, their

Truth consists in nothing else, but in such Appearances, as are produced in us, and must be suitable to those Powers, he has placed in external Objects, or else they could not be produced in us: And thus answering those Powers, they are what they should be, *true Ideas.*[48]

Locke takes it that simple ideas can be taken to be true because God has made it that objects external to us have a power (that we cannot comprehend) to produce ideas in us that answer those powers. Even once we understand that this is so, however, the question may still press: Why do we take it that different men have the *same* idea when presented with the same objects? Only if the ideas here are the same, can we say with some assurance that men communicate about the same simple ideas. We get the answer we seek when we look again at the passage in Book II where Locke considers the possibility that the idea produced in one man's mind by a violet might not be the same as that produced in another's mind by a marigold. Towards the end of that passage Locke writes:

I am nevertheless very apt to think, that the sensible *Ideas,* produced by any Object in different Men's Minds, are most commonly very near and undiscernibly alike. For which Opinion, I think, there might be many Reasons offered: but that being besides my present Business, I shall not trouble my Reader with them; but only mind him, that the contrary Supposition, if it could be proved, is of little use, either for the Improvement of our Knowledge, or Conveniency of Life; and so we need not trouble our selves to examine it.[49]

Finally we arrive at an answer to the question whether different men might not have different ideas. Locke allows that we cannot have proof that men's ideas are alike, but he thinks that there are reasons for thinking they are. Unfortunately, he does not explain what those reasons are. Perhaps Locke thinks that God would not have arranged things so that the same objects should give rise to different ideas in different men (God's laws are uniform). This may be. However, as Malebranche points out, despite the uniformity in God's laws, it may be that there are subtle differences in the sense organs of different men. Malebranche concludes that, in the case of sensations at least, it is highly likely that different men have different sensations when they come in contact with the same object (*vide supra*, Chapter III). Locke appears to think that men's sense organs do not differ in this subtle way.

The explanation Locke gives for omitting to give us his reasons for taking it that objects produce similar ideas in different men's minds is an interesting one: the belief that men's ideas are *not* alike would be of little use to us. Locke makes this point clear a few lines earlier when he considers what would happen if, because of a different structure in their sense organs, different men saw different colours when faced with the same object. Locke claims that such a situation need not bother us, just so long as there is a certain constancy or regularity in the ideas that are produced by any given object for any given man. He writes:

> For all the Things, that had the Texture of a *Violet*, producing constantly the *Idea*, which he called *Blue*; and those which had the Texture of a *Marigold*, producing constantly the *Idea*, which he as constantly called *Yellow*, whatever those Appearances were in his Mind; he would be able as regularly to distinguish Things for his Use by those Appearances, and understand, and signify those distinctions, marked by the Names *Blue* and *Yellow*, as if the Appearances, or *Ideas* in his Mind, received from those two Flowers, were exactly the same, with the *Ideas* in other Men's Minds.[50]

Locke's point is that it need not be the case that all men receive the same ideas from objects, just so long as the ideas a man does receive are constant. So Locke does recognize that different men can have different ideas. Nevertheless, he believes that there is reason to think that this is not the case, and that, even if it were the case, it would not matter – it would not matter to the conduct of our lives. So we *can* raise a question about the ideas in another man's mind, just as we can raise a question about the ideas in the minds of other kinds of creature. It is just that, while Locke holds that we can have no idea of the ideas that are in the minds of other kinds of creature, we have reason to suppose that the ideas in other men's minds are the same as those in our minds. Notice that no argument by analogy is here used to come to this conclusion. It is true that Locke does not fully explain what our reason is, but it is more likely that Locke thinks that it is based on the thought that there is a similar structure in the sense organs of all men than that it is based on analogy.

In any case, it does not matter if different men do have different ideas when faced with the same object. Throughout the *Essay* Locke emphasizes, on the one hand, what we can know or understand and, on the other hand, what is requisite for the conduct of life. In Book IV he writes,

The Understanding Faculties being given to Man, not barely for Speculation, but also for the Conduct of his Life, Man would be at a great loss, if he had nothing to direct him, but what has the Certainty of true *Knowledge*. For that being short and scanty . . . he would be often utterly in the dark, and in most of the Actions of his Life, perfectly at a stand, had he nothing to guide him in the absence of clear and certain Knowledge.[51]

According to Locke, the greater part of our actions is guided, not by knowledge, but by opinion. The division Locke draws here is not in all places clear, but of the importance of the distinction Locke is insistent. Let us now turn to an examination of the distinction Locke draws between knowledge and opinion.

KNOWLEDGE AND OPINION

Locke devotes Book IV of the *Essay* to a discussion of knowledge and opinion. Locke begins that book by writing,

> *Knowledge* then seems to me to be nothing but *the perception of the connexion and agreement, or disagreement and repugnancy of any of our Ideas.* In this alone it consists. Where this Perception is, there is Knowledge, and where it is not, there, though we may fancy, guess, or believe, yet we always come short of Knowledge.[52]

Locke then elaborates on what might be called various dimensions of knowledge: one dimension is its extent and another its degree. I shall first look briefly at these and then turn to consider our opinions – our beliefs, guesses, and fancies that fall short of knowledge.

Strictly speaking Locke allows for only two degrees of knowledge: intuition and demonstration. Through intuition we have knowledge of, among other things, our own minds, and through demonstration we come to know the existence of, among other things, God. In the case of intuition the mind 'is at no pains of proving or examining, but perceives the Truth, as the Eye doth light, only by being directed toward it'.[53] Further to this Locke writes of this degree of knowledge that it is 'like the bright Sun-shine', that it 'forces itself immediately to be perceived', and that it 'leaves no room for Hesitation, Doubt, or Examination'.[54] Intuition yields the highest degree of certainty that we can have. As well as the knowledge a man has of his own mind, he has knowledge in this way of the agreement or disagreement of certain ideas, such as that 3 is greater than 2, or that black is not white. Intuition also has a part to play in that other degree of knowledge, demonstration. For this reason the certainty we can have as the result of demonstration is great, but not as great as the certainty yielded by intuition alone. At this second degree knowledge is not immediate, but must proceed along a series of ideas which Locke calls demonstration or proof. The mind arrives at certainty here only after it follows a progression of steps. In this way the mind arrives at much mathematical and scientific knowledge, as well as at knowledge of God. Locke ends his discussion of these two degrees of knowledge by writing that 'whatever comes short of one of these, with what assurance soever embraced, is but Faith, or Opinion, but not Knowledge'.[55]

Having drawn such a clear line between knowledge and opinion, Locke adds that this line exists in this way only for general truths. When we consider particular truths – truths concerning the particular existence of finite beings – things are a little different. In the case of particular truths we find that, while our perceptions do not reach the degree of certainty of either intuition or demonstration, nevertheless they go 'beyond bare probability'.[56] Locke is very clear about what is at issue here: the question is not about the existence of an idea, but about the existence of anything 'without us, which corresponds to that *Idea*'.[57] It is over just such corresponding objects that Descartes raised his sceptical questions in his first *Meditation*. Considering such scepticism Locke asks,

> Whether he be not invincibly conscious to himself of a different Perception, when he looks on the Sun by day, and thinks on it by night; when he actually tastes Wormwood, or smells a Rose, or only thinks on that Savour, or Odour? . . . If anyone say, a Dream may do the same thing, and all these *Ideas* produced in us, without any external Objects, he may please to dream that I make him this Answer, 1. That 'tis no great matter, whether I remove this Scruple or no: Where all is but Dream, Reasoning and Arguments are of no use, Truth and Knowledge nothing. 2. That I believe he will allow a very manifest difference between dreaming of being in the Fire, and actually being in it.[58]

And he follows this up a few chapters later by writing,

> That *the certainty of* Things existing *in rerum Naturâ*, when we have *the testimony of our Senses* for it, is not only *as great* as

our frame can attain to, but *as our Condition needs.* For our Faculties being not suited to the full extent of Being, nor to a perfect, clear, comprehensive Knowledge of things free from all doubt and scruple; but to the preservation of us, in whom they are; and accommodated to the use of Life.[59]

Once again we find Locke putting an emphasis on what is required for the conduct of life. He makes it clear that intuition and demonstration do not provide us with knowledge sufficient for the conduct of life. The knowledge we have here must be supplemented. It is Locke's view that opinion provides the needed supplementation. In the matter of particular truths, however, Locke allows that we can have what he calls 'sensitive knowledge'. Despite the fact that our ideas of particular bodies lack the certainty of intuition and demonstration, Locke holds that we can also be said to have knowledge here.[60] So, to the two degrees of knowledge – intuition and demonstration – Locke adds another: sensitive knowledge.

Locke is very clear about the limits of sensitive knowledge. He writes: 'But *this Knowledge extends as far as the present Testimony of our Senses,* employ'd about particular Objects, that do then affect them, *and no farther.*'[61] He gives as an example of these limits the existence of men that are no longer in our company or men that we have never set eyes on but believe exist in the world. Locke insists that we cannot say that we know these men exist, although it is highly probable that they do. He writes:

Though the great likelihood of it puts me past doubt, and it be reasonable for me to do several things upon the confidence, that there are Men (and Men also of my acquaintance, with whom I have to do) now in the World: But this is but probability, not Knowledge.[62]

Thus I conduct my life as though there are other men, but my conduct is guided, not by knowledge, but by opinion based on probabilities. If we think of our epistemic relations as ranging on a scale from intuition, down through demonstration, and sensitive knowledge, and then on to opinions of various sorts, what we find is that Locke holds that our epistemic relations to absent men falls below the level of our epistemic relations to the world around us. Likewise, Locke holds that my conduct regarding the existence of other minds or spirits is guided not by knowledge but by opinion. Locke allows that our opinions here may, in some cases, be highly probable, but he insists that they cannot rise to knowledge. Locke writes: 'For we can no more know, that there are finite Spirits really existing, by the *Idea* we have of such Beings in our Minds, than by the *Ideas* any one has of Fairies, or Centaurs, he can come to know, that Things answering those *Ideas* do really exist.'[63] Although we cannot have knowledge here, Locke holds that we can have the assurance of reasons, backed by revelation. It is through God's revelation, and our assent to it that is called 'faith', that we come to be assured that those things that reason teaches us to believe to exist, really do exist.[64]

Later in Book IV Locke explains that, just as there are degrees of knowledge, so there are degrees of probability that correspond to degrees of assent. Our assent can range from 'assurance' and 'confidence' down to '*Conjecture, Doubt,* and *Distrust*'.[65] In this connection Locke considers the probabilities that are associated with things that are not capable of observation because they do not fall under the reach of our senses. (These he clearly differentiates from things that we can observe but, for one reason or another, we are not at a given time in a position to observe.) Locke explicitly considers the probabilities associated with the existence, nature and operations of immaterial beings such as angels and devils, as well as of material beings that are either too small for us to see or too remote from us. In connection with the latter Locke considers whether there be any 'intelligent Inhabitants in the Planets, and other Mansions of the vast Universe'.[66] Locke then explains that we draw our reason for believing in the existence of such beings from *analogy*. The analogy Locke has in mind works in the following way: we notice the way things operate at the level of what we can observe, and we conclude by analogy that things are similar at the level of things that we cannot observe. Thus, we notice that there is a gradual connection between things that we can observe in this world – that there are no discernible gaps – and we conclude by analogy that there is a similar gradual change in things in what Locke calls the 'intellectual world'. Locke writes:

> The difference is exceedingly great between some Men, and some Animals: But if we will compare the Understanding and Abilities of some Men, and some Brutes, we shall find so little difference, that 'twill be hard to say, that that of the Man is either larger or clearer. Observing, I say, such a gradual and gentle descents downwards in those parts of the Creation, that are beneath Man, the rule of Analogy may make it probable, that it is so also in Things above us, and our Observations; and that there are several ranks of intelligent Beings, excelling us in

several degrees of Perfection, ascending upwards towards the infinite Perfection of the Creator, by gentle steps and differences, that are every one at no great distance from the next to it.[67]

It should be clear from what Locke says about the rule of analogy that he is not making use of the argument from analogy that philosophers today are so familiar with. Locke does not suggest that I come to believe that other spirits exist because I observe their behaviour and reason that it must be the product of a mind in the way that my behaviour is the product of my mind. For Locke the rule of analogy helps us to form opinions where our knowledge cannot extend. And our knowledge cannot extend to the existence of these intelligent beings precisely because they are unobservable – too small, too far away from us, or exist without a body. It is because we are unable to observe the bodies of these creatures that we must employ the rule of analogy. Notice that Locke says that it is the *bodies* of these creatures that are unobservable not their *minds* or *spirits*. And yet we know from what he says elsewhere that he also thinks that minds are unobservable (or 'invisible'). Nevertheless, Locke does not suggest that I employ the rule of analogy to come by my belief that there are minds in other bodies – be they observable or unobservable. As we have seen, Locke is not altogether clear why we come to believe that there are minds in any other bodies. In the case of other men, he does say that we are satisfied that they have minds from their words and actions. In the case of animals whose bodies are not too small or too remote from us he presumably thinks we come to believe that they have minds because we can see that they have sense organs which give them ideas of the world around them. Presumably, Locke would say that the assent we give to propositions that assert the existence of minds in other men is at the top of the range: we are confident that there are minds in other men. However, our belief in the existence of any other minds – including those in men – cannot reach the full confidence of knowledge. Man is limited in what he can know. Concerning this limitation Locke writes:

I am not here speaking of Probability, but Knowledge; and I think not only that it becomes the Modesty of Philosophy, not to pronounce Magisterially, where we want that Evidence that can produce Knowledge; but also, that it is of use to us, to discern how far our Knowledge does reach; for the state we are at present in, not being that of Vision, we must, in many Things, content our selves with Faith and Probability.[68]

On matters relating to the existence of another mind, as well as those relating to the condition of that mind, we must rest content with opinion.

CONCLUSION

It is notable that Locke believes that our relations to others are founded on probabilities. Although we can have assurance that other minds exist, this assurance falls short of the assurance we have when we consider the existence of the world of bodies. Where Locke writes about our beliefs concerning the existence and condition of other minds, he largely discusses those minds that are different from our own. He considers incorporeal minds, and minds in creatures whose bodies and sense organs are very different from ours, as well as minds in beings whose bodies we cannot observe because they are too small or are too remote from us. He says very little about the minds of other men. Perhaps this is because Locke believes that the existence of these minds is relatively uncontroversial. Yet, as we have seen, even my belief in the existence and condition of other men's minds may be thought to raise questions. These are questions that Locke touches on without directly addressing. And these questions arise because the mind of *any* other being is 'invisible'. This Locke explicitly recognizes in the case of men, when he says that we satisfy ourselves that they have minds by observing their words and actions. Given the invisibility of another mind, however, it is presumably possible that another's words and actions may lead us wrongly to conclude that they have a mind. Locke appreciates that some animals – he gives the example of parrots – may utter the same sounds as men without these sounds functioning as words, as signs of ideas.[69] Yet he does not consider the possibility that a *man* may so utter these sounds. Locke writes with assurance that when men utter words they utter them as signs of ideas.

The lack of interest that Locke shows in the possibility that a man's words and actions may not signify ideas reminds one of the lack of interest that he shows in sceptical questions concerning the external world (*vide supra*). Concerning the existence of objects without us Locke writes,

> If we persuade ourselves, that our Faculties act and inform us right, concerning the existence of those Objects that affect them, it cannot pass for an ill-grounded confidence: For I think no body can, in earnest, be so sceptical, as to be uncertain of the Existence of Things which he sees and feels.[70]

Perhaps Locke would say something similar if pressed about our belief in the existence of other men's minds. However, given the conceptual divide of mind from body that Locke inherits from Descartes, the confidence we may have in the existence of other minds cannot be as great as that which we have in the existence of particular things. Locke himself recognizes this when he says that we can have only opinions about the existence of another mind. The mind of another is invisible even if we allow that we can be confident that the body of the other exists. Perhaps Locke would say that no man can in earnest be so sceptical as to be uncertain that his friends, his sister, or his mother has a mind. But if this is so, why does Locke draw a distinction between knowledge and opinion, allowing that we can only be of the opinion that there are other minds?

I want to end by considering what Locke has to say in response to the question raised by Augustine (*vide supra*): How can we account for the belief that there are other minds? This question can be understood to raise a conceptual problem about other minds. Augustine takes it that this problem arises because, although the mind is able to know itself, it is not similarly able to know others. The reason is that, according to Augustine, while the mind knows itself because it is present to itself, 'it is utterly impossible for us either to perceive or to understand [another's] will unless he makes it known by some corporeal signs, and even then we believe rather than understand'.[71] Augustine recognizes that we need to understand why, given that I know what a mind is by reflection on my own mind, I so much as believe or think that there are other minds. We need to understand how I come to conceive of mind as something general, something that can exist in others as well as myself. I suggested that it is to this end that Augustine proposes an argument from analogy. What is Locke's response to Augustine's question? Locke, after all, is insistent that I come to have my complex idea of spirit by combining various simple ideas, which simple ideas I come to have by reflection on my own mind. But if this *is* how I come to have my complex idea of mind, how do I come to have a general idea of mind?

In IV.xi.13, Locke writes concerning my idea of men: 'I have made an abstract *Idea* of such a Species [*Man*], whereof I am one particular.' Abstraction is one of the operations that Locke thinks the mind can perform on its ideas. According to Locke it is by the application of abstraction that the mind is able to move from having a particular idea to having a general one. Locke suggests that the mind observes a number of particulars that are alike in certain respects, and abstracts from them to form an idea that brings together just the similarities while leaving out all the differences. Locke's doctrine of abstraction is fraught with difficulties. However, whatever difficulties there may be in understanding how the process of abstraction works to give us a general idea of, say, white or snow or man, the process faces an additional difficulty when we consider how it can work to give us a general idea of mind. In the case of mind, I can have only one particular example, my own. The question then arises, how does abstraction work in this one case to give us a quite general idea of mind? I shall not press this question further here. In Part Three, I shall return to this question and consider the difficulties one encounters when trying to respond to it.

CHAPTER V

Berkeley and knowledge of other finite spirits

INTRODUCTION

Locke's interest in questions concerning the existence and condition of other minds or spirits is secondary to his interest in knowledge and its extent. Locke draws a clear distinction between the opinions we can have concerning other minds and the knowledge (he calls it 'sensitive knowledge') we can have of particular bodies. In the case of particular bodies the evidence rises above mere probability and so can be counted as knowledge, but this is not so in the case of other minds. We could say that, for Locke, our relationship to the world of bodies is more secure than our relationship to other minds.

Berkeley (1635–1753) is an inheritor of Lockean empiricism. However, Berkeley is unable to accept what he sees as the sceptical consequences of a philosophy like Locke's. Although Locke does allow that we can have knowledge of things actually presented to the senses, he admits that this knowledge is not direct. Locke writes,

'Tis evident, the Mind knows not Things immediately, but only by the intervention of the *Ideas* it has of them. *Our Knowledge* therefore is not real, but only so far as there is a conformity between our *Ideas* and the reality of Things.[1]

Locke's point is that, despite the fact that we cannot know things directly, we can be sure that our knowledge is real because we must take it that our simple ideas are 'the product of Things operating on the Mind in a natural way'.[2] Locke also points out the manifest difference that exists between ideas that arise as the result of the corresponding object affecting our senses and ideas that arise in dreams or memory. Berkeley is unpersuaded. He detects in such a philosophy a gap between our ideas and what they are ideas of, and insists that this gap will lead to scepticism – whether or not we *say* that we can have knowledge. In the preface to his *Three Dialogues Between Hylas and Philonous* Berkeley writes,

> Upon the common principles of philosophers, we are not assured of the existence of things from their being perceived. And we are taught to distinguish their real nature from that which falls under the senses. Hence arises *scepticism* and *paradoxes*. . . . We spend our lives in doubting of those things which other men evidently know, and believing those things which they laugh at, and despise.[3]

Berkeley takes it as a hallmark of his work that it shows how genuine knowledge of both mind and body is possible. As he writes in the introduction to his *Principles of Human Knowledge,*

> We should believe that God has dealt more bountifully with the sons of men, than to give them a strong desire for that knowledge, which he had placed quite out of their reach.[4]

According to Berkeley God has not placed certain things out of the reach of our knowledge, nor are our faculties limited. Rather, we are led to believe in these limitations on the possibility of knowledge when we insist on false principles. It is precisely these principles that Berkeley intends to examine in his work. Despite an emphasis on what we can know, however, Berkeley is, as I shall explain below, content to allow that our knowledge of the mind of another is merely probable.[5] When it comes to our epistemic relations to other finite minds, Berkeley's views do not appear to differ greatly from Locke's.

As with all the philosophers whose views I have considered thus far, Berkeley's comments on our knowledge of other finite minds are few and scattered throughout his works. Unlike the comments of these other philosophers on this topic, however, Berkeley's are more than peripheral to his overall interest and aims. Berkeley's rejection of so much as the idea of material substance, along with his recognition that our ideas of sense are not 'the creatures of my will', lead him to conclude that 'there is therefore some other will or spirit that produces [our ideas]'.[6] The topic of other minds and our knowledge of them is, thus, central to Berkeley's work. One commentator on Berkeley's work, Jonathan Bennett, claims that Berkeley was 'arguably the discoverer of the problem of other minds'.[7] It should be clear from the work of the previous chapters that Bennett can have no argument here at all. It is true that Descartes did not discuss the issue, but Malebranche is very careful to differentiate our knowledge of other minds from all other kinds of knowledge. And Arnaud is even clearer than Malebranche about what is involved in our conjecture that there are other minds. Furthermore, Locke carefully differentiates our opinions concerning other minds from our knowledge concerning particular things. Berkeley was, thus, certainly not the first philosopher to address issues that arise concerning the minds of others. Nor can it be said that Berkeley – or any other philosopher of this period – finds anything particularly *problematic* about our knowledge of the mind of another. Berkeley recognizes that our knowledge of other minds needs some special account, but, like Malebranche, Arnaud and Locke, he sees no difficulty in providing such an account. None of these philosophers writes in such a way as to indicate that they believe that there is any outstanding or lingering difficulty attending our knowledge of other minds once their account is in place.

As we have seen in previous chapters, many commentators have been quick to claim to find an argument from analogy to the existence of other minds in the history of philosophy. I have argued that, of all the philosophers whose work I have discussed thus far, only Arnaud's work can be said to contain an argument that bears any significant resemblance to this familiar argument. Several commentators claim to find this argument in Berkeley's work.[8] It is true that, when one first looks at the passages where Berkeley explains how we come by our knowledge of the existence of another mind or spirit, it is tempting to understand them as giving an early statement of the argument from analogy. I shall argue below, however, that what Berkeley says in the text falls short of that argument. Interestingly, Bennett is one of the very few commentators on Berkeley's work who does not attribute to him an argument from analogy. Bennett gives a causal interpretation of those passages that mention our knowledge of the existence of others. I am inclined to find Bennett's interpretation more to the point. Before we can be in a position to assess what Berkeley has to say about our knowledge of other finite minds, it is necessary to have some understanding of how he thinks it is that we come to have knowledge of bodies and of mind. Let us turn now to a brief review of Berkeley's principles of human knowledge.

THE OBJECTS OF HUMAN KNOWLEDGE: IDEAS AND SPIRIT

The opening lines of the First Principle in Part I of Berkeley's *Principles* are reminiscent of Locke's *Essay*. Berkeley writes,

It is evident to anyone who takes a survey of the objects of human knowledge, that they are either ideas actually imprinted on the senses, or else such as are perceived by attending to the passions and operations of the mind, or lastly ideas formed by the help of memory and imagination.

By the time one has read Berkeley's Second Principle, however, one is reminded not so much of Locke but of Malebranche. In the Second Principle Berkeley writes,

But besides all that endless variety of ideas or objects of knowledge, there is likewise something which knows or perceives them, and exercises divers operations, as willing, imagining, remembering, about them. This perceiving active being is what I call *mind*, *spirit*, *soul* or *myself*. By which words I do not denote any one of my ideas, but a thing entirely distinct from them, wherein they exist, or, which is the same thing, whereby they are perceived.

While it may be tempting to read the First Principle as suggesting that Berkeley accepts Locke's distinction between ideas of sensation and ideas of reflection, this would not be correct, as the Second Principle makes clear. Berkeley in fact rejects Lockean ideas of reflection and, along with them, the Lockean doctrine that all knowledge is founded on ideas. From the outset of his *Principles* Berkeley is keen to emphasize a distinction between objects that are known and the knowing subject. Furthermore, Berkeley insists that the knowing subject – the mind, spirit, or soul – is not itself known through ideas. Berkeley appears to be reviving the Malebranchean observation that there are different kinds of knowledge; not all knowledge is through ideas.

You will recall from Chapter III that Malebranche holds that men do not have ideas of mind: I know my own mind through sensation and the mind of another through conjecture. Nonetheless, Malebranche does not deny that there can be ideas of mind. Indeed, he holds that God has ideas of mind but that He has chosen not to give these ideas to men. Berkeley agrees that knowledge of mind is not through ideas, but his reason for this is quite different from Malebranche's. According to Berkeley, we do not have an idea of mind, and we could not have such an idea. Berkeley writes that 'it is manifestly impossible there should be any such *idea*'.[9]

Berkeley considers two objections that might be made to this claim. First he considers the possibility that we are unable to have the idea of spirit or mind only because we lack a sense appropriate to know it. There may be an idea of mind, but we are unable to perceive it. To this Berkeley replies,

> In case we had a new sense bestowed upon us, we could only receive thereby some new sensations or ideas of sense. But I believe nobody will say, that what he means by the terms *soul* and *substance*, is only some particular sort of idea or sensation. We may therefore infer that, all things duly considered, it is not more reasonable to think our faculties defective, in that they do not furnish us with an idea or spirit or active thinking substance, than it would be if we should blame them for not being able to comprehend a *round square*.[10]

Next Berkeley considers the possibility that, although it may be that an idea cannot resemble a spirit in certain respects, yet it may perhaps resemble a spirit in *other* respects. Berkeley himself admits, after all, that an idea need not resemble its original in *all* respects. Thus, while we may agree that an idea cannot resemble a spirit in its thinking, acting or perceiving ideas, it may be said to resemble a spirit in all its other respects. To this Berkeley responds by pointing out that, if you leave out the power to think, act, and perceive ideas, there is nothing left of spirit – 'this alone, constitutes the signification of that term'.[11]

Berkeley's point is that mind or spirit is not the sort of thing to be comprehended by an idea. He reiterates the point in Principle 142 where he summarizes the difference between spirits and ideas. He writes,

> *Spirit* and *ideas* are things so wholly different, that when we say, *they exist, they are known*, or the like, these words must not be thought to signify anything common to both natures. There is nothing alike or common in them: and to expect that by any multiplication or enlargement of our faculties, we may be enabled to know a spirit as we do a triangle, seems as absurd as if we should hope to *see a sound*.

Berkeley does not just insist on a difference here; he offers a reason to support this difference and refers to it repeatedly throughout the *Principles*. Consider, for example, Principle 139:

> All unthinking objects of the mind agree, in that they are entirely passive, and their existence consists only in being per-ceived: whereas a soul or spirit is an active being, whose

existence consists not in being perceived, but in perceiving ideas and thinking. It is therefore necessary, in order to prevent equivocation and confounding natures perfectly disagreeing and unlike, that we distinguish between *spirit* and *idea*.[12]

Berkeley first introduces the point in Principle 27 where he writes,

> A spirit is one simple, undivided, active being: as it perceives ideas it is called *understanding*, and as it produces or otherwise operates about them, it is called the *will*. Hence there can be no idea formed of a soul or spirit: for all ideas whatever, being passive and inert . . ., they cannot represent unto us, by way of image or likeness, that which acts. A little attention will make it plain to anyone, that to have an idea which shall be like that active principle of motion and change of ideas, is absolutely impossible. Such is the nature of *spirit* or that which acts, that it cannot be of itself perceived, but only by the effects which it produceth.

So the reason why it is absurd to think that we could have an idea of mind is that mind is an active principle while ideas are passive and inert. We cannot have an idea of that which acts. We cannot perceive that which acts, but can only perceive the effects produced.

Now Malebranche thinks that it follows from the fact that we do not have an idea of mind that we cannot know the nature of mind (*vide supra*, Chapter III). Berkeley, by contrast, does not think it follows from the fact that we cannot have an idea of mind that we cannot know the nature of mind. In Principle 135 he writes that 'perhaps human knowledge is not so deficient as is vulgarly imagined'. Berkeley believes we can know of the mind both *that* it is and *what* it is. We know *that* it is by 'inward feeling or reflexion'.[13] Considering *what* it is Berkeley writes: Spirit is 'that indivisible unextended thing, which thinks, acts, and perceives. I say *indivisible*, because unextended; and *unextended* because extended, figured, moveable things, are ideas; and that which perceives ideas . . . is plainly itself no idea.'[14]

Berkeley admits that there are those who will object to his saying that we cannot have an idea of mind by pointing out that, without an idea, words such as 'soul' or 'spirit' are without meaning. Berkeley turns this objection on its head: it is manifest that these words are significant and that we do understand their significance. It follows that ideas are not strictly necessary in order that words are significant. In Principle 139 he writes,

Those words do mean or signify a real thing, which is neither an idea nor like an idea, but that which perceives ideas, and wills, and reasons about them. What I am myself, that which I denote by the term I, is the same with what is meant by *soul* or *spiritual substance*.

And in another place Berkeley is clear that I know what is denoted by the term 'I' through reflection. When I reflect what I find is that

I know what I mean by the terms *I* and *myself*; and I know this immediately, or intuitively, though I do not perceive it as I perceive a triangle, a colour, or a sound.[15]

In order to accommodate the knowledge that we manifestly do have, while at the same time registering the particular nature of spirit, Berkeley introduces the term 'notion'. In Principle 27 he writes,

The words *will*, *soul*, *spirit*, do not stand for different ideas, or in truth, for any idea at all, but for something which is very different from ideas, and which being an agent cannot be like unto, or represented by, any idea whatsoever. Though it must be owned . . ., that we have some notion of soul, spirit, and the operations of the mind, such as willing, loving, hating, inasmuch as we know or understand the meaning of those words.

Berkeley makes it clear that to have a notion of spirit is one and the same with having an idea 'in a large sense indeed'.[16] He thinks it best, however, not to use the term 'idea' in this connection as its use is likely to mislead, and we are liable to forget that the natures of spirit and idea are utterly different. It is clear just what work Berkeley wants from the introduction of this new term, 'notion'. He wants to be able to affirm that when we use terms like 'soul, 'mind or 'spirit' we are not merely raising a dust and speaking sounds that are empty of meaning. Furthermore, he wants to allow that we can have knowledge of mind despite the fact that the nature of mind is not compatible with the having of an idea of mind. Whatever a notion is, it has a clear role to fulfil.

There is evidence from his early Notebooks that Berkeley struggled for some time over the question of our knowledge of mind.[17] In Notebook 490 Berkeley asks, 'whether it were not better not to call the operations of the mind ideas, confining this term to things sensible?' By the end of the Notebook Berkeley arrives at the position he is to adopt throughout his written work: the mind is an immaterial substance that we can know about without the intervention of ideas. It is not, however, until the second edition of the *Principles* that Berkeley first introduces the term 'notion' in connection with our knowledge of spirit. In the first edition he is equally adamant that we can have no idea of mind, but he stops short of offering the alternative of notions.

The introduction of the term 'notion' into Berkeley's work raises several questions. First of all there is the question how we are to think about notions. All Berkeley tells us is that, not being an idea, a notion is not an image or a likeness. Furthermore, he tells us that having a notion goes along with the understanding of words. Harry Bracken suggests that Berkeley's use of the term 'notion' may hark back to the scholastics, and even perhaps the Stoics, who say that having a notion of a thing is to understand it.[18] In that tradition, to have a notion of a thing is distinguished from having an image of it; to have a notion of a thing is to know something of it as a substance or active being. Furthermore, a notion is the bearer of linguistic meaning. Peter Geach speculates whether the origin of Berkeley's 'puzzling talk' about notions and the distinction between notions and ideas might be found in Augustine who distinguishes between *notiones* and *imagines*. *Imagines* are the mental images of something, while *notiones* are the exercise of a concept in judgement. Geach says that Augustine uses the term *notiones* to denote the mental act involved in the understanding of such words as 'fear', 'pain' and 'grief'. According to Augustine, were we to have *imagines* associated with such words – as opposed to *notiones* – they should arouse in us faint reproductions of those experiences.[19]

However we are to understand notions, the introduction of them gives rise to a potentially damaging objection to Berkeley's work. I want to consider this objection in a moment, but first I need to look at something else that Berkeley has to say about ideas and spirits: ideas and spirits are the only two kinds of thing that exist. The former are dependent beings that exist in, or are supported by, minds or spiritual substances. What drops out of the picture that Berkeley sketches is material substance. Ideas are modifications of mind, and they are caused by mind – not by inert matter. This leads to Berkeley's doctrine that *esse ist percipi* (to be is to be perceived).

The important point about material substance, as far as Berkeley is concerned, is that the very notion involves a contradiction. Berkeley's argument against material substance comes at the beginning of the *Principles*, and it is swift. The starting point is to be found in the opening lines: the objects of human knowledge are ideas. Berkeley then points out that ideas cannot exist without the mind; they cannot exist unperceived: 'For as to what is said of the absolute existence of unthinking things without any relation to their being perceived, that seems perfectly unintelligible.'[20] Berkeley is quick to consider the possibility that, while ideas are clearly in the mind, what they are *of* may exist in independence of the mind. Ideas are to be thought of as copies or resemblances of things in the world. To this Berkeley replies that 'an idea can be like nothing but an idea'.[21] In an attempt to get around the point, Berkeley considers introducing a distinction between the primary qualities of a thing (its extension, figure, motion, number and solidity or impenetrability) and its secondary qualities (its colour, sound, taste and the like). Only the primary qualities of things are then said to be *of* something existing without the mind. But Berkeley does not think that the introduction of such a distinction will help the materialist, for the reasons already given: ideas of primary qualities exist only in a mind, and an idea can be like nothing but another idea. He concludes that the very notion of matter or material substance is incoherent. Finally, Berkeley considers that the existence of material being is the best explanation of the ideas in our mind. To this Berkeley responds by pointing out that, even if material being were granted to exist, the materialist cannot explain *how* such bodies produce ideas in our minds. The *Dialogues* add another consideration. It is, says Berkeley, possible to believe in the existence of things that we do not perceive if we have some reason to do so. He then allows that there are two reasons for coming to have such a belief. The first is that we have a direct intuition of the thing, and the second is that we infer it as either a necessary or probable consequence of the idea I have. Berkeley then insists that, as neither reason exists in the case of unthinking matter, we have no reason to believe in the existence of material beings.[22]

With this very sketchy understanding of Berkeley's rejection of material substance, we can now return to consider the objection to his work that the introduction of the term 'notion' suggests. The objection, put bluntly, is this: Berkeley first insists that we have no idea of spirit; he then allows that, while we can have no idea of spirit, we can have some *notion* of spirit. The question then arises, why does Berkeley not allow that we can have some notion of material substance? Berkeley considers the objection in his *Dialogues*. There Hylas puts the objection to Philonous, the exponent of Berkeley's own views: 'To act consistently, you must either admit matter or reject spirit. What say you to this?'[23] What Berkeley, in the voice of Philonous, says in reply to this objection is the following. First of all, he reminds Hylas that he does not reject matter because he has no idea of it but because the idea is 'repugnant' or 'inconsistent'. The notion of spirit, Philonous points out, is neither inconsistent nor repugnant. Furthermore, we not only have no idea of matter, but no reason to believe in it. In the case of spirit or immaterial substance, however, we do have reason to believe in it. Philonous then cites two reasons for this, latter, belief: one reason for the belief in my own mind, and another for the belief in *another* mind. Of the reason for the belief in my own mind Philonous points out: 'Whereas the being of myself, that is, my own soul, mind or thinking principle, I evidently know by reflexion.' Of my reason to believe in the existence of another mind Philonous points out:

> It is granted we have neither an immediate evidence nor a demonstrative knowledge of the existence of other finite spirits; but it will not thence follow that such spirits are on a foot with material substances: . . . if the one can be inferred by no argument, and there is a probability for the other; if we see signs and effects indicating distinct finite agents like ourselves, and see no sign or symptom whatever that leads to a rational belief of matter.[24]

Berkeley's point is that spirit and matter are *not* on a par. I have a reason to believe in the existence of spirit, whereas I have no reason to believe in the existence of material substance. And, interestingly, Berkeley recognizes that the reason I have to believe in the existence of spirit in myself (i.e. reflection) does not give me a reason to believe in the existence of other spirits. Nevertheless, just as matter and my mind are not on a par, matter and other minds are not on a par. In the case of other minds or spirits I do have a reason to believe in their existence: the reason is that I see the effects and signs which indicate to me that there are distinct finite agents like myself. Thus, while I have no reason to believe in the existence of material substance, I do have reason to believe in the existence of both my own and other minds.

Ideas and spirits alone are the objects of human knowledge and the subject of discourse; matter or corporeal substance is a nonsense in which we have no reason to believe.[25] This is the crux of what we need to appreciate in order to avoid scepticism. Berkeley writes,

> Nothing seems of more importance, towards erecting a firm system of sound and real knowledge, which may be proof against

the assaults of *scepticism*, than to lay the beginning in a distinct explication of what is meant by *thing, reality, existence*.[26]

OUR (PROBABLE) KNOWLEDGE OF OTHER FINITE SPIRITS

Berkeley is clear about the difficulties involved in coming to know another mind or spirit. First of all he recognizes that reflection gives me evidence only of my own mind. Thus, I need an additional reason to believe in the existence of another mind. Second, Berkeley recognizes that I cannot have immediate evidence of another mind, and that I cannot demonstrate the existence of another mind from what I do know immediately. Berkeley is careful to explain just why these sorts of reason are not available here. In Principle 148 he writes,

> A human spirit or person is not perceived by sense, as not being an idea; when therefore we see the colour, size, figure, and motions of a man, we perceive only certain sensations or ideas excited in our own minds: and these being exhibited to our view in sundry distinct collections, serve to mark out unto us the existence of finite and created spirits like ourselves. Hence it is plain, we do not see a man – if by *man* is meant that which lives, moves, perceives, and thinks as we do: but only such a certain collection of ideas, as directs us to think there is a distinct principle of thought and motion like unto ourselves, accompanying and represented by it.[27]

Berkeley is making several points in this passage. The first is that all we ever see are the colours, figure and motions of a man; we do not perceive a *man*. And Berkeley is clear about what he means by the word 'man'. A man is 'that which lives, moves, perceives and thinks as we do'. A man is more than a body, more than a human form. We use the term 'man' to refer to an active principle that we take to inform the human forms that we do see. And this touches on the second point that Berkeley is making in this passage: a human spirit, or person, or man is not an idea. Although we may have ideas of a human body, we can have no idea of what makes this body a *man*; we can have no idea of a soul or spirit, as a spirit is an active principle. The final, and main, point that Berkeley is making in this passage is that, as we know other finite spirits, so we know the Infinite Spirit that is God. As with another man, we cannot see God. In all cases of mind distinct from my own, I know them from their effects.

In the case of another finite spirit we have an idea of the body of the other that 'directs us to think' that there is a spirit in the other as there is in ourselves. How we come to be so directed is explained by Berkeley in Principle 145 where he writes:

> From what hath been said, it is plain that we cannot know the existence of other spirits, otherwise than by their operations, or the ideas by them excited in us. I perceive several motions, changes, and combinations of ideas, that inform me there are certain particular agents like myself, which accompany them, and concur in their production. Hence the knowledge I have of other spirits is not immediate, as is the knowledge of my ideas; but depending on the intervention of ideas, by me referred to agents or spirits distinct from myself, as effects or concomitant signs.

In the *Dialogues* Berkeley explains that I reason that there are other minds from the 'signs and effects' that I perceive. In the *Principles* and in the *Dialogues* Berkeley concentrates on the case of other men, but in a later work, the *Alciphron*, Berkeley also mentions non-human animal spirits. In the following exchange between Euphranor and Alciphron, it is clear that he thinks that we come to believe in the existence of non-human animal spirits in the same way as we do any other spirit:

> *Euphranor*: What! Do you believe then that there are such things as animal spirits?
> *Alciphron*: Doubtless.
> *Euphranor*: By what sense do you perceive them?
> *Alciphron*: I do not perceive them immediately by any of my senses. I am nevertheless persuaded of their existence, because I can collect it from their effects and operations.[28]

Non-human animals have what Berkeley calls 'a living soul', while men have 'a thinking and reasonable one'.[29] The effects of the latter can be distinguished from those of the former. The operations and effects of a thinking, reasonable soul are speech. Berkeley writes:

> Upon . . . a minute examination of this point, I have found that nothing so much convinces me of the existence of another person as *his speaking to me*. It is my hearing you talk that, in strict and philosophical truth, is to me the best argument for your being.[30]

Berkeley is clear that the end result of this reasoning in either case is that there is 'a probability for the other'.[31] Berkeley thinks that I have good, but not certain, grounds for taking other minds or spirits to exist.

How are we to understand the argument that Berkeley thinks we use to come to believe in the existence of other finite spirits? Principle 145 has been taken by many commentators as showing that Berkeley here introduces an argument from analogy to the existence of another finite mind.[32] It certainly is the case that Berkeley says that I perceive certain motions and changes in the body of the other, and as a result come to think that there is an agent that accompanies them. And he also says that I think of the accompanying agency as *like myself*. But it is a real question whether the reference to *myself* here should be taken to introduce an analogy between the case of the other and my own case in order to show the existence of another mind. Here is a reason for thinking that it should not: Berkeley does not make any mention of a resemblance between the motions of your body and the motions of mine. Nor does he say that we observe in our own case that our mind is responsible for the movements of our body, and then argue from this to what is responsible for the movements of this other body. Rather, what Berkeley does is note the ideas of the motions of certain bodies and from this infer to the cause of these ideas. But if we are not to read this passage as offering an argument from analogy to the existence of another finite spirit, how are we to read it?

I am inclined to follow those commentators who suggest that what Berkeley is here offering is a causal argument to the conclusion that other finite spirits exist. Jonathan Bennett suggests that we read Principle 145 as proposing a causal argument. Bennett also suggests that this argument fails. According to Bennett, Berkeley's system shows that sensible things exist, that my mind exists and that God exists; but that system gives us no reason to suppose that other finite minds or spirits exist. According to Bennett, 'Berkeley is in fact deeply committed to saying: "I am alone in the universe with God".'[33] Lorne Falkenstein follows Bennett's interpretation of Principle 145, but thinks that Berkeley can avoid the criticism that Bennett levels against him.[34] I shall present Bennett's criticism of Berkeley's argument, understood as a causal argument to the existence of other finite spirits, and then I shall explain Falkenstein's defence of that argument. If Falkenstein's defence of Berkeley succeeds then, within Berkeley's system, there can be shown to be a reason to believe in the existence of other finite spirits.

According to Falkenstein, Berkeley's argument for the existence of other finite spirits is merely the last in a series of causal arguments used by him to establish increasingly specific claims about the metaphysical principles and agencies that produce our ideas. Other finite spirits are the cause of certain ideas I have of motion and change. Although this interpretation has a certain plausibility, it requires much work before we can rest content with it. Let us look at how Berkeley comes to suggest that it is other finite spirits who are the cause of certain of my ideas. Very early on in the *Principles* Berkeley takes it that he has established that all we perceive are ideas. He notes that the ideas that we perceive are continuously changing, appearing and disappearing, and he asks what may be thought to be the cause of these ideas. He considers several possibilities. First, there is the possibility that the cause of our ideas is an idea or combination of ideas. But Berkeley points out that this cannot be as it is manifest that ideas are entirely passive. Second, there is the possibility that the cause of these ideas is some substance. And here there are two possibilities: the cause is either corporeal substance or spirit. Berkeley takes it that he has just finished showing that there is no corporeal substance, so he concludes that the cause of ideas is spirit or incorporeal substance. Having established that the cause of our ideas is spirit, Berkeley notes that the cause cannot always be our own spirit, since so many of our ideas are manifestly not dependent on our will. He therefore concludes that 'There is therefore some other will or spirit that produces them.'[35] Berkeley strengthens his argument by pointing out in Principle 30 that ideas of sense are 'more strong, lively and distinct' than those of the imagination, and that the former are not excited at random but have a 'steadiness, order and coherence' that the latter often lack. Our ideas of sense are the product of some other will or spirit. Berkeley then suggests that our ideas of sense have an 'admirable connexion whereof sufficiently testifies the wisdom and benevolence of [their] Author'.[36] In other words, Berkeley takes it that the cause of our ideas is God. The ideas that we perceive bear testimony to His existence. The cause we postulate should be equal to effects that we observe; the characteristics of our ideas should lead us to believe that God is their cause.

Berkeley admits that most people have less trouble believing in the existence of their fellow beings than they do believing in God.[37] But he points out that, just as we observe the 'effects and concomitant signs' of our fellow beings, so we observe the effects and signs of God's existence. In the case of our fellow beings what we observe are the movements of their bodies, what we hear are their words; in the case of God the signs exist all around us: 'everything we see, hear, feel, or any wise perceive by sense, being a sign or effect of the Power of God; as is our perception of those very motions which are produced by men'.[38] Our reasons for believing in God's existence are, therefore, greater than those we have for believing in our fellow men.

It is at this point that Bennett thinks that Berkeley overplays his hand. Whereas Berkeley begins by trying to show that we know God as well as we know another mind or spirit, he ends by saying that we know God better than other finite spirits because the effects of nature are more numerous than the acts of man. And Berkeley continues,

> There is not any one mark that denotes a man, or effect produced by him, which doth not more strongly evince the being of that spirit who is the *Author of Nature*. For it is evident that in affecting other persons, the will of man hath no other object, than barely the motion of the limbs of his body; but that such a motion should be attended by, or excite any idea in the mind of another, depends wholly on the will of the Creator. He alone it is who *upholding all things by the Word of his Power*, maintains that intercourse between spirits, whereby they are able to perceive the existence of each other.[39]

If this is true, then, says Bennett, there is no room in Berkeley's system for other finite spirits after all. Berkeley uses our belief in our fellow beings to show us that we have the same reason to believe in God, but God then usurps the place of our fellow beings.

Falkenstein suggests that Berkeley does have a way of showing that, for all that God may be the cause of all of my ideas, we still have reason to believe in the existence of other finite spirits. Falkenstein goes back to Principle 145 and notes that Berkeley is careful there not to suggest that finite spirits are the sole cause of our ideas of animated bodies. What Berkeley in fact writes is that I perceive certain combinations of ideas that 'inform me there are certain particular agents like myself, which accompany them, *and concur in their production*' (my emphasis). Falkenstein understands Berkeley to be saying that, while God is the only true cause of motion, there is a secondary sense in which finite agents may act as the cause of the motions of their bodies. But now Berkeley runs up against another problem: if finite spirits are the secondary cause of our ideas of animated bodies, must we not conclude that God is determined by our wills to cause certain ideas in others? Falkenstein suggests that the postulation of secondary causes need not be taken to lead to this conclusion. Rather, we could say that

God is kindly disposed towards us, and as a result, when we will the motions of our bodies, He causes the appropriate ideas in our minds and the minds of other finite spirits. It is in this way that Berkeley can say that God 'maintains that intercourse between spirits'. Falkenstein's defence of Berkeley, then, relies on a distinction between the immediate cause of our ideas (God) and the concurring – or secondary – cause of the idea (another finite spirit).

Although Falkenstein's work goes some way towards allowing Berkeley to assert the existence of both God and other finite spirits, a problem still remains. Berkeley claims that we have *good reason* to take it that some of our ideas indicate the existence of other finite spirits, but it is not at all clear that we do have a good reason for this belief. If Falkenstein is right, there may be room in Berkeley's system for other finite spirits; but do we have a good reason to believe that other finite spirits exist? After all, if all that we see is the result of God's activity, then why do we think that there are other finite spirits who concur in causing some of my ideas? Another way of making the point is to ask, if God could make us think that other finite minds exist when in fact they do not, why do we take it that there really are other finite minds? It would appear that the postulation of other finite spirits is an extravagant proposal – all we need to explain our ideas is God.

In order to help us to see that we may indeed have reason to believe in the existence of *both* God *and* other finite spirits, Falkenstein refers us to something that Berkeley writes in the *Third Dialogue*. At one point Hylas accuses Philonous of making God the author of all sin – 'the author of murder, sacrilege, adultery, and the like heinous sins'.[40] In response, Philonous says:

> I have nowhere said that God is the only agent who produces all the motions in bodies. It is true, I have denied there are any other agents beside spirits: but this is very consistent with allowing to thinking rational beings, in the production of motions, the use of limited powers, ultimately indeed derived from God, but immediately under the direction of their own wills, which is sufficient to entitle them to all the guilt of their actions.[41]

Falkenstein concludes that Berkeley gets around the problem of God's responsibility for evil in the world by postulating the existence of other finite spirits. By indulging the wills of these finite spirits God can be the cause of all our ideas while avoiding being held responsible for the evil in some of those actions. And Falkenstein points out that it is not just evil that God is able to duck in this fashion. As Falkenstein reminds us, Hylas could just have easily have charged Philonous with making God the immediate cause of indecision, inconstancy of purpose and sheer stupidity. As it is, Falkenstein believes Berkeley has a way around all these objections.

There is one further objection that Falkenstein must defend against if his defence of Berkeley is to survive immediate criticism. On Falkenstein's reading of Berkeley it looks as if we have to say that we will our actions and God indulges us by causing ideas in our minds and the minds of others. But if this is so, then it looks like Berkeley has resurrected a form of occasionalism – the doctrine that reserves causal efficacy to God's acts, with spirits providing the occasion for those acts. The problem is that occasionalism is a doctrine that Berkeley himself firmly rejects. Falkenstein plausibly argues, however, that while Berkeley rejects occasionalism with regard to matter, his reason for rejecting it does not extend to the case of spirit. Falkenstein takes it that one of Berkeley's reasons for rejecting matter as the occasion of God causing ideas in us is that it is absurd to think that God requires reminding by matter to cause an idea in our mind. But if spirits are the occasion for God's actions, it is not that spirits *remind* God when to act. Rather, freely acting agents request that God produce ideas and God indulges these requests – not because agents remind Him to act but because they bring Him to behave differently from how He would if He were simply motivated by considerations of wisdom and benevolence.

Falkenstein could equally have pointed to another of Berkeley's reasons for rejecting matter as the occasion of God's actions: unperceived matter is senseless, and so cannot be the occasion of anything. This reason for rejecting matter-occasionalism also does not carry over to spirit-occasionalism, for spirit is not senseless. We understand what spirit is, at least in one case, because we are one. Thus, just as Berkeley argues that we are in a position to have a notion of mind, but not of matter, he could equally have held that matter is not the occasion of God causing ideas in my mind but another finite spirit's will may indeed be the occasion of God's causing an idea of change in me. And, as we have just seen, there is good reason – from the existence of sin and other imperfect acts – to think that other finite minds *are* the occasion of God's action.

If Falkenstein's defence of Berkeley is along the right lines, it may then be possible to defend Berkeley's causal argument to the existence of other finite spirits. Finite spirits, *along with God*, are the cause of certain of my ideas: my ideas of motion and change in human bodies other than my own. God is the sole cause of all the rest of my ideas. If, however, Falkenstein's argument can be shown to fail, we have to conclude along with Bennett that Berkeley's philosophy leaves me alone in the universe with God. Even if Falkenstein's argument succeeds, however, it should be noted that we can do no better in Berkeley's philosophy than to conclude that the existence of another finite mind is probable. Certain knowledge of another mind is not within our grasp.

I have been defending a causal interpretation of Berkeley's argument to the existence of another mind. This causal interpretation is intended to usurp the analogical interpretation of that argument. Although Berkeley's argument for the existence of another mind or spirit is not by analogy, it may be possible to find *an* argument from analogy in Berkeley's work. That argument comes in Principle 140 where Berkeley writes,

> Moreover, as we conceive the ideas that are in the minds of other spirits by means of our own, which we suppose to be resemblances of them: so we know other spirits by means of our own soul, which in that sense is the image or idea of them, it having a like respect to other spirits, that blueness or heat by me perceived has to those ideas perceived by another.[42]

Berkeley is not here considering the existence of another mind but its content. His point is that, by reflection, we come to have a notion (or idea 'in a large sense indeed') of our own mind, and we use this to conceive the ideas that are in the minds of other spirits. Just as I have an idea or notion of heat or blue, so, by analogy, we can think of another mind having similar ideas or notions.

Now this comment of Berkeley's may be thought to raise the following question: we may use our own mind as the model for thinking about other minds (for, after all, this is all we have to go on), but why do we think it is *correct* to do this? All reflection can do is give us a way of thinking and talking about another's mind as though it were like our own. But what reason can we have to think that the other's mind *is* like my own? Whether or not things actually are the way we think they are is very much an open question.

Berkeley touches on this problem in another context, in a discussion over the existence of material substance. Let me explain how the problem arises in that connection. In the *Three Dialogues*, Hylas is discussing with Philonous the existence of material substance. Philonous has been trying to persuade Hylas that material substance is a nonsense. Hylas cannot accept this conclusion, and he points out that, unless material substance can be said to exist, we will have to say that no two persons see the *same* object. To this objection Philonous replies that different persons may be allowed to see the same object, if we use the word 'same' in its 'vulgar acceptation'; that is, where the word 'same' is a synonym for 'similar'. If, however, we insist on using the word 'same' to denote what philosophers call identity, then Philonous admits that it may not be possible for different persons to perceive the *same* object. In short, Philonous sees the objection as turning on the meaning of a word. Philonous concludes his defence of his position by saying:

> But whether philosophers shall think fit to call a thing the *same* or no, is, I conceive, of small importance. Let us suppose several men together, all endued with the same faculties, and conse-quently affected in like sort by their senses, and who had yet never known the use of language; they would without question agree in their perception. Though perhaps, when they came to the use of speech, some regarding the uniformness of what was perceived, might call it the *same* thing: others especially regard-ing the diversity of persons who perceived, might choose the denomination of different things. But who sees not that all the dispute is about a word?[43]

Philonous' argument appears to be this: men who have the same fac-ulties and are stimulated in a like manner, have the same ideas. Whether we choose to call their ideas 'the same' is neither here nor there.

As I said, the dispute between Hylas and Philonous here is about whether we can all be said to perceive the same objects. But if we look at the issue closely, we can see that the dispute here has a further dimension – one not remarked upon by Berkeley. What Hylas cor-rectly observes is that according to Philonous we perceive only ideas in our own minds – that is, we cannot actually perceive the ideas that are in another's mind. It is because of this limitation that we must con-ceive of the ideas in another's mind by means of our own (cf. Principle 140). However, once we see that another *may* have ideas very differ-ent from those that we have, it becomes a very real question just what it is that reflection on our own mind helps us with. All reflection can do is give us a way of thinking and talking about another's mind as though it were like my own. But why should I think this?

As we saw in Chapter III, Malebranche considers the possibility that different men have different sensations. Unlike Berkeley, how-ever, Malebranche recognizes that God could have made it the case that similar causes do *not* have similar effects. And even if we believe that God did not set things up in this way (as Malebranche does), Malebranche points out that it is not at all clear that there is a perfect resemblance in the sense organs of all men. Malebranche concludes that it is most unlikely that different men have the same sensations. Malebranche's considerations help us to see that there is a real question whether we *can* conceive of the minds of others on the model of our own. At the end of the day, any analogy that Berkeley may be proposing between ourselves and others, must be backed up by an empirical claim about the way we are similarly constructed, along with some principle to the effect that the same causes produce the same effects. Only then can we rely on our own mind to serve as the model for what is going on in another's mind. And, of course, we might ask whether the same-causes-same-effects principle can be thought to hold in the case of minds. I may observe the principle to hold in the case of the world of bodies, and I may observe it to hold in the case of *my* mind, but it is a real question why we take it to hold across minds.

CONCLUSION

Berkeley's work is a rich source of discussion of other minds or other finite spirits. Although his work leaves many questions unanswered, it does raise and address two important issues relating to the mind of another: why do I think that another mind exists?; and, how are we to think of the content of another mind? Concerning the first issue, Berkeley points out that I do not have either direct or demonstrative knowledge of another mind. That another mind or spirit exists is the conclusion of reasoning on my part. Concerning the second issue, Berkeley suggests that we know the content of another mind by the resemblance we take it to bear to our own mind.

Berkeley – like Locke, Malebranche and Arnaud – takes it that another's mind is invisible to us. My belief in the existence of another mind – and my belief about what the content of another mind is like – goes beyond what I can experience. As far as experience is concerned, I can only have experience of my own mind. Nevertheless, all these philosophers hold that I have reason to go beyond my experience and conclude that other finite spirits also exist. In Chapter IV, I explained how Locke draws a distinction between our sensitive knowledge of material objects and our opinion that other spirits exist. Sensitive knowledge rises above mere probabilities, while opinion is founded on probabilities. Berkeley firmly rejects Lockean materialism and the scepticism to which he thinks it leads. Nevertheless, Berkeley's conclusion concerning the existence of other finite spirits is not dissimilar to Locke's. Berkeley concludes that we can have only probable knowledge of the existence of another finite mind. In saying this he would appear to accept the possibility of a sceptical doubt about the mind of another: things might be exactly as I perceive them to be and yet no other finite mind exist. Thus, Berkeley is content to accept the possibility of a scepticism about other finite minds that he finds so profoundly unacceptable about the world of bodies.

There are philosophers who find the possibility of both forms of scepticism unacceptable. Thomas Reid, for one, writing soon after Berkeley, considers Berkeley's conclusion that I can have probable knowledge of the existence of another finite mind and he writes:

> This seems to promise some comfort in my forlorn solitude. But do I see those minds? No. Do I see their ideas? No. Nor do they see me or my ideas. They are then no more to me than the inhabitants of Solomon's Isles, or of the moon; and my melancholy returns. Every social tie is broken, and every social affection stifled.[44]

Reid cannot accept the conclusion of Berkeley's philosophy, which he – like Bennett – takes to be solipsism. Even if Berkeley could show that we have reason to believe in the existence of another mind, that reason would, on Berkeley's own admission, afford only *probable* evidence that other minds exist, and Reid cannot accept that my relations to my children, my lover, my sister and the like are founded on probabilities. In the next chapter I shall examine just how Reid thinks it is that I come by my knowledge of other intelligent beings. But first I want to raise a final difficulty for Berkeley's account of our (probable) knowledge of other minds.

Although Berkeley's work clearly raises, and addresses, two issues relating to our knowledge of another mind, it fails to address another, arguably more important, issue. The issue that is neglected in Berkeley's work is that raised by Augustine's question, the question of how to account for the very belief that another finite being has a mind. Berkeley's question concerning the existence and content of another's mind presupposes a capacity to think of another mind, but it is a question how this is possible. This is the problem I referred to in earlier chapters as the conceptual problem of other minds. There is a passage in the *Third Dialogue* that may be thought to touch on this issue. In this passage Berkeley writes,

My own mind and my own ideas I have an immediate knowledge of; and by the help of these, do mediately apprehend the possibility of the existence of other spirits and ideas.[45]

If Berkeley is meaning to address the conceptual question here, then it would appear that his reply is that we get our conception of another mind with the help of what I know from my own case. I understand the meaning of 'mind' or 'spirit' from my own case, and understand the possibility of another mind on this basis. But how, exactly, am I to have the conception of another mind from the starting point of my own mind? How does the understanding I get when I contemplate my own mind generalize to include others as well as myself?

In order to see what response Berkeley might give to this question, we should look to his work on generality. Berkeley devotes the entire introduction of his *Principles* to an attack on Locke's doctrine of abstraction. Berkeley can make no sense of Locke's doctrine, nor can he see the need for it. Where Locke suggests that the mind abstracts from particular ideas to form general ones, Berkeley insists that all ideas are particular and that generality is introduced through the use of words. Where Locke holds that words become general by being made the signs of general ideas, Berkeley holds that a word becomes general by being made the sign 'of several particular ideas, any one of which it indifferently suggests to the mind'.[46] Concerning the generality of ideas Berkeley writes:

> *Universality*, so far as I can comprehend, not consisting in the absolute, positive nature or conception of anything, but in the relation it bears to the particulars signified or represented by it: by virtue whereof it is that things, names, or notions, being in their own nature *particular*, are rendered *universal*.[47]

When we attempt to apply what Berkeley writes about generality to our conception of mind, we immediately encounter difficulties. First of all, as Berkeley insists that we can have no idea of mind, it is not clear how generality is here to be achieved. Perhaps Berkeley thinks that we have a notion of mind and that this notion just *is* completely general. This, however, would go against Berkeley's insistence that all ideas (and notions?) are particular. Furthermore, given that Berkeley says that I know the meaning of the terms 'mind' and 'spirit' immediately or intuitively – that is, not by reference to anyone other than myself – it is hard to see how the notion we have of mind *can* be completely general. It may be, however, that Berkeley intends notions to operate precisely in the same way as ideas, and that generality is here achieved in the same way that it is in the case of any other idea. That is, generality is achieved by the use we make of the term 'mind'. But now we run into another difficulty: How, we may ask, *do* we use words in connection with mind? Well, I use the word 'mind' in connection with my own mind; I understand the word immediately. I do not have the same immediate understanding of another mind. But if this is so, I do not have a range of uses to lend generality to my use of the word 'mind'. It may, however, be said that I do use the word in connection with others. But notice that Berkeley holds that my use of the term in connection with others is based on what I observe about the behaviour of the other's body. But this means that my two uses of the word 'mind' are different – sufficiently different to prompt the question, Is the word being used with the same meaning in each case? Unless we can explain why we take it that the word *is* being used with the same meaning in both cases, we are not entitled to say that our word has the requisite generality. I shall not pursue this question now, but will return to it in Part Three.

This brings to a close the first part of the history of the problem of other minds. In Part One, I have looked at the work of some philosophers from the ancient Greek sceptics to Descartes, and from Descartes to Berkeley. I have argued that it is characteristic of philosophers of these periods not to find other minds particularly problematic. If we look at the work of the ancient Greek sceptics, there is little interest in the question of whether or not others have minds. I have suggested that this is due, in part, to the fact that the sceptic of ancient times assumed the existence of other minds in formulating his scepticism about the external world. It is Descartes who put in place the metaphysical framework that made it possible to question the very existence of the world. Scepticism concerning the existence of another mind is a consequence of this kind of radical scepticism. Despite operating within a Cartesian framework, none of the philosophers whose work I considered in Chapters II–V find our knowledge of the mind of another particularly problematic. Descartes does not acknowledge any issue here at all. Malebranche and Arnaud recognize that our knowledge of the mind of another needs to be given special consideration; but neither of these philosophers thinks there is any difficulty whatever in giving an account of our knowledge here. As they see it, we come to have knowledge of another mind by conjecture (Arnaud being clearer than Malebranche about the exact nature of that conjecture). While Descartes confines minds to men, Locke allows that there are minds in other creatures as well as men. He considers the possibility that there are minds in creatures smaller than ourselves, in creatures who may inhabit remote regions of the universe, and in incorporeal beings. Wherever minds may exist, however, I cannot know them to exist. I can only form the opinion that minds exist beyond my own. Berkeley follows Locke in this: of the existence of another finite mind I can have only probable knowledge.

In Part Two, I shall turn to the work of two philosophers, Thomas Reid and Ludwig Wittgenstein, who claim to find a problem about our knowledge of other minds in the work of philosophers from Descartes onwards. Reid and Wittgenstein emphasize what they see as our unselfconscious acknowledgement of others in our everyday lives, and both claim that a Cartesian philosophy makes that acknowledgement problematic. (According to Wittgenstein, the problem may be thought to go even deeper than this.) Unlike philosophers before them, Reid and Wittgenstein detect a deep and difficult problem about other minds that they think can be avoided only if we move away from a certain way of doing philosophy. Their work, then, marks a turning point: from now on philosophers, if they are not careful, must see themselves as faced with a serious problem about the mind of another.

Part Two

The problem of other minds

CHAPTER VI

Thomas Reid and knowledge of other intelligent beings

INTRODUCTION

Thomas Reid is the first major figure in the history of philosophy to notice a profound difficulty with respect to our knowledge of others. Philosophers from Descartes to Berkeley may have recognized that our knowledge of the mind of another is distinctly different from our knowledge of bodies and our knowledge of our own mind, but they did not think it too difficult to give an account of this knowledge. Malebranche, Arnaud, Locke and Berkeley each recognize that, in Locke's words, the mind of another is 'invisible'. In the light of this, Malebranche and Arnaud claim that our knowledge of another mind is by conjecture, Locke holds that we can only be of the opinion that there are other minds, and Berkeley says that we can have probable knowledge of another mind. Once we recognize the Cartesian framework which operates at the heart of the work of each of these philosophers, we see that it is possible to raise a certain scepticism about the mind of another. However we come to know about the external world, our knowledge of another's mind is not as secure as this.

Thomas Reid is impatient with *all* forms of scepticism. Indeed, it is arguable that he is *more* bothered by scepticism with respect to other intelligent beings than he is by scepticism about the world of bodies.[1] In any case, he rejects both forms of scepticism. According to Reid, it is deeply problematic that a philosophical system should come to the conclusion that our relations with others are founded on mere conjecture or grounded only on probability. We need to be able to say how a more secure knowledge of other intelligent beings is possible. The problem, as Reid sees it, is that philosophers will be unable to say how such knowledge is possible so long as they insist on starting where Descartes starts, with the theory of ideas. It is only if we reject this starting point that we can re-establish our relations with

139

others on a firm foundation. Reid looks back over an entire tradition in philosophy and notices that that tradition leads to profoundly unacceptable conclusions concerning our relationship to others. Reid's response is not to tinker at the margins of this system in the hope of avoiding these conclusions, but to suggest that we reject the root assumption of this system.

Thomas Reid (1710–1796) set up his philosophy in opposition to what he saw as the philosophy of scepticism.[2] It was not long, however, before Reid's insights were lost to philosophy. From the time of their eighteenth century editions, Reid's collected works remained out of print until 1967. Keith Lehrer has suggested several reasons for the decline of Reid's influence in philosophy.[3] One reason that Lehrer offers is that Reid's work to combat scepticism was overshadowed by the work of Immanuel Kant. Furthermore, Kant himself rejected Reid's common sense approach to philosophy as an uncritical acceptance of the views of the vulgar and a betrayal of the critical function of philosophy.[4] Another reason that Lehrer suggests for the decline of Reid's influence in philosophy is the fact that for a long time philosophers tended to make their acquaintance with Reid's work through the writing of Sir William Hamilton. Hamilton was a Reid scholar, but his characterization of Reid's work had a tendency to distort rather than elucidate. It is arguable that this impure Reid proved to be an all too easy target for criticism. One critic of Reid's work was John Stuart Mill. Mill's *An Examination of Sir William Hamilton's Philosophy* is, in effect, a critique of Reid's work. In this work Mill exposes what he takes to be the errors of Reid's thinking on the issue of other minds. According to Mill it is possible to prove the existence of other minds. Mill is clearly unimpressed by the profound difficulties that Reid sees for our relation to others in the philosophical system of earlier philosophers. One could see Mill's critique of Reid's work as contributing to the loss to philosophy of Reid's insights here.[5]

Reid's works include *An Inquiry into the Mind on the Principles of Common Sense*, *Essays on the Intellectual Powers of Man* and *Essays on the Active Powers of Man*. As is evident from the titles of these works, Reid's central concern is with the operations of the human mind. He is interested in these operations both from their active side, as they involve the exercise of will and action, and from their passive side, as the mind is engaged in knowledge and understanding. As well as these two, Reid recognizes yet another operation of the mind which he labels the 'social' operation, and which he separates from what he calls the 'solitary' operations of understanding and willing. By social operations Reid means 'such operations as necessarily suppose an intercourse with some other intelligent being'.[6] While the operations of willing and understanding may occur 'though [a man] should know of no intelligent beings in the universe besides himself', the social operations are 'acts of social intercourse between intelligent beings [which] can have no place in solitude'.[7] The social acts include the asking for or receiving of information, the bearing or receiving of testimony, the asking for or receiving of a favour, the giving or receiving of a command, and the making of a promise. These acts require will and understanding, but they require something more; they require the society of other intelligent beings. According to Reid, the social operations of our mind are on a par with the solitary operations, and the attempt to reduce the former to the latter will lead only to contradictions and difficulties. The important thing to notice about these social operations, says Reid, is that they 'suppose a conviction of the existence of other intelligent beings'.[8] These operations and their attendant convictions appear very early in life. Reid writes,

> When a child asks a question of his nurse, this act of his mind supposes, not only a desire to know what he asks; it supposes likewise a conviction that the nurse is an intelligent being, to whom he can communicate his thoughts, and who can communicate her thoughts to him.[9]

Reid sets out in his *Essays* to provide what other philosophies have failed to provide: an understanding of how it is that such conviction, at such a young age, is possible.

The philosophical figure against whom the greatest part of Reid's intellectual energies is directed is the sceptic. Reid finds the figure of the sceptic in the work of philosophers from Descartes to Hume. He holds that, if one starts where these philosophers all start – with the theory of ideas – one will inevitably be led into scepticism. The theory of ideas is, according to Reid, most pernicious because it can be shown to lead to conclusions that are not just false, but 'absurd'.[10] One of the absurd conclusions to which this theory leads can be found in the work of Berkeley. According to Reid it is a consequence of Berkeley's philosophy that 'what I call a father, a brother, or a friend, is only a parcel of ideas in my own mind'.[11] Reid explains how, by careful attention to first principles, philosophers can avoid the absurd conclusion to which Berkeley was led. The philosophy that Reid presents is both anti-sceptical and profoundly wedded to common sense.[12]

Reid, like Locke, is what I called in Chapter IV a robust or 'hard' realist with respect to other minds. That is, Reid holds that there exists what he calls a 'whole system of bodies in the universe' as well as a 'whole system of minds'.[13] And, again like Locke, Reid holds that we are capable of knowing only a small part of these systems. Concerning minds Reid writes,

> What variety there may be of minds or thinking beings through-out this vast universe, we cannot pretend to say. We dwell in a little corner of God's dominion, disjoined from the rest of it. The globe which we inhabit is but one of seven planets that encircle our sun. What various orders of beings may inhabit the other six, their secondaries, and the comets belonging to our system; and how many other suns may be encircled with like systems, are things altogether hid from us.[14]

Although we may be limited in what knowledge we may have of intelligent beings in the far flung reaches of the universe, Reid – unlike Malebranche, Arnaud, Locke and Berkeley – has no hesitation in affirming our knowledge of those individuals with whom we inter-act and converse. In this chapter I want to give a brief introduction to Reid's anti-sceptical philosophy, paying special attention to the ques-tion of our knowledge of other intelligent beings.

FIRST PRINCIPLES OF COMMON SENSE

Reid begins his *Essays* by asserting that all reasoning must be grounded on first principles. That this must be so, he takes to be the lesson of Newton and the scientists. Reid holds that, as definitions and axioms are the foundation of all science, so must philosophy build on a similar foundation if it wishes to enjoy the success of the sciences.[15] Philosophers must be careful to define their words, but they must also recognize that definitions come to an end; we must not attempt to define that which cannot be defined. Furthermore, philosophers must take care either to use words as they are commonly used, or to make it clear that they are introducing a term of art and explain these terms so as to avoid misunderstanding. Just as there are words common to men that admit of no definition, so, according to Reid, there are principles common to men that admit of no – and need no – proof. These principles, says Reid, are the foundation of all reasoning. Such are these principles that Reid takes it that, if someone were to deny them, we would consider him a lunatic, or at the very least hold him to be lacking in common sense. Reid asks,

Thus, if a man were found of so strange a turn as not to believe his own eyes; to put no trust in his senses, nor have the least regard to their testimony; would any man think it worth while to reason gravely with such a person, and, by argument, to convince him of his error?[16]

Reid acknowledges that it is possible to be mistaken about first principles or to doubt them, but he insists that when first principles are brought into dispute 'they require to be handled in a way peculiar to themselves'.[17] As Reid points out: 'Their evidence is not demonstrative, but intuitive. They require not proof, but to be placed in a proper point of view.'[18] He observes that

Very ingenious men, such as Des Cartes, Malebranche, Arnaud, Locke, and many others, have lost much labour, by not distinguishing things which require proof, from things which, though they admit of illustration, yet being self evident, do not admit of proof.[19]

According to Reid first principles must take the place of hypothesis and analogy; these methods of reasoning yield unstable and insecure foundations for knowledge. Reid once again shows his admiration for the science of Newton and his associates when he writes: 'Indeed, whatever is built upon conjecture, is improperly called science; for conjecture may beget opinion, but cannot produce knowledge.'[20] And the same can be said for reasoning by analogy; this, too, can lead only to probabilities. Reid admits that there is some place for reasoning by analogy in medicine, politics and in the study of the planets, but he holds that we will be led into error if we employ such reasoning in connection with the mind. Analogy is a weak form of reasoning and we use it to effect only where we can find no other evidence. Reid notes that men are particularly prone to use analogies when thinking about the mind. Because of the difficulty that attends reflection on the mind's operations, there is a tendency to think that the required evidence is lacking and that we must think about the mind on analogy with body. About this tendency Reid writes:

We form an early acquaintance with material things by means of our senses, and are bred up in a constant familiarity with them. Hence we are apt to measure all things by them; and to ascribe to things most remote from matter, the qualities that belong to material things.[21]

One of the errors that we make when we think of mind on analogy with body is this: we take it that, just as a body is affected by the contact and pressure of another body, so the mind is similarly affected by its object in thought. Reid acknowledges that, when we perceive something, an impression is made upon the organs, nerves and brain of the perceiver (the human mind would be unable to perceive objects unless this were so). Nevertheless, it would be a mistake to say that the eye sees. Where we go wrong, says Reid, is when we think that, as the object makes an impression on the organs of perception, so it also makes an impression on the mind. He writes: 'A telescope is an artificial organ of sight. The eye is a natural organ of sight, but it sees as little as the telescope.'[22] Just as it is a mistake to say that the eye sees, so it is a mistake to say that the object makes an impression on the mind. The object makes an impression on the eye, and the mind perceives the object. In perception the mind is aware of the object and is unaware of the impressions made by the object on the organ of sensation. We must jettison analogy and hypothesis, and in their place we must make careful observations. When we do this, what we will observe is that in the act of perception an object produces an impression only on the organ of perception – say, the eye. This impression is followed, in accordance with the 'laws of our nature', by certain operations in our mind.[23] And while we know this to be the case, we are unable to comprehend this act of perception. Reid writes:

> The perception of external objects is one main link of that mysterious chain, which connects the material world with the intellectual. We shall find many things in this operation unaccountable; sufficient to convince us, that we know but little of our own frame; and that a perfect comprehension of our mental powers, and of the manner of their operation, is beyond the reach of our understanding.[24]

While we may be unable entirely to comprehend how it is that mind connects with body, yet there is much that we can comprehend. We will only understand aright, however, if we jettison analogy and hypothesis in favour of careful observation.

Observation or reflection on the operations of mind is, Reid admits, difficult. First, there are many such operations, and they pass very quickly. Second, from our earliest infancy we are accustomed to attend to the objects of sense; it is less common for the understanding to take notice of itself. Connected with this is the fact that it is the nature of mind that it should cease when attention is drawn to it. For these reasons it is not surprising that we turn to analogy and hypothesis. But, although observation of the mind's operations is difficult, it is not impossible. Careful attention will reveal, says Reid, that we have indeed been led into error by analogies and hypotheses.

As perception is properly an act of mind, in order to gain knowledge of it we must appeal, not to the testimony of the senses (as we might if it were the sense organs that perceived), but to consciousness. Reid writes:

> In speaking of the impressions made on our organs in perception, we build upon facts borrowed from anatomy and physiology, for which we have the testimony of our senses. But being now to speak of perception itself, which is solely an act of mind, we must appeal to another authority. The operations of our minds are known not by sense, but by consciousness, the authority of which is as certain and as irresistible as that of sense.[25]

Reid is careful to explain what he means by 'consciousness'. This term does not admit of definition, but we can be clear about our use of it. According to Reid, we apply the term 'consciousness' to things that are present, and not to things that are past. To do otherwise would be to confuse consciousness and memory. Furthermore, we use the term to speak of things in the mind and not of things external to the mind. Thus, it would be improper to say, 'I am conscious of the table before me'; rather we say, 'I see the table; I perceive it'. In sum, we know external objects through perception and we know the operations of the mind through consciousness.

If we are clear about the meaning of our words, language can lead us to those first principles upon which the science of philosophy can be built. If, however, we are not clear about the meaning of our words, there is a danger that we will be led to mistaken principles. Reid takes the word 'idea' to be a case in point. This word, according to Reid, has a clear usage in our common language, it is also a word that has been appropriated by philosophers. The philosopher's use of the word, however, is unclear and often ambiguous. Insofar as Reid is able to understand the philosopher's use of the term, he takes it to be at odds with common usage. According to Reid, 'in popular language, *idea* signifies the same thing as conception, apprehension, notion'.[26] To have an idea is the same as to conceive or to apprehend; a man who thinks is having ideas. These are acts of mind that are expressed in language by the employment of an active verb. When we turn from common to philosophical usage, however, we notice an alteration in the way this word is used. According to philosophical usage, 'idea' does not signify an act of mind but an object of thought. Where the common man would say that he is thinking or having an idea, the philosopher says that ideas are the immediate objects of thought. Reid concludes that the philosopher's use of the word 'idea' is a 'fiction' – a fiction that confounds an operation of the mind with the object upon which that operation is directed. Reid then notes an important consequence of the philosopher's use of the word 'idea': as an idea is taken to be the internal and immediate object of our thought, so the object in the world is taken to be the remote or mediate object. But if the only thing that the mind is in contact with is an idea, the existence of the material world remains to be proved. It is precisely such a proof that philosophers have tried, and failed, to find. Reid writes: 'Des Cartes, Malebranche, and Locke, have all employed their genius and skill to prove the existence of a material world; and with very bad success.'[27] Berkeley may have been impatient with the scepticism of his predecessors, but his attempt to banish scepticism led him to reject the existence of a material world. This scepticism and this idealism are both, as Reid sees it, absurd consequences of the philosophical theory of ideas. To avoid these absurdities, we must take care how we use our words and discover the true first principles upon which all human knowledge depends.

SCEPTICISM AND THE EVIDENCE OF THE SENSES

Reid traces the origins of what he calls the 'ideal system' back to Descartes and beyond that to Aristotle. About Descartes he writes,

> The arguments of the ancient skeptics here occurred to [Descartes]; that our senses often deceive us, and therefore ought never to be trusted on their own authority: that, in sleep, we often seem to see and hear things which we are convinced to have had no existence. But that which chiefly led Des Cartes to think that he ought not to trust to his senses without proof of their veracity, was, that he took it for granted, as all philosophers had done before him, that he did not perceive external objects themselves, but certain images of them in his mind, called *ideas*. He was certain, by consciousness, that he had the ideas of sun and moon, earth and sea; but how could he be assured that there really existed external objects like to these ideas?[28]

Descartes is certain, through consciousness, of his own existence. From this slender foundation, he attempts to re-build the whole of human knowledge. Reid attributes Descartes' failure in this enterprise to the fact that the foundation he uses is altogether too slender. According to Reid, we must look to build our knowledge upon a broader foundation. Where Descartes admits only the evidence of consciousness, Reid holds that we must admit as well the evidence of sense. Reid writes: 'A man cannot be conscious of his own thoughts, without believing that he thinks. He cannot perceive an object of sense, without believing that it exists.'[29] Where philosophers from Descartes onwards assume without question the existence of the mind and its operations and proceed on this basis to prove the existence of the material world, Reid proposes to assume without question *both* the existence of the mind *and* the existence of the material world.

Reid's starting point involves a rejection of the Cartesian ideal theory. To the sceptic – that creature born of the theory of ideas – Reid responds by insisting that reason and perception are on an equal footing. He suggests that philosophers have been hindered from appreciating the equality of reason and perception by the theory of ideas:

> The sceptic asks me, Why do you believe the existence of the external object which you perceive? This belief, sir, is none of my manufacture; it came from the mint of Nature; it bears her image and superscription; and, if it is not right, the fault is not mine: I even took it upon trust, and without suspicion. Reason, says the sceptic, is the only judge of truth, and you ought to throw off every opinion and every belief that is not grounded on reason. Why, sir, should I believe the faculty of reason more than that of perception? – they came both out of the same shop, and were made by the same artist; and if he puts one piece of false ware into my hands, what should hinder him from putting another?[30]

Reid's acknowledgement of a symmetry between the deliverances of reason and those of perception is importantly different from anything that philosophers working with the theory of ideas accept. In particular, it differs from David Hume's response to the sceptic. In his *Treatise of Human Nature*, Hume investigates the role of reason in his attempt to reply to scepticism. Hume concludes that it is not reason but nature which 'cures [the philosopher] of this philosophical melancholy and delirium'.[31] But Hume's appeal to nature here should not be confused with Reid's. Reid claims that Hume's appeal to nature comes too late; nature, for Hume, is an antidote to reason. Reid, however, argues that reason has no place here. According to Reid, perception is on an equal footing with reason, and if we understand this there is no sceptical problem to be solved. In response to Hume's appeal to nature Reid writes:

> But what a pity it is, that nature, whatever is meant by that personage, so kind in curing this delirium, should be so cruel as to cause it. Doth the same fountain send forth sweet waters and bitter? Is it not more probable, that if the cure was the work of nature, the disease came from another hand, and was the work of the philosopher?[32]

Reid identifies three things in the act of perception: The first is that, whenever we perceive an object, we come to have some conception, notion or idea of the object perceived.[33] The second is that, as well as perception of the object perceived, we come to have a 'strong and irresistible conviction and belief' in the existence of the object perceived.[34] And the third is that we come to have this conviction or belief immediately and not as a result of reasoning or argument. Where Descartes holds that we are aware of our thoughts in consciousness and immediately come to believe in our own existence, Reid holds that we are aware of objects in perception and immediately come to believe in their existence.

Where Reid insists on a symmetry between reason and perception, philosophers have found an asymmetry. To the philosopher there is a crucial difference between the deliverances of consciousness and the deliverances of perception: while there is a certain infallibility that attends our consciousness of mind, we are, says the philosopher, undeniably fallible in our acts of perception. For this reason philosophers have learned not to trust the deliverances of the senses. The discovery of truth, then, is considered by philosophers to be the province of reason alone. One might conclude from the work of philosophers that 'the senses are given to us by some malignant demon on purpose to delude us, rather than that they are formed by the wise and beneficent Author of nature, to give us true information of things necessary to our preservation and happiness'.[35] And Reid adds:

> It seems to be a very unfavourable account of the workmanship of the Supreme Being, to think that he has given us one faculty to deceive us, to wit, our senses, and another faculty, to wit, our reason, to detect the fallacy.[36]

Reid rejects the philosopher's doctrine of the fallacy of the senses. He begins by pointing out that it is not possible for there to be any fallacy in sensation, for we are conscious of all our sensations, and they can 'neither be any other in their nature, nor greater or less in their degree than we feel them'.[37] Reid gives as an example here the sensation of pain. When a person is in pain he feels it, and when he feels pain his pain is real. The same, says Reid, is true of all sensations. Insofar as our senses are in error, says Reid, the error must be in the perception of objects external to us. He then explains the different reasons why our perception may be thought to be in error. First of all, we must remember that the perception of objects external to us takes place by means of the organs of perception – Reid here includes the nerves and brain as well as, e.g., the eye – and that these organs are liable to disorder. Disorder in the organ of perception will affect the mind's perception of its object. And Reid points out that reason, as well as perception, can be affected by such disorders. But to say that the organs of our body may suffer from disorders is not the same as to accuse them of being fallacious. Reid then goes on to consider three different kinds of case where fallacy has been imputed to the senses and explains what is going on in each case. In each case, Reid concludes that error is falsely attributed to the senses.

Reid first considers cases where rash conclusions are drawn from the testimony of the senses. For example, a man's senses are presented with a painted apple and he takes the presented object to be a real apple. Where is the deception? The man's senses testify to a certain colour, figure, taste and the like. This is all the senses testify to. From the deliveries of the senses, the man concludes, erroneously, that he is being presented with a real apple. It is the judgement that is precipitous, not the senses that are deceptive. The error is not one of false information but of mistaken reasoning. After this, Reid considers the errors that can arise in perceptions that he labels 'acquired' as opposed to 'original'. While original perception is properly the testimony of the senses, acquired perceptions are not; acquired perceptions are based on conclusions drawn from testimony. Thus, the senses testify to a certain conjunction of events, and we come to believe that there is a conjunction in nature. We then take the testimony of the first event to be a sign of the second. For example, our senses testify to a circular form having a certain distribution of light and we say that we see a spherical object. Error may introduce itself here, and we are inclined to attribute it to our original perception when it is justly attributed to our acquired perception. Finally, Reid suggests that error is imputed to the senses which in fact is the product of our ignorance of the laws of nature.

Ignorance of the laws of sound leads to our being deceived by echoes, whispering galleries and ventriloquists; and ignorance of the laws of sight lead us to be deceived by magic lanterns, camera obscuras, telescopes and microscopes. As our knowledge of these laws increases, so does our deception decrease. In conclusion Reid writes:

> There is nothing so absurd which some philosophers have not maintained. It is one thing to profess a doctrine of this kind, another seriously to believe it, and to be governed by it in the conduct of life. It is evident, that a man who did not believe his senses, could not keep out of harm's way an hour of his life; yet, in all the history of philosophy, we never read of any skeptic that ever stepped into fire or water because he did not believe his senses, or that showed, in the conduct of life, less trust in his senses that other men have.[38]

Contrary to the dictates of the philosophers, the senses do not deceive us. In the act of perception we come to have a conception of the object perceived as well as an immediate and irresistible conviction that the object exists. This is how we observe perception to operate. That it operates in this way is, says Reid, 'part of the original constitution of the human mind'.[39] How it operates is not something we can comprehend. Here we come upon one link in that mysterious chain between the material and the intellectual world. Reid sometimes writes in such a way as to suggest that we are unable to unravel the mystery here *because* the way perception works is simply an original constitution of the mind.[40]

Philosophers, however, resist the idea that perception operates in this way. They insist that our belief in the existence of material objects must be grounded in evidence. Reid agrees; however, he insists that we must be careful to distinguish different kinds of evidence: there is the evidence of sense, the evidence of memory, the evidence of consciousness, the evidence of testimony, the evidence of axioms and the evidence of reasoning. Each kind of evidence grounds its own belief. We could say that the evidence is suited to the belief. However, where Reid finds distinct kinds of evidence, philosophers look to find one thing which they can call 'evidence'. The philosopher attempts to find some factor common to all the different kinds of evidence. Where others attempt to reduce the several different kinds of evidence to one, Reid insists that such a reduction is not possible. Reid then considers the evidence of sense and he writes:

I shall take it for granted, that the evidence of sense, when the proper circumstances concur, is good evidence, and a just ground for belief.[41]

Reid accepts that, whereas the evidence of reason commands our assent without question, the evidence of sense does not reach this peak of perfection. What we must understand, says Reid, is that the evidence of reason and the evidence of sense are distinct. If we insist on comparing the two, and hanker for evidence from the one that properly belongs to the other, we will be led astray into scepticism.

To those philosophers who would insist that our belief in the existence of objects must be grounded in reason, Reid draws attention to the pre-rational child. He points out that we learn from experience long before we learn from reason. In one place Reid writes:

[The child's] activity and credulity are more useful qualities, and better instructors than reason would be; they teach him more in a day than reason would do in a year; they furnish a stock of materials for reason to work upon; they make him easy and happy in a period of his existence, when reason could only serve to suggest a thousand tormenting anxieties and fears: and he acts agreeably to the constitution and intention of nature, even when he does and believes what reason would not justify.[42]

In another place Reid explains that the adult's beliefs, just as much as the pre-rational child's, are regulated not just by reason but by certain *principles*, which principles are part of our constitution. He writes: 'Whether they ought to be called animal principles, or instinctive principles . . . is of small moment; but they are certainly different from the faculty of reason.'[43] Our nature is regulated by these principles. And there is no *proof* that can be offered of these principles: 'To judge of first principles, requires no more than a sound mind free from prejudice, and a distinct conception of the question'.[44] It is time now to look a little more closely at some of these principles.

FIRST PRINCIPLES AND OTHER INTELLIGENT BEINGS

The principles that most interest Reid are the first principles of *contingent* truths.[45] In his *Essays on the Intellectual Powers of Man*,

Essay VI, chapter v, Reid lists twelve such principles, but lays no claim to this being an exclusive list. I shall here mention only seven:

(i)   Everything of which I am conscious exists.
(ii)   The thoughts of which I am conscious are the thoughts of a being that I call 'myself', my 'mind' or my 'person'.
(iii)   Those things that I distinctly remember did really occur.
(iv)   Those things that I distinctly perceive by my senses do really exist and are as I perceive them to be.
(v)   There is life and intelligence in our fellow men with whom we converse.
(vi)   Certain features of the countenance, sounds of the voice and gestures of the body, indicate certain thoughts and dispositions of mind.
(vii)   There is a certain regard due to human testimony in matters of fact.[46]

These principles are the foundation of all our reasoning. They are not something a child is taught, but are a matter of 'common understanding'.[47] First principles need only be proposed to be understood and assented to. This is not to say that people cannot be mistaken in their judgement concerning first principles. Reid writes:

> We do not pretend, that those things that are laid down as first principles may not be examined, and that we ought not to have our ears open to what may be pleaded against their being admitted as such. Let us deal with them, as an upright judge does with a witness who has fair character. He pays a regard to the testimony of such a witness, while his character is unimpeached. But if it can be shewn that he was suborned, or that he is influenced by malice or partial favour, his testimony loses all its credit, and is justly rejected.[48]

This is sometimes referred to as Reid's fallibilism. Fallibilism is the doctrine that our judgement that something is a first principle can be overturned by contrary evidence. Reid's point is that these first principles must be taken for granted, and corrected in the appropriate manner if needs be. Ultimately, however, their evidence is intuitive, not demonstrative.

To the above list of first principles Reid adds another, which he says has a claim to being prior to all others. This all-important principle is the following:

(viii) The natural faculties, by which we distinguish truth from error, are not fallacious.

This principle cannot be proved because any attempt to prove it will only call upon the very point in question. It is because some philosophers (Reid here draws particular attention to Descartes) refuse to acknowledge this principle that they are led into impossible scepticisms. According to Reid, a denial of this first principle does 'violence to our constitution'.[49] He compares the denial of this principle to a man's feat of walking on his hands – it is something a man can do on occasion as an exhibition, but it is not something any man can sustain. ('Cease to admire his dexterity, and he will, like other men, betake himself to his legs.')[50] It is a refusal to acknowledge this principle that leads philosophers into conflict with common sense.

According to common sense objects in the world exist, a being who is conscious of thought exists, things that I can now distinctly remember did once happen, and other intelligent beings exist. These are all things that common sense accepts, but that some philosophers have found occasion to doubt. Concerning the clash that some philosophers see between philosophy and common sense, Reid writes:

> It may be observed, that the defects and blemishes in the received philosophy concerning the mind, which have most exposed it to the contempt and ridicule of sensible men, have chiefly been owing to this – that the votaries of this Philosophy, from a natural prejudice in her favour, have endeavoured to extend her jurisdiction beyond its just limits, and to call to her bar the dictates of Common Sense. But these decline this jurisdiction; they disdain the trial or reasoning, and disown its authority; they neither claim its aid, nor dread its attacks.
>
> In this unequal contest betwixt Common Sense and Philosophy, the latter will always come off both with dishonour and loss; nor can she ever thrive till this rivalship is dropt, these encroachments given up, and a cordial friendship restored. . . . Philosophy (if I may be permitted to change the metaphor) has no other root but the principles of Common Sense; it grows out of them, and draws its nourishment from them. Severed from this root, its honours wither, its sap is dried up, it dies and rots.[51]

This is a strong endorsement of common sense against philosophy, with its emphasis on reason. Reid's point is that reason has its place, but that the deliverance of common sense must not be judged only by the measure offered by reason.

Let us now look in more detail at principle (v), the principle that asserts a life and intelligence in our fellow men with whom we converse. Reid is clear about the reason why we must accept this first principle as something that is antecedent to all reasoning. The knowledge that there are other intelligent beings is essential to our ability to receive information and instruction, without which we would be unable to acquire the use of our reasoning.[52] This knowledge is, Reid points out, the province of all children long before the age of reason. Before a child is capable of reason it can ask, refuse and beg – the child, of course, achieves all this non-linguistically. Even before a child reaches its first birthday, it 'clings to its nurse in danger, enters into her grief and joy, is happy in her soothing and caresses, and unhappy in her displeasure'.[53] Furthermore, whatever conclusions the growing child may come to as the result of reason, she is unable to shake off her conviction that there are other intelligent beings. Indeed, if a man were to be asked his reason for this conviction Reid says that he 'perhaps could not give any reason which would not equally prove a watch or a puppet to be a living creature'.[54] This is not to deny that even the child can be in error here and attribute intelligence to something that is inanimate. But, according to Reid, the error that is possible here is of 'small consequence', and is soon corrected by 'experience and ripe judgement'.[55] Reid then repeats that, despite the possibility of error, we must acknowledge that, if reason is to be possible, such conviction in the existence of other intelligent beings is 'absolutely necessary'. Like principle (viii), principle (v) is fundamental to all reasoning and, hence, to all knowledge.

If we set natural conviction aside, Reid admits that 'the best reason we can give, to prove that other men are living and intelligent, is, that their words and actions indicate like powers of understanding as we are conscious of in ourselves'.[56] Reid thus acknowledges that those who deny first principles their rightful place have indeed found reason for our belief in the existence of other men in the only place they are able: in their words and actions. We do not need to rely on reason, however; our belief in the existence of other intelligent beings has yet a firmer foundation in our natural conviction. But notice that, while Reid does not hold that we employ reason in coming to believe that other intelligent beings exist, he does hold that our belief in the existence of other intelligent beings is the result of the operations of our senses. He writes that

It is evident we can have no communication, no correspondence or society with any created beings, but by means of our senses. And until we rely upon their testimony, we must consider ourselves as being alone in the universe, without any fellow creatures, living or inanimate, and be left to converse with our own thoughts.[57]

Our belief in these other beings depends upon the observation – and existence – of their bodies.[58] Our senses testify not just to the existence of certain bodies, but also to the existence of those we call 'father, mother, and sister, and brother, and nurse'.[59]

The dependence that our knowledge of the existence of other intelligent beings has on our knowledge of the existence of bodies is further brought out in principle (vi). This principle is concerned not with the existence of other intelligent beings but with what they are thinking and feeling. Reid accepts that one intelligent being cannot directly perceive the thoughts and feelings of another. Rather, one intelligent being perceives the countenance of the other, the gestures of the other's body and the sounds of the other's voice. And these, says Reid, are natural signs of other intelligent beings: 'the features of the person is the sign, and the passion or sentiment is signified by it'.[60] I do not see the features and infer the sentiment. Rather, I see the features and by the constitution of my nature I understand what sentiments they signify. Reid takes it that no one will dispute that the things I observe in the body of the other are signs, and thinks that the only question that arises is whether we understand these signs because we have learned them from experience (in the way that we learn that smoke is a sign of fire) or because this understanding is part of the constitution of our nature. It is Reid's belief that we must understand these signs by the constitution of our nature, 'by a kind of natural perception similar to the perceptions of sense'.[61] The alternative – the suggestion that we learn these signs – seems to Reid 'incredible'.[62] Again, Reid cites the evidence of infants and children. We can say when it is that children learn that smoke is a sign of fire, but is it possible to say when a child learns how to understand the expression in its mother's face? Surely this is not learned but is part of the child's natural constitution. Reid insists: 'Children, almost as soon as they are born, may be frightened, and thrown into fits by a threatening or angry tone of voice. I knew a man who could make an infant cry, by whistling a melancholy tune in the same or in the next room.'[63] And the same can be said for the child's observation of countenance and gesture: an angry countenance will frighten an infant in the cradle and a gentle expression will soothe her. Reid points to a very important difference between learned and natural signs: in the case of learned signs we are able to experience both the sign and what is signified, while in the case of natural signs we experience only the sign. Reid writes: 'But how shall experience instruct us when we see the sign only, when the thing signified is invisible?'[64] The thoughts of another are invisible, so how can experience establish a connection between these thoughts and the things that we see?

The understanding of natural signs is fundamental to our nature. It plays a part in our perception of objects, as well as in the information we receive from human testimony. About these signs Reid writes,

> Nature hath established a real connection between the signs and the things signified; and Nature hath also taught us the interpretation of the signs – so that, previous to experience, the sign suggests the thing signified, and creates the belief in it.[65]

We are fit by our natures to understand the signs delivered by the senses. When I have, for example, the feeling of hardness and roundness, I am led by the constitution of my nature to form a conception of a hard round body and to have the belief that a hard round body does really exist. Likewise, when I see the features of the face and the gestures of the body or when I hear the modulations of the voice, I am led by the constitution of my nature to understand them. All signs – both the signs of our original perceptions and the signs of the human countenance – are, says Reid, common among men of all nations. It is because we share a common human nature that men who share no mother tongue are still able to communicate. Reid notes that, although an actor who practises pantomime must work hard to learn his art, his audience requires no study to understand it.[66]

According to Reid, our ability to understand natural signs is important in itself, but it is also important because, without this natural understanding, human language would not be possible. He writes,

> I think it is demonstrable, that, if mankind had not a natural language, they could never have invented an artificial one, by their reason and ingenuity. For all artificial language supposes some compact or agreement to affix certain meaning to certain signs; therefore, there must be compacts or agreements before the use of artificial signs; but there can be no compact or agreement without signs, nor without language; and, therefore, there must be a natural language before any artificial language can be invented.[67]

Reid points out that all creatures have a natural language; all are fit to receive the testimony of their fellow creatures. Dogs, horses and chicks can understand each other, as well as some of the expressions of the human voice. Man has both a natural and an artificial language.[68]

In order to be capable of profiting from the testimony of our fellow creatures through the use of artificial language, Reid holds that God must have planted in our nature the following two principles: the principle of veracity and the principle of credulity. Without the principle of veracity no word could become a sign of a thought, and human testimony would be considerably weakened. Reid writes that 'truth is always uppermost, and is the natural issue of the mind. It requires no art or training, no inducements or temptation, but only that we yield to natural impulse.'[69] Without the principle of credulity we would not be fit to receive the information that others are in a position to give us and, as a result, many of the benefits of society would elude us. Credulity is our starting point, and it is strongest in children who have not yet learned to have reasons to distrust the words of others. Without the twin principles of trust and credulity we would be unable to profit from the signs of human testimony, and without the prior existence of natural language we would not be able to employ and profit from the use of an artificial language.

Principles (v) and (vi) are, together, fundamental to our well being. We know that other intelligent beings exist and we understand their thoughts and feelings. It is not enough that we hold the existence of other intelligent beings to be the result of reasoning. The mistake of philosophers – why they are unable to account for our knowledge here – is that they give reason pride of place over perception, and they take ideas to be intermediaries in the act of perception. From the starting point of an ideal theory, philosophers from Descartes to Berkeley are unable to give a proper place to our knowledge of other intelligent beings. Once philosophers understand that perception is on an equal footing with reason, they will also find that other intelligent beings are on an equal footing with me. On Reid's way of doing philosophy solipsism is no longer a threat.

REID VERSUS BERKELEY

Reid finds the full absurdity of the ideal theory manifest in the writings of Bishop Berkeley. Reid summarizes Berkeley's main philosophical doctrine thus:

[Berkeley] maintains, and thinks that he has demonstrated, . . . that there is no such thing as matter in the universe; that sun and moon, earth and sea, our own bodies, and those of our friends, are nothing but ideas in the minds of those who think them.[70]

The problem is the starting point, the assumption that what is before the mind in perception is an idea. Reid refers us to the opening lines of Berkeley's *Principles* where we find a statement of the basic premise of the ideal theory. According to Reid, once we allow Berkeley this starting point, his system is 'impregnable'.[71] Reid points out that, despite the importance of this starting point, Berkeley provides no argument in support of it; he simply takes it to be 'evident to anyone who takes a survey of the objects of human knowledge'.[72] Reid challenges Berkeley here. According to Reid, a self-evident proposition is one that is evident to every man of sound judgement who attends to it without prejudice; but the principle with which Berkeley begins his work is not self-evident in this sense. In order to find Berkeley's principle self-evident, says Reid, one would have to be steeped in philosophy.

Despite his disagreement with the premise, it is not so much the premise of Berkeley's work as its consequences that Reid thinks is the real sign of a philosophy gone wrong. Concerning one of these consequences Reid writes:

But there is one uncomfortable consequence of [Berkeley's] system, which he seems not to have attended to, and from which it will be found difficult, if at all possible, to guard it.

The consequence I mean is this, that, although it leaves us sufficient evidence of a supreme intelligent Mind, it seems to take away all the evidence we have of other intelligent beings like ourselves. What I call a father, a brother, or a friend, is only a parcel of ideas in my own mind; . . . I am left alone, as the only creature of God in the universe, in that forlorn state of *Egoism*, into which, it is said, some disciples of Des Cartes were brought by his philosophy.[73]

It is an interesting biographical fact that Reid was at one time a follower of Berkeley's work. In one place he writes:

I once believed this doctrine of ideas so firmly, as to embrace the whole of Berkeley's system in consequence of it; till, finding other consequences to follow from it, which gave me more uneasiness than the want of a material world, it came into my mind . . . to put the question, What evidence have I, for this doctrine, that all the objects of my knowledge are ideas in my own mind?[74]

Thus we can see that the turning point in Reid's thinking on these matters is not a reflection on the theory of ideas as such, but a reflection on the consequences of that theory. And it is interesting that it does not appear to be the ideal theory's consequences concerning the material world that most bothered Reid. Although Reid is not here explicit about which conclusions most bother him, we know from what he writes in other places that Reid is deeply exercised by the ideal theory's conclusions concerning the existence of other intelligent beings. Reid notes – and rejects – these consequences and then traces the fault back to the theory itself. According to Reid, philosophers who hold the ideal theory fail to distinguish between perceiving and sensing. Reid takes this mistake to be particularly evident in Berkeley's writing.

To see how this mistake arises it is necessary to go back to Berkeley's work and recall the distinction that Berkeley draws between our knowledge of objects and our knowledge of minds.[75] According to Berkeley, while we have an idea of body, we can have no idea of mind or spirit. The reason Berkeley gives for this is that ideas are passive and inert, while spirits are active beings. Nevertheless, Berkeley concludes that, inasmuch as we understand the meaning of the words 'spirit' and 'mind' we have some *notion* of spirit. Thus, Berkeley allows that there are things that can be known without the intervention of ideas. Reid examines Berkeley's work and asks why, given that it is possible to know spirit without ideas, we cannot be said to know the material world in a similar manner. Now Reid recognizes that Berkeley considers, and replies to, this objection in the *Third Dialogue*. In the *Third Dialogue* Reid's question is given voice by Hylas thus: given that we can conceive of the mind of God without having any idea of it, can we not allow that we can conceive of matter without having an idea of it? Philonous replies:

> You neither perceive matter objectively, as you do an inactive being or idea, nor know it, as you do yourself by a reflex act: neither do you mediately apprehend it by similitude of the one to the other: nor yet collect it by reasoning from that which you know immediately.[76]

Reid agrees that one does not apprehend matter by perceiving a similarity between it and an idea, and he also agrees that one does not reason to the conclusion that matter exists. However, Reid disagrees with Philonous when he says that one does not perceive matter objectively. This, according to Reid, is precisely what we do. And Reid thinks that it is because Berkeley does not appreciate this that he is led to his immaterialism. Berkeley concludes that we perceive ideas and not matter; Reid holds that we perceive matter and not ideas.

Here we find Reid asserting his philosophy of first principles in the place of a theory of ideas. Once we accept first principles, there is no need to distinguish (what in any case our language does not distinguish) between notions and ideas. Ideas are simply notions, and to say that we have a notion of something is to say no more than that we conceive it or apprehend it – in short, that we think of it.[77] Where Reid finds only notions or ideas, Berkeley insists there are notions *and* ideas. Reid sets out to understand what Berkeley could mean by *idea* in contradistinction to *notion*. To this end Reid notes that Berkeley writes that ideas are imprinted on the senses and excited in the imagination. As far as Reid is able to make out, what Berkeley calls 'ideas of sense' are nothing other than what we might otherwise call 'sensation'. And 'sensation', says Reid, 'is a name given . . . to an act of mind, which may be distinguished from all others by this, that it hath no object distinct from the act itself'.[78] This is just common language. Reid then notes that this account of sensation, taken from common language, fits Berkeley's description of an idea. It is at this point that Reid discerns Berkeley's mistake: Berkeley insists that we can have knowledge *only* of sensations or ideas. Once we agree with this, however, then Berkeley's 'system must be admitted, and the existence of a material world must be given up as a dream'.[79] But Reid does not think that we do have to agree with Berkeley. By our senses we have knowledge not of sensation only, but also of objects. It is this that Berkeley misses. Berkeley's mistake is to confound sensation with perception.

This confounding of sensation and perception is, according to Reid, 'the occasion of most of the errors and false theories of philosophers with regard to the senses'.[80] Sensation, according to Reid, is an act of mind that has no object distinct from itself. Perception is an act of mind which always has an external object, and which also has associated with it a belief or conception. Thus, when we perceive an object we have an immediate conviction and belief of something external. Reid writes:

> Sensation, taken by itself, implies neither the conception nor belief of any external object. It supposes a sentient being, and a

certain manner in which that being is affected; but it supposes no more. Perception implies an immediate conviction and belief of something external; something different both from the mind that perceives, and from the act of perception.[81]

Sensation does play a role in perception, but it is not the role Berkeley understands. Berkeley takes it that we perceive our sensations, when in fact what we perceive, according to Reid, are objects. The conception of the object and the belief in the existence of the object are both the result of the sensation. This conception and this belief are not the result of experience or of reason, but are simply 'the immediate effect of my constitution'. An object makes an impression on the organs of perception, which in turn produce sensations in the mind. These sensations are taken by us as signs of objects external to us. The sensation is in our mind, but the perception is of something external to the mind. Sensation and perception are distinct acts of mind.

Reid admits that Berkeley's mistake is an easy one to make. First of all, although the perception of an object is almost always accompanied by a sensation, we are not always aware of this. Many sensations that accompany the perception of an object are agreeable or disagreeable to us, but there are a great many sensations to which we are indifferent. Where we are indifferent we are apt to think there is no sensation. With a little effort, however, we can recognize that the sensation does in fact exist. Sensations – whether agreeable, disagreeable or indifferent – serve as the signs of the existence of objects. Another reason we are liable to confuse sensation and perception is that we are misled by language. Reid notes that we speak, for example, of the smell of the rose, and by this we refer both to the sensation and the perception of the rose. For this reason we are liable to be confused by the question, Is the smell in the rose or in the mind? The proper answer to this question is that the sensation of the rose is in my mind, while the object of my perception is external to me. Furthermore, the same mode of expression is used to denote both the sensation and the perception. Thus, we say, 'I feel a pain', and 'I see a tree'. Just as the latter expression distinguishes an act of perception from the object of perception, so we are apt to think that the former expression distinguishes an act of sensation and an object of sensation. But language misleads here; in the case of the expression of sensation, the distinction between the act and the object is not real but grammatical. Despite the way language may mislead us, sensation must be distinguished from perception. It is only if they are that we can avoid the absurd consequences of the theory of ideas.

If we now return to the opening lines of Berkeley's *Principles* we find that it is possible to reject what is written there. The objects of human knowledge include – as well as sensations and ideas – objects. Reid says that Berkeley's immaterialism may look like a bold and daring philosophy, but in truth it is no more than the end result of the theory of ideas that Descartes introduced into philosophy. Philosophers begin by exploring ideas in order that they may explain perception, but in the end these ideas 'usurped the place of perception, object, and even the mind itself, and have supplanted those very things they were brought in to explain'.[82] As Reid sees it, philosophers must reject Cartesian ideas if they wish to avoid Berkeleian solipsism.

CONCLUSION

Once reason and perception are placed on an equal footing, no sceptical problem will arise either concerning the existence of external bodies or concerning the existence of other minds. What stands as an obstacle to knowledge is the intervention of ideas. It is the ideal theory, first proposed by Descartes and inherited by philosophers from Descartes' time onwards, that Reid sees as the enemy of knowledge. By rejecting this theory Reid is able to assert the existence of other intelligent beings.

Although Reid is most perceptive in his identification of the problems inherent in the ideal theory, it is arguable that he has not yet managed to free himself entirely of the Cartesian influence. By this I mean that Reid is still operating within what I have been calling the Cartesian framework. Although Reid is able to account for our knowledge of the world and other intelligent beings, his conception of the subject in relation to her world is still such that it is possible to raise a question concerning the subject's knowledge of the world beyond her own mind. The logical or conceptual divide between the subject and her world is still in place. Reid's point is that we in fact have a way of reaching across that gap. The theory of ideas is only one way of characterizing that gap, and, as Reid rightly points out, the introduction of ideas only brings in its wake an impossible scepticism. But Reid's rejection of the theory leaves the Cartesian conceptual divide still intact. And so long as this conceptual divide is in place, the *possibility* of scepticism threatens still.

Evidence of this conceptual divide is littered throughout Reid's work. Take, for example, *Essay* I, chapter viii where Reid insists that we must supplement the solitary operations of the mind with the social ones. The solitary operations are the ones recognized by philosophers like Locke; they include the operations of understanding and willing. The social operations are the ones that philosophers like Locke overlook; they include all operations that presuppose intercourse with other intelligent beings (such as giving and receiving testimony). Of the solitary operations Reid writes: 'A man may understand and will; he may apprehend, and judge, and reason, though he should know of no intelligent being in the universe besides himself.'[83] This characterization shows that Reid takes the social operations as merely supplementary, and not essential, to the solitary operations. There is no conceptual connection between the subject and her world. The subject may exist, with all her solitary operations intact, but no world or other beings exist.

In Reid's philosophy, as much as in Descartes', the subject of experience is conceived of in isolation from the world and other minds. Where Descartes appeals to God to guarantee our clear and distinct ideas in order to be able to have knowledge of the world on the other side of the gap, Reid appeals to our nature.[84] If Reid is right to appeal to first principles then knowledge is possible, but knowledge here can still be thought of as an isolated subject's way of reaching across to the world and other subjects. As Reid sets things up we can imagine the following possibility: a creature may be endowed with a certain set of sensations, and its constitution may be such as to give rise to the belief in objects and minds external to itself, while no world and no other minds exist. This subject would live in a solipsistic world. It may be that God did not in fact set things up this way, but such a conception of a subject makes sense on the picture of things with which Reid is working. The existence of the world and other minds is still conceived of as something additional to the existence of a subject who has sensations of that world.

I want to end by considering Reid's reply to what I have been calling Augustine's question: What account does Reid give of the very belief that there are other intelligent beings? Of course, Reid looks as if he has a reply to this question. Our perception of the countenance and gestures of certain bodies gives me both the conception of another intelligent being and a belief in his or her existence. But this does not answer the question where we get our *general* conception of mind. According to Reid, we come by our general conceptions as the result of a two-stage operation of mind. At the first stage the mind focuses attention on some quality (Reid calls this operation 'abstraction'), and at the second stage the mind generalizes from these qualities in accordance with the demands of utility to form a general conception of a common attribute.[85] Let us now ask, How do we come by our general conception of *mind*? Reid thinks that we know clearly the attributes of mind and its operations in our own case. But he also makes it clear that the 'thoughts and passions of [another] mind, as well as the mind itself, are invisible'.[86] How then does the mind form a general conception of a *common* attribute? In the case of another, all I can do is listen to her voice, observe her countenance, and watch her actions, while in my own case I know my own mind through consciousness. Why, then, do we take it that there *is* anything in common between such different qualities? The problem is not dissimilar to the one I raised for both Locke and Berkeley. I shall not pursue these questions now, but shall return to them in Part Three.

I want now to consider most briefly the work of three philosophers: John Stuart Mill, Rudolph Carnap and Moritz Schlick. Mill is important in this story because of his attempt to reject Reid's philosophy, and in its stead to offer what he takes to be a 'proof' of the existence of other minds. Carnap and Schlick provide an interesting propaedeutic to the more profound philosophy bequeathed to us by Wittgenstein, whose work I discuss in Chapter VII.

BRIEF INTERLUDE: JOHN STUART MILL

According to Reid, Berkeley's system leads at best to the conclusion that the existence of other intelligent beings is merely probable, and at worst to the conclusion that I am alone with God in the universe. Neither conclusion is acceptable to Reid. In order to avoid Berkeley's unacceptable conclusion concerning other intelligent beings, Reid argues that we must reject the theory of ideas. John Stuart Mill (1806–1873) believed he could avoid these unacceptable conclusions concerning other intelligent beings without having to abandon the Cartesian Ideal Theory. Mill accepts the deliverances of consciousness, but he rejects Reid's attempt to put the evidence of the senses on an equal footing with the evidence of consciousness. According to Mill, all truths are known in one of two ways: either directly, through the authority of consciousness, or indirectly, by inference from truths known directly. Mill takes it to be the job of metaphysics to determine which part of human understanding is known by intuition or consciousness and which is known through inference. Where Reid (and others) holds that there are the deliverances of consciousness and a reality distinct from these, Mill thinks there are the deliverances of consciousness and inference from these. In his *System of Logic* he writes:

But we may fancy we see and feel what we in reality infer. A truth, or supposed truth, which is really the result of a very rapid inference, may seem to be apprehended intuitively.[87]

Mill sets out to give a psychological account of these inferences. Mill's account postulates first, that we are capable of forming a conception of possible sensations – that is, 'sensations which we are not feeling at the present moment, but which we might feel, and should feel if certain conditions were present' – and second, that there are laws of the 'association of ideas'.[88] Mill takes it that from these premises we are capable of generating our belief in a world external to consciousness. As Mill thinks that it is possible to show how these beliefs can be internally generated, he holds there is no need for Reid's account of these beliefs.[89] Matter, according to Mill, is to be defined as the permanent possibility of sensation.

Mill intends his psychological theory to apply to our belief in mind, just as much as to our belief in matter – or, as Mill sometimes writes, to apply to ego just as much as non-ego. Where Reid takes it that our belief in mind is a first principle, Mill holds that we can account for this belief in terms of the permanent possibility of those states. Mill writes,

There seems no hindrance to our regarding Mind as nothing but the series of our sensations (to which must now be added our internal feelings), as they actually occur, with the addition of infinite possibilities of feeling requiring for their actual realization conditions which may or may not take place, but which as possibilities are always in existence, and many of them present.[90]

Having proposed his account of mind and matter – of ego and non-ego – Mill turns to consider an objection that he takes it Reid would make to this account:

If this is all that Mind, or Myself, amounts to, what evidence have I (it is asked) of the existence of my fellow creatures? . . .
    Dr. Reid unhesitatingly answers, None. If the doctrine is true, I am alone in the universe.
    I hold this to be one of Reid's most palpable mistakes.[91]

Mill does not take himself to be a solipsist; he believes that there is evidence for a belief in the existence of our fellow creatures. There is, then, on Mill's view an asymmetry between our belief in objects external to us, on the one hand, and our belief in intelligent beings other than ourselves, on the other. While the former belief is merely a construction out of groups of possible sensations, the latter corresponds to the existence of other, quite separate, minds. Mill is explicit about this asymmetry in his response to an objection by H. B. Smith. Smith claims that Mill's account of our belief in external bodies offers us no proof that such bodies exist. In response to Smith, Mill writes,

> I never pretended that they do. I am accounting for our conceiving or representing to ourselves, the Permanent Possibilities as real objects external to us. I do not believe that the real externality to us of anything, except other minds, is capable of proof.[92]

As we have seen earlier, Reid holds that there is a dependence of our belief in the existence of other intelligent beings on our belief in the existence of bodies external to the mind. Reid takes it that Berkeley deprives us of external bodies, and so deprives us of other intelligent beings. Mill, by his own admission, deprives us of external bodies. Mill is right, then, to think that Reid would say that Mill's system deprives us of the company of other intelligent beings. Yet Mill insists that his system does not have this consequence. Let us now look at Mill's proof of the existence of other minds. Because of the importance of Mill's proof I shall quote it at length:

> By what evidence do I know, or by what considerations am I led to believe, that there exist other sentient creatures; that the walking and speaking figures which I see and hear, have sensations and thoughts, or in other words, possess Minds? . . . I conclude it from certain things, which my experience of my own states of feeling proves to me to be marks of it. . . . I conclude that other human beings have feelings like me, because, first, they have bodies like me, which I know, in my own case, to be the antecedent condition of feelings; and because, secondly, they exhibit the acts, and other outward signs, which in my own case I know by experience to be caused by feelings. I am conscious in myself of a series of facts connected by an uniform sequence, of which the beginning is modifications of my body, the middle is feelings, the end is outward demeanour. In the case of other human beings I have the evidence of my senses for the first and last links of the series, but not for the intermediate link. I find, however, that the sequence between the first and last links is regular and constant in those other cases as it is in mine. In my

own case I know that the first link produces the last through the intermediate link, and could not produce it without. Experience, therefore, obliges me to conclude that there must be an intermediate link; which must either be the same in others as in myself, or a different one: I must either believe them to be alive, or to be automatons: and by believing them to be alive, . . . I bring other human beings, as phaenomena, under the same generalizations which I know by experience to be the true theory of my own existence. . . . We know the existence of other beings by generalization from the knowledge of our own: the generalization merely postulates that what experience shows to be a mark of the existence of something within the sphere of our consciousness, may be concluded to be a mark of the same thing beyond that sphere.[93]

Mill holds that this proof is constructed entirely on the basis of our sensations and the possibilities of sensations; it in no way depends upon the separate existence of either mind or matter. First of all I notice that among the possibilities of sensation is one group which I call my own body, and I notice, further, that this group of sensations is 'in a peculiar manner' connected with all the sensations I call my own. I next notice that when I look about me there are a great number of other bodies which closely resemble those I refer to as my body, and that the modifications in these (other) bodies are not connected with feelings or sensations in my consciousness. I infer, says Mill, that, since the modifications are not connected with sensations in my consciousness, they are connected with sensations that are 'out of my consciousness, and that to each [group of sensations] belongs a world of consciousness of its own, to which it stands in the same relation in which what I call my own body stands to mine'. Mill concludes:

Having made this generalization, I find that all other facts within my reach accord with it. Each of these bodies exhibits to my senses a set of phaenomena (composed of acts and other manifestations) such as I know, in my own case, to be effects of consciousness, and such as might be looked for if each of the bodies has really in connexion with it a world of consciousness.[94]

Most philosophers take this passage to offer the argument from analogy to the existence of another mind; and some philosophers have claimed that we find in these pages the first statement of that argument.[95] Mill's proof certainly does contain all the elements of such an argument: an assumption about the way things are in my own case, a noted correlation between my own sensations and my behaviour, a recognition of a similar behaviour that is not connected with my sensations, and a conclusion that this behaviour which I observe is connected with sensations in another human being. Of course, insofar as Mill is offering us an argument from analogy, we must be sure to remember to interpret that argument in the context of his phenomenalism. If we do this, however, a certain difficulty becomes apparent. This difficulty was pointed out to Mill by a critic of his day, Mr H. F. O'Hanlon. O'Hanlon notes that Mill's psychological theory 'inserts an alien consciousness between two consciousnesses of my own, as the effect of one of them and the cause of the other'. O'Hanlon gives the example of a boy who cuts his finger and screams. According to Mill's psychological theory the knife, the blood, and the boy's body are all groups of possible sensations, the boy's scream is an actual sensation, and in between all these sensations of mine is a feeling which belongs to a consciousness which is not mine. O'Hanlon points out that, had I not been present, the boy, the knife, the blood and the scream would only exist 'potentially' while the boy's sensation is actual, and he asks whether this is not absurd. Mill responds to O'Hanlon by pointing out that, on his psychological theory, although the actual sensation is not common to himself and the boy, the permanent possibilities of sensation are common to both of them. Mill writes: 'Other people do not have our sensations exactly when and as we have them: but they have our possibilities of sensation; whatever indicates a present possibility of sensations to ourselves, indicates a present possibility of similar sensations to them, except so far as their organs of sensation may vary from the type of ours.'[96]

The argument from analogy is no doubt present in Mill's argument. Mill even refers to analogy in the course of his discussion of his proof.[97] Nevertheless, Mill insists that, taken in its entirety, his is *not* an argument from analogy. Rather, analogy forms a proper part of Mill's argument to prove the existence of other minds. What makes it the case that the argument, taken as a whole, is not just an argument from analogy is the fact that the conclusion we reach by analogy can be verified by subsequent observations. All in all what Mill takes himself to be offering is not an argument from analogy, but a good inductive argument. About the conclusion we draw from analogy Mill writes,

If the evidence stopped here, the inference would be but an hypothesis; reaching only to the inferior degree of inductive

evidence called Analogy. The evidence, however, does not stop
here; for . . . I find that my subsequent consciousness presents
those very sensations, of speech heard, of movements and other
outward demeanor seen, and so forth, which, being the effects or
consequents of actual feelings in my own case, I should expect
to follow upon those other hypothetical feelings if they really
exist: and thus the hypothesis is verified. It is thus proved inductively that there is a sphere beyond my consciousness.[98]

What Mill claims to be presenting is an inductive argument which has
at its core a conclusion drawn from analogy. What makes the argument an inductive one is the fact that, once I posit the hypothesis that
there is another consciousness besides my own, the hypothesis is con-
firmed in subsequent sensations. Thus, although it is true that we find
in Mill an early statement of the argument of analogy, this analogy is
used as only part of what Mill takes to be a good inductive argument.
It is this inductive argument which is meant to prove the existence of
other intelligent beings. Mill takes it that, with this inductive argument, he has answered Reid's objection to his psychological theory.
The psychological theory, although it deprives us of an external reality, does not deprive us of other intelligent beings. If Mill's inductive
argument works, then solipsism is avoided.

The question, then, is whether the inductive argument that Mill
offers can indeed prove the existence of other intelligent beings. The
question for Mill is whether it is possible to argue inductively to a conclusion about something that never has been *and never could be* a part
of my consciousness. That I can never experience the sensations that
belong to another consciousness is something that Mill readily admits.
Mill considers the question, and responds as follows:

Facts of which I never *have* had consciousness are as much
unknown facts, as much apart from my actual experience, as
facts of which I cannot have consciousness. When I conclude,
from the facts that I immediately perceive, to the existence of
other facts such as *might* come into my actual consciousness
(which the feelings of other people never can) but which never
did come into it, and of which I have no evidence but an induction from experience; how do I know that I am concluding
rightly – that the inference is warranted, from an actual consciousness to a contingent possibility of consciousness which
has never become actual? Surely because this conclusion from
experience is verified by further experience; because those other

experiences which I ought to have if my inference was correct, really present themselves. This verification, which is the source of all my reliance on induction, justifies the same reliance wherever it is found.[99]

But it is not clear that Mill is right to say that facts of which I have never been conscious are on a par with facts of which I *could* never be conscious. And if this is not right, then it looks as if the conclusion that is being verified falls short of the desired conclusion. Mill appears to want to say that it is the predictive success of my hypothesis that proves its correctness, but all that Mill's induction can do is entrench a habit within my experience. The problem is that another's experience is precisely *not mine*. The problem is evident if we recall the first of the two postulates of Mill's psychological theory: that we are capable of forming a conception of possible sensations, of 'sensations we are not feeling at the present moment, but which we might feel, and should feel if certain conditions were present'. Mill says nothing here of our capacity to form a conception of sensations which we are not now feeling and which we might never feel.

Mill's insightful critic O'Hanlon attempted to put the point to Mill. O'Hanlon argues that Mill assumes that we can simply extend the principles of inductive inference beyond our own sphere of consciousness, whereas the existence of another sphere of consciousness is precisely the thing Mill wants to prove. To O'Hanlon's objection Mill writes:

> To this I reply, that it does not postulate [this], but, to the extent required by the present question, proves [it]. There is nothing in the nature of the inductive principle that confines it within the limits of my own consciousness, when it exceptionally happens that an inference surpassing the limits of my consciousness can conform to inductive conditions.[100]

It is hard to avoid the conclusion that Mill has missed the point of O'Hanlon's objection. And if we do not have an inductive argument to the existence of the mind of another, we are left just with the conclusion drawn from analogy. However, as Reid has pointed out (and Mill agrees), an argument from analogy can yield nothing better than probabilities. And, as Reid has also pointed out, it is difficult to accept that our social relations are all based on probabilities.[101]

I want, finally, to raise another difficulty for what Mill has to say about other minds. Mill considers the question of our knowledge of the existence of other minds, and offers what he takes to be a proof of their existence. What he does not do is consider Augustine's question, Why do I so much as think that others may have minds? In order to believe that other minds exist I must have a completely general conception of mind, and the question is how I can account for the generality of the concept of mind.

In his discussion of the topic of generality Mill builds on some of the work of Sir William Hamilton. He agrees with Hamilton that the formation of general notions comes in four stages: first, a plurality of objects is presented; second, the objects presented are compared and judged to be similar or dissimilar by an act of the understanding; third, an act of volition which he calls 'attention' concentrates on those qualities recognized as similar; and fourth, the qualities judged similar are 'constituted into an exclusive object of thought'.[102] Mill then notes that, although we are able to synthesize into an object of thought those qualities judged similar, strictly speaking we have no general concept. Generality is maintained and utilized by the introduction of words. This is Mill's nominalism. Now the question arises, How would Mill apply this process to minds? A problem may be thought to emerge at the very first stage: what is the plurality of objects that the understanding judges for similarity and dissimilarity? The only objects there can be are the series of feelings that do not surpass *my* consciousness. But if I come to have my conception of mind by attending to this series of feelings, why should I take it that the concept I end up with has any application outside this series? It is not at all clear what reply Mill could give to this question. Like the philosophers whose views I considered in earlier chapters, Mill's account of how we achieve generality in our concepts encounters difficulties over our concept of mind.

BRIEF INTERLUDE: CARNAP AND SCHLICK

With the work of John Stuart Mill philosophy returns to its condition of finding nothing particularly problematic about our knowledge of the existence of another mind. The problem that Reid finds in the philosophical system that runs from Descartes to Berkeley is dismissed by Mill. There is no problem; we can prove the existence of other minds. With this proof Mill expects that he can avoid solipsism. Mill holds that there is an important asymmetry between the existence of an external world and the existence of other minds: our belief in the external world can be constructed within his psychological theory, while the existence of other minds (considered as nothing but a series of sensations) can be proved to exist in independence of our belief. As it is unclear that his proof is successful, it is also unclear whether Mill manages to avoid solipsism. The question of solipsism continues to hang over philosophy. I want now to turn very briefly to look at the work of two philosophers working in the early part of the twentieth century, Rudolph Carnap and Moritz Schlick, and to see how this work tries to account for our knowledge of other minds.

In the early part of the twentieth century a group of mathematicians, scientists and philosophers – later to be known as the Vienna Circle – came together to discuss matters of joint interest. A certain approach to philosophical issues was adopted by this group, which approach came to be known as logical positivism. In its 1929 manifesto the group traced its philosophical roots back to, *inter alia*, the empiricism of Berkeley and Hume.[103] In 1922 Moritz Schlick was appointed to a chair in philosophy at the University of Vienna and joined the group, soon establishing himself at its centre. About his philosophy Schlick once wrote:

In former days, philosophy used to ask about the ultimate ground of what exists, about the existence of God, the immortality and freedom of the soul, the meaning of the world and the guiding principle of conduct – but we ask nothing at all except: 'What do you really mean?'[104]

One reason for asking this question is to distinguish between those questions which have meaning and those that do not – metaphysics is then associated with the latter. The philosophy of the Vienna Circle came to be associated with a rejection of traditional metaphysical questions.

In 1926 Rudolph Carnap was invited by Schlick to Vienna and likewise became a member of the group. Carnap soon became one of the foremost exponents of the group's ideas. In *The Logical Structure of the World* Carnap writes that his concern is in the main 'with questions of epistemology, that is with questions of the reduction of cognitions one to another'.[105] Carnap takes the purpose of this reduction to be twofold: on the one hand, it simplifies some philosophical problems and, on the other, it shows that some philosophical problems are mere 'pseudoproblems'. Let us look briefly at the work of each of these philosophers in turn to see how it accommodates the mind of another.

At the start of *The Logical Structure of the World* Carnap recognizes three main types of known object: psychological objects, physical objects and cultural objects.[106] He then proposes to begin with psychological objects and to construct the other two from this. Carnap insists that nothing hangs on the identification of the starting point as psychological; all that is important is the very possibility of a logical construction. Although we can characterize the basic elements in this system as psychological, the system as a whole is, says Carnap, formal and neutral. Carnap recognizes the tendency of reductions of this sort to fall into the trap of behaviourism – of reducing the existence of introspectable minds to observable behaviour – and he wishes to avoid this trap. It is his belief that science must recognize both behaviour and introspection. In order to do this, he intends that his system accounts for others, not just as physical objects but as bearers of minds. To this end Carnap divides the psychological into what he calls the 'autopsychological' and the 'heteropsychological', which refer to one's own and another's mind respectively.[107] Carnap then proposes to begin with an autopsychological basis and to construct the heteropsychological out of this. Carnap's *method* is unashamedly solipsistic (he refers to it at one point as 'the position of *methodological solipsism*'),[108] but the end result is meant as an account of other minds. It is Carnap's view that a construction of other people that takes them to be purely physical things is an incomplete construction. Let us see how Carnap proposes to complete this construction.

Carnap insists that the heteropsychological can only be constructed through the mediation of a body. As things stand, what we observe are the gestures, facial expressions and vocal expressions of another body, and our construction is based on this. These physical processes stand in what Carnap calls an 'expressive' relation to the other's psychological processes.[109] While Carnap is clear that the assignment of the heteropsychological can only be to the body of the other and not to his mind, he also continues to insist that it is possible to distance his position from behaviourism. He writes, 'the entire *experience sequence of the other person consists of* nothing but *a rearrangement of my experiences and their constituents*'.[110] In other words, although what we are constructing is the experience of another, '*even here we do not desert the autopsychological basis*'.[111] Carnap takes it that understanding this will help us to appreciate that his system can avoid the trap of behaviourism. Carnap continues, 'all of "M's [the other's] objects" are still objects of the one constructional system and thus go back ultimately to the basic object of that system, i.e. to a relation which holds between elementary experiences (my experiences!)'.[112]

At the point that we construct the heteropsychological we have, says Carnap, a choice of two languages with which to talk about the other. We can choose to speak a purely physical language and mention the expressive gestures and words of the other, or we can choose to speak a psychological language. If we choose to speak a psychological language, however, we must be very careful. It may be true that this psychological language expresses something more than is expressed in a purely physical language (we express, for example, the other's joy), but this 'something more' must not be taken to be a fact. Carnap writes:

> By saying 'A is joyful' and not merely 'A shows facial expressions of such and such a form', I express that I have a representation of a feeling of joy, although a feeling of joy in the autopsychological sense, since I cannot know any other. However, to assume that by using the psychological instead of the physical language . . . we express a fact which goes beyond the physical state of affairs, is [a confusion].[113]

When pressed to accept that there is a difference here – the difference between solipsism and realism – Carnap remains unmoved. He asks us to consider two scientists – one a solipsist and one a realist – who want to know whether a certain subject, A, is really joyful or is merely simulating joyfulness. Carnap claims that, on the basis of the empirical criteria of psychology, these two scientists can reach an agreement. If these two scientists now put on their philosophers' hats, however, the realist will insist that, as well as the observed behaviour, A *really* has consciousness. Carnap then considers an objection which is designed to further the realist's position. He labels it the 'worm objection', and it is the following. There *is* a difference between the case where the other behaves in a joyous manner and is joyful, and the case where that joy is absent but the manner unaltered; the difference is this: if I know that an animal is conscious, it affects my actions. Thus, if I know that a worm feels pain, then I will refrain from stepping on it; the mere observation of writhing – without this knowledge – does not necessarily result in similar behaviour on my part. Carnap's response to the worm objection is to differentiate between empathy and cognition. He accepts that empathy may be produced where there is knowledge of consciousness, but this, he claims, is a practical and not a theoretical matter. One may adopt a practical position *vis à vis* the other as the result of thinking that the worm really has consciousness, but one's thought does not express anything that can be evaluated for truth and falsehood. In response to the realist position Carnap writes,

As concerns the physical and observable, hence only the testable, both psychologists agree. . . . The divergence between the two standpoints occurs beyond the factual, in a domain where in principle no experience is possible; hence, according to our criterion, they have no scientific significance.[114]

The realist's statement is what Carnap labels a 'pseudostatement', and pseudostatements are the product of metaphysics. A rejection of metaphysics, in this case, is a rejection of any *problem* concerning the mind of another. All that matters is what we can observe – the rest may add to our practical, but not to our theoretical, knowledge.

Like Carnap, Schlick rejects the realist's statement. The realist is here raising a question that can be seen to fall squarely within the metaphysical tradition. In an early paper, Schlick considers the question whether the colour that I experience when I look at a red object is the same that another experiences when she looks at the same red object (the problem sometimes referred to as the 'problem of the inverted-spectrum'). In response to this question Schlick writes:

It is generally admitted that the question . . . is [one] that absolutely cannot be answered. There is no method, nor can any be imagined, whereby the two reds could be compared and the question settled. The question has therefore no specifiable meaning. . . . It would in any case be pointless to raise such questions in science or philosophy, for it is certainly pointless to ask where we know that we can get no answer.[115]

Just as it is pointless to ask whether another has the *same* experience as I do, so it would be equally pointless to ask whether the other is experiencing anything at all. Schlick writes that questions about the existence of other minds are like questions about the existence of an external world: both are pointless. All we can say is how it is that we distinguish in science and in real life between the 'really existent' and the merely 'illusory'. Schlick, like Carnap, admits that to say this leaves one feeling that something has been left out. In the case of other minds what one feels to be left out is the other's consciousness. In response to this Schlick explains that what we feel is left out is 'wholly inexpressible'. He writes,

We have nothing against anyone attaching meaning to such a question, but must insist with all emphasis that this meaning cannot be stated.

These questions arise . . . by wrongly taking what can only be the content of acquaintance for the possible content of a cognition, that is, by attempting to communicate the essentially incommunicable, to express what cannot be expressed.[116]

Where Carnap distinguishes between empathy and cognition, Schlick distinguishes between acquaintance and knowledge. Schlick takes the distinction between acquaintance and knowledge to correspond to the distinction between what is incommunicable and what is communicable. Schlick explains the distinction in the following way. What I am acquainted with is the intrinsic content of experience, and this 'must forever remain private and can in no way be known in common to many individuals'; it is incommunicable.[117] What can be communicated, what can be known, are formal relations only. These formal relations have absolutely nothing of the quality of experience about them.[118]

Schlick recognizes that physics is often criticized for being concerned only with abstract formulae, and leaving out the qualitative aspect of the world. He believes, however, that once we understand the distinction between acquaintance and knowledge, we will come to see that the statements of physics are on an equal footing with the statements of the human sciences and the statements of daily life. Schlick writes, 'However paradoxical it may sound, it is literally true that all our statements, from the commonest utterances of daily life to the most complex assertions of science, reflect only formal relations of the world, and that absolutely nothing of the quality of experience enters into them.' And he continues:

For the meaning of those words employed by the poet or the psychologist can under all circumstances be stated and explained only by reverting to the formal relations between objects. The word 'green' is no richer (on the contrary, it is actually poorer) than the concept of the frequency of light-waves, which the physicist puts in its place.[119]

Schlick's point is that the humane sciences seek to do more than express certain truths; they aim to arouse and evoke experiences. He writes,

Deep experience is not of more value because it signifies a higher sort of knowledge – it has nothing at all to do with knowledge; and if worldly knowledge is not identical with worldly experience, this is not because knowledge has but poorly performed its task, but because by its nature and definition knowing is allotted from the outset a specific task lying in a direction entirely different from that of experience.[120]

Schlick ends his paper with some comments on metaphysics. The problem with the metaphysician, as Schlick sees it, is that he confuses living with knowing. If the metaphysician would simply confine himself to living, he would be fulfilled; what turns out to be a will o' the wisp is the metaphysician's insistence on knowing what can only be experienced.

In a later paper, Schlick considers the objection that the positivist programme of constructing all concepts out of the elementary data of consciousness amounts to an endorsement of solipsism. He admits that this objection is fuelled by Carnap's reference to his method as that of 'methodological solipsism', and by Carnap's talk of reducing all concepts to the autopsychological. However, Schlick reminds us that Carnap's solipsism is entirely dispensable; what is essential to his programme is the possibility of a logical construction, and that construction might have just as easily had a quite different starting point. The key to understanding that positivism need have no truck with solipsism is, according to Schlick, to recognize that primitive experience is neutral, it 'has no owner'. Schlick writes,

To see that primitive experience is *not* first-person experience seems to me to be one of the most important steps which philosophy must take towards the clarification of its deepest problems.[121]

In order to help us to see that primitive experience is not first-person experience, Schlick asks us to consider the following proposition:

(I)   I can feel only my pain.

(I) is sometimes taken to express the basis of the solipsist's position. The solipsist is a sceptic about the mind of another, and he bases his scepticism on the truth of the proposition expressed in (I). Schlick asks how we are to understand (I), and he offers two suggestions. First of all, (I) may be thought to be equivalent to:

(II)   I feel pain only when the body of M is hurt.

Schlick then considers (II) and shows that the proposition there expressed is false. To see this we need only imagine a world in which I feel pain whenever the body of my friend is hurt. This is not an empirically possible world, but it is a logically possible world. In such a world the proposition expressed by (II) would be false. But if (II) can be false, then it cannot be the basis for solipsism. The formulation of solipsism depends upon what Schlick calls the 'egocentric predicament', and, if (II) is meant to be a formulation of that predicament, it turns out to be an illusion.

The solipsist may insist that (II) is simply not equivalent to (I), and that it is indeed a correct statement of the egocentric predicament. The solipsist may insist that, in a logically possible world, when I feel pain in my friend's body, this must never be expressed thus: 'I feel my friend's pain.' The solipsist's point is that, although the place of the pain may be said to be my friend's body rather than my own, the pain I feel is *mine* and not my friend's. The solipsist expresses this in the following way:

(III)   I *can* only feel *my* pain.

The emphasis in (III) is designed to differentiate it from (I). But now Schlick asks the solipsist what the pronoun 'my' signifies in (III). He writes,

> It is easy to see that it does not signify *anything*; it is a superfluous word which may as well be omitted. 'I feel pain' and 'I feel my pain' are, according to the solipsist's definition, to have identical meaning; the word 'my', therefore, has no function in the sentence. If he says, 'The pain which I feel is my pain', he is uttering a mere tautology, because he has declared that whatever the empirical circumstances may be, he will never allow the pronouns 'your' or 'his' to be used in connection with 'I feel pain', but always the pronoun 'my'. This stipulation, being independent of empirical facts, is a logical rule . . .; the word 'can' in [III] (together with 'only') does not denote empirical impossibility, but *logical* impossibility. In other words: it would not be false, it would be *nonsense* (grammatically forbidden) to say 'I can feel someone else's pain'.[122]

Schlick concludes that the proposition which the solipsist uses as the basis of his position is 'strictly meaningless', and that consequently solipsism itself is meaningless. Experience is absolutely neutral, it 'has no owner' or bearer. Once we see this, we can see as well that positivism is not a form of solipsism. Schlick writes, 'This neutrality of experience – as against the subjectivity of the idealist – is one of the most fundamental points of true positivism.'[123] The positivist reduction is a construction based on neutral data.

The positivism of Carnap and Schlick needs to be differentiated from Mill's phenomenalism. Schlick himself characterizes the difference in the following way. Phenomenalism is a form of idealism that recognizes only sensations, and attempts to account for belief in an independent world of body in terms of various associations of sensations. Another form of idealism that Schlick identifies recognizes as well the existence of a distinctively mental or spiritual substance. What unifies both forms of idealism, as Schlick sees it, is that both tend to view the mental or spiritual, 'not as some late product brought forth by nature, but rather as the true material of which the world essentially consists'.[124] What Schlick opposes to idealism, then, is naturalism. According to naturalism, it is not the mind that is the starting point, but the natural world. What, then, can we say about the mind? Schlick responds, 'The mind, so to speak, would have its seat in the human body, and by means of the latter would experience the effects of external nature and elaborate them into ingenious theories and into the world-picture of which we have spoken.'[125] This is old-fashioned empiricism formulated in purely naturalistic terms.

Insofar as Schlick's philosophy can be seen to have its roots in earlier empiricism, it can be seen to have inherited the Cartesian framework of its predecessors. That framework may not be evident, however, because of the avowed naturalism of its exponents. Nevertheless, the framework can be detected at the heart of the neoempiricist's work. The Cartesian framework, as I have explained, introduces a logical divide between the subject and the world of bodies. In Schlick's work there is no examination of this logical divide, there is simply a rejection of one half of it. The mind is now to be taken to have 'its seat in the human body'. Just *how* the mind has this seat is not at all clear. It is arguable that, in their rush to banish traditional philosophical problems, the logical positivists simply adopt a naturalist stand from which the mind has been extruded. True, the positivists do not think of the mind existing in an immaterial substance, but how we are to think of mind's place in nature is entirely unresolved. Until philosophers examine – and reject – this logical division between the mind and its body, the Cartesian framework can be said still to be exerting its influence. It is this framework that bequeaths to philosophy a problem about other minds, and it is arguable that until philosophy rejects this framework it will continue to find other minds problematic. Schlick neither solves the problem nor explains why we think it arises in the first place. All he does is dismiss the problem as 'meaningless'.

Schlick's work contains a particular picture of the philosophical enterprise. To understand this picture, one must understand that to which it is opposed. Schlick looks back on the history of philosophy and identifies throughout this history a certain battle with the questions of the metaphysician. Waismann summarizes Schlick's attitude towards such questions thus:

> Such questions give rise to a peculiar mental uneasiness. Philosophy is the alleviation of this unrest. But in what does such alleviation consist? At this point it seems quite obvious to answer, in knowledge. . . . Profounder consideration shows that the road to a solution points in a different direction: In order to track it down, we must go back to the source the problem springs from, we must penetrate to the inner meaning of the terms employed, we must illuminate the darkness that lies about our concepts. This getting down to the roots of our uneasiness permits us to see that in all cases where an insoluble problem appears to be present, either the meaning of the question has been still unclear, or the problem is in principle soluble, since a statement of the meaning coincides, at bottom, with an indication of the road that leads to an answering of the question.[126]

Philosophy is to be cured of its metaphysical questions by a particular blend of naturalism and clarity about meaning. As we have seen above, one metaphysical problem that Schlick thinks philosophy will be cured of in this way is the problem of other minds. So what we need to ask ourselves is this: Is our mental uneasiness over other minds alleviated by the work of the logical positivists? The work of philosophy since the first quarter of the twentieth century attests to a negative reply to this question. If alleviation from unrest is the goal, philosophy clearly did not achieve it with the work of the logical positivists. One philosopher whose work may be taken to have shown just how difficult it is to identify the source of this unrest in philosophy is Wittgenstein. Let us now turn to an examination of Wittgenstein's work, paying particular attention to what he has to say about other minds.

CHAPTER VII

Wittgenstein and living with others

INTRODUCTION

In a series of remarks published posthumously under the title *Culture and Value* Wittgenstein writes:

> Nearly all my writings are private conversations with myself. Things that I say to myself *tête-a-tête*.[1]

This conversation is represented in Wittgenstein's writings by an interplay of voices: on the one side there is the voice that represents a particularly tempting line of thought, on the other side there is the voice that tries to draw us away from that thought. We could say that certain philosophical systems embody these tempting lines of thought, but this would be to restrict the temptation. As Wittgenstein sees it, there are certain lines of thought that have proved seductive not just to the philosopher but to us all. Wittgenstein finds that he himself is drawn to these thoughts. It is for this reason that his writings are a conversation with himself: they represent his struggle to resist these thoughts. By engaging in this struggle on the page, Wittgenstein invites us to engage in our own struggle with these thoughts.

It may be asked just why one should struggle so hard to resist a line of thought that *is* so natural – that is so hard to resist. The impetus to this struggle can be found in the philosophical problems that such a so-called 'natural' line of thought generates. Scepticism about the mind of another is one of the many philosophical problems that may be thought to be generated in this way. In order to appreciate how Wittgenstein's work engages with this problem, it is necessary to understand Wittgenstein's attitude towards philosophy. On occasion Wittgenstein compares his work to that of Sigmund Freud: Freud aimed to dissolve problems through psychoanalysis; Wittgenstein aimed to dissolve

181

philosophical problems with his work. After the struggle comes the peace, and the peace Wittgenstein wants to help us to find in philosophy will be measured by our ability to engage in our activities without the interruption of philosophical questions. Wittgenstein has compared the doing of philosophy with the untying of a knot: once we have done it – once we have untied the knot – we are no longer bothered by the questions. It is not that philosophical questions will have received an adequate reply; rather, the questions no longer arise.

In his work Wittgenstein contrasts the work of philosophy with that of science. Science, he says, can be characterized as an activity with the objective of *explanation*: first a phenomenon is identified and then an explanation of its nature is sought. Where we are unable to offer an explanation, we expect some future discovery will fill in the gap; what is now hidden will one day be revealed. Where science seeks explanation, philosophy looks for description. Where science looks to penetrate the phenomenon, philosophy seeks to engage with it. Where science craves generality, philosophy must look for individual differences. In the *Blue Book* Wittgenstein writes:

> Philosophers constantly see the method of science before their eyes, and are irresistibly tempted to ask and answer questions in the way science does. This tendency is the real source of metaphysics, and leads the philosopher into complete darkness. I want to say here that it can never be our job to reduce anything to anything, or to explain anything. Philosophy really *is* 'purely descriptive'.[2]

Wittgenstein had not always fully appreciated these differences. In his early work, the *Tractatus Logico-Philosophicus*, Wittgenstein holds that the essence of language lies hidden and that philosophers have to work to uncover it – if not today, then tomorrow. In time, however, he came to believe that the essence of language lies before us in the use we make of our everyday language. In conversations recorded by Waismann, Wittgenstein insists,

> The answers to philosophical questions must never be surprising. In philosophy you cannot discover anything. I myself, however, had not clearly enough understood this and offended against it. . . .
> The truth of the matter is that we have already got everything, and we have got it actually *present*; we need not wait for anything. We make the moves in the realm of the grammar of our

ordinary language, and this grammar is already there. Thus we have already got everything and need not wait for the future.[3]

One reason we don't appreciate that everything we need *is* present, is that the essence of language is often obscured by various illusions that language itself throws up. There are, for example, misleading analogies between the forms of expression in different parts of our language. We find Wittgenstein writing of our 'bewitchment' by language, and of philosophy as the struggle against this. Language bewitches us when it idles; we need to use language and observe our use.[4] When we do observe use we achieve an understanding of the phenomena that leaves us with no inclination to ask philosophical questions. We reach that peace which is free from philosophical perplexities.

The language that Wittgenstein is asking us to observe has both a spatial and a temporal dimension.[5] By recognizing this we move away from thinking of language as fixed, as something on which we can take up an objective perspective. We appreciate language's dimensions by appreciating our employment of it. Throughout his work, we find Wittgenstein emphasizing that, if we want to understand the phenomenon of language, we must reflect on the grammar of our ordinary language. Consider, for example, the opening remark of Wittgenstein's *Philosophical Remarks*:

A proposition is completely logically analysed if its grammar is made completely clear: no matter what idiom it may be written or expressed in.[6]

Wittgenstein's appeal to grammar here can be misleading. Traditionally, what philosophers have understood by 'grammar' is something along the lines of a hidden structure or rules. Waismann gives a good account of this traditional use of the term:

By 'grammar' we mean everything to do with language that can be laid down even before language is employed. The opposite to it will be the *employment* of language.[7]

Wittgenstein in effect asks us to reverse Waismann's understanding of grammar. Waismann's understanding of grammar leads to the formulation of formal languages, which in turn become the object of our study. What Wittgenstein asks us to notice is that, while the logician's symbol is fixed, the grammar of our language is fluid. Instead of developing a symbolism, we need to chart the movement of our language. The grammar of our language is not hidden from us, but lies before us in our use of language. This grammar – this use – is highly diverse. We do not need to try and unify differing parts of our use and ask what makes them all the same (the old mistake which comes from the 'craving for generality' which, in turn comes from 'our preoccupation with the method of science').[8] What we need is a correct description of this grammar.

In this chapter I want to look at the grammar of our talk about sensations and experiences – our own and that of others. In the following section I shall concentrate on what Wittgenstein has to say about this in the *Philosophical Remarks* and in his conversations recorded by Waismann. In the subsequent two sections I shall look at what I shall call the 'mature view' which is largely centred around the *Philosophical Investigations*.

EARLY THOUGHTS

The period from 1929 until 1937 marks a period of profound development in Wittgenstein's thoughts on a number of topics. Among the issues that preoccupied him during this time are the twin problems of solipsism and behaviourism.[9] The topic of solipsism surfaces most clearly. In his conversations with Waismann, Wittgenstein considers two propositions which the solipsist may use to express his position:

(i)   I cannot feel pain in your tooth; and
(ii)   I cannot feel your toothache.

Wittgenstein remarks that the proposition expressed in (i) has a clear sense and expresses empirical knowledge which we can imagine to be false. Thus, I can imagine feeling a pain and pointing to your tooth in answer to the question, 'Where does it hurt?' It must be remembered, however, that, although I might feel pain when your tooth is touched, the pain I feel is *my* pain. This, in effect, is what the solipsist is trying to express in (ii). But what the solipsist fails to appreciate is that the proposition in (ii) has no clear sense; it is 'sheer nonsense'.[10] Wittgenstein then points out that the word 'I' belongs among those that can be eliminated from our language. And he remarks,

We could adopt the following way of representing matters: if I, L. W., have toothache, then that is expressed by means of the proposition 'There is toothache'. But if that is so, what we now express by the proposition 'A has toothache', is put as follows: 'A is behaving as L. W. does when there is toothache'.[11]

Now, of course, this way of speaking must be mirrored in each speaker. In his conversations with Waismann, Wittgenstein speaks of 'many different languages, each of which has a different man at its centre'.[12] Wittgenstein then makes several observations about these languages. The first is that we can translate these languages into one another. The second is that only what these languages have in common mirrors anything. And the third is that one of these languages has 'a distinctive status, namely that one in which I can as it were say that I feel *real* pain'.[13] The third observation is connected to the second, for Wittgenstein claims that the distinctive status that each language has does not mirror anything; it cannot be expressed in language but lies in its application.[14] Wittgenstein then elaborates the point. He attempts to explain the way our language misleads us – with its inclusion of the personal pronoun – into either solipsism or behaviourism. We have just seen how the personal pronoun is exploited by the solipsist. In *Philosophical Remarks* 65 Wittgenstein tries to show the way it is exploited by the behaviourist. He writes:

> The logic of our language is so difficult to grasp at this point: our language employs the phrases 'my pain' and 'his pain', and also the expressions 'I have (or feel) a pain' and 'He has (or feels) a pain'. An expression 'I feel my pain' or 'I feel his pain' is nonsense. And it seems to me that, at bottom, the entire controversy over behaviourism turns on this.

Wittgenstein here appears to be explaining the consequences of not appreciating that the sense of any distinctive status is something that can only be expressed in an individual's application of his language. What we must remember is that '"I have a pain" is a sign of a completely different kind when I am using the proposition, from what it is to me on the lips of another; the reason being that it is senseless, as far as I'm concerned, on the lips of another until I know through which mouth it was expressed.'[15]

Wittgenstein's rejection of behaviourism is made explicit in his 1930–1933 lectures which are recorded by G. E. Moore.[16] Moore reports Wittgenstein as asking whether when we say 'He has toothache' his toothache is only his behaviour, whereas when I say, 'I have toothache' I am not talking about my behaviour. To this question Wittgenstein answered, 'no', and Moore reports that Wittgenstein 'implied' that when we pity someone who has a toothache we do not pity him for putting his hand to his cheek. Moore then reports Wittgenstein as introducing another question, namely, Is another person's toothache 'toothache' in the same sense as mine? To this question Wittgenstein answered, 'yes'. One can see Wittgenstein's negative reply to the first question as connected to his positive reply to the second. We can see Wittgenstein here drawing attention to the fact that, despite an asymmetry in our use of the phrase 'has toothache' in the first person case and the third, there is nonetheless a univocity of meaning. This is something we need to understand: how can there be univocity of meaning where there is an asymmetry of use? The behaviourist fails to appreciate the univocity and so misunderstands the asymmetry. The solipsist wants to say that the univocity is an illusion because there can only be *my* pain.

The language whose centre I am has a distinctive status, and so does the language whose centre you are. If this distinctive status cannot be expressed in language, however, then there is an inclination to think that communication in language between individuals is limited: individuals may communicate about the world they inhabit, but they cannot talk about their experiences. In *Zettel* 87 Wittgenstein writes:

> This is likely to be the point at which it is said that only form, not content, can be communicated to *others*. – So one talks to oneself *about the content*.[17]

This is a very tempting picture. Once it is clear that communication between individuals is limited in a certain way, it is very natural to concentrate on one's *own* relationship to what cannot be expressed in language. As David Pears points out: it may be fair enough to hold that when two people communicate, reference to sensations drops out of the picture, but sensations are real enough to the subject *before* she begins to communicate.[18] It is as if we confront the experience directly in our own case, and we try to find a form of words to express this. The problem is that, every time we try to formulate a description of this experience, we end up leaving something out. It soon begins to look as if nothing descriptive can ever be as immediate as we want. In *Philosophical Remarks* 68 Wittgenstein writes:

Instead of a description, what would then come out would be that inarticulate sound with which many writers would like to begin philosophy. ('I have, knowing of my knowledge, consciousness of something.')

You simply can't begin before the beginning.[19]

What we notice is that, not only do we attempt again and again to express that which cannot be expressed, but we do this because we have a feeling that there is something there to be expressed if we could only figure out a way to do it.

By the time Wittgenstein comes to prepare his 'Notes for Lectures on "Private Experience" and "Sense Data"' (that is, sometime between late 1934 and early 1936) we find him writing:

It is as though, although you can't tell me exactly what happens inside you, you can nevertheless tell me something general about it. By saying e.g. that you are having an impression which can't be described.

As it were: There is something further about it, only you *can't say* it; you can only make the general statement.

It is this idea which plays hell with us.[20]

It would appear that the distinction between what can be described in language and what can be expressed in its application does not so much banish metaphysics as invite it. There is the ever-present temptation to think that there is *something* that simply defies description. And once we allow this, we find ourselves once again with a problem about the mind of another: 'I know what I mean by "toothache" but the other person can't *know* it.'[21] We notice an asymmetry between what we observe in the case of the other and what we feel in our own case, and we 'look on this as a mirror image of the nature of things'.[22] We give this asymmetry a metaphysical underpinning; we take it to reflect the nature of things. The asymmetry, understood in this way, leads us to talk of the immediate experience of one's own pain and of behaviour that shields the other's experiences from me. I can only know of another's experiences indirectly. In this way we are led to talk of conjecture, of hypothesis; we feel the need to rely on analogies and induction. Wittgenstein writes:

I wished to say that talking about his toothache at all was based upon a supposition, a supposition which by its very essence could not be verified.[23]

All I have to go on in the case of the other is his behaviour, while in my own case I know that there is something more than behaviour – there is something *inside*. I am led to wonder whether or not there is something inside the other too; and I think that my idea of another is somehow bound up with the idea of myself. With what knowledge I have from my own case, the best I can do in the case of another is form an unverifiable hypothesis. About all this Wittgenstein writes:

> But if you look closer you will see that this is an entire misrepresentation of the use of the word 'toothache'.[24]

We observe the asymmetry in our language use and we are led into the murky depths of metaphysics. Language is bewitching us. In the next section I want to look at Wittgenstein's proposal for how to avoid these murky depths.

THE MATURE VIEW

In the *Philosophical Investigations* 116 Wittgenstein writes,

> When philosophers use a word – "knowledge", "being", "object", "I", "proposition", "name" – and try to grasp the *essence* of the thing, one must always ask oneself: is the word ever actually used in this way in the language-game which is its original home?
>
> What *we* do is try to bring words back from their metaphysical to their everyday use.

As we can see from the previous section, the process of bringing words back from their metaphysical to their everyday use is an arduous process. It is arduous because language leads us astray – or rather it leads us astray when we try to impose certain ideas upon it. As we have just seen, one idea which, if imposed on our language, will lead us into difficulties is that of insisting that the asymmetry we observe in our use of sensation words must mirror something about the nature of sensation. Wittgenstein takes it that the imposition of ideas on language is the result of our seeing philosophy on the model of science: we yearn for deep explanations and in our yearning we spurn the surface descriptions. In *The Blue Book* Wittgenstein writes,

> But let's not forget that a word hasn't got a meaning given to it, as it were, by a power independent of us, so that there could be

a kind of scientific investigation into what the word *really* means. A word has the meaning someone has given to it.[25]

Once again, Wittgenstein urges us to look for the meaning of our words and sentences in language use. Only if we do this can we begin to move away from metaphysical problems. What we begin to realize as we study Wittgenstein's work is that language can bewitch us in a myriad of ways. We must work very hard to avoid the fascinating depths into which certain understandings of language lead. We must remember that what we need to observe in order to achieve peace and freedom from philosophical problems is something ordinary. However, even once one has accepted the idea that use is what is important in the study of language, one can be led astray about just what this use consists of. There is a constant temptation to think of use as something that co-exists with the sign. What we must appreciate is the following:

> The sign (the sentence) gets its significance from the system of signs, from the language to which it belongs. Roughly: understanding a sentence means understanding a language. As part of the system of language, one may say, the sentence has life.[26]

In his work around this time we find Wittgenstein connecting language use to the playing of a game – what he calls a 'language game'. Language games are many and various; they come into existence, alter, and go out of existence. In the *Philosophical Investigations* 23 Wittgenstein writes:

> Here the term "language-*game*" is meant to bring into prominence the fact that the *speaking* of language is part of an activity, or a form of life.[27]

Language-games are connected to the whole, and if we want to understand the use of any particular word or phrase we must understand the whole into which it fits. In *The Blue Book* Wittgenstein connects language-games with the more primitive activity of a child beginning to learn a language. If we start by examining these more primitive activities we find, he says, they are continuous with more complex activities, and that we can 'build up the more complicated forms from the primitive ones by gradually adding new forms'.[28]

Let us, for now, put aside temptation, and look at that segment of our language which is connected with sensation and experience. Let us see how we operate with sensation and experience words, starting with the way that a child comes to learn the use of these words. And as we examine our 'system of language' here, let us pay particular attention to the fact that, despite the asymmetry in their use, these words mean the same thing when used in connection with me as when used in connection with another. It is Wittgenstein's belief that a proper description of our use of these words should leave us with no temptation to raise any questions about the mind of another.

Wittgenstein begins by considering situations in which we might teach a child to use sentences incorporating words and phrases such as 'so-and-so has a toothache' or 'so-and-so sees red'; in other words, he begins by considering our use of such words and phrases in connection with others. This may seem a curious place to start, since we might think that it is precisely the case of others that is problematic. If we look back at the work of philosophers from Descartes to Mill (excluding Reid), we find that they all begin by considering what they take to be the unproblematic case, my own. As we have seen, however, this starting point raises certain questions about our knowledge of *another* mind. These questions, on the whole, are then answered by appeal to conjecture, hypothesis, analogy, induction and the like. As we saw towards the end of the previous section, Wittgenstein takes this way of thinking about the mind of another to be connected with a mistaken understanding of the asymmetry which we rightly observe our words to have when used in connection with myself and others. In *The Blue Book* Wittgenstein raises a serious question about the attempt to start from one's own case and to understand our knowledge of another mind from this basis. He asks, How can I *believe* that another has an experience of, say, pain? The question Wittgenstein raises here is the one I attributed to Augustine in Chapter II. Wittgenstein is even clearer about the question:

> Also I am told: 'If you pity someone for having pains, surely you must at least *believe* that he has pains'. But how can I even *believe* this? How can these words make sense to me? How could I even have come by the idea of another's experience if there is no possibility of any evidence for it?[29]

These are questions asked by a conceptual solipsist. The conceptual solipsist takes it that I know what pain is by some sort of inward reflection, and that words relating to experience in my own case are unproblematic because they have their meaning immediately. It is the very picture of what makes the use of these words unproblematic in my own case that makes my use of those same words in connection with others problematic. The conceptual solipsist is to be distinguished from the epistemological solipsist, and his question is prior to the one raised by the epistemological solipsist. Augustine raises this question in order to respond to it; Wittgenstein raises this question in order to point up the difficulty inherent in answering it.

Immediately upon posing the conceptual solipsist's question Wittgenstein writes:

> But isn't this a queer question to ask? *Can't* I believe that someone else has pains? Is it not quite easy to believe this? – Is it an answer to say that things are as they appear to common sense? – Again, needless to say, we don't feel these difficulties in ordinary life.[30]

When we do look at our language-games that incorporate words relating to sensations and experiences we find that we unselfconsciously and unproblematically use these words in connection with others. To understand how this is possible, we need to look at what we do. If we see someone crying, holding his cheek, and refusing to eat, we might say, 'Poor Nick, he has a toothache'. And we might do this as much in the presence of the language-learning child as we do in the presence of someone who already has a good grasp of language. In saying what we do in these circumstances we expose the child to our use of language and, as a result of this exposure, the child comes in time to be able to use this language for himself. At this point, however, we have exposed the child to only the smallest fragment of our language in connection with sensation words. A child who understands only that certain behaviour is connected with our use of these words understands next to nothing about our use of them. We need to fill out our description.

One way in which we need to fill out the description of the language-game with sensation words is to take account of its complexity. When we teach a child about the behaviour that we associate with sensation and experience words we also teach the child that there are times when this behaviour may be lacking and the other may still be in pain, and we also teach the child that there will be times that we will think that the relevant behaviour is present and yet the other is not in pain. The child also comes to learn the contexts and situations which give rise to these anomalies. Thus, for example, the child is taught that a person crying out on the television is not *really* in pain, or that mummy is only pretending to cry, or that sometimes people are very brave and do not shout out in a library even though they may have hurt themselves. A child who has not learned about these possibilities has not fully understood our use of sensation words.

Although we can say that concealment and pretence are very much part of our use of sensations words, we must understand how these words are *normally* used. It is for this reason that we begin with straightforward and genuine cases of the expression of pain and complicate the picture from there. Thus we find Wittgenstein writing:

> It is clear that we in our language use the words "seeing red" in such a way that we can say "A sees red but doesn't show it"; on the other hand it is easy to see that we should have no use for these words if their application was severed from the criteria of behaviour. That is to say: to the language game which we play with these words it is both essential that the people who play it behave in the particular way we call expressing (saying, showing) what they see, and also that sometimes they more or less conceal what they see.
>
> Balance. The point of the game depends upon what *usually* happens.[31]

Universal mendacity, then, has no place in our language-game. Of course, this is not to deny occasional mendacity. Occasional mendacity is one of the complications in our use of language that the child must learn. The child must learn that sometimes people lie about whether or not they are in pain if she is to learn our language. Wittgenstein writes:

> When I say that moaning is the expression of toothache, then under certain circumstances the possibility of its being the expression without the feeling behind it mustn't enter my game.
>
> It is senseless to say: the expression may always lie.[32]

Wittgenstein points out that the fact that language requires a background of truth does not help us to know when someone is speaking the truth and when they are telling a lie. We can still, in certain circumstances, question whether the person who is holding his cheek *really* has toothache, or whether the person who appears to be acting quite normally is *really* suffering from toothache. This is just what our use of sensation words allows.

Even with the introduction of the possibility of pretence, we have so far only given a very partial description of our language in connection with sensation words. The child who uses sensation words only in connection with others has not yet learned our language-game. Sensation words are also used in connection with oneself. Now there is something of the utmost importance that the child must understand who is learning to use sensation words in connection both with herself and with others and it is this:

> My own relation to my words is wholly different from other people's.[33]

Or as Wittgenstein writes in another place:

> I do not listen to [my words] and thereby learn something about myself. They have a completely different relation to my actions than to the actions of others. . . .
>
> My words and my actions interest me in a completely different way than they do someone else. (My intonation also, for instance.) I do not relate to them as an observer.[34]

Wittgenstein is here reminding us of the asymmetry in our use of sensation and experience words.

This asymmetry must be borne in mind when we turn from consideration of the ascription of sensations to others to a consideration of sensations to oneself. But although this asymmetry must be borne in mind, we need not take it that there is anything surprising or problematic about what is going on in one's own case. The asymmetry is only problematic if one begins, as philosophers working in the Cartesian tradition do, by reflecting on one's own case. But Wittgenstein does not begin here. He begins by describing the way we use our words – pointing out how we teach the use of words to children – and there is an acknowledgement in this that our use of words involves an important asymmetry. It is this that we must teach our child. Once Annie has learned when it is appropriate to say, 'Nick is in pain', she also must learn when it is appropriate to say that she herself is in pain. Say we see Annie fall over, hit her head on a stone and cry out. We pick her up and say, 'Ow, that must hurt – that must be painful; Annie hit her head on a hard stone.' We might ask Annie, 'Does that hurt?', 'Are you in pain?' In due course Annie will come to learn to say that she is in pain in these and similar circumstances. In fact Wittgenstein claims that we teach the child to replace her crying with these words. He writes,

We teach the child to use the words "I have toothache" to replace its moans, and this was how I too was taught the expression.[35]

Once the child can use sensation words in her own case, she must also learn that she can lie to others about whether or not she is in pain: she can say she is in pain just to get attention, and sometimes she can be a very grown up girl and not make any fuss at all even though it hurts a lot. The child is now really beginning to use sensation and experience words in the same way we do. She appreciates the asymmetry in use between the application of these words in her own case and in the case of another, and she understands as well the way these words can be used by both parties to conceal and to deceive. The child is beginning to play a rather complex and elaborate language-game with these words. And we are beginning to have a rather complex description of the language-game that the child is beginning to learn.

So far I have concentrated on the first two features of what Wittgenstein calls our language-games: their connection with the way a child learns a language, and the way we move from more primitive to more complex language-games by a process of accretion. Wittgenstein also mentions another feature of a language-game. In one place he writes: 'If he is to play a language-game, the possibility of this will depend upon his own and other people's reactions.'[36] These reactions play a crucial part in the development of that activity we call speaking a language. Let us now describe the role they play.

References to our nature are scattered throughout Wittgenstein's later writing. In one place he writes:

Suppose I said: The expressions get their importance from the fact that they are not used coolly but that we can't help using them. This is as though I said: laughter gets its importance only through being a *natural* expression, a natural phenomenon, not an artificial code.[37]

How are we to understand this reference to our nature? Before we try to answer this, let us look at two other places where Wittgenstein talks of nature. One place is in the course of a discussion about teaching a child to use experience words in connection with behaviour. Wittgenstein looks at the way we teach a child to say that someone is blind, and then he asks the following question about our use of the word 'blind': 'What if [a man] saw all the time but nevertheless behaved exactly like a blind man?' In response to this question Wittgenstein writes:

> Or should we say: "Nature wouldn't play such tricks on us!"[38]

Another place where Wittgenstein makes reference to nature – this time to *our* nature – is in the course of a discussion of different possible ways of teaching sensation words to a child. He considers that from the beginning, instead of teaching the child to say 'he has toothache', we should simply teach him the less committal 'I think he has toothache'. But he immediately follows up this consideration with another: consider that, instead of teaching the child to say 'I have toothache' in circumstances where she is liable to cry out whenever she has a cold drink and bites sweets and the like, we teach her to say, 'I believe I have toothache'. In response to the latter way of speaking Wittgenstein writes,

> But why not in the child's own case? Because there the tone of voice is simply *determined* by nature.[39]

How are we to understand these references to nature? What is Wittgenstein saying about the part that nature – *our* nature – plays in our language game? It is important to remember that our concern is with our everyday use of language – not some formal or invented language. And we must also remember that we are interested in a philosophical understanding of language, not a scientific one. Now it is a notable feature of our language that it is something that comes to us quite naturally. This is not to say that we do not develop and invent the signs of our language, but that the urge to do this at all is part of our nature. Furthermore, the impetus to use language can be seen to be part of a larger natural impulse we all have to react to the world – the world including other people – in certain ways: we incline our heads to hear sweet sounds; we bend to sniff an aromatic flower; we jump when we are approached unexpectedly from behind; we reach out to help someone who has hurt themselves. These reactions are not imposed; they are most natural to us. This is the context in which we develop language. Thus, if we think about the way the child cries when it has been wounded by a sharp object – or has a sharp toothache – it would not be appropriate for us to teach the child to say, 'I believe I have a pain/toothache'. In these circumstances, given our nature, we teach the child to say in no uncertain terms, 'I am in pain/have toothache'. If we consider the blind man, and then we consider the possibility that the man may be normally sighted and only acting like a blind man, we must recall the following: The world and the people in it are such that some are normally sighted and some are blind; furthermore, people are such that sometimes they play act and sometimes they lie and sometimes they want to fool those around them – this is all part of human nature. The world and the people in it are *not* such as to behave at absolutely *all* times as if blind while being normally sighted. If this had been the world we found ourselves in, we would not have developed the everyday language that we in fact developed. (Indeed, it is hard to see how we could have developed any language at all in these circumstances.) But for now it is best not to dwell on what might have been. Our nature forms part of the context – the circumstances – in which we come to develop our language.

When Wittgenstein calls our attention to the place in our language-games of our natural activities and reactions, he does not intend simply to draw our attention to our reaction to, say, pain; he also intends to call attention to the way we react to each other when we are in pain. We share *these* reactions just as we do all others, and these shared reactions are equally fundamental to our language-game. The child behaves in a certain way and another responds to this behaviour in a certain way. *All* these reactions form part of the context in which we learn to use sensation and experience words. Wittgenstein writes:

> It is only in the normal case that the use of a word is clearly prescribed; we know, are in no doubt, what to say in this or that case. The more abnormal the case, the more doubtful it becomes what we are to say. And if things were quite different from what they are – if there were for instance no characteristic expression of pain, of fear, of joy; if rule became exception and exception rule; or if both became phenomena of roughly equal frequency – this would make our normal language-games lose their point.[40]

There is a further point to notice about what Wittgenstein has to say about nature in connection with our use of language. Wittgenstein notes that we have reactions to things and to other people, and he also notes that we agree in these reactions. This is at least as important as that we have these reactions in the first place. Again, we might ask what would have happened had we not agreed in our reactions, but, as before, we needn't dwell on this situation; it is not the situation we find ourselves in. We do agree in our reactions, and this is an important part of our coming to have the language that we do. Wittgenstein writes:

> If language is to be a means of communication there must be agreement not only in definitions but also (queer as this may sound) in judgements.[41]

We have, we might say, a natural involvement with the world and with others, and this natural involvement forms part of the context in which we come to speak a language. Now there is something we need to notice about all this: given the importance of the world and others in the development of language, it is hard to see how there is going to be room for the sceptic to come along and question the very existence of this world and these others. But let us not now worry about the sceptic. Let us get on with the job of describing our use of that portion of language that involves sensation and experience words.

Let us look a little more closely at some of the reactions we naturally have – and naturally share – towards each other. Wittgenstein writes,

> We want to say: "When we mean something, it's like going up to someone, . . ." We go up to the thing we mean.[42]

Wittgenstein is here talking about the connection between meaning and the way we react to both people and things. Now there are two questions we might ask about what Wittgenstein is saying here in connection with our use of sensation words: (i) Who is it that we 'go up to'? ; and (ii) How is it that we go up to someone? In response to (i) we might consider what Wittgenstein writes in *Philosophical Investigations*, 281:

> It comes to this: only of a living human being and what resembles (behaves like) a living human being can one say: it has sensations; it sees; it hears; is deaf; is conscious or unconscious.

This response raises some interesting further questions. We want to ask, What about non-human animals?; What about machines and other automata?; What about plants? We must recall, however, that the original question asked who is it that we *naturally* react to – 'go up to' – with our use of sensation words. If we observe ourselves, what we find is that we react to living human beings with our use of these words, and we also react to *some* non-human animals that behave in

197

ways that resemble the ways that living human beings behave. We must, however, be careful here: what we will find is that only *some* of our sensation words will apply outside the human sphere. We find, for example, that we say of some non-human animals that they may be angry, frightened, happy or unhappy, or startled. The patterns into which these words fit are such as to apply to more than human animals. But there are limits – both to how far into the animal kingdom even these words may apply, and to the range of experience words that apply outside the sphere of human interactions. There are some animals that exhibit a pattern that is too simple even for us to speak of them as 'angry' (the behaviour of an ant, perhaps, or an amoeba); and words like 'hopeful' and 'worried' appear only to apply to human beings.

Let us now turn to the second of the questions identified above: *How* do we 'go up to someone'? Again, we must look at our natural reactions to people, to animals, to automata. One thing we notice about the way we go up to another human being is that we react, not just to their facial expression, but to their whole body: to the tilt of the head, the sway of the hip, the slump of the shoulders and the like. In fact, we take in a much wider context even than this. Wittgenstein writes in one place:

> I see a picture which represents a smiling face. What do I do if I take the smile now as a kind one, now as malicious? Don't I often imagine it with a spatial and temporal context which is one either of kindness or malice? Thus I might supply the picture with the fancy that the smiler was smiling down on a child at play, or again on the suffering of an enemy.[43]

Here we find our reactions shifting as the wider context shifts. The smile takes on different meaning for us – we react differently to it – depending upon the circumstance.

We are now at the point where we can appreciate a further – very important – complexity in our use of sensation and experience words. If we look carefully at the way we react to one another – at how we interact with one another – we will find that our reactions take on a certain quality. Consider, for example, that you are in pain and shout out. I react. *How* do I react? Well, this depends upon how I hear the shout. If I see a sharp object piercing your flesh as you shout, I react in a way we call 'assuredly': I am sure you are in pain. If, however, I see no sharp object I may react in a way we call 'hesitantly': I am unsure whether you really are in pain or are trying to fool me for some reason. I can imagine a situation where I might move from a hesitant reaction to an assured reaction. For example, I notice that you are holding your jaw and that there is a half-eaten bowl of ice-cream on the table. Now I can see a reason for your shout, and I react to you with more assurance. I can also imagine becoming more deeply hesitant. For example, I see nothing that could be taken to have caused you pain and I remember that you are a well-known practical joker. Now my hesitancy is not dispelled; I react in a way we call 'doubting': I doubt that you are in pain. Wittgenstein writes in one place:

> Being sure that someone is in pain, doubting whether he is, are so many natural, instinctive, kinds of behaviour towards other human beings, and our language is merely an auxiliary to, and further extension of this relation. Our language-game is an extension of primitive behaviour. (For our *language-game* is behaviour.) (Instinct).[44]

Doubt (and its opposite) is embedded in our (now rather complex) language-game. Doubt is as much a part of our reaction to another's behaviour as assurance is. Both are rooted in our reactions to one another's behaviour. Our reaction may begin as one of assurance, but waver; or it may begin as doubt, but become assured. And these are not the only reactions we may have to the behaviour we encounter. My reaction to the possibility of pretence in another may be complicated, as this description brings out:

> Uncertainty: whether a man really has this feeling, or is merely putting up an appearance of it. But of course it is also uncertain whether he is not merely putting up an appearance of pretending. This pretence is merely rarer and does not have grounds that are so easily understood.[45]

The end result of this endless complexity in our responses to one another is that we can say of some people that they are transparent to us, while we say of others that they are a complete enigma.[46] And we can also say that some people are better than others at understanding other people. Despite the fact that we generally are in agreement in our reactions, there will be individual differences. Some people have a better knowledge of mankind. This is why Wittgenstein can write,

> There is in general no such agreement over the question whether an expression of feeling is genuine or not.[47]

What about teaching someone to understand those around him? This is possible – up to a certain point. One can give another tips, point them in the right direction, and the like. But we cannot teach just anyone in this way. If, perchance, there was a person whose nature was deficient with respect to their natural reactions to others, we would be very hard pressed to teach this person. What we can teach must be rooted in our nature. And what we teach is both the understanding of others and the use of language in connection with experience and sensation words. What we must remember is that, just as that understanding is fluid, so that use is ambiguous:

> A picture is conjured up which seems to fix the sense *unambiguously*. The actual use, compared with that suggested by the picture, seems like something muddied.[48]

At least *our* use is ambiguous, *our* nature is such that it does not fix our reactions to things. There is, however, a limit to this ambiguity. The ambiguity we have been describing has all been in relation to living things. But we may ask, what is our natural reaction to a machine, or an automaton? Wittgenstein says this:

> Our attitude to what is alive and to what is dead, is not the same. All our reactions are different. – If anyone says, "That cannot simply come from the fact that a living thing moves about in such-and-such a way and a dead one not", then I want to intimate to him that this is a case of the transition 'from quantity to quality'.[49]

But what about the possibility that the people around me now are automata – can't I imagine this? To this Wittgenstein responds,

> If I imagine it now – alone in my room – I see people with fixed looks (as in a trance) going about their business – the idea is perhaps a little uncanny. But just try to keep hold of this idea in the midst of your ordinary intercourse with others, in the street, say! Say to yourself, for example, "The children over there are mere automata; all their liveliness is mere automatism." And you will either find these words becoming quite meaningless; or you will produce in yourself some kind of uncanny feeling, or something of this sort.[50]

Once again we see how what we say is rooted in our natural responses. We do not respond to people and to automata in the same way. If you ask, 'But how do you know that that individual over there isn't an automaton?', the only reply one can give is that that is not what we call 'an automaton'.

Time and again Wittgenstein draws our attention to how we use our language – the complexity of that use – and to the way that use is rooted in our natures. If you ask how I know that someone is in pain, or that someone is pretending to be in pain, or is in a drugged trance, or is not an automaton, the answer is always the same: 'I have learned English.'[51] As Wittgenstein writes at one point,

> You learned the *concept* 'pain' when you learned language.[52]

At this point we probably have enough of a description of our language to understand the asymmetry that exists in connection with our use of sensation and experience words. If we look at how we use these words, the asymmetry can receive a very full description. Furthermore, the description we have given of the asymmetry is such as to make it clear how it is that the word 'pain' has a univocal meaning. Given this description it is hard to see how any *problem* can arise about others. My concept of a sensation such as pain is shaped by all the different things I have learned to do with the word 'pain'. My concept is, no doubt, a little rough around the edges, but so is the use that shaped it. In *The Blue Book* Wittgenstein says that 'when we look at such simple forms of language the mental mist which seems to enshroud our ordinary use of language disappears'.[53] This may be true, but the mists can roll in again almost imperceptibly. In order to keep them at bay, it may be necessary to do more than describe what we do. This is the part of Wittgenstein's work that has come to be known as 'the private language argument'. I turn in the next and last section of this chapter to an examination of that argument.

THE PRIVATE LANGUAGE ARGUMENT

> Philosophy, as we use the word, is a fight against the fascination which forms of expression exert upon us.[54]

In the previous section we began a description of our use of sensation and experience words which looked to give us an understanding of the univocity of these words in the face of an asymmetry in their use. A certain amount of natural doubt is embedded in this use. But it is not the traditional doubt of the sceptic. The traditional sceptic asks us why we think that there are sensations and experiences where we can only see a moving body. The body we see might have sensations and experiences very different from our own, or it may have none at all. Wittgenstein proposes an analogy for the way the sceptic thinks we use experience and sensation words:

> Suppose everyone had a box with something in it: we call it a "beetle". No one can look into anyone else's box, and everyone says he knows what a beetle is only by looking at *his* beetle. – Here it would be quite possible for everyone to have something different in his box. One might even imagine such a thing constantly changing.[55]

We could substitute 'pain' for 'beetle' in the above paragraph and we would have a picture which would explain the asymmetry which we observe in our use of sensation words. Thus, pain is something I *have*, it is *mine* – like an object I keep tucked away inside me in that box I call 'my mind'. This picture would explain why another would have to look at my moving body if she wanted to know whether I was in pain: as the pain is inside me, you can only know whether it is there if I let you know through my movements. Of course, my movements can indicate that I have a pain inside me when I don't, and I might have a pain inside me that my movements don't indicate. More extreme situations can be envisaged: I might have a completely empty mental box, but my body always moves in the same way as someone whose box is full of sensations and experiences; or the pain in my box might disappear and be replaced by a feeling of elation, even as I am crying out; and, of course, each of us might have something very different in our box, although we continue to use words like 'pain' in all the same situations. This picture supports all these situations. It supports them because on this picture there is an insurmountable barrier between people that makes it the case that people are unable to look inside another mind to see if there really is a pain there and what it is like. On this picture my relationship to others is tenuous: it can slip away at a moment's reflection. Indeed, this is precisely what the sceptic about other minds urges me to acknowledge. Solipsism, the thought that only *my* experiences exist, is a real possibility on this picture. This picture of how we use sensation and experience words has two sides: on the one side it shows us to have a most intimate contact with something in our own case, and on the other side it shows us that a consequence of this intimacy is a certain detachment from others. In the case of another, all I can do is form a hypothesis – come up with a conjecture – about their sensations and experiences based on the movements I see. Hypothesis and conjecture take the place of the access that is denied us. This tenuous grasp on others is the price we have to pay for getting things right in our own case.

Philosophers have become surprisingly comfortable with this picture of our language use in connection with sensations and experiences. And they have grown accustomed to the sceptic's questions. Some philosophers even go so far as to insist that scepticism is the price we pay for a certain kind of realism.[56] But, as we have seen in Part One, there is a real question how the sceptic can raise his doubt about the mind of another: the hypothesis that there is another mind must be meaningful but, if my sensation words get their meaning from their connection with the sensation that exists in my mental box, how does my talk about another mind come to be meaningful? It can begin to look as if the only meaning we can give our sensation words in connection with others is a meaning which has to do with their bodily movements. But if this is so then we have to accept that there is no univocity of meaning, since we do not use these words in our own case in connection with bodily movements. The word 'pain' has to be taken to be ambiguous: sometimes I use it to talk about what is going on inside me, and sometimes I use it in connection with the other's bodily movements. But this does appear to be at odds with our actual use of these words: when we use words like 'pain' we do suppose a univocity in its meaning across different persons. Where the sceptic challenges us to show how we know that another is in pain, ordinary language, in turn, challenges the sceptic to account for the apparent univocity in our language use.

Despite these and other problems, it must be admitted that the picture that lies behind the sceptic's challenge is a powerful one. We feel that this picture *must* be correct, and as a result we brush aside questions about meaning and univocity. The pull of the first-person is so strong that we are sure that our words must be rooted in this. The model of a private object that we name by some sort of inward reflection is one that seems to fit the way things are in our experience. It may take more than an alternative picture here to loosen the grip that this picture has on us. In fact Wittgenstein sees another problem lurking in the sceptic's picture of the asymmetry in our use of sensation and experience words. The problem is brought to light in a series of remarks that collectively have become known as the private language argument. The argument may be taken to undermine the sceptic's position and, with this, any problem there may be about other minds.

In *Philosophical Investigations*, 243 Wittgenstein asks,

But could we also imagine a language in which a person could write down or give vocal expression to his inner experiences – his feelings, moods and the rest – for his private use? – Well, can't we do so in our ordinary language? – But that is not what I mean. The individual words of this language are to refer to what can only be known to the person speaking; to his immediate private sensations. So another person cannot understand the language.

Wittgenstein calls a language in which the words refer to what can only be known to the person speaking a 'private language'. What Wittgenstein sets about investigating is whether we can imagine such a language. The question is particularly pressing given that the sceptic looks to be speaking just such a private language. In *Philosophical Investigations*, 244 Wittgenstein begins his investigation by asking how it is that words refer to sensations, but immediately switches to the more general question: how does any word manage to refer? Wittgenstein first addresses the more general question before coming to the more specific question in connection with sensations. Let us begin where Wittgenstein begins and return to the question about sensations only once we have a better idea how we are to answer the more general question.

To the general question about how the connection between a name and a thing is set up the private linguist gives the following answer: 'naming is something like attaching a label to a thing'.[57] And, importantly, this naming is taken by the private linguist to be preparatory to the use of the word. On this model we might think of the situation of a child learning language in the following way: I point to a certain object, say an apple, and utter a certain sound, say, 'apple'. The child is expected to understand that the direction of my finger is towards the apple and that I am placing the label 'apple' on this object. At a certain point in this process of naming objects, we can imagine the child going up to a new item – a ruler, say – and asking what it is called. We, then, reply by providing the appropriate label – we give what Wittgenstein calls an 'ostensive definition'.

Having explained the model, Wittgenstein asks us to reflect on it. He admits that one can come into a strange country and ask questions about the meanings of the words that the inhabitants of this strange country use. One can point to an object and ask what it is called – just like in the private linguist's picture. But Wittgenstein points out that the stranger can do this only because she already speaks a language. He writes: 'We may say: only someone who already knows how to do something with it can significantly ask a name.'[58] But the original question about how the connection between a word and object is set up was not about how one learns *another* language. That was a question about one's own language, one's first language. The private linguist is thinking of the child as someone who already understands a language, or, perhaps, as someone who can *think* but not yet speak.[59] But if we think of the *first* language, then we can see that it is not at all clear that when, in the first instance, one points to an apple and says 'apple' the child is in any position to appreciate what one is doing. What is the child to understand by this pointing? To what is she to take you to be pointing? – to the apple, or to its colour, or to its shape? As Wittgenstein writes at one point: 'an ostensive definition can be variously defined in *every* case.'[60] It is only if the child already understands the role of the word in the language that she is then in a position to understand and ask for ostensive definitions. A great deal of 'stage setting' must already be in place.[61] The private linguist's picture of meaning puts the cart before the horse: we don't first name objects in order to use words; rather, we need to use words in order to be in a position to name objects. It is our use of language that provides the needed stage setting. The development of language is the development of a language-game – and it is a game we play with others.

If we concentrate on this use that Wittgenstein takes to be fundamental to meaning, what we notice is that use is fluid; in some cases (say our use of sensation and experience words), we must conclude that our use is ambiguous.[62] This idea can seem difficult to accept. Wittgenstein connects the difficulty we have accepting this with our tendency to be in thrall to the method of science with its search for generality and tidy pictures, its search for essences that can explain what different cases have in common. And he reminds us that science is not our project here. Wittgenstein writes in one place:

> One might say that the concept "game" is a concept with blurred edges. – "But is a blurred concept a concept at all?" – Is an indistinct photograph a picture of a person at all? It is even always an advantage to replace an indistinct picture by a sharp one? Isn't the indistinct one often exactly what we need?[63]

The use people make of language in the course of their everyday activities may be fluid, but this should not be taken to stand in the way of an appreciation of the way use gives shape to meaning.

We can now return to the question with which we began: How do words refer to sensations? The private linguist's picture has an equal (if not greater) pull on us in connection with these words. His picture, applied to the case of sensations, is this: the child fixes its inward gaze upon an object inside itself and labels this object, say, 'pain'. The process is parallel to the one described above in connection with the naming of an apple – except in this case the object is inner, and the teacher and the one taught are collapsed into one and the same person. Once we see that the cases are parallel, then we can also see that the problems that Wittgenstein raises for the first case apply equally to the second. In *Philosophical Investigations*, 257 Wittgenstein reminds us of his earlier discussion of naming in connection with the case of a child naming its sensations:

> But what does it mean to say [the child] has 'named his pain'? – How has he done this naming of pain?! And whatever he did, what was its purpose? – When one says, "He gave a name to his sensation" one forgets that a great deal of stage-setting in the language is presupposed if the mere act of naming is to make sense. And when we speak of someone's having given a name to pain, what is presupposed is the existence of the grammar of the word "pain"; it shews the post where the new word is stationed.

Wittgenstein follows this reminder with a discussion of the following imaginary case:[64] Say I want to keep a diary about the recurrence of a certain sensation. Every day that I experience the sensation I writes 'S' in a calendar on the day I have the experience. As I write 'S' I concentrate very hard on the experience I am having (for I have the impression that this concentration has the effect of making a connection between the experience and 'S'). All this is in line with the private linguist's picture of how a sensation word manages to refer to its object. Now Wittgenstein raises a question about this 'ceremony': what is it for? Why do I want to make this connection between the word and the sensation? He concludes that the purpose of the ceremony is to bring it about that I 'remember the connexion *right* in the future'. In other words, I want to be sure that the next time I use 'S' I use it to name *that* sensation. But now Wittgenstein remarks,

> But in the present case I have no criterion of correctness. One would like to say: whatever is going to seem right to me is right. And that only means that here we can't talk about 'right'.[65]

What exactly is the problem that Wittgenstein wants us to recognize in the private linguist's ceremony? What Wittgenstein says is that this ceremony alone fails to give us the very thing we wanted: a standard of correctness for our future use of 'S'. But why does the ceremony fail to give us what we want? Is it because the ceremony needs some supplementation by memory, and memory is unreliable? Or does the problem go even deeper than this? Is the problem that we never managed to name anything here in the first place? If we recall Wittgenstein's discussion of the attempt to set up a connection between a word and an external object, then we know that the act of naming requires the prior 'stage-setting' of use. This stage-setting is absent in the case of naming an inner sensation, so how can there *be* anything to get right in the future? The very thing the private linguist wants from his ceremony is what that ceremony fails to provide.[66] In *Philosophical Investigations*, 260 Wittgenstein warns: 'Don't consider it a matter of course that a person is making a note of something when he makes a mark – say in a calendar. For a note has a function, and this "S" so far has none.' In an attempt to rescue his account of naming, the private linguist might insist that, even if I cannot manage to refer to a particular sensation by my act of concentration, I can nonetheless refer to *something* in this way. What the mark records is that the person has something. To this Wittgenstein responds: '"Has" and "something" also belong to our common language.'[67]

Wittgenstein emphasizes the sterility of the private linguist's exercise in *Philosophical Investigations*, 268 where he writes:

> Why can't my right hand give my left hand money? – My right hand can put it into my left hand. My right hand can write a deed of gift and my left hand a receipt. – But the further practical consequences would not be those of a gift. When the left hand has taken the money from the right hand, etc., we shall ask: "Well, and what of it?" And the same could be asked if a person had given himself a private definition of a word; I mean, if he has said the word to himself and at the same time has directed his attention to a sensation.

Wittgenstein here exposes the emptiness of the private linguist's exercise. At the same time, Wittgenstein reminds us that what we need to make this a meaningful exercise is attention to the use the person makes of these words in the context provided by others with a similar nature. As with the case of outward objects, what is missing here is the use we make of the sensation word in our language-game. And once we have that use, what we notice is that the object that the private linguist thinks is so important drops out as unnecessary. The object has no role to play in that portion of our language-game that concerns itself with sensation. Wittgenstein makes this point in *Philosophical Investigations*, 271 when he writes:

> "Imagine a person whose memory could not retain *what* the word 'pain' meant – so that he constantly called different things by that name – but nevertheless used the word in a way fitting in with the usual symptoms and presuppositions of pain" – in short he uses it as we all do. Here I should like to say: a wheel that can be turned though nothing else moves with it, is not part of the mechanism.

The image of a machine piece that plays no part in the machine's operations is one that recurs throughout much of Wittgenstein's writings. If we return to the analogy of the beetle in a box we find Wittgenstein writing in *Philosophical Investigations*, 293:

> The thing in the box has no place in the language-game at all; not even as a *something*: for the box might even be empty. – No, one can 'divide through' by the thing in the box; it cancels out, whatever it is.
> That is to say: if we construe the grammar of the expression of sensation on the model of 'object and designation' the object drops out of consideration as irrelevant.

In the case of sensation, all this emphasis on what we do – on our use of the word 'pain' – has led some philosophers to interpret Wittgenstein as advancing some kind of behaviourism. Wittgenstein himself recognizes the danger of being misinterpreted in this way. In *Philosophical Investigations*, 307 he considers being asked: "'Are you not a behaviourist in disguise? Aren't you at bottom really saying that everything except human behaviour is a fiction?'" This worry seems to arise as soon as we wean ourselves off the idea that sensation words act like labels for private objects. And it can feel as if the only way to avoid this behaviourism is to go back to the private linguist's picture of how sensation words get their meaning. The only way to be sure our use of sensation words isn't empty is to fill them with the objects that we find inside our mental boxes.

To think that behaviourism is the only alternative to the private linguist's picture is to ignore so much of our use of sensation words. In *Philosophical Investigations*, 288 Wittgenstein considers someone who says that he does not know if what he has got is a pain or something else. We might understand such a person to be telling us that he doesn't know what the English word 'pain' means. Wittgenstein then considers how we might go about teaching this word to this person. He suggests that we might prick him and say, 'That's what pain is'. But if this person were now to say to us, 'Oh, I know what "pain" means; what I don't understand is whether *this*, that I have now, is pain.' To this Wittgenstein responds:

> We should merely shake our heads and be forced to regard his words as a queer reaction which we have no idea what to do with. (It would be rather as if we heard someone say seriously: "I distinctly remember that some time before I was born I believed . . . . .".)

Here we can see that Wittgenstein has no intention of leaving the pain out: if we want someone to know what 'pain' means, we prick him – we don't say he must jump up and down. The point about behaviour is not so much that it is publicly available but that it is the behaviour of a certain sort of person.

In *Philosophical Investigations*, 283 Wittgenstein asks, 'What gives us *so much as the idea* that living beings, things, can feel?' Is it that I have learned to look inside myself, find my feelings, and thereby come to have my idea of feelings that I then transfer to others – to other people, but not to plants and stones? Wittgenstein is here in effect raising two questions. The first echoes a question that he raises in *The Blue Book*, and which I mentioned in the previous section: why do I so much as think that *another* has sensations and experiences given that I don't have the same consciousness of another's pain that I have of my own? The second question Wittgenstein raises concerns the limit of our idea: why do I extend my idea to other people but not to plants and stones? And further, why do I extend it only to living things and not to dead ones? We find we can answer these questions if we look at the use we make of our sensation words. In *Philosophical Investigations*, 310 Wittgenstein writes:

> I tell someone I am in pain. His attitude to me will then be that of belief; disbelief; suspicion; and so on.
>
> Let us assume he says: "It's not so bad" – Doesn't that prove that he believes in something behind the outward expression of pain? – His attitude is a proof of his attitude. Imagine not merely the words "I am in pain" but also the answer "It's not so bad" replaced by instinctive noises and gestures.

Here we see that it is not the outward expression alone that is important, but also the attitude we take towards the expression. Our nature is such that we respond in a certain way to that expression, and we respond in a slightly different way when the expression alters even slightly. How we respond is reflected in our language. The significance of our words lies before us in what we do as a result of the way we are. Once again we find that Wittgenstein can avoid the charge of behaviourism, as he can avoid the charge that he has misunderstood the nature of the first-person perspective.

As we have seen in the previous section, if we describe what we do as the result of the way we are – rather than think that what we do with our words is use them as labels for objects – we will have no inclination to raise certain philosophical problems. On *this* picture there is no problem about the mind of another. I use my sensation and experience words in such a way that they reflect the fact that I talk of another's sensations in response to the other's behaviour, and I talk of my own sensations without reference to my behaviour. There is an asymmetry in our use of sensation words, and that asymmetry is part of what we are describing when we describe our use of these words. There not only is no need for the sceptic's picture, but that picture turns out, upon examination, to be shot through with difficulties. The privacy of our sensations to which the sceptic draws our attention turns out to be something that we can describe as part of the language-game we play with sensation and experience words. At the end of the day what Wittgenstein urges us to recognize is this:

> What we are supplying are really remarks on the natural history of human beings; we are not contributing curiosities however, but observations which no one has doubted, but which have escaped remark only because they are always before our eyes.[68]

CONCLUSION

I have now come to the end of the second part of this book. It is time to take stock. Parts One and Two have been concerned with the history of our knowledge of other minds. This is not a straightforward history. I divided the history into two parts in order to reflect a certain point. In the first part I showed how a problem about our knowledge about the mind of another may be thought to have arisen in the history of philosophy. It can be seen to be the result of a certain way of approaching and formulating a sceptical question concerning our knowledge of the external world. Scepticism about the mind of another rides piggy-back on a certain sceptical question about the world. I argued in Chapter II that there is a way of raising the sceptical question about the world that does not give rise to this consequential scepticism about the mind of another. This is the scepticism that we find in the writings of the ancient Greek sceptics. It is a scepticism that raises only the universal possibility of doubt – a doubt about this or that claim to knowledge. It is not a scepticism that questions all our beliefs at once. This ancient scepticism is motivated by a desire to achieve a way of living in our ordinary lives that is free from unhappiness. The sceptics of ancient times perceive dogma – the pursuit of knowledge – as the root of unhappiness. Tranquillity is the aim, and tranquillity will only come if we give up the search for knowledge and opt instead for the life of pure scepticism.

Descartes believed he could put to rest once and for all the doubts of the sceptic. But the sceptical doubts that Descartes believed he could put to rest were more serious and profound than those of his predecessors. Descartes introduces the possibility of universal doubt – the possibility that all my beliefs may be false. A consequence of this doubt is a radical – logical – divide between the mind and the world of bodies. Knowledge comes to be seen as our way of reaching across this gap to the world. In an attempt to achieve this knowledge, Descartes puts aside all action. Descartes' scepticism is incompatible with ordinary life; it must be overcome. However, Descartes' own attempt to reach across this gap with the help of a non-deceiving God has proved untenable. The result of Descartes' sceptical question, then, is to leave philosophers looking for a knowledge without which they would be confined within the limits of their own minds.

The attempt to account for our knowledge of the external world is a dominant theme in the work of philosophers from Descartes' time onwards. Alongside the task of accounting for our knowledge here, some philosophers recognized the need also to give some account of our knowledge of the mind of another. As with the external world, there is a need to account for our knowledge of both the existence and the nature of another mind. The need to account for our knowledge here remains even once our knowledge of the external world of bodies has been accounted for. Once a radical – logical – divide is introduced between a subject's mind and her body, even if we can give an account of how such a subject manages to come by knowledge of the world of body, there remains the further question of how she manages to come by any knowledge of the mind of another. From Malebranche onwards there is a recognition that the knowledge we have of another mind is by conjecture, or hypothesis. There is also a recognition that the knowledge we can achieve in the case of another mind is somewhat weaker than the knowledge we can achieve concerning bodies. This is particularly clear in the work of Locke, who allows that we can have sensitive knowledge of the world of bodies (that falls short of certainty but yet deserves to be called 'knowledge'), but who holds that we can reach nothing more than opinion when it comes to other minds. Berkeley rejects Locke's idea that sensitive knowledge is to count as knowledge. In Berkeley's opinion knowledge can only be achieved if we let one half of the Cartesian logical divide fall away: material substance is a nonsense. Everything that exists is either mind or ideas in a mind. We understand what it is to be a mind from our own case, and we have reason to believe that there are other minds in addition to our own. As Berkeley admits, however, we have no more than probable grounds for believing in the existence of these other minds or finite spirits. Mill, in a manner not entirely unreminiscent of Berkeley, holds that the only real externality we can prove to exist is that of other minds. Objects external to us are nothing more than the permanent possibilities of sensation, but there really do exist series of feeling other than my own. Mill thinks that he can prove the existence of other minds. Philosophers since, however, have not been persuaded by Mill's proof. And without such a proof Mill is left having to say, as Reid once observed about Berkeley, that my sister, mother, friend and lover are all just parcels of my own mind.

As we follow this Cartesian tradition we find that there is no recognition of any particular *problem* about our knowledge of another mind. There are in effect two ways of accounting for our knowledge here. First, there are those who hold that we can have knowledge of the world of bodies, and that we can use this knowledge to form a conjecture about the existence and nature of minds that may exist in some of these bodies. And then there are those who deny the existence of body, but find reason in the mind's ideas to conclude that there may be other minds.

In Part Two I introduced the work of two philosophers who discern a problem in the Cartesian tradition over our knowledge of the mind of another. The first of these philosophers is Reid. Reid looks back over a tradition of philosophy initiated by Descartes and finds that it culminates in the absurd conclusion that the existence of another mind is either a parcel of my own mind or merely probable. To avoid this conclusion we must, according to Reid, reject the theory of ideas that lies at the heart of the Cartesian tradition. I argued that, despite his perspicacity over the role of the theory of ideas and the conclusions to which it leads, Reid is still in the grip of the Cartesian framework. What he objects to in the Cartesian system is the interposition of ideas between the knowing mind and the external world, but rejecting the theory of ideas is rejecting only a manifestation of the Cartesian framework. According to Reid, our constitution is such that certain sensations give rise in us to certain conceptions and certain beliefs. In the case of bodies we form beliefs about what we can experience, but in the case of another mind we form beliefs about things which Reid takes to be invisible to us. In the case of another mind, we see only the countenance, hear only the voice; nevertheless, our nature is such that, when we hear the voice or see the countenance, we take it to be a sign of another mind. It is here that we find the Cartesian framework in Reid's work. The subject of experience is still conceived as something essentially distinct from the world of bodies and other minds. Reid's rejection of the theory of ideas still leaves the basic Cartesian framework in place.

Naturalists such as Schlick would no doubt take themselves to be free of what I have been calling the Cartesian framework, but it is not clear that they are. Schlick takes the mistake of his idealist predecessors to be that they take mind as basic and look to construct the world and other minds from this. The naturalist turn that Schlick and other members of the Vienna Circle introduce is an attempt to start in a different place: we must start with the natural world, and account for the mind in terms of this. But the language of Descartes is still to be found here; the only difference is the starting point. The litmus test of this Cartesian framework is that there is still some difficulty encountered over our knowledge of the mind of another.

It is only with Wittgenstein's work that we find the Cartesian legacy finally beginning to fade. In Wittgenstein's work there are no logical divides, no gaps that need to be reached across by the achievement of knowledge. There are just language users who act together in the world. What Wittgenstein shows is that a correct description of the way a community uses language can bring understanding of that use which raises none of the traditional philosophical problems. In particular, it raises no problem concerning our knowledge that another, for example, feels pain or has sensations more generally. That we take another to be in pain is a quite natural reaction we have to a certain sort of living being. Our concept of pain is revealed to be such that it applies to others as well as to myself, and it applies in such a way as to leave room for a certain amount of hesitation or doubt about whether or not the other really is in pain. Reid identified the ideal system to be the real problem in the Cartesian system, but we can now see that Reid did not dig deep enough. It is not just that the Cartesian system introduces ideas as a veil which ultimately cuts us off from reality and other minds. The real problem is that the Cartesian system introduces a logical divide in the first place. Once such a divide is in place we need to come up with some way of reaching across it – or else knowledge of the world becomes impossible. And whatever we say about our knowledge of the world of bodies, it looks like our knowledge of another mind is liable to raise further problems. In his work, Wittgenstein turns his back on this divide. Because there is no divide, there are no bridges that need to be built. In Wittgenstein's work we begin as a community of language users, and we come to understand our world and the world of other experiencing beings by looking at the way in which we interact with one another.

Part Three

The conceptual problem
of other minds

CHAPTER VIII

The conceptual problem of other minds

INTRODUCTION

In Chapter I, I suggested that there is an understanding of the work of the ancient Greek sceptics which takes them to be realists about the world of material objects and about the minds of others. This is a realism that is undermined by the philosophical work of Descartes. Of course, Descartes is also a realist about the world of material objects and the minds of others, but his conception of a subject and of an object is such as to make a subject's knowledge of the world of objects difficult – if not impossible – to come by. Descartes and his followers may be realists, but it is a realism that brings in its wake various radical sceptical questions. Indeed, several philosophers have insisted that this realism and this scepticism are made for each other. Thus, we find Thomas Nagel claiming that 'realism makes skepticism intelligible', and Colin McGinn writing that 'a prima facie vulnerability to . . . a [sceptical] challenge should be regarded as an adequacy condition which any formulation of realism is required to meet'.[1] I shall refer to the realism that allows for such radical scepticism as 'hard realism'. According to this variety of realism, the world consists of mind-independent objects whose existence can be thought of from a God's eye perspective, that is, a perspective external to the minds of men (or any other thinking creature).

The realism of the ancient sceptics, it has been argued, does not admit of this radical sceptical possibility. It would appear from the way that the ancients formulated their scepticism that the existence of the world and other minds is taken to be there from the start (so to speak). The ancient sceptics despaired of discovering that the world is determinately this way or that – but the existence of the world they did not doubt. If we consider this less radical sceptical challenge, the pronouncements of Nagel and McGinn must be understood in a different light: a realism that is not based on a metaphysical or conceptual gap between the subject and its objects will allow for only a moderate or weak scepticism. I shall refer to this realism as 'soft realism'. Soft realism allows only for a moderate form of scepticism; hard realism opens up the possibility of a more radical scepticism.

In Chapter I, I also suggested that, whereas Descartes can be seen to have given prominence to knowledge over action, the sceptics of ancient times tempered their pursuit of knowledge by an acknowledgement of the need to live in the world. Thus, where knowledge is given prominence, we find a picture of isolated subjects reaching out to the world and other subjects. From this privileged position of isolation, the subject needs somehow to find a reason to believe – or support his belief – in the existence of anything and anyone beyond himself. Knowledge, as Bernard Williams has said, is, on this picture, taken to be of what is *there anyway* – independent of any particular subject's thoughts about it. Knowledge is taken to be an individual's way of getting in touch with things and minds other than his own. When the pursuit of knowledge is tempered by an acknowledgement of action, the picture we form is very much altered. On this other picture the subject is not conceived of as isolated from the world of objects and other subjects. The question I raised right at the end of Chapter I is this: How can we plausibly maintain this second picture? In particular, how can we forbear from taking seriously the radical sceptical questions that Descartes raised – especially once they have been formulated? I ended Chapter I with the following question: Can we find a 'postlapsarian counterpart' to the ancient sceptic's realism concerning the mind of others? It seems to me that there are pressures that force us to look for such a counterpart. Without it we do not just face epistemological questions over our knowledge of other minds but we are left with a conceptual picture that harbours a very serious difficulty. I have touched on this difficulty at several points throughout Parts One and Two. In what follows I want to clarify just what this difficulty is, and show how attention to it will help us to fill out the postlapsarian picture whereby the concept of knowledge is tempered by an acknowledgement of action.

THE CONCEPTUAL PROBLEM

When we reflect back over the history discussed in Part One, above, it is easy to be struck by the following: running throughout this work there is an assumption that I can know from my own case what it is to be in pain, see red, believe there is a round object before me, and the like. Given this knowledge, two questions are asked: (i) how can I know that another individual has sensations, sees, believes, and the like?; and (ii) even if I can know *that* another has sensations, sees and believes, how can I know just *what* the other feels, sees and believes? A question that has received less attention, however, is this: what puts us in a position to so much as raise these questions about the mind of another? In order to raise these epistemological questions I must have a quite general concept of mind – a concept that applies to others as well as myself. The question is whether I can give a plausible account of my possession of such a general conception of mind. This question can be distinguished from the question, raised by Wittgenstein's private language argument, that I considered in the final section of the previous chapter. One upshot of that argument is to shed doubt on the possibility of coming to have a concept of *my* mind in advance of fulfilling the conditions that make it possible for one to think of the possibility of the existence of others. This is undeniably a most powerful argument, and it has been put forward by many as showing up the major problem with the position advocated by philosophers who work within the Cartesian framework. It is, however, not an argument that has found favour with some, and where that argument has not found favour there is a tendency to return to thinking of the other minds issue as a purely epistemological one. And where the issue is viewed as an epistemological one, it is not taken to be particularly problematic. Where questions concerning the mind of another are taken to be epistemological, there is not only an assumption that it makes sense to think about one's own mind in advance of others, there is also an assumption that the concept one comes to have in this way is entirely general.[2] It is this, further, assumption that I want now to address. For the purposes of what follows I shall allow that it may be possible somehow to come, by reflection, to have a concept of my mind. What I want to question is whether the concept one comes to have in this way can be thought to have the generality required to permit one to raise questions about the mind of another. This question has come to be known as the conceptual problem of other minds, and it is a question that (some) philosophers of more recent times take to be the important question facing us with respect to other minds.[3] It is a question that, as I argued in Chapter II, can be traced back to Augustine; however, the question does not figure in the concerns of philosophers again until it emerges in the work of Wittgenstein in the early part of the twentieth century.

The conceptual question may, however, seem a curious one. Surely we can, and do, raise questions about the minds of others. The problem is not so much whether we do this, as whether the account we give of how we come to have our concept of mind in the first place may be thought to raise questions about our claim to have a quite general concept of mind. The point of raising these questions is not to show that they *cannot* be answered (although the problems are sufficiently pressing to raise a doubt about the possibility of answering them), but to point out that they *have not* been answered. Until such time as a reply to these questions is forthcoming it must be taken that there is a *prima facie* doubt about our entitlement to say that the concept of mind we have is entirely general.

To see how a problem may be thought to arise here, let us begin by considering the following principle:

(P)   A concept is general insofar as several distinguishable individuals can fall under it.

Principle P is not to be taken to say anything about what individuals in fact do fall under a given concept. It is simply a claim about the applicability of the concept to a distinguishable range of individuals. In his important work on persons, P. F. Strawson reminds us of the importance of recognizing this principle in connection with our ascription of states of consciousness and experience. Referring to this principle in its linguistic mode, Strawson writes:

> The idea of a predicate is correlative with that of a *range* of distinguishable individuals of which the predicate can be significantly . . . affirmed.[4]

The principle has been incorporated by Gareth Evans into what he calls the 'generality constraint'. Evans writes:

> We cannot avoid thinking of a thought about an individual object x, to the effect that it is F, as an exercise of two separable capacities; one being the capacity to think of x, which could be equally exercised in thoughts about x to the effect that it is G or H; and the other being a conception of what it is to be F, which could be equally exercised in thoughts about other individuals, to the effect that they are F.[5]

220

My interest is not so much in (P), but in its application to one particular kind of concept, the concept of mind or mental concepts.
Ultimately, my interest is less in (P) than in (PM):

(PM)   A mental concept is general just in case several distin-
       guishable individuals can fall under it.

I have formulated (PM) in terms of mental concepts generally, but I
could equally have formulated it in terms of the concept of mind, and
in what follows I shall alternate indiscriminately between talking
about the concept of mind and talking about that concept's instantia-
tion in a single mental concept. As I have said, the conceptual problem
of other minds is connected with the worry that there is a *prima facie*
problem about understanding how our concept of mind (or mental
concepts) can be general.

In order to be in a better position to understand how there may be a
difficulty with (PM), let us begin by considering another instance of
(P). Suppose Annie comes to have the concept duck (or learns to use
the predicate 'is a duck') as the result of being taken to feed a certain
animal that lives on a pond in the University Parks. Annie's understanding of this concept should allow her to appreciate that there may
be ducks in other times and places – say, in Central Park in New York,
tomorrow. Indeed, unless Annie did understand these possibilities, we
would not say that she possessed the general concept of duck.

Principle (P) seems fairly straightforward in application to a concept like duck. Things look less straightforward, however, if we
consider a mental concept, for example, the concept of pain. Let us
say that Annie comes to have the concept of pain as the result of cutting her finger with a sharp knife at breakfast; in other words, she
understands what it is to be in pain from her own case. By application
of (PM) we should be able to say that, if the concept Annie now possesses is a quite general one, then she should have no trouble
extending this concept to include her own pain at different times and
in different places (as a pain in her foot when a heavy object falls on
it after dinner) *as well as* extending this concept to include the pain of
another who is not herself (as in Mummy's pain or Grandpa's pain).
This much is just what (PM) requires. Yet a problem can be raised for
experiential concepts that makes it difficult to see *how* a child who has
come to have the concept of pain as the result of feeling pain in her
own case is able to extend this concept to others. Some philosophers
have taken this to be what Wittgenstein is getting at in *Philosophical
Investigations* 302, where he writes:

If one has to imagine someone else's pain on the model of one's own, this is none too easy a thing to do: for I have to imagine pain which I *do not feel* on the model of the pain which I *do feel*. That is, what I have to do is not simply to make a transition in imagination from one place of pain to another. As, from pain in the hand to pain in the arm. For I am not to imagine that I feel pain in some region of his body. (Which would also be possible).

Wittgenstein appears to be pointing up a *special* difficulty concerning our concept of pain, and it is a difficulty connected with our ability to comply with principle (PM). Furthermore, it appears to be a difficulty that is not experienced when we employ the concept in connection with different parts of one's own body. The difficulty arises when we attempt to make the transition from my pain to someone else's.

One response to the question how I extend my concept of mind – which can be seen to lie at the heart of the work of philosophers from Malebranche to Mill (the work of Reid excepted) – is simply to say that I suppose that the other has what I have had on so many occasions. But this simple response appears to miss the difficulty. Considering this response Wittgenstein writes in *Philosophical Investigations*, 350:

It is as if I were to say: "You surely know what 'It's 5 o'clock here' means; so you also know what 'It's 5 o'clock on the sun' means. It means simply that it is just the same time there as it is here when it is 5 o'clock." – The explanation by means of *identity* does not work here. For I know well enough that one can call 5 o'clock here and 5 o'clock there "the same time", but what I do not know is in what cases one is to speak of its being the same time here and there.

In exactly the same way it is no explanation to say: the supposition that he has a pain is simply the supposition that he has the same as I.

I claim to have raised the same problem, to which Wittgenstein may be thought in these passages to be adverting, in terms of a difficulty for principle (PM). But someone may query this. *Philosophical Investigations*, 302 and 350 are addressing the question of the extension of my concept of pain from myself to *others*, whereas it is not at all clear that satisfaction of (PM) requires *this* sort of extension. Why not say that (PM) is satisfied just in case there is no difficulty in extending one's concept to cover different parts of oneself at different times and in different locations. In this case, the term 'individuals' in (PM) is to be interpreted loosely to cover oneself in different times and places. Interpreted in this way, there does not appear to be any difficulty: Annie's extension of the concept she learned from the morning's episode with the knife at breakfast to cover an episode with another knife at dinner would seem no more difficult than imagining the transition of a pain in her hand to a pain in her arm. If this is right, then there is no difficulty for (PM). One may wish to accept that (PM) is satisfied under such circumstances; however, one would then have to accept that the satisfaction of (PM) is compatible with conceptual solipsism. In other words, despite the fact that one's concept satisfied (PM), one would nevertheless be unable to understand or comprehend the extension of that concept to any but one's own self – albeit oneself at different times and in different places. In order to avoid conceptual solipsism, (PM) would need to extend to include individuals that were not one self. Whether or not (PM) demands it (and arguably it does), the avoidance of conceptual solipsism *does* demand that our employment of our mental concepts be capable of extension beyond the individual self. The rejection of conceptual solipsism requires that we can at least make sense of such an extension of our concept. I shall take it that conceptual solipsism is a position we want to avoid. (Certainly those who raise epistemological issues about other minds are not conceptual solipsists.) Showing how we can satisfy (PM) with respect to other distinguishable individuals who are not oneself would be a way to avoid this kind of solipsism.

It may, however, still not be apparent why this is a *problem*. After all, the linguistically able person *can* comprehend what it is for a range of distinguishable individuals to be ducks, and such a person is likewise able to comprehend what it is for a range of distinguishable individuals to be in pain. We all use words connected with these concepts in ways that bear testimony to this. But philosophers see a problem here, and it is a problem that arises in connection only with mental concepts. In what follows I want to suggest an understanding of this problem; I want to show just *why* generality may be thought to be an issue in connection with the concept of mind.

Let us begin by considering again the application of the predicate 'is a duck', first to ducks in the University Parks and then to ducks on other ponds. Without looking into the question how it is that we achieve this, I want simply to point out that, when Annie does use this predicate in connection with what we all take to be a similar animal in another park we agree that she is using it correctly, but if she were to use the same predicate in connection with, say, a wooden platform raised off the ground and placed near the edge of the pond (what we call 'a bench'), we would be less inclined to think she has understood the correct application of this term. We can appreciate the similarities between the animals, and we find the park bench sufficiently dissimilar to them. When we turn to consider the application of the mental predicate 'is in pain', things may not be so straightforward. Say that one acquires the concept associated with this predicate from experience in one's own case; in other words, I come to have the concept of pain as the result of feeling pain. Now consider a generalization of this concept, or a use of this predicate in connection with others. The first thing we have to realize is that, where we are all in a position to experience lots of different ducks, none of us is in a position to experience another's pain. This is not to say that I might not experience pain in another person's body (recall the discussions of this in the work of Schlick and Wittgenstein, above). What I cannot do is get myself in a position to feel *another person's pain.* Nor can I directly observe another person's pain. This is something that all the philosophers whose work I considered in Part One would accept. Thus, we find Locke writing that the thoughts of another are 'invisible', and Berkeley writing that we do not see a 'man', if what we mean by that word is that which 'lives, moves, perceives, and thinks as we do'. But, as this is the case, we can ask why we take it that it is the concept of *pain* that is applicable in the case of another. Why do we take it that the concept I acquire from my own case is the very same concept I apply to the other? If we consider the issue in connection with the predicate 'is in pain', we can ask why we take our use of this predicate to be unambiguous. Consider the predicate 'is a bank'. Say I learn to use this predicate in connection with monetary transactions of a certain sort. When I use the same word in connection with the place on either side of a body of water, there is little temptation to say I am extending the very same concept. Here we accept that the predicate is ambiguous. Why, then, given the apparent difference in the way I apply the word 'is in pain' to myself and to others, do I not similarly conclude that this predicate is ambiguous?

I shall refer to this as the 'problem of unity'. It is the problem of whether or not, when we consider our concept of mind, we have before us one unified concept (or when we consider our mental predicates we are entitled to say that they are unambiguous). What I want to suggest is that the *prima facie* problem that we encounter over the generality of our mental concepts is connected with the unity of those concepts. The question is whether we are satisfied that the concept we have purported to generalize to others is indeed *the very same concept* that we apply in our own case. This is the question that, as I suggested in Chapter II, we find in the work of Augustine. Augustine appreciates that, given that I know what a mind is from my own case, we need to understand my belief that there are minds other than my own. Augustine's suggestion is that we believe that there are minds in others 'from a likeness to us'.

Augustine writes:

> We perceive something present in that mass such as is present in us to move our mass in a similar way; it is life and soul. . . . Therefore we know the mind of anyone at all from our own; and from our own case we believe in that which we do not know.[6]

Some philosophers have suggested that what we find in Augustine's work is an argument from analogy: it is by analogy with myself and what I know to be present in my movements that I believe that another has a mind on the basis of the bodily movements that I observe. I am now in a position to make good the promise I made in Chapter II to consider whether Augustine's response to this problem is a plausible one. There is no doubt that my observation of another's bodily movements inclines me to say that he has feelings, thoughts and emotions, but the question is whether it is plausible that the concepts I employ in connection with the other are extensions of the very same concepts I employ in my own case. There is nothing in what Augustine suggests to convince one that this is so. What we need to understand is why the person who uses the predicate 'is in pain', first in application to herself on the basis of introspection or reflection and then in application to others on the basis of their observed bodily movements, is not like the child who uses the predicate 'is a duck' first in response to the animal she observes on the pond and then in response to the raised platform of wood by the pond's edge. There is nothing in the argument from analogy that provides this understanding.

The problem is also present in Locke's work. Locke holds that ideas become general as the result of a process of abstraction. In Chapter IV I raised a question for Locke's account of abstraction as it may be thought to apply to the case of mind. Locke holds that one moves from having a particular to having a general idea by a process of abstracting similarities among various particulars. The question is how this process is meant to work in the case of mind, where the only particular I am in a position to have an idea of is my own mind. I want now to add to this objection. Given that what I do observe in the case of another is only her bodily movements, why do I say that the idea I come to have in connection with another is the very same that I have in connection with myself? It is the question of unity that makes the question of generality particularly pressing.

This Lockean problem has been nicely identified by Colin McGinn in his paper 'What is the problem of other minds?'. McGinn takes as his starting point, not the work of Locke, but section 302 from Wittgenstein's *Philosophical Investigations*. The question McGinn asks is why imagining someone else's pain on the model of one's own *is* 'none too easy a thing to do'. McGinn sees the problem as arising in the following way:

> It may . . . be that I have a way of thinking of my experiences which (a) only I have and (b) enters into my understanding of the concept in question. This distinctively first-person way of thinking (call it 'introspection') threatens us with ambiguity because it introduces an *un*common element. . . . Indeed it is the threat of this uncommon element that largely constitutes the central problem of other minds.[7]

McGinn takes it that what makes a concept like pain importantly different from a concept like duck is the presence of this 'uncommon element', which element is connected with a 'distinctively first-person way of thinking'.

In order to help us to see just how this uncommon element creates a problem McGinn suggests that we consider an analogous issue captured by Molyneux's question. The question that interests McGinn focuses on the conceptual predicament of a blind man. Say a man, born blind, comes to have a concept of square on the basis of tactual information; and say that this same man is somehow brought to sight at a mature age. The question Molyneux asks is this: Upon being visually presented with a square object – but before being able to touch it – can this newly-sighted man apply the concept he possesses? McGinn takes Molyneux's question to be a challenge to the unity of our concept: is it the same concept that gets applied on the basis of information from the different sense modalities? One answer to this question (favoured by Molyneux himself, as well as Locke and Berkeley) is 'no': until such a man is able to connect the information which his sight now presents to him with that which touch previously presented, he is not able to apply the predicate 'square' in a way which we can say is unambiguous. About this response McGinn writes,

Now this negative answer might be motivated by the thought that the blind man cannot *imaginatively extend* his tactually based concept of square in order to arrive at a visually based concept, simply because any image he may form will bear the inexpungible stamp of the tactual mode of presentation of the property of squareness with which he is acquainted. . . . The underlying issue here results from the fact that we apply 'square', a seemingly univocal word, on the basis of radically different sorts of sensory data, and this creates a *prima facie* problem about the unity of the concept and its extrapolability from one sense to another.[8]

The analogy intended should be clear: We get our concept of pain from our own case and then are presented with the task of extending this concept by use of the imagination to another. The task is 'none too easy' because the way we get our concept from our own case bears the 'inexpungible stamp' of the first-person mode of presentation by which we acquired our concept. And where extrapolation is not possible, neither is it possible for us to continue to view our concept as unitary.

Actually McGinn does not accept a negative reply to Molyneux's question. The reason is that he can see a way of forming a concept here that prescinds from the mode of presentation. There is nothing in the case of the concept of square that forces us to accept any particular mode of presentation as essential to the very nature of that concept. According to McGinn, we come to have a unitary concept of square by thinking of squareness *objectively*, that is, in independence of the particular ways it is given to us in sense. This might lead us to think that, in the analogous case of pain, we might also conceive of this property by prescinding from its sensory appearance to us. But the parallel move, McGinn argues, is not available in this case. The reason is that appearance-to-us is essential in the case of pain; this is why there is a special problem of other minds. This, concludes McGinn, is the problem being raised by Wittgenstein in section 302: it looks impossible to imagine pain which I do not feel on the model of pain which I do feel. And so long as this does look to be impossible, we must conclude that we do not operate with a univocal concept of pain; the predicate 'pain' is ambiguous. At least this must be our conclusion until such time as we can see how we can extend our concept from the first person without loss of that perspective.

McGinn takes it that he has made it clear just what the problem of other minds is. In terms of the principle (PM) we could say that the problem of other minds is that of understanding how several distinguishable individuals can fall under a mental concept in such a way that we can understand the unity of that concept. It is the question of unity that makes the generality of mental concepts particularly problematic. We could say that at the heart of the problem of generality is the problem of unity. Notice that the conceptual problem of other minds runs deeper than any epistemological problem we may think we encounter with respect to others. Until we are in a position to understand how our concepts can be general, we are not in a position to even raise the question how we know whether other minds exist. And, of course, if it should turn out that the unity we impart to our concept is only apparent, then there is no epistemological problem concerning other minds at all – when I speak of another's pain I am simply referring to her behaviour and this is observable.

Earlier I said that the linguistically able among us do appear to use words like 'duck' and 'pain' in such a way as to indicate that there is no ambiguity here. P. F. Strawson points out that the non-philosopher has no trouble with the thought that the predicate 'in pain' means the same whether one says 'I am in pain' or 'He is in pain'. Strawson writes:

> The dictionaries do not give two sets of meanings for every expression which describes a state of consciousness: a first-person and a second-person meaning.[9]

As Strawson correctly notes, it is the *philosopher* who identifies a problem here. Given the observations made about our concept of pain above, it is hard to see how our use of mental predicates can be unambiguous. Yet no speaker would admit to such an ambiguity. That is why no dictionary records two meanings for the word 'pain'. If mental predicates really are like the predicate 'is a bank', why do we not acknowledge this in the way that we do the ambiguity in the latter predicate? We could say that our interactions with others are a living example of our collective rejection of conceptual solipsism.

When Strawson says that it is the philosopher who sees a problem, one could understand this in the following way: given a certain philosophical view about our concept of pain, it looks like there is a serious problem about the extension of this concept to others. Notice the way McGinn begins his discussion of the matter by drawing our attention to what he calls an 'uncommon element' – a distinctively first-person way of thinking. McGinn not only attaches importance to the first-person perspective, but also assumes that the only way to be true to this perspective is to assume that I come to have my concept of pain as the result of an experience of my own pain. We have already seen how this assumption gives rise to the conceptual problem before us. We could also say that it is this assumption that gives rise to a conclusion concerning our use of mental predicates that is at odds with our actual use of mental predicates. This starting point threatens to leave us in a position that none of us would recognize – the position of the conceptual solipsist. McGinn might say that this is precisely the philosophical problem before us: to understand how it is possible for us to reject conceptual solipsism given a certain view of the essential nature of our concepts. The problem with this position is that it threatens the *possibility* that we are in fact conceptual solipsists and what we believe about our position in relation to others is merely imaginary. It is possible that our mental predicates are in fact ambiguous.

It should be clear how a certain philosophical starting point looks to land us with the possibility of conceptual solipsism. We do better to reject the philosophical starting point and begin with the position we would all maintain is ours: the position that distances itself from conceptual solipsism and asserts a generality for our mental concepts. In other words, instead of beginning with a philosophical position about our own case, we should assert the lived position of true generality that we all operate with every day. The problem, after all, seemed to arise because we could not see a way of moving from our philosophical starting point to the position of conceptual generality. We avoid this problem if we assume a different starting point.

McGinn might argue that his is not just a philosophical starting point, but it, too, has a claim to being called a 'lived position'. It is the starting point of the individual in touch with his or her experiences. But this starting point acknowledges only *part* of what we might label the 'lived position'; it acknowledges only the experiences of an individual who is conceptually isolated from the world and other minds. The true lived position embraces the world and others, as well as the subject's experiences.[10] Such a starting point does not harbour any conceptual problem of the sort we have been describing. There is, nevertheless, philosophical work to be done here. We must be careful not to adopt this position dogmatically, refusing to acknowledge the difficulties it may be thought to harbour. What this starting point begs is the question, How is this starting point possible? I want to take it that this is the question that faces us, rather than the question of how generality is possible given a certain *philosophical* starting point. I take it that one of the lessons to be learned from McGinn's discussion is that understanding that a problem of other minds confronts us when we make certain philosophical moves gives us a reason to distrust those philosophical moves. We need to re-orient ourselves. Rather than taking it that philosophy gives us our starting point and, thereby, bequeaths to us a problem, we should take our cue from what I am calling the lived position and use philosophy to understand this. The philosophical task is that of understanding how the lived position is possible.

OUR CONCEPTUAL STRUCTURE

I ended the previous section with the claim that it is the job of philosophy to acknowledge a certain non-solipsistic starting point and to say something about how this starting point is possible. Following the work of P. F. Strawson, I want to suggest that a certain philosophical understanding will come from an investigation into the structure of our concepts. Such an investigation is relatively modest work; it will not explain how our concepts work to someone who is not *au fait* with them. Nevertheless, the results of such an investigation should be such as to be acceptable to someone who has the concepts and operates with them. In other words, the results of this sort of investigation should be recognizable by anyone who operates with these concepts as a correct account of what he does. Furthermore, once this structure has been unveiled, certain questions should no longer seem pressing. In particular, we should no longer be troubled by the question, How is a general concept of mind possible?

In proposing such an investigation, Strawson places his work somewhat at odds with that of Wittgenstein. Strawson agrees in large part with the work of his predecessor, and in particular with the thought that it is the job of philosophers to show how philosophical problems can arise through the imposition of false pictures. However, where Wittgenstein takes the job of philosophy to be purely descriptive and therapeutic, Strawson takes it that there is more that philosophy can do. In his review of Wittgenstein's *Philosophical Investigations* Strawson writes: 'Now even if we *begin* with the therapeutic purpose of the philosopher's work, our interest might not exhaust itself when that purpose is achieved; and there can be an investigation of the logic of sets of concepts, which starts with no purpose other than that of unravelling and ordering complexities for the sake of doing so. The desire to present the facts systematically here becomes important in proportion as the therapeutic aims become secondary.'[11] As Strawson sees it, the philosophical urge to understand can be indulged without interfering with the therapeutic descriptive work that Wittgenstein provides. There will no doubt be those who will insist that there is no further work to be done, while still others will say that what Strawson is proposing is fine as far as it goes, but that it does not go far enough; what we need is to engage in a more explanatory task. Notice that, like Wittgenstein, Strawson also sees the task of philosophy to be descriptive – but Strawson labels his work as an exercise in 'descriptive metaphysics'. It is not altogether clear what Strawson means by this, but he explains the work in one place as that of describing the actual structure of our thoughts about the world. He contrasts this exercise with another that he labels 'revisionary metaphysics', which seeks to produce a better structure.[12] Strawson's exercise is not Wittgenstein's. Where Wittgenstein insists that we must 'bring words back from their metaphysical to their everyday use', Strawson is content to re-introduce the metaphysical.[13] Nevertheless, for all Strawson's talk of metaphysics, he never re-introduces the logical divide between the subject and her world that is characteristic of the problematic metaphysics.[14] Once this is understood, one can look at Strawson's descriptive task as an extension of Wittgenstein's. Strawson takes the work of the descriptive metaphysician to be recognizable by those who operate with that conceptual structure, and in this respect his work does not depart from the everyday. Nevertheless, although we operate with these concepts in our daily lives, their *structure* is not apparent until the philosopher uncovers them.[15]

As part of his descriptive metaphysics Strawson considers mental concepts – concepts associated with our ascribing to individuals predicates of the following sort: 'being in pain'; 'forming an intention'; 'having a belief'; and the like. Strawson considers, *inter alia*, two important aspects of our use of such predicates: first, that I use these predicates with the same meaning in connection with myself as with others; and second, that the use of these predicates in my own case does not require me to identify who is, for example, in pain, while my use of these predicates in connection with another does require that I identify whose pain it is. Thus we can see that, like Wittgenstein, Strawson is concerned to understand, in connection with mental predicates, the unity of meaning across an asymmetry of use.

Donald Davidson is another philosopher who is concerned to reconcile the asymmetry in our use of mental predicates with the unity of their meaning across these different uses. Davidson raises the issue in the following way: 'If the mental states of others are known only through their behavioural and other outward manifestations, while this is not true of our own mental states, why should we think our own mental states are anything like those of others?'[16] The striking asymmetry in our use of mental predicates calls the assumed unity of their meaning into question. Like Strawson, Davidson approaches these questions in a way that can be taken to be compatible with the descriptive therapeutic work that Wittgenstein urges. And also like Strawson, Davidson attempts to go beyond that work. However, where Strawson takes his work to be descriptive, Davidson looks for explanations. According to Davidson, it is only explanations that can silence the sceptic who dogs our every move here: if we begin with a secure knowledge of our own mental states, the sceptic questions our knowledge of the mind of another; and if we connect the mind of another with the behaviour of the other, the sceptic will ask why we take it that we use the very same predicates in connection with the other as we do in connection with ourselves. It is in order finally to silence the sceptic that Davidson seeks an explanation of the asymmetry in our use of these predicates that can help us to understand the unity in their meaning. Davidson acknowledges Strawson's work in this connection, but wants to go beyond it. Thus Davidson writes that while 'Strawson may have correctly described the asymmetry between first and other person ascriptions of mental predicates, he has done nothing to explain it'.[17] This strikes me as unfair to Strawson.[18] It is possible to see Davidson's work as continuous, rather than at odds, with that of Strawson. In what follows I shall attempt to show that Davidson's philosophical task is very much along the same lines as Strawson's, and that the work that Davidson does to 'explain' the asymmetry in our use of mental predicates dovetails nicely with that done by Strawson in his attempt to 'describe' the asymmetry. When one puts together the work of these two philosophers, what one gets is a picture of the structure of our concepts that should be acceptable to all those who operate within it. This picture should make it clear to us how the asymmetry in our use of mental predicates is compatible with a unity in their meaning.

What is striking about the work of both Strawson and Davidson is that it begins, as Wittgenstein's work begins, by looking at the way we operate with our mental concepts in our everyday lives. In other words, the work of all three philosophers takes as its starting point what I have labelled 'the lived position'. And the result of the work of all three is meant to be such as to lay to rest any queries we may be inclined to raise with respect to this starting point. In particular, once we understand the way our concepts fit together, we should feel no need to ask how a general concept of mind is possible. In the use we make of our mental concepts, their generality should appear unproblematic. Any temptation that one may have had to be sceptical about our starting point should be laid to rest by this picture. That, at least, is the aim.

STRAWSON AND DESCRIPTIVE METAPHYSICS

We find in Strawson's work a clear statement of the generality of our mental concepts and the unity of meaning in our mental predicates. Strawson writes:

> It is a necessary condition of one's ascribing states of consciousness, experiences, to oneself, in the way that one does, that one should also ascribe them, or be prepared to ascribe them, to others who are not oneself. This means not less than it says. It means, for example, that the ascribing phrases are used in just the same sense when the subject is another as when the subject is oneself. Of course, the thought that this is so gives no trouble to the non-philosopher.[19]

The generality of our mental concepts is unproblematic to the non-philosopher, that is to all of us in our daily lives. Nevertheless, the unproblematic can come to seem problematic to the philosopher. The philosopher notes that we use our mental concepts in very different ways in connection with ourselves and in connection with others, and then questions why we say it is the very same concept we are employing. Strawson also detects another problem for the philosopher – especially for the Cartesian philosopher who thinks he can identify states of consciousness within himself before identifying them in others. The problem Strawson sees is this: if one ascribes mental predicates to oneself as the result of inward reflection, it looks difficult – if not impossible – to distinguish one's own mental experiences from those of another. Strawson writes: 'We must know the difference between *one* such item and *two* such items. We must know, that is, on what principle such items are to be counted.'[20] Until we can identify several different individual consciousnesses, it is hard to see how we can speak of any individual consciousness. Although Strawson puts the point in terms of our capacity for the self-ascription of mental concepts, the point is related to the one I raised earlier: how can we account for the generality of our mental concepts?[21]

Strawson suggests a way to avoid the philosopher's problems. Where the Cartesian philosopher starts with the individual subject of consciousness, Strawson suggests that one begins with the whole person. And he explains, 'What I mean by the concept of a person is the concept of a type of entity such that *both* predicates ascribing states of consciousness *and* predicates ascribing corporeal characteristics, a physical situation etc. are equally applicable to a single individual of that single type.'[22] This concept of a person with which one begins must be taken, says Strawson, to be 'logically prior' to that of an individual consciousness. In other words, the primary concept is that of a person, and it is only once that concept is in place that we can understand the concept of an individual consciousness. Accepting the primitiveness of the concept of a person in our conceptual structure makes it possible for me to ascribe psychological predicates both to myself and to others. This is because a person has, as well as states of consciousness, corporeal characteristics. We can avoid one of the philosopher's difficulties: the identification of consciousness is the identification of a person, and where we are identifying a person we are identifying something that has a body as well as states of consciousness. When we ascribe states of consciousness to another we do this on the basis of our observation of the other's behaviour.

The starting point that Strawson urges avoids the problems of the philosopher's starting point. As well as avoiding the problem of identity, it avoids the problem of the generality of our concept. Generality is guaranteed because it is the starting point. This starting point leaves no room for either conceptual solipsism or conceptual scepticism; the concept of mind with which we operate applies to others as well as to oneself. Conceptual scepticism is precluded once we recognize that the logically dominant concept is not that of a mind but that of a person – the concept of a type of entity to which both mental *and* physical predicates can be ascribed.[23] The important thing about this, Strawsonian, move is that the concept of mind is no longer the concept of a thing apart. This is an explicit challenge to the Cartesian framework that is so dominant in the work of the philosophers considered in Part One. Where Cartesian philosophy introduces a logical gap between the mind and its body, Strawson is proposing that we start with a whole to which different types of predicate are applicable.[24] The asymmetry in our use of mental concepts can then be taken to be part of one unified concept. What we need to understand is the concept of a person that has pride of place in our conceptual scheme.

When we attribute various mental concepts to another person, we do so on the basis of the other's behaviour. We must, however, remember that things are importantly different with the self-ascription of these mental concepts. When one ascribes mental concepts to oneself one does *not* observe one's behaviour. This is the asymmetry in our use of mental concepts that leads the sceptic to raise questions about the unity of these concepts. Strawson's reaction to this asymmetry (like Wittgenstein's) is to say that this is simply characteristic of our mental concepts. Our mental concepts are such as to apply to others on the basis of the observation of behaviour while being such as to apply to oneself without the observation of any behaviour. Understanding that our mental concepts operate in this way is part of the description of our concepts. As Strawson says, 'If there were no concepts answering to [this] characterization . . ., we should indeed have no philosophical problem about the soul; but equally we should not have our concept of a person.'[25] A correct description of our concepts must acknowledge the asymmetry in our use, but, as Strawson notes, this description may be thought to give rise to philosophical problems. Problems arise when philosophers, as a result of observing this asymmetry, emphasize one or the other use as more basic: emphasizing self-ascription leads to problems about the ascription of the very same concept to others, while emphasizing other-ascription leads to worries that one has left out the very thing that makes this a *mental* concept that is being ascribed. If we avoid the philosophical moves that lead to these problems – if we refuse to take either ascription as more basic, what can we say about the observed asymmetry in our use of mental concepts? A mere description of the asymmetry does nothing to help us to understand why we continue to insist that it is the same concepts we are using in these very different ways. Without some kind of understanding here, the philosophers' moves can appear tempting.

It is at this point that Davidson thinks we need an explanation. Without an explanation, the sceptic will continue to press his question. Davidson is right to insist that something more needs to be said, although it is a question whether the something more that is needed should take the form of an explanation that will satisfy the sceptic. Perhaps what is needed is an extension of our description. This extended description may give us the intellectual satisfaction we seek, while turning us away from the temptation to make the philosophers' moves. This is what Strawson believes. While Strawson proposes that our concept of a person is fundamental in our conceptual structure, he also acknowledges the difficulties inherent in holding this. He writes:

Now our perplexities may take . . . the form of the question: 'But how can one ascribe to oneself, not on the basis of observation, the very same thing that others may have, on the basis of observation, reasons . . . for ascribing to one?' This question may be

absorbed in a wider one, which might be phrased: 'How are
P[sychological]-predicates possible?' or: 'How is the concept of
a person possible?'[26]

Strawson is raising a question that can be seen to be at one with the
question that I said earlier should replace that asked by those philosophers who take it that one begins by reflecting on how things are in
one's own case. Where one begins with inward reflection, the question
that arises is how generality is possible; where one begins with the
lived position, the question that arises is how the lived position – the
position that includes others as well as oneself – is possible. As with
Strawson's claim about the centrality of our concept of a person, the
mere assertion of the lived position can leave one feeling that there are
questions still to be answered. In both cases it can look as though one
is dogmatically asserting a starting point and refusing to answer the
questions it raises. It is in order to alleviate this feeling that I said the
philosopher must answer the question how the lived position is possible, and Strawson asks how the concept of a person is possible.
Now Strawson does not think we have to abandon the exercise of
description in order to give a satisfactory reply to his question; what
we must do is extend our description. It is hoped that this extended
description should satisfy our need to understand. Strawson makes a
move in the direction of such a description when he re-phrases his
question thus:

> We may still want to ask what it is in the natural facts that
> makes it intelligible that we should have this concept [that is, the
> concept of a person], and to ask this in the hope of a non-trivial
> answer, i.e. in the hope of an answer which does not *merely* say:
> 'Well, there are people in the world'.[27]

With this question Strawson is attempting to extend the description he
has thus far given of our practices, and to do so in a way that will help
us further understand the asymmetry that we find in our practices
that incorporate these concepts. We might hope that this further
description will make it less likely that we should be tempted to abandon our starting point and join the ranks of sceptics demanding a
justification of our practices.

Having raised our hopes, Strawson proceeds to outline what he
describes as 'beginnings or fragments of an answer' to the question
he has posed.[28] It is these beginnings that Davidson overlooks.
Furthermore, it is these beginnings that Davidson unwittingly builds

on, as I hope to show in the next section. Strawson begins by drawing our attention to that class of predicates which, while they may not indicate any definite sensation or experience, nonetheless imply consciousness. Examples of this kind of predicate include: 'going for a walk', 'playing ball', and 'writing a letter'. It is important that we see that such predicates do exhibit the asymmetry in question: although one does need to observe another's behaviour in order to ascribe them to another, one does not need to observe one's own behaviour before ascribing them to oneself. Despite this asymmetry of use, however, the temptation to suggest that what is being ascribed in each case is different is slight. This, says Strawson, is because of the 'marked dominance of a fairly definite pattern of bodily movement in what [these predicates] ascribe'.[29] These predicates show a little of the common territory occupied by both uses of our predicates. My writing a letter and your writing a letter both necessarily involve the movement of our bodies. I see your movements as actions, and I interpret them in terms of your intentions; I see your writing a letter as a token of the type of bodily movement which in my case I know to be the writing of a letter without the observation of the movement of my body. I see and understand your actions, and I know my actions. Most importantly, Strawson points out that our understanding of another's movements bears on and conditions our understanding of our own; we are in a position to understand the other's movements 'only by seeing them as elements in just such plans or schemes of action as those of which we know the present course and future development without observation of the relevant present movements'. And he continues, 'But this is to say that we see such movements as *actions*.'[30] Strawson summarizes his brief remarks thus:

> What I am suggesting is that it is easier to understand how we can see each other, and ourselves, as persons, if we think first of the fact that we act, and act on each other, and act in accordance with a common human nature.[31]

Notice that when Strawson asks the question, How is our concept of a person possible?, he asks specifically, What is it in the *natural facts* that makes this concept possible? His reply to this question stems from a close examination of the ways in which we interact with one another. We quite naturally respond to one another in a certain way. When we observe these interactions what we find is that there is a seamless flow between my actions in the world, my actions towards another and my recognition of the actions of another. Where the

Cartesian goes wrong is in thinking that this seamless flow can be broken up into separate moments. Where the behaviourist goes wrong is in thinking he can omit part of the flow. What Strawson points out is that, if you try to break up this flow, the movements you are left with are unintelligible. They are unintelligible because they no longer have any place in our conceptual scheme.

The further, expanded, description of our practices that Strawson provides includes reference to our nature, the nature each of us has and that each of us shares with others. It is observing this shared human nature that helps us to understand what makes our concept of a person possible; it also helps us to understand the asymmetry in our use of mental predicates. With our use of mental predicates we draw together our understanding both of ourselves and of others. The expanded description that Strawson offers bears a marked resemblance to that offered by Wittgenstein (*vide supra*). Like Wittgenstein, Strawson takes a description of our practices to include a reference to those who engage in the practice: our understanding of that practice is dependent upon our understanding of the shared nature of those who engage in it. With this description of things, we move closer to an understanding of the asymmetry in our use of mental predicates. We come closer to understanding both how our concept of a person is possible and how the lived position is possible. And understanding these things should wean us away from the temptation to raise sceptical questions. In particular, we should not be tempted to ask why we believe that there are other minds, or why we take there to be one unified concept of mind that applies both to ourselves and to others. The reason is that, on this picture of things, there is no logical gap for the sceptic to exploit between the subject and her world and, hence, between the behaviour and the mind of another. That this is the gap that the sceptic about other minds is exploiting is nicely captured by Davidson when he writes, 'If there is a logical or epistemic barrier between the mind and nature, it not only prevents us from seeing out; it also blocks a view from outside in.'[32] To paraphrase Davidson we could say, following Strawson, that if there is *no* logical gap between the subject and her world, this relieves us both of a problem of seeing out and of a block in our view from the outside in. What Strawson provides us with is an examination of the structure of our concepts that, it is hoped, will make it intelligible to us how things can be the way they manifestly are.[33] His examination first recognizes the logical priority of the concept of a person over that of an individual consciousness. It then reveals that our concept of a person is bound up with our concept of action. Persons act and they see the movements of others as of the same type that they produce when they are minded in a certain way. This, in turn, helps us to understand the asymmetry in our use of mental predicates. This asymmetry emerges from the nature that we share with others. There need be no temptation to say that our predicates are ambiguous; and there need be no temptation to question the unity in our mental concepts.

DAVIDSON AND INTERPRETATION

Davidson begins his discussion of these matters with what on the surface looks like an acknowledgement of the sceptic's question, 'Why do we take it that our use of mental predicates is unambiguous?' What Davidson appears to want is an explanation that will, once and for all, silence the sceptic.[34] In contrast to this I have been arguing, following Strawson, that we should ignore the sceptic's starting point and the questions to which it gives rise. We should start with a recognition of the lived position that takes it that our use of mental predicates is unambiguous. What we need to understand is not how, from the standpoint of the sceptic, these predicates can be unambiguous, but how, assuming these predicates to be unambiguous, the lived position is possible. In what follows I will try to show that, despite many of the things he has written, Davidson is not after all hospitable to the sceptic. Davidson himself has come more recently to describe his work as giving a theory about our beliefs which is such that 'scepticism cannot get started'.[35] Insofar as Davidson's work does have this result, it can be placed alongside Strawson's. Furthermore, despite the fact that Davidson rejects all talk of conceptual schemes, his work can be described as that of a descriptive metaphysician.[36] The reason is that Strawson's talk of conceptual structure need not – indeed, should not – be taken to have any truck with a dualism between conceptual scheme and content (*vide supra*). If we do see Davidson's exercise as continuous with Strawson's, we can also see it as building on the 'beginnings or fragments of an answer' that Strawson offers in response to the question, How is our concept of a person possible? Although Davidson's work can be seen to build on Strawson's, the question Davidson sets out to answer is not the same as Strawson's. The question Davidson asks is this: How do our beliefs and utterances come to have the content they do? Despite the difference in their questions, what I hope to show is that their responses share something in common; and what the responses share in common can help us to fill out the conceptual picture that Strawson began to describe. The result of putting together Davidson's work with that of Strawson's is a description of the concepts with which we operate in our everyday lives – and this description is such as to leave no temptation to raise the various sceptical questions about others. I want now to explain how Davidson proposes to answer the question he raises.

Davidson conducts his exercise in terms of an examination of our mental predicates. Davidson's question is why we take it that our mental predicates are unambiguous. Now it is interesting to note that, where I have been considering this question in connection with what I have been calling the conceptual problem of other minds, Davidson raises the question in connection with the traditional epistemological problem of other minds. The difference here may be seen to be connected with Davidson's inclination (at least much of the time) to take the sceptical challenge seriously and to explain things in such a way as to satisfy the sceptic. As Davidson sees it, the question over the ambiguity of our mental predicates arises in the context of traditional sceptical questions.[37] The sceptic about other minds begins by accepting without question our entitlement to talk of our knowledge of our own mental states, and questions our entitlement to talk of our knowledge of other minds. In an attempt to answer the sceptic's question the philosopher may reply that we know that another has a mind because of our observation of the other's behaviour. At this point the sceptic will press his question, thus: 'If the mental states of others are known only through their behavioural and other outward manifestations, while this is not true of our own mental states, why should we think that our own mental states are anything like those of others?'[38] Davidson takes it that, until we can give some explanation here, we have no answer to the question why we take our mental predicates to be unambiguous. Notice that, while the first sceptical question is an epistemological one, the second sceptical question is concerned with the very meaning of the words involved in raising that epistemological question. Until the second sceptical question is answered, it is not clear that the first sceptical question can even be raised. It is this that Davidson appears to miss. When I raised the question of ambiguity earlier, I did not raise it in the traditional sceptical context; rather, I raised it in the context of a *conceptual* difficulty, as a question concerning the generality of our mental concepts and, correspondingly, the univocity of the mental predicates we use to ascribe them. I argued that there is a *prima facie* difficulty with the traditional sceptic's entitlement to raise the questions he does about the minds of others. The *first* question is the conceptual one, and the answer we give to it must make it clear why we take it that it is the very same concept we apply to others that we apply in our own case. Until the conceptual question has been answered, we are in no position to raise the traditional sceptical question about our knowledge of another mind. Given this, we can see the series of sceptical questions that Davidson poses leads him away from epistemological issues and towards conceptual ones.

Let us now proceed to see how Davidson proposes to answer the question he asks. Davidson begins by listing three varieties of empirical knowledge: our knowledge of our own mind, our knowledge of the world and our knowledge of other minds. He then explains that philosophers have often attempted to understand the relationship between these varieties of knowledge by taking one variety as primary, and attempting a reduction of the other forms to this. One familiar exercise of this response is the Cartesian attempt to take self-knowledge as primary and to try to derive our knowledge of the external world from this – adding a further step to other minds based on observation of behaviour. Concerning such exercises Davidson writes, 'Scepticism in various of its familiar guises is our grudging tribute to the apparent impossibility of unifying the three varieties of knowledge.'[39] Davidson diagnoses the philosophers' failure to defeat scepticism as resulting from a tendency to consider these problems separately. He suggests that we eschew reductions. What we must appreciate is the way that these three kinds of knowledge relate. About this Davidson writes,

> In trying to form a picture of the relations among the three kinds of knowledge we must do much more than show *that* they are mutually irreducible; we must see *why* they are irreducible. This in turn will involve bringing out the respective conceptual roles played by each of the forms of knowledge, and showing why each of the three sorts of knowledge is indispensable – why we could not get along without all of them.[40]

This, then, is Davidson's project: to show the indispensability of each form of knowledge; to show the conceptual role played by each. Davidson begins his project by considering, not one or another form of knowledge, but belief which is a condition of knowledge. What Davidson wants to understand is how our beliefs come to have the content that they do. His answer to this question is such as to link beliefs to language. The discriminating behaviour of a non-linguistic creature is, according to Davidson, insufficient for belief. The sunflower turns towards the light, the earthworm makes its way along the ground towards a source of food and a dog can forage for a bone by the garden gate, but none of these creatures can appreciate the difference between the real and the apparent, between what they think and what is the case. It is the capacity to appreciate this contrast that Davidson thinks distinguishes those with from those without beliefs. Davidson holds that this capacity comes about as the result of communication through language. Language puts us on the path that makes belief possible. What we need to understand is how language does this.

In order to explain just how communication can be the source of objective truth Davidson sketches a picture of how a competent speaker of a language comes to understand – to interpret – a speaker of an alien tongue. If we consider a competent speaker's utterance of a sentence, what we find is that the meaning of that utterance is a function of that speaker's intentions and beliefs. The radical interpreter knows neither what the speaker's utterances mean nor what his intentions and beliefs are. If the interpreter could get a handle on the speaker's intentions and beliefs she could work out the utterance's meaning; or if she knew the utterance's meaning she could work out the speaker's intentions and beliefs. Davidson suggests that the interpreter breaks into this circle of meaning and belief by first identifying which utterances the speaker *holds true*. The reason why this helps is that the attitude of holding true can be identified without having to know what the utterance means.[41] Once the interpreter knows which utterances the speaker holds true, she can proceed to separate out the two components of belief and meaning. She does this by applying to those utterances identified as held true by the speaker two principles: the principle of coherence and the principle of correspondence.[42] The principle of coherence encourages the interpreter to attribute a certain degree of logical consistency to her subject; while the principle of correspondence encourages the interpreter to find her subject rational and largely correct in his beliefs about the world. Davidson explains this second principle by saying that it encourages the interpreter to take the speaker to be 'responding to the same features of the world that [the interpreter] would be responding to under similar circumstances'.[43] Thus, interpretation proceeds under an assumption of shared logical consistency and shared responses to the world.

It is at this point that questions – and eyebrows – are raised. Davidson accepts that there is a very important challenge to this line of thought, which is this: Why should what people agree upon be true? Or, to put the question another way, Why should an interpersonal standard be an objective one? Surely there is more to our picture than what goes on in interpretation; surely it is the world that constrains what we can say about it. Interpretation yields only an interpersonal standard, not an objective one. Davidson's reply to these questions is to emphasize the importance of shared responses to mutual understanding.[44] In talking about shared responses Davidson is careful to distinguish between responses that are *de facto* shared and those that are acknowledged as shared. It is the latter that are fundamental to interpretation. The acknowledgement of one speaker by another of the similarity in their response is what makes it possible to say that these individuals are in fact responding similarly. If we trace back out from this shared response to the world we can then identify the source of this response. Davidson writes,

> Until the triangle is completed connecting two creatures, and each creature with common features of the world, there can be no answer to the question whether a creature, in discriminating between stimuli, is discriminating between stimuli at the sensory surfaces or somewhere further out, or further in. Without this sharing of reactions to common stimuli, thought and speech would have no particular content – that is no content at all. . . .
> We may think of it as a form of triangulation: each of two people is reacting differently to sensory stimulation streaming in from a certain direction. If we project the incoming lines outward, their intersection is the common cause. If two people now note each other's reactions (in the case of language, verbal reactions), each can correlate these observed reactions with his or her stimuli from the world. The common cause can now determine the contents of an utterance and a thought. The triangle which gives content to thought and speech is complete.[45]

So the world does constrain what we can say about it, but our knowledge of the world is necessarily conditioned by our knowledge of other minds. As Davidson writes in one place: 'A community of minds is the basis of knowledge; it provides the basis of all things. It makes no sense to question the adequacy of this measure, or to seek a more ultimate standard.'[46] We are back with an intersubjective standard; we are back with interpretation. What all this shows, says Davidson, is the way we 'see through language'.[47] We must, however, be careful how we understand this. Davidson compares the way we see through language with the way we see through our eyes. Both our language and our eyes can be thought of as organs with which we come into 'direct contact' with our environment; as with our eyes, we perceive the world with language. We must, however, be very careful how we understand the idea that we see through language. We must be careful not to think that our language mediates between us and the world; that it represents or mirrors the world. *This* understanding of the way we see through language leaves the door open for sceptical attack: as there is a gap between the representation and what it represents, a justification is required of any step we might take from the representation to the purported object presented. Our perceptions and our language are seen as barriers between us and reality. Davidson wants to close this gap. There are no barriers – logical or epistemic; language does not represent reality, it presents reality. In the place of a gap that we must somehow reach across if we are to account for knowledge, what we have is three kinds of knowledge – knowledge of our own mind, of the world, and of other minds – each supporting and making possible the other.

Davidson represents these kinds of knowledge, and their dependence on one another, by a triangle, thus:

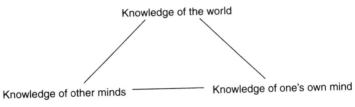

Whichever way one turns this triangle one finds that one can only make sense of one angle (kind of knowledge) by reference to the other angles (kinds of knowledge). Thus, while we find that our knowledge of the world depends on communication between persons, we also find that communication between persons depends on our recognition that we occupy a shared world. Furthermore, it is not possible to speak of the propositional contents of our own mind until we acknowledge our mind's interaction, in communication, with another mind. The line that connects one's own mind to other minds forms what Davidson calls 'the base line'. Appeal to a base line is not intended to imply any conceptual priority, but is intended as a starting point. We come full circle; or rather, Davidson has shown how the three angles of the triangle each depend essentially on the other two angles.

Once we appreciate the way in which our knowledge of other minds, of the world, and of our own mind hang together, we can also appreciate how it is that Davidson can write: 'the nature of correct interpretation guarantees both that a large number of our simplest beliefs are true, and that the nature of these beliefs is known to others'.[48] Notice that it is 'a large number' of our beliefs that can be taken to be true. Of course there is always room for error. What this way of looking at things rules out is the possibility of massive, or global, error. In other words, what this picture rules out is the possibility of radical, Cartesian, scepticism. As Davidson writes: 'What cannot be the case is that our general picture of the world and our place in it is mistaken, for it is this picture which informs the rest of our beliefs, whether they be true or false, and makes them intelligible.'[49]

Of course the label 'Cartesian scepticism' is, as we have seen, misleading. Descartes himself is not a sceptic. According to Descartes knowledge is possible; its possibility rests on the existence of a non-deceiving God. One could represent Descartes' account of knowledge as a triangle with knowledge of God in place of knowledge of other minds. Contrasting the Cartesian and the Davidsonian representations of knowledge we could say that, where Descartes relies on God to guarantee our beliefs about the world, Davidson relies on other speakers; where Descartes relies on God to ensure the veridicality of our beliefs, Davidson relies on the nature of belief itself. The nature of belief is such that we can be assured, not only that the world exists, but that most of what we believe about it is true. And it is the nature of belief that makes interpretation possible. Thus we find that Davidson answers his original question (How is belief possible?) by appeal to the nature of belief. Davidson holds that the nature of belief is such as to be veridical, and we can see that this is so when we consider the way that beliefs come to have the contents that they do.

Let us now turn to the way that Davidson proposes to explain the asymmetry that we find in our use of mental concepts. Thus far I have been discussing the asymmetry in terms of our reference to behaviour in the use of predicates such as 'beliefs that p' in connection with another, and the absence of any such reference in the use of such predicates in one's own case. Connected with this is a certain assurance in the way I use this predicate in my own case which is not matched in the way I use it in connection with another. Davidson talks of a certain authority or privilege which attaches to the first-person use of such a predicate.[50] This is the asymmetry that Davidson sets out to explain. He proposes that we find the explanation we need when we look more closely at the situation of the radical interpreter. The asymmetry we find in our use of mental predicates can be explained by the following feature of the interpretative situation. On the one hand, an interpreter must always be open to the possibility that, although she may have done her best to understand the utterances of another, further evidence may require her to reassess her interpretation. A speaker, on the other hand, can do no better than to say what he means. The interpreter – if she is to be in a position to interpret at all – must take it that the speaker wishes to be understood and, as a result, that the speaker knows what he means.[51] It is the constraints on interpretation, then, that can be taken to explain the asymmetry in our use of mental predicates. Davidson thinks that it is possible to understand the asymmetry between first- and third-person uses of mental predicates if we follow through a certain way of understanding how it is possible for beliefs to have the contents that they do; i.e. if we follow through our account of how belief is possible.[52]

STRAWSON AND DAVIDSON

Strawson and Davidson have each, in their own way, arrived at an understanding of the asymmetry that is involved in our use of mental concepts. Let us recall the reason we set out in search of such an understanding. I argued above that the need for an understanding of this asymmetry formed part of the need for us to understand how our general concept of mind is possible. I claimed that it is only by assuming that our mental concepts are in fact general that we can avoid what has come to be called the conceptual problem of other minds. We must begin by noting the generality of our concept and then try to understand our concept in such a way that there can be no temptation to ask the question, Why do we assume that we are working with one concept here and not two? (Or, in the linguistic mode: Why do we assume that our mental predicates are unambiguous?) I suggested that both Strawson and Davidson could be seen as offering a defence of our general concept of mind in the work that each does to make comprehensible to us the asymmetry that lies at the heart of our use of mental predicates. If we can accept what they show us about our mental concepts, we should no longer be tempted to take the fact that there is an asymmetry in our use of mental predicates to be in any kind of tension with the generality of our starting point. The end result of all this work would be to make the lived position comprehensible.

It should be clear, then, the way I see the work of Strawson and Davidson as fitting in with the overall position I wish to adopt. I now want to explain why I take it that, despite some of the things that Davidson has said, his approach to the understanding of this asymmetry is in line with Strawson's. As I said above, both Davidson and Strawson could be taken to be engaged in the exercise that Strawson once labelled 'descriptive metaphysics', and it is possible to see Davidson's work as an extension of Strawson's here. I want now to spell out the way the work of these two philosophers overlaps.

Strawson traces the asymmetry in our mental concepts to the centrality of our concept of a person (*vide supra*). Strawson does not stop here, but asks how it is possible that we should ascribe the very same thing to ourselves, not on the basis of observation, that we ascribe to others on the basis of observation. Strawson takes this question to be equivalent to asking how the concept of a person is possible. Thus, by enquiring further into our concept of a person Strawson aims to shed further light on the asymmetry that lies at the heart of our mental concepts. Interestingly, Strawson pursues the question about persons by asking what it is in the natural facts that makes it intelligible that we should have the concept of a person that we have. His answer is that we are in a position to see each other as persons from the natural fact that we 'act, and act on each other, and act in accordance with a common human nature'. Ultimately, then, we must understand our mental concepts by reference to action. By 'action' Strawson is careful to point out that he does not have in mind mere movement. An action is something that only subjects are in a position to carry out, and to observe.

Davidson sees the asymmetry in our ascription of mental states as connected to the nature of interpretation. There is a presumption that the speaker knows what he believes when he speaks. This is a presumption without which interpretation could not proceed, and interpretation lies at the heart of our understanding of the way beliefs come to have the contents they do. So, the asymmetry is connected with interpretation which, in turn, is connected with belief. It would be possible to understand what Davidson is doing here by approaching it from a slightly different angle. Let us begin once again with the question Davidson asks, How is belief possible? Following Strawson let us expand this question thus: What is it in the natural facts that makes it intelligible that we should have the concept of belief that we have? Let us now use the reply that Strawson gives to a parallel question about persons in response to this question. Thus we could say:

> We have the concept of belief that we do because we are creatures who act in the world, and act on each other, and act in accordance with a common human nature.[53]

This reply dovetails perfectly with what Davidson actually does say in reply to his question. Davidson links belief content with interpretation and then shows how interpretation proceeds. When we interpret, what we interpret is the behaviour (the actions) of subjects. Our actions – linguistic and otherwise – form the subject matter of interpretation. Now Strawson connects our concept of a person with the same natural facts: our actions and interactions with others. Once we see this we can see that our concept of a person connects with our concept of belief via that of an action. The concept of action is a sort of pivot concept. We could say that, ultimately, it is by reference to action that we are able to understand the asymmetry that lies at the heart of our mental concepts. If we want to understand how our mental concepts can be general we must understand that we are creatures who 'act, act on each other, and act in accordance with a common human nature'.[54] Our concept of action is such as to draw together one's idea of oneself as a subject of action, one's idea of others as subjects of action, and our idea of the world. The activity of a subject is engaged *in* the world and *with* other subjects. Knowledge is the upshot of this activity.

What can we say about the knowledge that is the upshot of this activity? Towards the close of Chapter I, I suggested that there are two distinct ways of thinking of the relationship between our concepts of knowledge and action. On one way of thinking the concept of knowledge takes precedence over that of action. Thus we find that Descartes sees knowledge as a subject's way of reaching out to a world that lies beyond him – as forming a bridge between the metaphysically distinct worlds of the subject, on the one hand, and the object, on the other. On this model action is suspended for the time of the *Meditations*, until such time as the metaphysical gap is bridged and knowledge established on a firm foundation. We can now see that this way of thinking about knowledge is very much opposed to the model I am urging (and that we can find in the work of, *inter alia*, Strawson and Davidson). On this *other* model our concept of knowledge is tempered by action. Our concept of action joins together mind and body. Action is the business of a subject engaged in communication with other subjects who interact with the world. This is what we understand when we explore the lived position. And if we do adopt the lived position we are able to avoid the conceptual problem of other minds.

ANOTHER SCEPTICAL CHALLENGE

I want now to consider an argument designed to show that, although there may be reasons to hold that we must believe that there are others and a natural world that we share with them, the requirement that we believe this is consistent with the falsity of our beliefs. According to this argument, it may be true that our beliefs hang together in a certain way, but none of this guarantees the truth of our beliefs. Scepticism in its traditional guise is still a possibility. This sceptical position has been defended with great persuasive force over the years by Barry Stroud.[55] Stroud's attack on the form of argument employed by the likes of Strawson and Davidson has softened somewhat over the years. Where Stroud once challenged the very idea that such arguments could be effective against Cartesian style scepticism, he now wants to allow that such arguments are effective – but only up to a point. Stroud believes there is still room here for *a* sceptical challenge.

Before we turn to Stroud's challenge, let us consider what Strawson and Davidson say about the sceptic. Both Strawson and Davidson begin by raising the conceptual problem of other minds. This conceptual question is prior to epistemological questions about the existence of the world and other minds. Nonetheless, the result of the work by both Strawson and Davidson is such that we can say that, if they are right about our mental concepts, then there is no need to ask the traditional epistemological questions. The reason is particularly clear in Davidson's work. The conclusion of Davidson's line of thought is that there is a way to understand the asymmetry in our use of mental predicates that makes it plausible to maintain that our use of these predicates is unambiguous. The story Davidson tells involves a description of the interpretive exercise that gives content to our beliefs: the world and others figure in the way that all belief comes to have content. Once we understand the way others and the world figure in belief content in the first place, the traditional questions asked by the sceptic no longer arise. Strawson is clear that the end result of his descriptive exercise is that traditional sceptical questions have been pre-empted. Once we understand how our concepts work, we see that the sceptic's questions depend on the very structure that he purports to call into question.[56] In the case where someone loses sight of the way our mental concepts tie up with our action in the world, what we must do is once more to take them through the descriptive exercise outlined above; what we do *not* do is take their worry seriously. The descriptive exercise helps us to understand the concepts with which we operate in our daily lives. Notice that, although the exercise begins as a way of understanding the generality inherent in our mental concepts, the description we give is such as to take for granted the existence of others and of a world. We come to have an understanding of the unity of our concept of mind that leaves no room either for a question about the unity of that concept or for a question about the existence of another mind. On this way of proceeding, there is no conceptual problem and there is no epistemological problem about other minds.

For these reasons it is misleading for Davidson to talk as he does in several places of the need to give explanations to the sceptic. When Davidson complains that Strawson does nothing to explain the asymmetry in our use of mental concepts it can look as if he is complaining that Strawson has not said enough to refute the sceptic here. This way of setting out the problem may lead one to think that Davidson's project is that of showing the sceptic where he goes wrong. This would place Davidson on the side of philosophers, like Descartes, who listen patiently to the sceptic and then set out to provide an explanation of matters that is intended to show him the error of his ways. The temptation to read Davidson in this way is reinforced when we read him writing the following: 'how about . . . [the] admonition to stop trying to answer the sceptic, and tell him to get lost? A short response would be that the sceptic has been told this again and again over the millennia and never seems to listen; like the philosopher he is, he wants an argument.'[57] Despite the fact that it looks as if Davidson is here setting himself on the side of those who attempt to engage with the sceptic, we also find him writing just a few lines later: 'I did not set out to "refute" the sceptic, but to give a sketch of what I think to be a correct account of the foundations of linguistic communication and its implication for truth, belief and knowledge. If one grants the correctness of this account, one *can* tell the sceptic to get lost.'[58] Here we find Davidson writing in a manner more reminiscent of Strawson than Descartes. One way to place Davidson more firmly on the side of Strawson here would be to modify his complaint against Strawson over the issue of the asymmetry in our mental concepts. Rather than complain that Strawson does nothing to *explain* the asymmetry, he should say that Strawson has not done enough to *describe* it. An expanded description should help us to understand why there is an asymmetry in our use of mental predicates. Dropping all talk of explanation here would strengthen Davidson's hand and help him to repel Stroud's attempt to mount a further sceptical challenge.

As I have said, Stroud wants to agree with the work of both Davidson and Strawson – up to a certain point. He agrees that it may not be possible for us to have any thoughts unless we take it that there is a world and others with whom we are in communication. And if this is the case, we may conclude that it is not possible for us to take the sceptic's questions seriously. This is how Stroud understands the Strawsonian idea that any sceptical challenge is idle: it is idle because nothing can move us from our belief in the world and others. As Stroud sees it, what philosophers like Strawson and Davidson have shown is that we are secure against, or invulnerable to, the sceptic's challenge. What provides us with this security is pre-cisely what must be in place in order for us to have any thoughts in the first place. However, Stroud carefully peels off the question of our security or invulnerability here from the question of what he calls 'positive metaphysical results'.[59] Stroud takes it that what Strawson has shown is that the sceptical question is idle 'because . . . nothing could ever lead us to change our minds on such fundamental matters; there is simply no point in considering it'.[60] These 'fundamental mat-ters' will include that there is an external world and that there are other minds. But Stroud does not see that the sceptic's challenge is to get us to change our minds about such things. We can leave our beliefs in place; we are secure. The point is that we should find a reason for holding these beliefs to be inviolable. This is the sceptical challenge. Our beliefs remain in place, but we must have a reason for our beliefs. This is the positive metaphysical result that is quite separate from the security we have in our beliefs. Thus Stroud can agree that the scep-tic's challenge is impotent to challenge our beliefs. What the sceptic does, however, is benefit human reason by challenging us to defend these beliefs by appeal to positive metaphysical results. What we must accept, according to Stroud, is that all our beliefs might be the way they are and yet be false.

Stroud's position here might be thought to parallel Descartes'. Before the sixth *Meditation*, Descartes is in a position to have what he calls 'moral certainty' that the world exists. Following Stroud we could say that it is Descartes' recognition of the *logical* possibility that everything that he believes may be the result of the machinations of an evil demon that spurs him on to his proof of the existence of a non-deceiving God, and hence the position (at the end of the *Meditations*) that *absolute* knowledge is possible. We could say, following Stroud, that moral certainty is not something that we abandon in the face of the sceptic. Indeed, the sceptic is not out to diminish this certainty. What the sceptic has succeeded in forcing Descartes to do is find a reason that might be thought to support this certainty, thus upgrading it to absolute knowledge. With his proof of the existence of a non-deceiving God, Descartes claimed to have found the positive metaphysical result Stroud thinks is needed. Stroud does not accept Descartes' defence of our beliefs, but he holds that we must not lose sight of what is required for us to be in a position to say of our beliefs that they are true. Security is one thing, positive metaphysical results another.

But where Stroud sees two questions there is only one. When Strawson claims that the sceptic's question is idle, he does not leave

251

the door open for 'positive metaphysical results'. And when Davidson claims that we can see from the way that content is possible that knowledge of our own mind, other minds and of the world stand together, he does not leave it open that we can move from this to a more secure form of knowledge. The kind of positive metaphysical results that Stroud takes to be in the picture are part of a picture that Davidson rejects. Stroud still sees the sceptic as demanding a response, if not because he threatens our security, then because he challenges our right to believe that our beliefs are largely correct. But providing an explanation that will satisfy either kind of sceptic is not how we should understand the work of either Strawson or Davidson. If we take it that what both Strawson and Davidson are doing is describing the structure of our concepts in order to make understandable to us what I have called the lived position, then there is no room for either of the sceptical questions that Stroud identifies. The starting point is the world I live in with others. The single question before us is the one with which I began this chapter: How are we to understand this starting point? The question that bothers Stroud simply doesn't arise. Thus we can see that (*pace* Stroud) conceptual considerations leave us secure in our knowledge that we co-exist with others in a natural world. There is no room on this picture of things for a logical or metaphysical gap between me and everything else. With his insistence on a rational defence of all of our beliefs at once – and from the outside – Stroud is endorsing a picture that, like Descartes', takes knowledge to have primacy over action. An isolated subject reaches out with this knowledge to a world that is (in the words of Bernard Williams) *there anyway*. The kind of realism that Stroud is defending is the one I earlier labelled 'hard', and it gives rise to a radical form of scepticism. The conception of knowledge that is tempered by agency yields what I earlier labelled 'soft realism' – a realism that allows for uncertainty but not radical scepticism. These labels are a handy device for referring to positions here, but ultimately it may be best to leave labels behind altogether, and talk simply of our actions in the world and with others.[61]

What we need to be clear about is the nature of our question. At the outset of this chapter I put to one side the question, Given a certain understanding of how I come by my concept of mind in the first place, how am I to understand the generality that this concept appears to have? I suggested that, if we think of the concept in this way, generality is difficult – if not impossible – to come by. The point is that the first-person orientation of the concept makes its generality difficult to understand. It is difficult to understand because of the problem of unity. In order to avoid this problem, I suggested that we begin with what I labelled the 'lived position'; that is, we begin with a concept that is already general. The question we then need to ask is, How are we to understand this lived position; how is this lived position possible? I outlined two different suggestions for how we might do this – one taken from Strawson and another from Davidson. I also suggested that the work of Strawson and Davidson can be understood to share a common descriptive aim. The work of these two philosophers shares another important element: the way they suggest for understanding generality leaves no room for epistemological questions concerning the existence of another mind. The lived position just is a position in which our concept is general and where we understand this generality by appeal to our actions and our common human nature. There is, on this position, no gap between myself and others that needs to be bridged (no gap arising from a Cartesian metaphysical divide). For this reason there is no room for the 'positive metaphysical results' that Stroud yearns for.

CHAPTER IX

The conceptual problem: another approach

INTRODUCTION

> The interesting problem of other minds is not the epistemological problem, how I can know that other people are not zombies. It is the conceptual problem, how I can *understand* the attribution of mental states to others. And this in turn is really the problem, how I can conceive of my own mind as merely one of many examples of mental phenomena contained in the world.[1]

These words might be thought to summarize the work of the previous chapter. I began that chapter by raising a serious conceptual problem in connection with the generality of our mental concepts given a certain starting point. I then suggested that we can avoid these problems if we take our concepts to have generality from the start. The upshot of a certain understanding of this starting point is that there is no room for any sceptical question concerning the existence of the mind of another. We could say that, once we sort out the interesting conceptual problem of other minds, we can see that the epistemological question was a red herring.

The author of the above quotation is Thomas Nagel, and the position he defends is in many ways opposed to the one I have been defending. When Nagel writes that the interesting problem of other minds is the conceptual, and not the epistemological, one he means something that cannot be understood in terms of the work of the previous chapter. Let me now explain what Nagel means when he writes this.

THE (UNINTERESTING) EPISTEMOLOGICAL PROBLEM

Let us begin by looking at the problem which Nagel wishes to place to one side, the problem he wishes to contrast with the interesting conceptual problem: the epistemological problem of other minds. Nagel does not find this an *interesting* problem. But the reason is not that he thinks that the epistemological problem is a red herring, but that he thinks it is unalterable. To see this, recall the relationship that Nagel believes to hold between realism and knowledge. In one place Nagel writes: 'The search for objective knowledge, because of its commitment to a realistic picture, is inescapably subject to skepticism and cannot refute it but must proceed under its shadow.'[2] On Nagel's picture of things, knowing is our way of reaching out across a divide (Nagel here – as in many other places – reveals his commitment to the Cartesian conceptual divide), and built into Nagel's picture of knowing is the possibility of falling short – of failing in our reach. It is for this reason that Nagel sees scepticism as a live threat. We can see from the way that Nagel sets things up that the scepticism he envisages here is *radical*: there is a real question how I know that other people are not zombies. This possibility – this threat – is part of the human condition; it is something we must live with. This scepticism is the flip side of what I earlier labelled Nagel's 'hard realism'. We could say that Nagel accommodates scepticism as part of his picture of knowledge and reality. Despite the ever-present threat of scepticism, however, we remain, according to Nagel, committed to our belief in the existence of other minds and we try to find out as much as we can about them. What we must accept is that, at the end of the day, there is what Nagel calls a 'gap' between our beliefs about others and the contents of those beliefs under a realistic interpretation.[3]

Hard realism is Nagel's starting point: other minds exist and it would be flying in the face of reality to deny this. Part of this hard realist picture is that other minds exist – not just in other human beings, and not just in creatures like ourselves, but in creatures in many respects dissimilar to ourselves. Nagel acknowledges this when he writes,

> I assume we all believe that bats have experience. After all, they are mammals, and there is not more doubt that they have experience than that mice or pigeons or whales have experience. . . . Bats, although more closely related to us than other species, nevertheless present a range of activities and a sensory apparatus . . . different from us.[4]

Nagel is not so much concerned to defend this realism as to accept a certain ignorance about those minds very different from our own. This ignorance is reflected in Nagel's claim that, although we can be confident that other animals such as bats have minds, we are unable to comprehend what things are like for bats. Nagel uses this observation to drive a wedge between our objective knowledge of the world and the bodies of, say, bats, and the subjective viewpoints which are theirs despite our inability to comprehend them. The point may be harder to see in the case of minds close to our own where, Nagel holds, we *can* comprehend the experiences of another.[5] What the contrast with the case of a bat shows us is that, when we do understand what another is experiencing, we do not do this on the basis of objective knowledge alone. We need to be able to occupy the relevant point of view, and we can only do this in the human case. (Perhaps we can go a little further than this, but not much.)

To someone who denies that we can believe in the existence of a mental reality whose nature we cannot comprehend, Nagel points out the following: denying this would be no different from an intelligent Martian who tried but failed to comprehend the nature of our mental lives, and thereby concluded that we have no mental life. The point here is that, although the Martian is doomed to failure, we are in a prime position to realize that his denial of the reality of our mental lives is a mistake. Similarly, just because we cannot ever hope to be able to give a detailed description of a bat's phenomenology, we should not conclude that it is meaningless to claim that bats have experiences fully comparable in richness of detail to our own.[6] Nor do we have to imagine Martians to make the point. In one place Nagel takes as his example the thinking of blind and deaf people. We have no problem saying that such people are unable to form conceptions of things that we, sighted and hearing persons, can know. And yet we are in a prime position to have the ideas that are denied to the blind and deaf.[7] Nagel takes the point about Martians merely to be an extension from this. He concludes: 'to deny the reality or logical significance of what we can never describe or understand is the crudest form of cognitive dissonance'.[8]

Nagel defends this position in his later work. His strategy is not so much to advance a positive argument here, as to defend hard realism against arguments that hold that it runs into insuperable philosophical problems which can only be solved by the abandonment of that position. Nagel's position is that 'realism makes as much sense as many other unverifiable statements, even though all of them, and all thought, may present fundamental philosophical mysteries to which there is at present no solution'.[9] In effect Nagel is starting from a position where he takes it that we believe certain things that we are not in a position to know, and there's an end on it. We can hope that someday things will be made clearer to us, but we may have to reconcile ourselves to this as part of the human predicament. It is for this reason that Nagel holds that the epistemological problem of other minds is not an interesting problem.

THE (INTERESTING) CONCEPTUAL PROBLEM

The interesting problem of other minds is, according to Nagel, the conceptual one, the problem captured by the question, How can I conceive of my mind as merely one of many examples of mental phenomena contained in the world? This is a problem philosophers *can* say something about; indeed, they must say something about it if they are not to fall into conceptual solipsism. In this connection Nagel cites a passage from Wittgenstein's *Blue Book*: 'If what I feel is always *my* pain only, what can the supposition mean that someone else feels pain?'[10] In this connection Nagel writes, 'the avoidance of solipsism requires that the *conception* of other persons like oneself (not necessarily the belief that there are any) be included in the idea of one's own experience from the beginning'.[11]

Conceptual solipsism, then, is a position Nagel is keen to avoid. In this respect he is in agreement with the position I outlined in the previous chapter. However, Nagel does not understand the relationship between conceptual and epistemological issues in the way outlined in that chapter. At the end of the previous chapter I explained that, on a certain understanding of the generality of our mental concepts, no epistemological – or sceptical – problems arise; that there are other minds is the starting point. Contrary to this, Nagel takes it that it is possible to give an account of the generality of our mental concepts that leaves room for radical epistemological scepticism. According to Nagel, the sceptic can legitimately claim to have a quite general conception of mind while at the same time allowing for the possibility of radical doubt concerning the existence of any mind other than his own. Far from holding that the generality inherent in our concept of mind cuts the ground from under the sceptic, Nagel sees no problem in saying that the concept that the sceptic employs in the formulation of his position is a perfectly general one. The question we need to ask, then, is: how is it that Nagel understands the generality inherent in our mental concepts?

Clearly Nagel cannot accept the understanding of the lived position that I outlined in the previous chapter. Nagel would no doubt consider my understanding of the lived position to be overly verificationist; that is to say, he would consider the conception of reality to emerge from this way of proceeding to be too closely tied to what we can know. If we do tie the reality of another mind too close to what we can know, we will end up with a position that is overly restrictive in its attribution of mind. The realism that Nagel envisages is hard – it allows for the possibility of minds in creatures far and wide. Nagel writes: 'There is probably a great deal of [conscious] life in the universe, and we may be in a position to identify only some of its forms.'[12] According to Nagel there may be creatures, sufficiently unlike ourselves, to whom we would be unable to attribute a mental life because their movements would not be recognizable by us. If, however, we understand the generality of our mental concepts by reference to the concept of action, as I suggested in the previous chapter, those concepts could only get a grip where we were in a position to recognize the behaviour of the other. It is because Nagel wishes to distance himself from positions that he labels 'verificationist', that he is forced to divorce our mental concepts from the concept of action. But if our mental concepts *are* divorced from the concept of action, how are we to understand the generality inherent in them?

Nagel does not present us with a developed proposal, but the broad outlines of his position are clear. Let us begin with what Nagel writes in *The View From Nowhere*:

> The beginning of an objective concept of mind is the ability to view one's own experiences from outside, as events in the world. If this is possible, then others can also conceive of those events and one can conceive of the experiences of others, also from outside. To think in this way we use not a faculty of external representation, but a general idea of subjective points of view, of which we imagine a particular instance and a particular form. So far the process does not involve any abstraction from the general forms of our experience. We still think of experience in terms of the familiar point of view we share with other humans. All that is involved in the external conception of mind is the imaginative use of this point of view – a use that is partly present in the memory and expectation of one's own experience.[13]

This is, as Nagel says, only the beginning of an answer. Ultimately, Nagel thinks that our concept can extend to cover even the subjectively *un*imaginable mental lives of other species. Thus, our concept extends to cover bats and cockroaches. We will identify such creatures by the way they behave, but our concept is in no way bound up with this method of identification. It is for this reason that our concept can extend to cover creatures whose behaviour is unrecognizable by us; our concept extends well beyond our capacity to apply it. This is a consequence of Nagel's hard realism.

Let us look a little more closely at the way Nagel thinks the imagination is involved in the objective conception of mind. First of all notice the direction that Nagel reaches when trying to account for the generality of our mental concepts: the appeal to the imagination is an appeal to something the understanding of which does not require that we go outside the subject. If the appeal to the imagination works, there is no need to assume the existence of others. Imagination yields generality *intra*-subjectively. Appeal to the imagination is compatible with the possibility that others are in fact zombies. Given that Nagel wants to be able to solve the conceptual problem while still being able to raise radical sceptical questions, it is not at all surprising that he looks to the imagination to account for the generality in our mental concepts.

Although it is clear why Nagel looks to the imagination in his account of the generality of our mental concepts, it is not at all clear just how appeal to the imagination is meant to work. It is tempting to read Nagel as holding that we begin with a concept of mind that is rooted in the subject and that, by employment of the imagination, we are able to extend this concept. This, however, does not appear to be what Nagel has in mind. Nagel recognizes that, if one does begin with an idea that one has by reflecting on one's own case, it is hard to see how one can extend out from here.[14] Nagel also appreciates that, if one relies on behavioural evidence to attribute minds to others, one runs up against the problem of the unity of our concept.[15] Concerning this starting point Nagel writes,

> If one begins with the sole idea of oneself and one's own experience as a model, one may not have sufficient material to extrapolate to a significant notion of other selves and their experiences. . . . If [this] is correct, then the avoidance of solipsism requires that the *conception* of other persons like oneself . . . be included in the idea of one's own experiences from the beginning. This is achieved by a conception which permits every feature of one's own situation and experience to be described and regarded, without loss of content, from the impersonal standpoint.[16]

Nagel does not propose that we start by extending out from our own case. Rather, he holds that we *begin* with a quite general conception of experience. And he thinks that appeal to the imagination can help us to understand this general conception of experience.

Another philosopher who thinks that appeal to the imagination can help us avoid the conceptual problem of other minds is Alec Hyslop.[17] Hyslop accepts that the problem of other minds is generated by an asymmetry. However, where Nagel takes the asymmetry to give rise to a *conceptual* problem, Hyslop takes it to give rise to an *epistemological* problem. Hyslop explicitly rejects what Nagel calls the 'interesting conceptual problem' of other minds. Indeed, Hyslop claims not to be able to understand what bothers Nagel (and others) here. Hyslop tells a story that he thinks can help us to see that there is no problem with the generality of our concept of mind. Hyslop's story makes essential reference to the imagination. If Hyslop's story is plausible, then perhaps we can use it to understand Nagel. Let us now consider Hyslop's attempt to solve the conceptual problem of other minds.

Hyslop considers the question of generality in connection with the concept of pain. He begins by suggesting that we can understand the generality of the concept of pain if we first consider our own remembered and anticipated pain. He continues:

In the case of memory, I think of a person, myself, feeling pain. I can then shift to imagining a person, myself, feeling pain. The shift from doing that to imagining another person feeling pain is manageable.[18]

Hyslop's point is that the required shift can be thought to take place in stages, each stage taking us some distance away from our starting point in ourselves until we reach the desired end point in another. In the case of remembered pain what one does is visualize oneself in pain (Hyslop takes visualizing to be a specific instance of imagining). When one does this, what one does is visualize oneself in pain from the outside. Once one does this, one can move on to visualize another as one does oneself; we can, thereby, come to visualize another in pain. In this way one moves – painlessly, we might say – from our own pain to that of another.

It is in this way that the conceptual problem is, according to Hyslop, easily solved. Hyslop thinks that the *interesting* problem of other minds is the epistemological one that Nagel puts to one side. But it is a real question whether Hyslop can dismiss the conceptual problem so easily. The problem I see for Hyslop's view concerns the way that he thinks about the imagination. Christopher Peacocke has suggested that, when we talk of imagining something or other, we use the term 'imagine' in two different senses. We sometimes mean something along the lines of supposing or supposing falsely, and we sometimes mean something that concerns the having of what Peacocke calls a 'phenomenologically distinct state'.[19] Thus a newly blind man can imagine (in the sense of suppose falsely) that there is a painting by David Hockney before him, or he may imagine (in the sense of having a phenomenologically distinct state) a Hockney painting visually presented to him. About the second sense of 'imagine' Peacocke suggests that it is plausible to say that to imagine something is 'always at least to imagine, from the inside, being in some conscious state'.[20] Now this kind of imagining involves the self in a particular way. About this Peacocke writes: 'imaginings always involve imagining from the inside a certain [type of] viewpoint, and someone with that viewpoint could, in the imagined world, knowledgeably judge "*I'm* thus-and-so", where the thus-and-so gives details of the viewpoint'.[21] It is, no doubt, the second of these senses of 'imagine' that Hyslop has in mind when he says that he can imagine being in pain. What is less clear is whether it is this sense of 'imagine' that is involved in Hyslop's proposed imagined move from himself to others. The problem is in Hyslop's account of memory. According to Hyslop, when I remember my pain, what I do is think of a person, myself, feeling pain. I then move from thinking about this person to imagining this person in pain. The act of imagining may be from the inside but the person I imagine to be in pain is a person I imagine from the *outside*. I imagine this person feeling pain in the same way that I can imagine watching myself typing this sentence. If I am imagining myself from the outside when I remember being in pain, it is no surprise that I can move from imagining this to imagining another person being in pain. The problem is not in imagining from the outside another person in pain; the problem is in imagining from the inside another person being in pain. If this is right then Hyslop has not managed to solve the conceptual problem of other minds by appeal to the imagination.

Although Nagel says very little about the work of the imagination, what he does say looks as if it can avoid the objection just given to Hyslop's suggestion. Nagel writes: 'When we conceive of the minds of others, we cannot abandon the essential factor of a point of view: instead we must generalize it and think of ourselves as one point of view among others.'[22] The generality that Nagel thinks we must begin with is designed to capture this subjective point of view; the general idea we have involves subjective points of view. Rather than abstract

261

from our experience, Nagel's idea is that we imaginatively use this point of view.

Now Nagel appears to thinks that this general conception of mind is innately given. This is not explicit in Nagel's work. Nevertheless, he is explicit about the innatism that lies at the heart of our thought about the world, and it is not implausible that he thinks that a similar innatism lies at the heart of our thinking about mind. Nagel writes in one place:

> This does not mean that we have innate knowledge of the truth about the world, but it does mean that we have the capacity, not based on experience, to generate hypotheses about what in general the world might possibly be like, and to reject those possibilities that we see could not include ourselves and our experiences. . . . The conditions of objectivity that I have been defending lead to the conclusion that the basis of most real knowledge must be a priori and drawn from within ourselves.[23]

And a little later he writes:

> When we use our minds to think about reality, we are not, I assume, performing an impossible leap from inside ourselves to the world outside. We are developing a relation to the world that is implicit in our mental and physical makeup, and we can do this only if there are facts we do not know which account for the possibility.[24]

Nagel is here talking about our capacity to think about the world, but it is easy to see how he would extend this to cover our capacity to think about other minds. Here, too, we have a capacity, not based on experience, to generate hypotheses about what might be going on with others. And this capacity is rooted in the general conception of mind that we innately possess. There is, however, an extra dimension to our thinking about other minds: minds have a subjective point of view. Nagel understands this. It is in order to ensure that our thoughts about others are thoughts about other subjective points of view that Nagel makes reference to the work of the imagination. Appeal to the imagination may be thought to help us to understand the innately general conception of mind – with its inherent subjectivity – that we possess.

I want now to raise two considerations designed to tell against an appeal to the imagination in this connection. The first consideration is due to Peacocke.[25] According to Peacocke, Nagel's appeal to the imagination here is circular. Peacocke's argument is as follows. Imagine, says Peacocke, seeing Manhattan from the bay to its south, or imagine being in pain. Now imagine *John's* seeing Manhattan from the same point, or imagine *John* being in pain. In both cases the image involved will be the same; any differences here will be part of what Peacocke calls the *S-imagined* conditions – conditions that go beyond the subject's images. Peacocke's point is that the imagined experience alone does not reveal whose experience it is; this is part of the S-imagined condition. Now about the S-imagined condition Peacocke writes: 'But this condition is intelligible only to, or is graspable only by, those who already have the conception that there may be many subjects all of whom have experiences in exactly the same sense.'[26] In other words, one cannot appeal to S-imagined conditions to explain the generality of our concept of experience, since those conditions presuppose the very thing we want to understand. Peacocke points out that the circularity objection holds even if one were to insist that it is possible to imagine a *type* of experience which is such as to apply to others as well as oneself. Just saying this gives us no understanding of the generality of our concept. If Peacocke is right, then appeal to the imagination cannot do the work Nagel requires of it. And if we cannot appeal to the imagination, we are left with a concept which is said to be innately general, but of which we have no understanding whatever.

I want now to raise a very different sort of objection to Nagel's proposal. For the moment I want to ignore the circularity that Peacocke sees here and to allow Nagel his appeal to the imagination. The question I want to raise is this: Even if the appeal to the imagination were not circular, can it give us the understanding of the generality of our concept that we require? I shall argue that it cannot. In order to see this one has to understand that what makes the generality problem so intractable is the problem of unity. Without the problem of unity we might simply accept Nagel's appeal to an innate conception, whether or not he was able to give any further characterization of it. The reason why we need to understand this conception is that we need to satisfy ourselves that what we have here is one unified concept; we need to understand why it is that the concept we apply in our own case is the very same one we apply in the case of another. But if this is what is required, then it is easy to see that appeal to the imagination will not work. The problem is particularly apparent when we consider that Nagel thinks that our concept of mind extends even beyond where we can go with our imagination. This is a point to which I have drawn attention several times. Nagel makes the point in one place, thus:

The pretheoretical concept of mind involves a kind of objectivity which permits us to go some way beyond our own experiences and those exactly like them.

The idea is that the concept of mind, though tied to subjectivity, is not restricted to what can be understood in terms of our own subjectivity – what we can translate into the terms of our own experience. We include the subjectively *un*imaginable mental lives of other species.[27]

So, the generality that Nagel takes to be inherent in our concept of mind from the outset is *greater* than that which we reach by appeal to the imagination. This is consistent with Nagel's hard realism. However, at the point that Nagel accepts the reach of our concept beyond the reach of our imagination, the unity question is particularly threatening. What allows us to say that the concept we apply to such creatures is *at one* with the concept we apply to those to whom our imagination does reach?

This problem is exacerbated when we remember just how far Nagel thinks our concept of mind extends. Nagel is extremely generous about where he finds mentality. We have already seen that he thinks our concept extends beyond the range of our imagination. This is how we come to attribute experience to a bat or a cockroach, while at the same time acknowledging that we are unable to know what things are like for a bat or a cockroach. Once we go down this route, however, it becomes a real question why we do not attribute experience far and wide; why we do not attribute experiences to, for example, trees and stoves. Actually, Nagel *does* hold that our concept extends quite a long way away from us – and even away from the bat. When it comes to attributing experience to the bat and the cockroach Nagel shifts attention away from the imagination and on to the behaviour and structure of these creatures.[28] But when he considers the full extent of the reach of our concept Nagel accepts that, although the intimate connection to behaviour, structure and circumstance must be present, we need not be in a position to recognize that they are present. He writes:

There is probably a great deal of [conscious] life in the universe, and we may be in a position to identify only some of its forms, because we would simply be unable to read as behaviour the manifestations of creatures sufficiently unlike us.[29]

Just as there may be minds we are incapable of imagining, so there may be manifestations of behaviour that we are unable to read as behaviour. And in doing this we have *not*, according to Nagel, illegitimately and irresponsibly made use of our concept. Furthermore, the concept we are employing in connection with these creatures is supposed to be the very *same* concept we use in connection with ourselves. But what evidence is there that the concept is the same? What can Nagel say to a sceptic who challenges him to show why the concept we apply to these creatures whose behaviour we are unable to identify is the same as the one we apply in our own case – or even the same as the one we apply to creatures such as bats? We may also ask why, once we have gone this far, we do not apply this concept to such things as stoves and rocks? What is there to stop us from doing so?

Perhaps it is Nagel's position that our concept of mind does extend far and wide, and that there is *no* limit to its extension. But this is not the case. In one place Nagel writes that 'some examples, like the ascription of pain to a stove, do pass the limits of intelligibility'.[30] I am inclined to agree. The question is whether Nagel is in a position to say that there is a limit here. The problem is that he has given us no understanding of the generality that our concept undoubtedly possesses such that we can intelligibly say that certain cases go beyond this. We need some understanding of our concepts here that can help us to see how we can plausibly maintain both their generality and their unity – and this understanding should help us to see the limits of those concepts. The problem is that Nagel offers us no understanding here.[31]

THE PROBLEM OF GENERALITY AND THE PROBLEM OF UNITY

When I introduced the generality problem I said that it is a problem that arises given a certain picture of how we come to have the concept in the first place. If we take it that I know what, say, a pain is by reflecting on the way it feels when I, say, cut my finger, then it can look problematic how we are to understand the application of that concept of another who is not me. When one does see the generality problem in this way, one can also appreciate that one must be careful that any purported extension of the concept will not be vulnerable to the question: Why do we take it that it is the very same concept that is being extended? In other words, one must be careful to respond to the generality problem without running into the unity problem.

Nagel recognizes the generality problem, but he characterizes it in a somewhat different manner from me. Nagel holds that the generality problem is the problem, 'how can I conceive of my own mind as merely one of many examples of mental phenomena contained in the world'.[32] In other words, Nagel wants to *begin* with an assumption of generality and he takes the problem to be how we can understand our own mind to be an instance of such a general phenomenon. Nagel does not see that he needs to worry about the unity problem because he doesn't think we achieve generality by extending out from our own case. But it is not clear that Nagel can avoid the problem in this way. Just because we begin with generality does not mean that we don't also have to worry about the unity of our concept. Indeed, the reason why we cannot simply take for granted the generality of our concept in these cases lies precisely in the fact that the unity of the concept is problematic. Let me explain why I say this.

Nagel takes it that it is empiricist assumptions about how we come to have our concept of mind (that we come to have the concept by reflection on our own case) that leads to problems about the unity of that concept.[33] I explained in the previous chapter how, precisely, this problem may be thought to arise on such assumptions. It is in order to avoid the problem of unity that Nagel adopts his innatist thesis: we innately possess a quite general conception of mind. As I understand it, he then appeals to the imagination to help us to understand this general conception which we innately possess. What Nagel does not appreciate is just how much rests on his being able to make good this appeal to the imagination. Without some understanding of the generality possessed by our innate concept of mind, it is a real question whether or not we innately possess one single concept of mind. Let me explain why I say this.

There are two ways of understanding the innatist's position. The first is sometimes called a dispositionalist understanding, and it is often argued that Descartes held a dispositionalist innatist thesis. This attribution rests on what Descartes writes in his *Comments on a Certain Broadsheet* when explaining what he means when he says that ideas are innate:

> This is the same sense as that in which we say that generosity is 'innate' in certain families, or that certain diseases such as gout or stones are innate in others: it is not so much that the babies of such families suffer from these diseases in the mother's womb, but simply that they are born with a certain 'faculty' or tendency to contract them.[34]

From this characterization of innate ideas it would follow that innate ideas are triggered at a certain point in the person's development by certain conditions. If we consider an innate idea of mind, we might ask just what conditions trigger this idea. Descartes would most likely reply that what triggers our idea of mind is our experience of our own mind. But he might equally respond that our idea of mind can be triggered by our experience of the linguistic and other actions of other human beings (*vide supra*, Chapter II). So there are two, quite different, ways of triggering our innate idea of mind. Once we see this, it is clear that we can raise the following question: Why do we take it that the idea that is triggered by experience of our own mind is the very same concept that is triggered by experience of another's behaviour? Descartes might answer that this is just the way things are, but we might think that the triggerings here are sufficiently dissimilar to warrant some further account of the unity in our idea.

The point is not dependent on the acceptance of a dispositional innatist thesis. There is a non-dispositional understanding of the innatist's position according to which we are possessed of a general idea or concept of mind and this idea is present to us prior to any sense experience. It is possible also to raise a *prima facie* difficulty for this understanding of the innatist's thesis. As I keep explaining, in order for the concept we possess to count as general it must be applicable to others as well as oneself. If, however, one considers the conditions of application for this concept in the case of another, one finds that it is quite different from the conditions of application in one's own case. The conditions for thinking that another is, say, in pain, is the way she behaves; in my own case I can apply the concept without any reference to behaviour. So different are the conditions of application in one's own case and in the case of another that we can raise a *prima facie* doubt about whether it is the very same concept that is being applied. In other words, we run up against the unity problem once again.

I conclude that the unity of our concept is an issue whether one begins with a concept of mind that applies in one's own case or one begins with a quite general conception of mind. In the one case the issue is how to achieve generality without violating unity; in the other case the issue is to defend the plausibility of the purported generality given the quite different conditions of applicability. The conceptual problem of other minds is, as Nagel recognizes, the problem of generality. It is less clear that Nagel recognizes that it is the unity problem that makes the generality problem really intractable. Nagel's failure to make clear just how appeal to the imagination can make it plausible for us to say that our concept of experience is general, leaves us with a very serious conceptual problem. It is precisely to solve this problem that I, following Wittgenstein, Strawson and Davidson, appeal to the concept of action. This is the all important concept that Nagel thinks he can shun. Until such time as a plausible alternative is forthcoming, however, we must accept that we are left with a conceptual problem of other minds.

THE RELATIONSHIP BETWEEN EPISTEMOLOGICAL AND CONCEPTUAL PROBLEMS

When Nagel writes that the interesting problem of other minds is the conceptual, and not the epistemological, one, he means that it is the conceptual problem with which philosophers can – and must – make some headway. Unless we can solve the conceptual problem of other minds, we are left in the position of conceptual solipsism; we are left in a position where it does not so much as make sense to raise a question about the mind of another. Once we can satisfy ourselves over the conceptual issue, we are left, it is true, with an epistemological problem of other minds. This, however, is not something philosophers can do much about; it is just the flip side of hard realism. And once we have solved the conceptual problem of other minds, we are in a position to raise questions about the existence of minds in creatures far and wide. These questions make good sense, despite the fact that we are not in a position to come to any definitive answers.

I have argued that Nagel makes no headway with the interesting conceptual problem which he raises. The reason can be seen to lie in the way in which Nagel understands the conceptual problem. He takes it that the conceptual problem is simply the problem of generality. Nagel acknowledges the unity problem, but thinks that it does not arise if one holds, *pace* the empiricists, that the concept of mind is not given in experience. I have argued that the unity problem is as much a difficulty for innatists as for empiricists. With his appeal to the imagination Nagel offers us no understanding of how it is that the concept I apply in my own case is the very same concept that I apply to bats, to cockroaches and possibly to oysters. Furthermore, Nagel gives us no understanding of the generality of our concept that makes it comprehensible why it is unintelligible to extend that concept to such things as rocks and stoves.

In order to make headway with the very important problem that Nagel has identified, I suggest we emphasize the element of behaviour in our concept of mind. Before I explain further what I mean here, let us return to Nagel's picture of things and identify in it the following three stages: At stage one it is the work of the imagination that gives us a concept that can be thought to extend to others like ourselves. At this stage we both observe the other's behaviour and employ the imagination. At stage two, we take off with our concept and apply it in cases where the 'behaviour, structure and circumstance' may be present, but where we are unable to employ the imagination.[35] Thus, we come to attribute minds to bats and even cockroaches. At stage three we allow that we may simply be 'unable to read as behaviour the manifestations of creatures sufficiently unlike us'.[36] It is in this way that we can consider the possibility of minds even in creatures who offer none of the behavioural criteria we relied on at stage two. Reference to behaviour is helpful, but not essential, for the attribution of mind to another; and the same can be said about the use of the imagination. Notice that, at stage two – when we are unable to use our imagination – Nagel places greater emphasis on the behaviour (structure and circumstance) of the other for the attribution of experience. I have argued that Nagel's appeal to the imagination does not help us to understand the unity that the generality of this concept requires. I now want to suggest that in order to preserve unity we should emphasize the role of behaviour even at stage one. When, at stage one, Nagel emphasizes the *intra*-subjective element of imagination, he should rather emphasize the *inter*-subjective element of behaviour. This suggestion may seem puzzling. After all, have I not just finished arguing that it is Nagel's appeal to behaviour at stage two that leads to the unity problem? If this is so, how can appeal to behaviour at an earlier stage do any more than raise the unity problem at an even earlier stage? The crucial issue here has to do with how we understand 'behaviour'.

In order to understand what I have in mind here, consider something that David Armstrong has written:

> We may distinguish between 'physical behaviour', which refers to any merely physical action or passion of the body, and 'behaviour proper', which implies relationship to the mind.[37]

Armstrong draws attention to this distinction in giving a functionalist account of mind. Unless it is going to beg some very important questions, it is important that a functionalist account of mind which makes reference to behaviour makes reference to what Armstrong calls 'physical behaviour'. When in his account of the generality of our concept of mind Nagel makes reference to behaviour he, too, must mean by this 'physical behaviour'. When we look at the behaviour of another, we must supplement what we see in some way; the behaviour of another indicates to us the presence of a mind, but that mind is quite distinct from the behaviour I observe. On the other hand, when I suggest, *contra* Nagel, that we should appeal to behaviour at an earlier stage, I mean that we must appeal to behaviour proper. Appeal to physical behaviour at any stage in one's account of the concept of mind will only give rise to a question about the unity of our concept; appeal to behaviour proper does not give rise to this problem.

To see why this is so, let us go back to Nagel's stage three where he says that we may be unable to 'read as behaviour the manifestations of creatures sufficiently unlike us'. What Nagel means by this is that, in the case of some creatures who have experience, we are unable to identify anything about them as behaviour. Where we are unable to identify behaviour, we are unable to attribute experience to them. However, our inability to make the attribution in no way touches the fact that such creatures do have experience. It is, however, tempting to read Nagel's phrase in a quite different way. It is tempting to take it as saying that we are unable to *read the behaviour* of the other; we are unable to see the manifestations of these creatures as behaviour that we can read. Now if we understand behaviour as the sort of thing one can 'read', we get closer to a meaning of 'behaviour' that does not leave us with a unity problem. Behaviour in *this* sense is behaviour proper; it is behaviour that implies (in Armstrong's words) 'a relationship to a mind'. This is behaviour that is intelligible to another subject. On this understanding of behaviour, it is not simply the physical movement of limbs; it is the action of a subject. The crucial point is that behaviour proper is the behaviour of a subject that is comprehensible to other subjects. This is the behaviour – the action – to which Strawson makes reference in his attempt to explain how our concept of a person is possible (*vide supra* Chapter VIII). It is also the behaviour that figures in Wittgenstein's description of how we teach a child how to use experience words (*vide supra* Chapter VII). Insistence that the concept of behaviour so understood lies at the heart of our concept of mind will lead us to understand the generality of that concept while at the same time acknowledging its unity.

An appeal to the inter-subjective notion of behaviour proper to solve the conceptual problem of other minds has two very important consequences. The first is that it restricts the attribution of mind. On this account it is not possible to say with assurance that minds may exist far and wide – regardless of our capacity to discern them. Our concept extends without any doubt to those nearest to us: to our parents, our children, our friends and foes and the like. And it extends as well to certain other animals whose behaviour is comprehensible to us. Our concept reaches its limit, however, at the point where behaviour is longer comprehensible to us. Rocks and stoves do not have experience; and we can now understand why this is so. Notice that this way of proceeding has the consequence that it is not always entirely clear just how far the concept of experience does extend. There is room for disagreement and discussion.

Another consequence of this way of solving the conceptual problem is that it leaves no room for the epistemological problem to arise. Where reference to behaviour proper forms an integral part of our understanding of the concept of mind, the existence of others cannot be in doubt. The notion of behaviour that is being appealed to here is precisely *inter*-subjective. On this way of understanding the generality of our concept, the existence of others is given from the start. Their existence provides the very condition for our understanding of that concept. By appealing to an essentially intra-subjective notion like imagination, Nagel hopes to establish generality without commitment to the existence of other minds. Appeal to an essentially inter-subjective notion like behaviour would lead us to see that a solution to the conceptual problem would leave no room for an epistemological problem here.

It is easy to miss the divorce of conceptual and epistemological issues in Nagel's work. When Nagel writes that the interesting problem of other minds is the conceptual one, he is saying something with which many philosophers would agree. Consider, for example, the following from John McDowell's *Mind and World*:

> We could not credit a subject with a capacity to use, say, the concept of pain in judgements of 'inner experience' if she did not understand how the circumstance that those judgements concern fits into the world at large. What that requires is that the subject must understand her being in pain as a particular case of a general type of state of affairs, *someone's* being in pain. So she must understand that the conceptual capacity drawn on in the relevant 'inner experience' is not restricted to its role in 'inner experience': not restricted, that is, to its first-person present-tense role.[38]

But the similarity between McDowell's work and Nagel's here is only superficial. It is true that both believe that the conceptual problem is the important one, and both believe that generality is inherent in our concepts from the start. But McDowell would not hold to the separation of conceptual and epistemological problems. Earlier I said that Nagel's attitude towards the sceptic is neither to reply to him nor to ignore him, but to acknowledge him and carry on regardless. This is not McDowell's response. McDowell writes in one place:

> The aim here is not to answer the sceptical questions, but to begin to see how it might be intellectually respectable to ignore them, to treat them as unreal, in the way that common sense has always wanted to.[39]

McDowell here considers the options of ignoring the sceptic or responding to him. Had he considered Nagel's option of acknowledging the sceptic and carrying on regardless, McDowell would no doubt have rejected this as well.

Nagel is right to say that the conceptual problem of other minds is the interesting problem. But it is interesting because it is the *first* problem. Once we attend to this, the epistemological problem need not arise. We are now in a position to appreciate that the conceptual problem of other minds is, ultimately, a problem that results once philosophers adopt what I have been calling a Cartesian framework. This framework introduces a radical conceptual divide between a subject and the world, which in turn brings with it a radical separation of one's own mind from other minds. It is this radical conceptual separation of subject from subject and each from the world that leads to the unity problem. And it is, as we have seen, the problem of unity that makes the generality of our concept so difficult to envisage. Descartes appears to have taken it for granted that our innately given idea of mind is inherently general, but this generality is in tension with the conceptual divide that his philosophy introduces between a subject and her world. Once this, Cartesian, framework is in place the generality in our concept is thrown into doubt. Nagel, too, accepts this Cartesian framework. This is evident from his acceptance of what he calls an 'unclosable gap' between the knowing subject and her world.[40] One way to reassert the generality of our concept – without threatening its unity – is to reject this Cartesian framework. An acceptance of the way our concept of mind is bound up with the concept of behaviour proper is one way of rejecting this framework. Behaviour proper straddles the gap. A correct understanding of the place of behaviour proper here can help us to see that these divisions are spurious.

We are now in a position to see a quite different relationship between conceptual and epistemological issues from the one Nagel urges. We are now able to say that attention to the conceptual problem puts us in a position to ignore the epistemological one. There is, of course, a certain fallout from this way of looking at things. We are no longer able to defend hard realism about other minds. The emphasis on behaviour proper which gives unity to our concept also restricts the range of its application. Our concept applies as far as we are able to understand its application – allowing a certain indeterminacy in the actual extent allowed for here. Where there is behaviour that we are able to find intelligible as behaviour expressive of mentality, there our concept reaches.

Nagel is right: the epistemological problem of other minds is *not* the interesting problem. But Nagel thinks it is not interesting because – at least for the present time – it is part of the human condition. I am suggesting that we should see that the epistemological problem is not interesting because it is the result of mistaken conceptual assumptions. Once the interesting conceptual issues have been properly attended to, the epistemological problem need not bother us. Solipsism – either in its conceptual or in its epistemological form – is not possible. This security is gained at a cost, no doubt. We are no longer in a position to attribute minds far and wide as the hard realist does. But it must be remembered that, while the hard realist is in a position to indulge in speculations about minds far and wide, he leaves us with a certain insecurity in the case of those others closest to us.

CHAPTER X

Rejecting behaviour

A CHALLENGE TO BEHAVIOUR

In the previous chapter I argued that the interesting problem of other minds is the conceptual one. I identified that problem as one of understanding the generality of our concept of mind, and I suggested that the problem of generality is at heart a problem over the unity of our concept. This conceptual problem is to be found in the work of those philosophers who operate within what I have been calling a Cartesian framework. If we abandon this framework we can solve the conceptual problem; furthermore, we can solve the conceptual problem in a way that does not leave room for any epistemological problem about the existence of another mind.

My suggestion for solving the conceptual problem is to appeal to the notion of behaviour proper which, I argued, is a concept that straddles the divide between the subject and her world. The appeal to behaviour in our account of mind has, however, been viewed with growing suspicion in recent years. In the previous chapter I explained Nagel's attempt to give an account of our general conception of mind without any appeal to behaviour. What is particularly interesting about Nagel's work here is the way he both takes seriously the conceptual problem of other minds and thinks that he can say something about this problem without reference to behaviour. In this chapter I want to consider the work of two philosophers who also reject reference to behaviour in their account of mind. Unlike Nagel, however, these philosophers do not recognize the importance of the conceptual problem of other minds. One could say that, according to these philosophers, there is *no* interesting problem of other minds.

An explicit, and extreme, statement of suspicion over appeal to behaviour in one's account of mind can be found in the work of Galen Strawson. Consider, for example, when Strawson writes:

[It is a mistake to think that] reference to behaviour enters essentially into the correct account of the essential nature of all or almost all types of mental state or occurrence (emotions, sensations, thoughts, imagining, fantasies, rememberings, beliefs, desires, etc.). . . .

To suppose that these epistemological facts about the publicly observable circumstances of language acquisition and use . . . dictate answers to questions about the nature of the things we talk about is (as far as I can see) to misunderstand the nature of language and the nature of reality and the nature of possibility. I think it is to misunderstand the scope and nature of philosophy, and to reduce it to a covert or indirect form of anthropology.[1]

Strawson is here opposing what he takes to be a neo-behaviourist strain in recent philosophy, a form of behaviourism that he takes to be fuelled in large part by Wittgenstein's later work. Strawson quite rightly sees that Wittgenstein's appeal to behaviour is connected with a certain view about the business of philosophy. As we saw in Chapter VII, Wittgenstein distinguishes the work of philosophy from the work of science: the former is purely descriptive, while the latter seeks explanations. The descriptions that philosophers give are of what lies open to view; while the explanations that scientists seek appeal to what is hidden, what is concealed from view. Following on from the work of Wittgenstein, P. F. Strawson engages in what he calls 'descriptive metaphysics' – describing the structure of our mental concepts. The aim of this work is to give a description of our use of mental concepts that makes it clear how there can be a unity to these concepts in the face of an asymmetry in their use. Both the unity and the asymmetry are taken as a datum that we observe; the description of how we employ these concepts is designed to make it intelligible to us that our concepts possess unity despite the asymmetry in their use.

Galen Strawson rejects this project, and with it any appeal to behaviour in our understanding of the nature of mental. As he writes: 'It is, no doubt, a natural fact that many mental phenomena have publicly observable causes and effects, but it is not part of their essence.'[2] Epistemology comes apart from ontology: how we come to know about mind is one thing, what the mind *is* is another. But if we are not to think of the mind in relation to behaviour, how, then, are we to think of it? Strawson's main concern is with the reality of experience or conscious experience. He wants to understand this experience against a background of naturalism. This leads him to a position that he labels 'agnostic materialism'.[3] Starting from the observation that people possess an unshakeable belief in both the reality and the physical nature of experience, agnostic materialism holds that experience, qua experience, is real and as such is physical. Despite the fact that conscious experience is physical, however, we are at present sufficiently ignorant of the physical as to be unable to understand just how this can be the case.[4]

Another philosopher to emphasize the subjectivity of the mental and its place in the natural world is John Searle. Searle, however, is less agnostic than Strawson. According to Searle consciousness is a 'higher-level or emergent property of the brain', or as he also sometimes puts it, 'the brain causes certain "mental" phenomena'.[5] Searle labels his position 'biological naturalism'. He believes that an understanding of how the brain causes mental phenomena is in principle no different from understanding how H_2O molecules cause the property of liquidity.[6] According to Searle, consciousness does not need to be naturalized because it is already natural. All we need to do is to understand the natural process of the brain that is consciousness much in the way that we have come to understand the natural process in the stomach that is digestion – and Searle can see no difficulty with that in principle. Thus, Searle and Strawson differ somewhat in their attitude towards naturalism; however, in their attitude towards the mental they agree entirely: they both hold that consciousness or the experiential is real and natural. Furthermore, both Searle and Strawson insist that the reality of the mental cannot be understood without reference to what things are like from the first-person point of view. One could say that both these philosophers accept Cartesian intuitions about the mental without accepting Descartes' substantial dualism. Searle writes: 'After all, one does not have to read [Descartes'] *Meditations* to be conscious that one is conscious or that one's desires, as mental phenomena . . ., are real causal phenomena. . . . [Nevertheless, philosophers] find it difficult to see that one could accept the obvious facts about mental states without accepting the Cartesian apparatus that traditionally went along with the acknowledgement of these facts.'[7] Searle and Strawson want to accept the 'obvious facts' about mental states, and they think that doing this requires that one divorce the ontology of mind from its epistemology. I shall refer to their position as naturalized Cartesianism.

Searle explains that it is because mental phenomena are essentially connected with consciousness, and because consciousness is essentially subjective, that the ontology of the mental is essentially a first-person ontology ('mental states are always somebody's mental states').[8] He believes that an acknowledgement of this fact has, ironically, led philosophers into a 'flight from subjectivity'. This flight involves philosophers in an attempt to redefine the ontology of the subjective in terms of third-person accessible facts about behaviour.[9] The results of this are evident in positions such as behaviourism (which holds that mental states are dispositions to behave in a certain way), functionalism (which holds that mental states are to be defined by reference to causal antecedents and consequents), and strong artificial intelligence or AI (which holds that mental states are computational states). Searle sees this flight as triggered by philosophy's inability to tolerate the following two things: one, the metaphysical conclusion that there are irreducibly subjective 'private' entities in the world; and two, the epistemological asymmetry between the way a subject knows about her own mental life and the way others know about her mental life. Searle thinks that philosophers should resist this flight. What they have to recognize is that there are empirical subjective facts as well as empirical objective facts. What stands in the way of a recognition of this is, according to Searle, an ambiguity in the word 'empirical': people sometimes use the word to refer to actual, contingent, facts about the world – as opposed, say, to the facts of mathematics or logic; and they sometimes use the word to talk about a method of knowing. Thus, empirical facts are said to be facts that are equally accessible to all competent observers. It is this second sense of 'empirical' to which Searle objects. There are, according to Searle, empirical facts that some of us may not be in a position to know about – at least, we may not be in a position to know about them *directly.*

Searle outlines various thought-experiments that are designed to illustrate this divorce of empirical subjective fact from third-person accessibility.[10] He first presents what might be called the base thought-experiment: Imagine a slow deterioration in your brain that super-neuroscientists are able to reverse with the introduction of silicon chips that are capable of maintaining your normal conscious experience and their usual output function. In other words, with these silicon chips in place your mental life and your behaviour remain unchanged. With this base thought-experiment in place, Searle then offers us two further thought-experiments:

Case I. Imagine that you are the subject of the operation described in the base thought-experiment. And imagine also that, instead of everything proceeding as normal you discover the following: as the silicon chips are implanted into your brain your consciousness diminishes, and that as this happens you also notice that you are no longer in control of your behaviour. Thus, when a doctor holds up a red object and asks you to say what you see, you want to say, 'I can't see anything. I am going blind.' But in fact you hear yourself say, 'I see a red object before me.' Searle takes it that we can imagine this going on until such time as the subject's consciousness has vanished entirely and yet his physical behaviour is unchanged from before the operation.

Case II. Imagine that silicon chips are being implanted into your brain as in the base thought-experiment. Imagine also that your consciousness is not affected by the operation, but that your physical behaviour is. As a result of this operation you end up in a state of total paralysis. However, your mental life continues as it did before the operation. In this case Searle imagines that you can hear doctors discussing your case and concluding that the silicon chips were unable to maintain your mental life although they were able to maintain your vital processes of respiration, heartbeat and the like. In the extreme case we are asked to imagine that the doctors discuss allowing you to die on the grounds that you are already mentally dead. Although you are paralysed we can imagine you wanting to shout out: 'I am not mentally dead. I am fully conscious; I just can't make the movements that would enable me to make this obvious to you.'

What these thought-experiments teach us, according to Searle, is that there is a sharp distinction to be drawn between the ontology of mind and the epistemology of mind. We may come to know about another's mental states by observing her behaviour, but *'behaviour, functional role, and causal relations are irrelevant to the existence of conscious mental phenomena'* (Searle's italics).[11] Behaviour is neither necessary (Case II) nor sufficient (Case I) for mental phenomena.

According to Searle, we must accept that the mental exists beyond our capacity to attribute it; we do not have *direct* access to certain empirical facts in all cases. What we have in those cases where direct access is lacking, however, is *indirect* access. Let us now look at what Searle takes the indirect evidence to be in the case of other minds. It is in specifying the indirect evidence that some philosophers who might otherwise agree with Searle about the ontology of mind are inclined to make reference to behaviour; I come to know about another's mental life (both that it exists and what it is like) by observing another's behaviour. (We find even Nagel making reference to behaviour – at least in a great number of cases.) All the arguments from conjecture, analogy and induction start with observations of the other's behaviour. Searle, however, rejects reference to behaviour even in the specification of the indirect evidence for mind. He writes: 'It isn't just because the dog behaves in a way that is appropriate to having conscious mental states, but also because I can see that the causal basis of the behaviour in the dog's physiology is relevantly like my own.'[12] In shifting the emphasis from behaviour to causal structure Searle does not mean to imply that we all go around with sophisticated neurophysiological theories about the causal origins of behaviour. Rather, he thinks that we note the structure of the other's skin, her eyes, ears, nose, hair and the like and we recognize the causal role played by such structures. Indeed, Searle makes the interesting observation that in characterizing certain structures *as* eyes, ears, etc. we are already attributing to them causal powers and functions similar to our own. As he writes:

The principle that warrants my complete confidence in the existence of other minds is not: similar-behaviour-ergo-similar-mental-states. Rather the principle is: similar-causal-structures-ergo-similar-cause-and-effect-relations.[13]

If I wish to know whether another individual feels pain, has a belief that the object before it is red, and the like, what I have to do is look at the causal basis of the behaviour that I observe. Observing this causal structure will reveal, not only *that* the individual has experiences and the like, but it will reveal as well *what* those experiences are like. Searle complicates things slightly at this point with his recognition that we cannot assume that consciousness will have the same causal structure in all individuals. He allows that we may find that there is, in fact, a great variety in the neurophysiological structures that are consciousness. Indeed, he allows that some of these structures may be such as to be unknowable by us. In a manner reminiscent of John Locke (*vide supra*, Chapter IV) Searle insists that 'it is inconsistent with what we know about the universe and our place in it to suppose that everything is knowable by us'.[14] Where we are unable to understand the neurophysiological structures, we do not have the indirect evidence that allows us to say that mental life exists and what it is like.[15] On Searle's picture of things – as on Locke's and

Nagel's – minds are taken to exist far and wide: well beyond our capacity to know about them. Searle is a hard realist about minds.

Searle concludes that once we understand the causal basis of the ascription of mental states to other animals, then 'several traditional skeptical problems about "other minds" have an easy solution'.[16] The several problems that Searle refers to here are: (i) the problem of whether other human beings have minds; (ii) the problem of whether other non-human animals have minds; and (iii) the problem of spectrum inversion (the problem of knowing whether others might not use colour words as we do and discriminate coloured objects as we do while at the same time systematically differing in the colours they see). The easy solution to these problems is as follows: In the case of other human beings we are warranted in thinking that they have minds because the causal basis of their experiences is 'virtually identical' to our own.[17] In the case of non-human animals we will be warranted in thinking that they have minds once neurophysiologists identify a causal basis for their experiences.[18] And the inverted spectrum problem will be ruled out once neurophysiologists uncover the difference in the structures responsible for our colour experiences. Once these structures are uncovered, we will have what Searle calls 'solid neurophysiological evidence' that things either look to others as they do to us, or they do not.

Notice that Searle takes it that the indirect evidence afforded by the causal structure warrants my 'complete confidence' in the existence of other minds. There are two things to note about this confidence. First of all, although one's confidence that there are other minds may be complete one's warrant may not be; and second, one's confidence in the existence of other minds is not to explained by reference to what warrants it. Let us first look more closely at the second of these. When Searle writes of my complete confidence that there are other minds in the absence of a warrant, what he wants to draw attention to is the fact that we don't need any warrant in order to be able to attribute minds to another. We all make such attributions throughout our daily lives. Searle's point is that scepticism with regard to the mind of another does not arise in our daily lives; we simply treat others as though they had minds. That we do this is part of what Searle calls 'the Background'. Searle writes:

> Except when doing philosophy, there really is no 'problem' about other minds, because we do not hold a 'hypothesis', 'belief' or 'supposition' that other people are conscious, and that chairs, tables, computers, and cars are not conscious. Rather, we

have certain Background ways of behaving, certain Background capacities, and these are constitutive of our relations to the consciousness of other people.[19]

According to Searle, the existence of such a Background is a precondition of any theory of mind; it is not possible to theorize about this Background. The existence of the Background is, in effect, a commitment to the existence of other minds. Neurophysiology may warrant my confidence in the existence of other minds, but the confidence itself is independent of the warrant – it is part of the crucial Background. It is for this reason that Searle can say that my confidence in the existence of another mind is not to be explained by reference to what warrants it. By divorcing my confidence that another has a mind from my warrant in this way, it is possible to say that, although my confidence that there are other minds may be complete, any warrant I may subsequently come to have is far from complete. From the point of view of my warrant, there is always *some* room for doubt. Searle, himself, acknowledges this in one place when he writes: 'If we had a rich enough theory so that we could identify XYZ as causally both necessary and sufficient for consciousness, then we might regard the hypothesis [that a certain animal had consciousness] as definitely established, pending, of course, the usual hesitations about the ultimate falsifiability in principle of any scientific hypothesis.'[20] The belief that another has a mind is, on Searle's picture of things, a hypothesis, and the important thing to recognize about this hypothesis is that it can never be definitely established. The hypothesis that another has a mind must be recognized to be merely probable – a hypothesis that may be overturned by subsequent neurophysiological research.

Despite the fact that the belief in another mind can never rise above an hypothesis, Searle does not recognize this as a problem. This is because of the existence of the Background. Like the philosophers I discussed in Part One, above, Searle finds nothing *problematic* about our knowledge of another mind. Searle, however, wants to say that there is nothing problematic because of the existence of the Background. Searle's attitude towards scepticism with respect to other minds differs sharply from Galen Strawson's. Where Searle wants to reject the sceptic's question by gesturing at the Background, Strawson takes it that the sceptic here cannot be defeated. Strawson writes: 'The mistake is to attempt to defeat skepticism. To think that skepticism must be defeated is to accord it too much force. To acknowledge that it is irrefutable is to keep it in proportion.'[21] Strawson asks us to imagine a race of individuals – he calls them 'Sirians' – who, under certain circumstances, have painful sensations that they can think about without producing any observable causes and effects in relation to them. This turns out to be just as well as there is, in Sirian society, a taboo on talking about these sensations. Strawson further asks us to consider that one of these Sirians should decide to break this taboo and write a book about his painful sensations. Novelist Sirian introduces words for the sensations he has been thinking about before deciding to write his book, and he correctly believes that other Sirians will be able to understand his words. Strawson takes it that this story will make sense to all of us, and that the reality of novelist Sirian's subject matter, pain sensation, can be taken for granted.[22] According to Strawson all that is required for this story to make sense is the following: 'that there exists a certain kind of general, interpersonal, de facto congruence in the character of the Sirian's (private) experience: all of them experience these highly unpleasant sensations in certain circumstances'.[23] Strawson admits, however, that he is not able to prove that such de facto congruence exists. He, thus, acknowledges that there is *a* problem of other minds and that it is, 'strictly speaking, insoluble'.[24] Like Searle, Strawson holds that the epistemology of mind has nothing to do with the ontology of mind: the epistemology of mind may be problematic (Strawson) or not (Searle), but none of this affects the ontology of mind. The epistemology of mind is one thing, its ontology another.

Returning to Searle what we find is that he, in effect, advances two arguments against epistemological discussions in the philosophy of mind. The first I shall refer to as the argument from thought-experiments, and it is this: because it is possible to imagine situations where one's mental life vanishes while one's behaviour remains the same and where one's behaviour vanishes while one's mental life remains the same, we can see that the ontology of mind comes clean away from its epistemology. Behaviour is neither necessary nor sufficient for mentality. Searle's second argument I shall refer to as the argument from indirect evidence, and it is this: once one accepts that the ontology of mind is distinct from its epistemology, one can also see that our indirect evidence for the existence of another mind is not behaviour but causal structure. Although the first argument may be thought to leave us prey to the sceptic about other minds, the second argument is designed as a reply to the sceptic. While others try to fend off the sceptic by appeal to conjecture, analogy and induction, Searle puts forward the argument from causal structure. With this argument Searle claims to have begun 'to break the hold of three hundred years of epistemological discussions of "the other minds problem", according to which behaviour is the sole basis on which we know of the existence of other minds'.[25] Searle addresses the following remark to the philosophical sceptic about other minds: 'a cloud of philosophical scepticism condenses into a drop of neuroscience'.[26]

Galen Strawson joins forces with Searle over the first of these arguments, the argument from thought-experiment. It is the argument here that leads both of these philosophers to hold that the epistemology of mind comes clean away from its ontology. It is unclear, however, whether Strawson would wish to join forces with Searle over the second of his arguments, the argument from indirect evidence. Strawson's commitment to materialism leaves it open that he could accept the argument from indirect evidence, but his agnosticism leaves it open that reference to behaviour may play some role in the way we come by our hypothesis that another has a mind, in our indirect evidence for other minds.

A RETURN TO BEHAVIOUR

In Chapter IX I said that the concept of behaviour proper (in Armstrong's sense) is a concept which straddles the divide between the subject and her world. To acknowledge a close conceptual relationship between our concept of behaviour proper and our concept of mind is to acknowledge that our concept of mind is such as to leave no room for a sharp divide between the subject and her world. With their rejection of behaviour in their account of the nature of mind, Searle and Strawson maintain a commitment to this conceptual divide. Despite the fact that both Searle and Strawson renounce Cartesian dualism, they both remain committed to a radical conceptual divide between a subject and her world; they both develop their philosophy within a Cartesian framework. This is clear in Strawson's work from the fact that he explicitly embraces scepticism about other minds. The subject and her world are metaphysically distinct, and this gives rise to a problem when it comes to our knowledge of the mind of another. Although Strawson assumes the existence of a 'de facto congruence' between individuals, he also admits that he cannot prove that this congruence exists. Strawson admits that this leaves us with the traditional, radical, epistemological problem of other minds, but he does not find this worrying or problematic. The existence of this problem in its radical form is evidence that Strawson is committed to the Cartesian framework that holds a conceptual divide between a subject and her world.[27]

Searle does not embrace the traditional epistemological problem of other minds. According to Searle the traditional problem does not arise because of the existence of the Background. For this reason, one cannot simply point to sceptical questions as evidence of Searle's commitment to the Cartesian framework. It is not clear, however, whether appeal to the Background really does rule out traditional sceptical questions about other minds. By appealing to the Background Searle is able to insist that our complete confidence in, and commitment to, the existence of other minds is constitutive of our relations with others. Despite the existence of the Background, however, Searle raises the question of our warrant for our complete confidence and commitment. Although Searle is not clear here, it is possible to see what he is doing in terms of Stroud's argument against P. F. Strawson and Davidson (*vide supra*, Chapter VIII). Strawson and Davidson also take our commitment to other minds to be constitutive of our relations with them, but their understanding of this commitment leaves no room for the further question of warrant. Stroud accepts this commitment, but insists that there is room for what he calls 'positive metaphysical results'. This, in effect, is Searle's point as well: commitment is one thing, warrant another. But the separation of the question of warrant from the question of commitment is evidence of the Cartesian framework in Searle's work. It is as a result of his adherence to this framework that Searle can write: 'Mental contents . . . are existence-independent, in the sense that one could have exactly the contents one has, and yet the objects referred to by one's representations might not exist.'[28] The conceptual divide that gives substance to the question of warrant may not undermine our confidence as we go about our daily lives, but it may undermine our confidence when we contemplate our actions. The confidence we have does not go deep; it does not push aside the question of warrant. And where our confidence does not reach deep, the sceptic can always raise his question. Thus we can, after all, find in Searle's work the scepticism that is evidence of a Cartesian framework.

Both Searle and Galen Strawson can be seen to accept the Cartesian framework. Searle, at least, is perfectly explicit about the Cartesian nature of his work, but he finds nothing to be worried about in this; like Strawson's, Searle's Cartesianism is *naturalized*. Both these philosophers believe that, once one introduces naturalism, there is nothing to worry about in Cartesianism. But it is not at all clear that this is the case. The really worrying aspect of Cartesianism is not its substantial dualism but the conceptual framework it assumes, the radical conceptual divide it introduces between a subject and her world.

The Cartesian conception of a subject in relation to her world is such as to give rise to a *prima facie* difficulty about the generality of our concept of mind, and this difficulty gives rise to a conceptual problem of other minds. It is interesting that there is no talk of *this* problem of other minds in the work of either Searle or Strawson. When they talk about the problem of other minds, it is always the traditional epistemological problem to which they refer. And their attitude towards this epistemological problem is explicit and clear. There is, however, no mention of what Nagel has labelled the 'interesting, conceptual problem of other minds' in their writings. I believe that it is attention to *this* problem that will reveal a serious difficulty at the heart of their respective pictures of mind.

The absence of attention to the conceptual problem of other minds in the work of Searle and Strawson is particularly notable when one considers how similar, in essential respects, their positions are to Nagel's. Like Nagel, Strawson and Searle emphasize the first-person element in their account of the nature of mind. Strawson writes, and all three might agree, that:

> Sometimes it seems that the only thing that is completely clear is that reference to experience must have a central place in [a positive account of the nature of mind]. By 'experience' I mean conscious experience, the phenomenon of life's having rich experiential content from moment to moment. The term 'experience' has no theoretical charge. It refers only to something with which every normal human being is profoundly familiar.[29]

It is this thought that leads Strawson, Searle, and Nagel to insist that the epistemology of mind has nothing to do with its ontology. Once experience is given central place, all else pales into insignificance. I can have knowledge of this experience from a first-person perspective, and all other knowledge falls behind this. Realism about other minds is fiercely proclaimed, but it is also admitted that our belief in the mind of another is an hypothesis (Searle),[30] or founded on a commitment to a 'kind of de facto, interpersonal, congruence' (Strawson), or dependent upon our ability to 'call whole worlds out of our heads' (Nagel). The realism that results is hard, and it allows us to contemplate the existence of minds far and wide without regard to what we can understand or know. Thus all three philosophers are unmoved by the radical sceptical problem of other minds. In one way or another they would all agree that such a scepticism is a correlate of their (hard) realism.[31] Searle and Strawson, each in his own way, could agree with Nagel when he writes that the interesting problem of other minds is not the epistemological one, how I can know that others are not zombies.

Nagel, however, after dismissing the epistemological problem, goes on to recognize the conceptual problem as the *interesting* problem of other minds. It is notable that neither Searle nor Strawson mentions this problem. As far as the *concept* of mind is concerned, Strawson is simply concerned to insist that reference to behaviour has no part in it.[32] Searle would no doubt agree. Let us remind ourselves just what the conceptual problem of other minds is. Nagel takes it that the problem is that of accounting for the generality of our concept. I have argued that what makes generality *problematic* is the unity problem. We need not only to understand how our concept of mind can be general, but to understand how it can be the very same concept that applies to others as well as myself. The first-person element that Nagel, Searle and Strawson are so keen to emphasize is precisely what makes it so hard to see just *how* we can have one unified general concept of mind. This is a point recognized by both Nagel and Colin McGinn (*vide supra*, Chapters VIII and IX). It is precisely because of the difficulties involved in extending our concept of mind out from its use in first-person ascription that I have suggested we must begin in another place, we need to begin with the lived position. Beginning here gives us an assurance of the generality of our mental concepts. But an assumption of generality is not enough; we need to understand this generality, to understand how it is possible in the face of the obvious asymmetry in the application of the concept across individuals. It is here that reference must be made to action or behaviour proper. In the words of P. F. Strawson, what we need to understand is that we 'act, and act on each other, and act in accordance with a common human nature'.[33] In other words, what we need to do is look at how we operate with our concept. A detailed description of what we do here should make the assumption with which we begin intelligible to us. It is important to bear in mind that there is nothing reductive in this proposal: the actions that each of us performs – and observes each other performing – are actions of minded individuals (see Armstrong's notion of 'behaviour proper'). We act in the way that we do because of the nature that we have, and we interact in the ways that we do because of the human nature that we share with one another. The non-reductive aspect of this proposal is crucial. Without it we are left requiring some *further* understanding of what we do (of our movements through the world). Once we jettison reduction what we are left with is a bunch of tightly knit concepts each of which sheds reciprocal light on the other. And chief amongst these is the concept of (inter)action.

Notice that acceptance of this suggestion for how we are to understand the generality of our concept of mind involves accepting that the concept of behaviour is essential to our concept of mind. If, however, we follow Searle and Galen Strawson and reject all reference to behaviour in our account of the nature of mind, it is a real question what understanding we can have of the generality that our concept of mind undoubtedly possesses. Strawson's reply to this question, like Nagel's, is to say that our concept of mind is simply *innately* general. Strawson does not explicitly consider our concept of mind, but he does say the following in response to the claim that one needs to be exposed to a certain form of experience in order to acquire a certain concept: 'the concept . . . in question may be innate'.[34] It is likely that, had he considered the question, he would have said that our concept of mind is innate, and innately general. There is, however, as I pointed out in connection with Nagel's appeal to an innate general conception of mind, a *prima facie* difficulty with any such appeal: given that there is an asymmetry in the application of the concept in one's own case and in the case of another, a sceptic can ask why we take it that it is the very same concept that we use in connection with ourselves as we do in connection with others (*vide supra*, Chapter IX). As far as I know, Strawson does not consider the unity problem.

It is much less clear what Searle would say to this conceptual problem. I don't think that he would want to move in the direction of postulating an innate general conception of mind; his appeal to the Background is in tension with this. The crucial Background is a pretheoretical condition for the existence of *any* concept. The concept of mind is not innately given, but emerges out of this Background. At the level of the Background there is no problem about other minds. Searle writes that 'we have certain Background ways of behaving, certain Background capacities, and these are constitutive of our relations to the consciousness of other people'.[35] What Searle says here would be in keeping with my appeal to behaviour: understanding our behaviour here leaves no room for any question about the existence of another mind; that there are others is a precondition of our appreciating our behaviour and capacities. The difference between my position and Searle's is that I believe that this all carries over to the conceptual level: the concept of mind that I possess has to be understood in relation to this background. Searle, however, draws a distinction between the Background and the theoretical/conceptual foreground. According to Searle, I form certain conscious beliefs and hypotheses against this

Background, and these can be warranted by appeal to the neurophysiological evidence. My concept of mind – which could not come into existence without the prior existence of the Background – is to be understood, not by reference to the behaviour and capacities that are so much in evidence in the Background, but by reference to an individual's causal structure. But at *this* level – the conceptual level, *not* the level of the Background – we can ask: how are we to understand the generality of our concept of mind? It is not at all clear to me what Searle would say in reply to this question. Searle insists on rejecting a reply that is already in place for him to make: as with the Background, we must understand our concept of mind in relation to the concept of behaviour and capacities that we share with others. But Searle explicitly distances himself off from this reply. If, however, our concept of mind emerges from this Background, why can we not appeal to it when trying to understand our concept? By cutting himself off from the Background in this way, Searle makes it entirely unclear how he is going to account for our concept of mind. In the absence of any alternative account, an appeal to behaviour here can make the concept we operate with intelligible.

It may be thought that Searle has an excellent reason for distancing himself from the kind of reply I am urging him to make. He may point to the argument from thought-experiments as showing that we must distance ourselves from this kind of reply. It is a real possibility that the implantation of silicon chips may diminish my consciousness while leaving my behaviour untouched or make behaviour impossible while leaving consciousness intact. What can we say about these cases if we insist on saying that reference to behaviour must form part of our conception of mind? The first thing to consider is just what kind of reply we are looking for here. When Searle introduces these thought-experiments he claims that his intuitions tell him that it is *clear* that consciousness may become extinct while behaviour remains as normal or that behaviour may be impeded with no diminution of consciousness. What Searle looks for is a physical fact to back up this clear intuition. But can the clear cut nature of this intuition not be seen to be an imposition or requirement of theory? If we consider the pretheoretical situation, *is* it completely clear what our response would be to a world in which we behaved and were conscious but others behaved and were *not* conscious – or where everyone behaved the same but some others were conscious and some not? Our responses to these situations might be thought to be ones that we may describe as 'hesitant' or 'uncertain'. And can we not accept that there is all the difference in the world between such imagined situations and the situation to which we do find ourselves responding? When Searle introduces his thought-experiments he is careful to point out that he does not think that it is even a remote empirical possibility that the world could be such as to maintain consciousness without behaviour; but he insists that such thought-experiments remain 'valid as a statement of logical or conceptual possibility'.[36] In other words, he thinks that our concept of mind is such as to allow for such possibilities. But once we accept that our concept of mind needs to be understood by reference to the concept of behaviour proper or action, it is not at all clear that our concept of mind does allow for such possibilities. We must go back to Descartes for a conception of mind that allows for the possibilities that Searle imagines. But if we do this, we will also find that this conception of mind is the product of very specific conceptual assumptions (*vide supra* Chapter I). Searle simply asserts that our concept of mind is such as to allow for the possibilities he describes, but it is perfectly in order to reject both the possibilities and the conception of mind that allows for them. I have been arguing that, unless we do reject this conception of mind, we encounter a serious conceptual problem about other minds.

Strawson and Searle would no doubt object that my approach denies the essential subjectivity of mind. They would insist that the only way to ensure that we do not end up denying the subjectivity of mind is to emphasize experience over behaviour; we must hold on to what we can know in our own case. In line with the Cartesian conception of mind which they inherit, Searle and Strawson emphasize knowledge over action – not knowledge of the world, but first-person knowledge of one's own mental states. To adopt an alternative conception of mind – one compatible with an emphasis on action over knowledge – looks to lose us the essential subjectivity of the mental. But there need be no such fear: subjectivity is part of our conception of action. The action being emphasized here is the action of subjects. It is because we are the subjects that we are that we have come to have the concept of a mind that we have. We could say that mind is what our concept of mind is a concept of, and this concept of mind is one fashioned by our interaction with others who share our nature. The important point is that we are subjects ourselves, and that we observe and react to the behaviour of other subjects. It will be objected that subjects need to be able to distinguish between behaviour proper and physical behaviour, and that in order to do this we must make reference to something other than the behaviour of the subject; and once we do this, we can see that reference to behaviour is inessential to what makes behaviour *proper*. In other words, all behaviour is taken in the first instance to be physical behaviour which somehow gets upgraded or converted to behaviour proper as the result of a causal antecedent. But is it true that we need to refer to a causal antecedent to make sense of the distinction between behaviour proper and physical behaviour? After all we all react quite differently when we come across a robot and when we meet our siblings. It may be that the robot has been very cleverly designed: at first we are fooled and react to it much in the way that we react to our siblings. But after a while the robot will do something that changes our attitude. But this sort of account of the difference between behaviour proper and physical behaviour can seem unsatisfying; we want to explain the difference by appeal to something more fundamental. But it is possible to be satisfied without recourse to this sort of explanation. Understanding the kinds of beings that we are and the way we act, with others, in the world can help to make the concept of mind that we operate with intelligible to us. Appreciating this can also help us to see that there is *no* problem of other minds – no epistemological problem and no conceptual problem.

Notes

OVERVIEW

1   I discuss this argument in the following section of this chapter and in Chapter II. Other arguments that are standardly proposed include inductive arguments (see Chapter VI, this volume, Brief interlude: John Stuart Mill), and arguments to the best explanation of the behaviour we observe (see this chapter, 16).

2   Malcolm 1966a.

3   This is taken directly from Malcolm 1966a: 371. For a fuller discussion of this passage from Mill see Chapter VI, this volume.

4   I argue in Chapter VI, this volume, Brief interlude: John Stuart Mill, that analogy is only *part* of Mill's argument here.

5   Sir William Hamilton was an expounder of Reid's work in the nineteenth century. Thus, much of Mill's *Examination of Sir William Hamilton's Philosophy* is devoted to consideration – and attack on – Reid's work.

6   Mill 1872: 242–243.

7   Mill, *op. cit.*: 239, footnote*. I explain what Mill means by this in Chapter VI, this volume, Brief interlude: John Stuart Mill.

8   Reid 1969 [1785]: Pt. II, ch. x, 179. For a discussion of Reid's interpretation of Berkeley see Chapter VI, this volume.

9   *Ibid.*: Pt. VI, ch. v, 633.

10 Mill, *op. cit.*: 243.

11 I am here referring to philosophers working in the analytic tradition. There is another tradition, the phenomenological one, that has run along side the analytic one since, roughly, the time of Kant. The phenomenological tradition is a rich source of discussion of other minds. I do not mean to deny this, but should make it clear that the concern of this book is the analytic tradition only.

12 Wittgenstein's work was followed by that of P. F. Strawson. Strawson's work here has been highly influential and, arguably, responsible for a certain way of understanding Wittgenstein's own ideas. I discuss Strawson's position in Part Three, Chapter VIII, this volume.

13 Perhaps more; perhaps one is forced to reassess one's entire approach to philosophy. See Chapter VII, this volume.

14 Descartes makes reference to the matter only in passing and in a very few places. See Chapter II, this volume.

15 I intend, for the moment, to continue to be vague about just what this alternative – or these alternatives – are. It is enough at this point that we note that it is the aim of such an alternative to find a satisfactory place for other minds. For more on this alternative, see Part Three, this volume.

16 Burnyeat 1982.

17 This is in the opening paragraphs of Fodor's entry under 'Fodor, J. A.' in Guttenplan 1994: 292.

18 Although I suspect that this fashion may be coming to an end. Recently there has been a revival of interest in issues having to do with self-knowledge, and questions here *should* make philosophers reflect also on the question of our knowledge of other minds. Furthermore, a current interest among philosophers and psychologists alike in the phenomenon of autism has begun to prompt reflection on this topic.

19 See Fodor 1994b: 88. One must be careful here, for Fodor's position is not Cartesian through and through.

20 *Ibid.*: 102.

21 In one place Fodor calls his position 'minimum scepticism'. See Fodor 1968: 61. Interestingly, Fodor invokes the idea of 'moral certainty' in this connection (see *Psychological Explanation*: 64). For a discussion of this idea, see Chapter II.

22 See especially Strawson 1959. Although Strawson's work is influenced by Wittgenstein's, it displays important differences. For a discussion see Chapter VIII, this volume.

23 See especially Nagel 1979a.

24 This term is often used by philosophers to embrace a variety of positions. From the point of view of the philosophers under discussion, the differences between positions is less important than the fact that all of them give prominent place to behaviour. It is *this* that they want to oppose.

I ANCIENT AND MODERN SCEPTICISM AND THE PROBLEM OF OTHER MINDS

1 For a discussion of Descartes' work in connection with this issue, see Chapter II, this volume.

2 The following story is an example of the Academic sceptic's method: While in Rome, serving as ambassador from Athens, Carneades gave two public lectures on the topic of justice. In the first lecture he undertook a detailed defence of the prevailing views of justice; on the following day he delivered a point-by-point refutation of the previous day's lecture. The story is cited in Hankinson 1995: 95.

3 Because of this the Academic sceptic is sometimes said to have held a *mitigated* scepticism. For a discussion of whether the Academic sceptic mitigated his scepticism or whether he was addressing the Stoic see Couissin 1983 [1929]. See also Burnyeat 1997.

4 It is sometimes said that, while the Academic sceptics formulated their scepticism in direct response to the Stoics, the Pyrrhonists allowed their target to range more widely. See, for example, Couissin 1983 [1929]: 57.

5 Both stories are related by P. P. Hallie 1985: 12.
6 David Hume 1975 [1748]: Section XII, Part II, 160.
7 The comparison is made by Sextus Empiricus in his *Outlines of Pyrrhonism*: Pt. I, ch. xii. See Hallie 1985: 41.
8 This is how Burnyeat understands the Pyrrhonist's commitment to the four-fold scheme of life. See his 'Can the skeptic live his skepticism', (1983: 131). On a variation of Hume's point Burnyeat argues that the element of belief that the Pyrrhonist urges us to renounce is the very thing that 'gives meaning and sense to life' (133).
9 See Annas and Barnes 1985, and also Hallie 1985.
10 Burnyeat 1982: 33. For a discussion of Berkeley's idealism see Chapter V, this volume.
11 Burnyeat 1982: 33. See also Williams 1981.
12 Burnyeat admits that Berkeley does allow that minds and ideas are different sorts of things and that ideas are dependent upon minds. What Berkeley fails to acknowledge is that minds have an essential relation to ideas. Burnyeat's point is that there is no *ontological* dependence of mind on ideas in Berkeley's work. See Burnyeat, *op. cit.*: 27.
13 Sextus, *Against the Professors*: VII, 196. This passage is quoted and discussed at length by V. Tsouna (1998a: 246).
14 For her argument in defense of this conclusion see Tsouna (1998a: 251). See also Tsouna 1998b.
15 Tsouna 1998a: 250.
16 Burnyeat 1983: n. 32.
17 Everson 1991: 146.
18 Striker 1983: 103–104.
19 Sorabji 1974: 88.
20 Popkin 1960: Chapter X. That Descartes would have disagreed with this accusation is clear from the following passage: 'What could be more perverse than to attribute to a writer views which he reports in order simply to refute? What could be more foolish than to pretend during the interval in which such views are being stated, pending their refutation, they are the doctrines of the writer, and hence that someone who mentions the arguments of the atheists is temporarily an atheist?' Descartes proceeds to write that, should the man who hopes to refute atheism die before doing so, we would not say he dies an atheist. One can only assume that Descartes would also insist that, should the author's refutation *fail*, we should not say he was, thereby, an atheist. If this is right, we should conclude that Descartes would not accept Popkin's claim that he is 'sceptic *malgré lui*'. See Descartes 1985 [1647]: 309.
21 In one place Descartes writes that doubt should be employed 'solely in connection with the contemplation of the truth'. As for the conduct of life, we are 'often compelled to accept what is merely probable' (1985 [1644]: 193).
22 Descartes 1984 [1641b]: 243, 'Author's replies to the fifth set of objections'.
23 Descartes 1984 [1641a]: 15.
24 Williams 1978: 47.

25 Descartes 1984 [1641a]: 12.
26 *Ibid.*: 13.
27 Michael Williams explains the significance that consideration of dreams – and of madness – has in the writings of the ancient Greek sceptics in contrast to Descartes' writings. See his 'Descartes and the metaphysics of doubt' (1986).
28 Descartes 1984 [1641a]: 15.
29 Popkin 1960: 182.
30 Descartes 1976 [1648]: 4.
31 Greg McCulloch (1995: 11) puts the point in the following way: 'Descartes not only supposed that mind is separable from all body, but also that individual minds *are self-contained with respect to body*, or capable of having the mental characteristics that they do, independently of the existence of any body'.
32 Burnyeat 1982: 44. Burnyeat does acknowledge that Augustine anticipated Descartes with his *si fallor sum* (if I am mistaken, I am), but he holds – along with Popkin and many others – that Augustine does not accord a privileged status to knowledge of our subjective states. For a consideration of Augustine's work in relation to Descartes' see Chapter II, this volume.
33 Descartes writes that 'the proposition, *I am, I exist*, [*cogito ergo sum*] is necessarily true whenever it is put forward by me or conceived in my mind' (1984 [1641a]: 17).
34 McDowell 1986: 146.
35 Williams 1981: 238.
36 Burnyeat 1982: 40.
37 *Ibid.*
38 Cf. J. W. Cook (1969: 122), who writes: 'With the suggestion that he is dreaming Descartes sees a place to enter a wedge between himself and his body, a wedge that is driven further in the remaining Meditations'.
39 J. McDowell 1986: 146.
40 Descartes 1985 [1644]: 213.
41 See Descartes 1984 [1641a]: 21.
42 Although it is not at all clear that Descartes intends the passage in the second *Meditation* to be raising a problem about our knowledge of another mind. For a discussion of this passage see Chapter II, this volume.
43 My reply here builds on the work of Burnyeat, especially 'Idealism and Greek Philosophy' (1982).
44 J. McDowell 1986: 147.
45 M. Williams 1986: 118.
46 *Ibid.*: 124.
47 See Descartes 1984 [1641a]: 12.
48 S. Everson 1991: 123.
49 M. McGinn, 'Pyrrhonism and the Cartesian sceptic', unpublished. In a similar vein, Daniel Garber describes Descartes' *Meditations* as 'a Trojan horse that Descartes is attempting to send behind the lines of Aristotelian science' (1986: 82).
50 McDowell 1986: 152. It should be noted that McDowell does not make this

point in order to illustrate the relative priority of the Cartesian conception of the world over that of the subject, nor does he wish to show the primacy of conceptual over epistemological issues.

51 Williams 1978: 66.
52 J. McDowell 1994: 109.

II DESCARTES AND KNOWLEDGE OF OTHER MINDS

1 Descartes, Letter to Colvius, 14 November 1640 (1991: 159).
2 Copleston 1962: 71. Other writers to understand Augustine's work in this way include Popkin (1960) and Matthews (1992).
3 Augustine (1974) *De Trinitate*, 15, 12, 21 (trans. M. Frede).
4 Augustine (1991) *Confessions*, IV, V, 7.
5 Augustine (1974) *De Trinitate*, 8, 6, 9: 120. Augustine does not think that the ability to recognize another is confined to humans. He writes: 'Neither is this the property of human foresight and reason, since brute animals also perceive that not only they themselves live, but also other brute animals interchangeably, and the one the other, and that we ourselves do so. Neither do they see our souls, save from the movements of the body, and that immediately and most easily by some natural agreement' (*De Trinitate*, 8, 6, 9).
6 In particular Matthews 1992: Chapter 9. Matthews explains that he was, for some time, convinced that Augustine did propose an argument from analogy to explain our knowledge of the existence of another mind and that he was in advance of his time in doing so. Matthews came to doubt this interpretation of Augustine's work, however, upon hearing a paper by T. M. McNulty (see McNulty 1970).
7 Augustine *De Trinitate*, 10, 9, 12: 140.
8 *Ibid.*
9 He writes: 'Augustine wants to explain how it ever occurs to us . . . to attribute minds, or souls, to other beings' (Matthews 1986: 150).
10 Matthews 1992: 122.
11 In correspondence Christopher Kirwan has indicated that he agrees that in *De Trinitate*, 8, 6, 9 Augustine appears to shift the question from (a) what *justifies* my belief in other minds? to (b) what accounts for my belief that others have minds, and that in doing so avoids the question of justification altogether.
12 Descartes 1984 [1701]: 409.
13 The temptation is mostly voiced by philosophers in discussion. In print philosophers are more careful and say that Descartes' work 'suggests' or 'approximates to' the argument from analogy. See, for example, Plantinga 1967: 191; Henze 1972: 43; and Ryle 1949: 16. If what I say in this chapter is along the right lines, it would explain these philosophers' reservations about assigning a full-blown argument from analogy to Descartes.
14 Descartes does not explicitly consider the matter. Nonetheless, it is likely that he would say this. In 'Descartes and the problem of other minds', Matthews (1986) suggests that the question which occupied Descartes is the question, assuming that others do have minds, *which* others have minds?
15 Descartes, *Meditations* 1984 [1641a]: 21.

16 *Ibid.*
17 *Ibid.*: 22–23.
18 *Ibid.*: 21.
19 *Ibid.*: 22.
20 It is important to note that, although it is our language which is mislead-
    ing, it is ultimately our judgement that is responsible for error, not our
    understanding. See Descartes, *Principles of Philosophy* 1985 [1644]: Part
    I, 33.
21 See Matthews 1977.
22 Descartes, *Objections and Replies* 1984 [1641b]: 246 Reply to Objection V.
23 Matthews 1977: 16.
24 Descartes, *Treatise on Man* 1985 [1664]: 108.
25 Matthews points out that this distinction was standardly – if not univer-
    sally – held by earlier philosophers. See Matthews 1977: 18.
26 See, however, Cottingham 1978.
27 Descartes, Letter to Reneri for Pollot, April or May 1638 (1991: 99).
28 Descartes here refers Reneri for Pollot to Part V of his [Descartes']
    Discourse on Method. I discuss the passage here referred to by Descartes
    below, 63.
29 Descartes, Letter to Reneri for Pollot: 100.
30 Descartes, *Discourse on Method* 1985 [1637]: 139. See also Descartes'
    Letter to Reneri for Pollot: 100.
31 The sort of machine that God could produce is described by Descartes his
    Treatise on Man: 99–110. It is interesting to note that in a footnote to their
    translation of this text, Cottingham *et al.* point out that the men to whom
    Descartes refers in the text are 'fictional men' that are 'intended to cast light
    on the nature of real men in the same way that the description of the "new
    world" in *The World*, Chapter 6, is intended to cast light on the real world'
    (99).
32 Much of this criticism drew on Montaigne's work, which details the
    sophistication of animal behaviour. See, in particular, Montaigne 1987
    [1576].
33 Descartes, *Discourse on Method*: 141.
34 Descartes, Letter to the Marquess of Newcastle, 23 November 1646 (1991:
    304).
35 Descartes, *Discourse on Method*: 141.
36 Descartes, Letter to More, 5 February 1649 (1991: 366).
37 Descartes, *Discourse on Method*: 139–140.
38 *Ibid.*
39 Descartes, Letter to the Marquess of Newcastle, 23 November 1646: 303.
40 Descartes, Letter to More, 5 February 1649: 366.
41 Descartes, *Discourse on Method*: 140.
42 *Ibid.*
43 Gordon Baker and Katherine Morris note that Descartes does not believe that
    the mind or soul can be united to anything other than a human body, and they
    cite Leibniz in this connection when he writes: 'Nature does not permit
    these fictions'. See Baker and Morris 1996: 188, n. 336. The quotation from
    Leibniz is from his *New Essays* 242.

44 I take the phrase 'test of a real man' from the translation of Descartes' *Discourse on Method* by Haldane and Ross (1970: 116).

45 Descartes, *Discourse on Method*: 139–140. Descartes is referring in this passage to his earlier work *The Treatise on Man*. Notice that where this translation writes of 'means of recognizing', the Haldane and Ross translation writes of 'tests'.

46 *Ibid.*: 141. In the same place Descartes writes: 'it is not sufficient for [the soul] to be lodged in the human body like a helmsman in his ship . . . but must be more closely joined and united with the body.'

47 In an interesting paper Stephen Voss (1994) charts Descartes' use of the term 'man' throughout his writings. Voss suggests that Descartes' use of the term can be seen to progress through three distinct stages: In stage one (which Voss takes to include Descartes' *Rules for the Direction of Mind*, his *Discourse on Method*, and his *Meditations*) Descartes takes a man to be composed of a body together with a soul. In stage two (which Voss dates from 1641–1642) Descartes writes in such a way as to suggest a substantial union between body and soul. 'Man' is the name for the substance generated by that union. In the third and final stage (which Voss takes to include Descartes' *Passions of the Soul* and *Principles of Philosophy*) Descartes ceases to use the term. The passages I am considering in this chapter all fall within what Voss identifies as stage one.

48 See note 19, this chapter.

49 Descartes, *Principles of Philosophy*: 290.

50 *Ibid.*: 289–290.

51 Descartes, *Meditations*: 55.

52 See Matthews (1986) for a similar understanding of Descartes' work here.

53 Descartes' Letter to More: 365.

54 See, in particular, Descartes' *Discourse on Method*: 140.

55 Baker and Morris speculate that Descartes holds that all and only men have minds because he believes that God is benevolent and would not have set up a world that would make the moral life impossible. Their point is that, just as Descartes contrasts the mechanical with the rational, he also contrasts the mechanical with the free, the morally responsible and the virtuous. This latter contrast lends an interesting twist to the Cartesian thesis that animals are mere mechanisms. Baker and Morris point out that, in saying this, Descartes is declaring that machines (or non-human animals) do not have free will and so cannot be praised and blamed for their actions. Furthermore, if you deny that animals are machines, then you would be allowing them free will and, hence, a moral life. As Baker and Morris write: 'you would have to accord to [the animal] all the moral rights and duties that are inseparable from having a rational soul'. And from this would follow that you would have a moral obligation to look after animals, and it would have to be considered murder to kill them for food. In this connection Baker and Morris cite Descartes' Letter to More (*op. cit.*) where he writes that 'my opinion is not so much cruel to animals as indulgent to human beings . . . since it absolves them from the suspicion of crime . . . when they kill or eat animals.' See Baker and Morris 1996: 89–91.

Notes

III MALEBRANCHE AND KNOWLEDGE OF OTHER MEN'S SOULS

1   This neglect is evidenced by the absence of much translation of his work. Until 1980 only one of his books, *Dialogues on Metaphysics and Religion* (1980 [1688]), had been translated into English. A translation of the *Search After Truth* in 1997, as well as books on Malebranche by Charles McCracken (1983) and Stephen Nadler (1992) has done much to provoke interest in Malebranche's work.
2   See McCracken 1983: 250; Luce 1934: 108; and Radner 1978: 76.
3   Malebranche, *The Search After Truth*, preface, xxxix.
4   *Ibid.*: Bk. I, ch. 1, 3.
5   *Ibid.*: 2.
6   See, for example, *The Search After Truth*: Bk. I, ch. 6, and also the preface xxxix.
7   Malebranche, *op. cit.*: Bk. III, Pt. ii, ch. 1, 218.
8   *Ibid.*: 217. This is not all Malebranche has to say about ideas. For more on Malebranche on ideas see below, 73.
9   *Ibid.*
10 See *The Search After Truth*: Bk. III, Pt. ii, ch. 6.
11 For a discussion of this debate see this chapter, Brief interlude: Arnaud and Malebranche on knowledge of other minds.
12 What Hume has to say about causation betrays the influence of Malebranche.
13 See Reid (1969 [1785]). In more recent times, A. A. Luce has argued that Malebranche was in many and important ways the philosophical precursor of Berkeley.
14 For a discussion of Berkeley's work, see Chapter V, this volume. I explain Malebranche's view in what follows in this chapter.
15 Malebranche, *op. cit.*: Bk. VI, Pt. ii, ch. 6, 480.
16 *Ibid.*
17 Malebranche, *op. cit.*, Elucidation 11: 637.
18 *Ibid.*: 634.
19 *Ibid.*: 634–635.
20 Malebranche, *op. cit.*, Elucidation 3: 561. For a good discussion of Malebranche's use of the term 'idea' see Nadler (1992), especially ch. 2.
21 *Ibid.*: Bk. III, Pt. ii, ch. 1, 237.
22 *Ibid.*: Elucidation 11: 635.
23 *Ibid.*: Bk. III, Pt. ii, ch. 1, 218.
24 *Ibid.*
25 See McCracken 1983: 58.
26 Malebranche, *Dialogues on Metaphysics and Religion*: I, ix, 37.
27 *Ibid.*: III, vii, 61.
28 Malebranche, *The Search After Truth*: Bk. I, ch. 13, IV, 62–63.
29 *Ibid.*: Bk. I, ch. 13, II, 61.
30 *Ibid.*: Bk. III, Pt. ii, ch. 7, IV, 239.
31 Cf. *The Search After Truth*: Bk. IV, ch. 11: 'God knows the nature of soul clearly because He finds in Himself a clear and representative idea of it.' Arnaud questions Malebranche's assurance that God has not given us an idea of mind.

298

Arnaud asks, 'And who taught him that God wished to reveal the one [ideas of bodies] but not the other [ideas of soul]?' Arnaud 1990 [1683]: 161. For a discussion of a part of the debate between Malebranche and Arnaud see this chapter, Brief interlude: Arnaud on Malebranche on knowledge of other minds.

32 Cf. *The Search After Truth*: Bk. III, Pt. ii, ch. 7, IV.

33 See *The Search After Truth*: Bk. III, Pt. ii, ch. 6.

34 *Ibid.*: Bk. III, Pt. ii, ch. 6, 233.

35 Doney 1967: 143.

36 Contrast Berkeley, see Chapter V, this volume.

37 Malebranche, *op. cit.*: Bk. I, ch. 14, 68. Strictly speaking, it is not the senses that are the locus of error but our natural judgement – or, rather, a certain intense feeling that is excited in us, which Malebranche chooses to call 'judgement' in order to emphasize the fact that we cannot cease to perceive these sensations as if they were of some objective quality in bodies. Interestingly, Malebranche acknowledges that these judgements are caused in us by God, but escapes the criticism that this makes God a deceiver by insisting that God does not intend for us to learn about the nature of body by the use of the senses. The purpose of the senses and of natural judgement is to *preserve* us, and for this the senses must inform us quickly, and, consequently, in a way that is liable to error. See *The Search After Truth*: Bk. I, ch. 7, IV.

38 *Ibid.*: Bk. III, Pt. ii, ch. 1, I, 219.

39 Reid, *op. cit.*: Essay II, ch. VII, 130.

40 Malebranche, *op. cit.*: 570.

41 Malebranche, *op. cit.*: Bk. I, ch. 10, 48.

42 *Ibid.*, Elucidation 6: 572.

43 Malebranche, *Dialogues on Metaphysics and Religion*: I, iv, 29–30.

44 Malebranche, *The Search After Truth*: Bk. III, Pt. ii, ch. 7, V, 239

45 It is interesting to note in passing that John Norris (1657–1711), in many respects a faithful follower of Malebranche's work, disagrees with Malebranche over his account of knowledge of other minds. According to Norris, all knowledge is either direct or by representation. As Norris accepts that our knowledge of other minds comes about in neither of these two ways, he is in a quandary how to account for it. On this see McCracken 1983: 173.

46 Malebranche, *op. cit.*: Bk. III, Pt. ii, ch. 1, I, 218.

47 *Ibid.*

48 See *The Search After Truth*, Elucidation 3: 561.

49 These are Malebranche's own examples, see *The Search After Truth*: Bk. III, Pt. ii, ch. 7, V, 239.

50 *Ibid.*

51 *Ibid.*: Bk. I, ch. 13, V, 63.

52 *Ibid.*

53 *Ibid.*: Bk. I, ch. 13, VI, 66.

54 *Ibid.*: Bk. III, Pt. ii, ch. 7, V, 239.

55 *Ibid.*: 240.

56 Cf. *The Search After Truth*: Bk. III, Pt. ii, ch. 7, I.

57 See McCracken 1983: 81.

58 For a discussion of the debate between Malebranche and Arnaud see Nadler 1989; and Church 1931.

59   Arnaud, *Of True and False Ideas* 1990 [1683]: 191–192.
60   *Ibid.*: 192.
61   See Descartes' *Discourse on Method*: 116. See also my discussion of
      Descartes in Chapter II, this volume.
62   Arnaud, *Of True and False Ideas*: 192.

IV   JOHN LOCKE AND KNOWLEDGE OF OTHER SPIRITS

1   Locke, *An Essay Concerning Human Understanding* 1975 [1689]: I.ii.15:
     55. All references to Locke's *Essay* will be to this edition, and all quotations
     from it will follow the seventeenth century spelling and punctuation, and
     Locke's use of italics.
2   *Ibid.*, I.i.2: 43.
3   Quoted by Woolhouse 1994: 147.
4   Locke, *op. cit.*, I.i.4: 45.
5   *Ibid.*, IV.iii. 23: 553–554
6   Locke's work here is reminiscent of the more recent work of Thomas Nagel.
     See especially Nagel 1979a: 165–181. See also Chapter IX, this volume.
7   Locke, *op. cit.*, I.i.3: 44.
8   *Ibid.*
9   *Ibid.*, IV.xvi.12: 665.
10   Locke, *An Examination of P. Malebranche's Opinion of Seeing All Things in
     God* 1824 [1706]: 249.
11   It is clear from Locke's discussion of Malebranche that he bases his under-
     standing of Malebranche's work on Bk. II, Pt. ii, ch. 7, v of the *Search After
     Truth*. Like most others, Locke does not consider what Malebranche writes
     in Bk. III, Pt. ii, ch. 1 to the effect that our knowledge of things outside us –
     including spiritual things – is through ideas. See Chapter III, this volume.
     Furthermore, as I explained in Chapter III, Malebranche is not addressing the
     question of our knowledge of the *existence* of another mind when he appeals
     to conjecture.
12   Locke, *Essay*, I.i.8: 47.
13   *Ibid.*, II.i.9: 108.
14   Although there are no innate ideas or principles of mind, yet Locke allows
     that babies may receive some ideas before they are born. Locke writes:
     'Therefore I doubt not but *Children*, by the exercise of their Senses about
     Objects, that affect them *in the Womb, receive some few Ideas*, before they
     are born, as the unavoidable affects, either of the Bodies that environ them,
     or else of those Wants or Diseases they suffer; amongst which, (if one may
     conjecture concerning things not very capable of examination) I think the
     Ideas of Hunger and Warmth are two' (*Essay* II.ix.5: 144).
15   *Ibid.*, II.i.4: 105.
16   See Locke, *op. cit.* II.xx. Interestingly, Locke claims that the latter two pas-
     sions have in them 'some mixed Considerations of our selves and others'
     (*Essay* II.xx.14: 231).
17   *Ibid.*, II.1.4: 105.
18   *Ibid.*, II.ix.11: 147.
19   *Ibid.*, II.ix.13: 148. Cf. II.xi.11: 160.

20   *Ibid.*, II.ix.13: 148–9.
21   *Ibid.*, II.xxiii.5: 297.
22   *Ibid.*, II.xii.6: 165.
23   *Ibid.*
24   For what Locke has to say about pure substance in general see *op. cit.*,
      II.xxiii.1 and 2.
25   *Ibid.*, II.xxiii.28: 311.
26   *Ibid.*, II.xxiii.11: 301.
27   *Ibid.*, II.xxiii.12: 302.
28   *Ibid.*, II.xxiii.13: 303–4.
29   *Ibid.*, IV.iii.23: 554.
30   *Ibid.*, II.xxiii.13: 304.
31   *Ibid.*, II.xxiii.29: 312.
32   *Ibid.*, II.xxiii.32: 314.
33   *Ibid.*, II.xxiii.15: 305–6.
34   *Ibid.*, II.xxiii.36: 315.
35   *Ibid.*, II.xxiii.36: 316.
36   *Ibid.*
37   *Ibid.*, IV.iii.27: 558.
38   *Ibid.*, II.xxxii.15: 389.
39   *Ibid.*, III.ii.1: 404–5.
40   *Ibid.*, III.ii.1: 405.
41   Cf. Locke, *op. cit.*, II.xxxii.15.
42   *Ibid.*, III.ii.8: 408. Cf. III.ii.4.
43   *Ibid.*, III.ix.18: 486.
44   *Ibid.*, III.ix.18: 487.
45   *Ibid.*
46   *Ibid.*, II.xxxii.3: 384.
47   *Ibid.*, II.xxxii.3: 385
48   *Ibid.*, II.xxxii.14: 388. This and other similar passages are taken by Michael
      Ayers to show that Locke revives in his work the Epicurean doctrine of
      ideas as signs. A simple idea is a natural sign of its cause. See M. Ayers,
      Locke, vol. I: Epistemology, London, Routledge 1991, especially Pt. I.
49   *Ibid.*, II.xxxii.15: 389.
50   *Ibid.*
51   *Ibid.*, IV.xiv.1: 653.
52   *Ibid.*, IV.i.2: 525.
53   *Ibid.*, IV.ii.1: 531.
54   *Ibid.*
55   *Ibid.*, IV.ii.14: 536–7.
56   *Ibid.*, IV.ii.14: 537.
57   *Ibid.*
58   *Ibid.*
59   *Ibid.*, IV.xi.8: 634.
60   Cf. *Essay* IV.xi.10: 636, where Locke writes: 'how foolish and vain a thing it is,
      for a Man of narrow Knowledge, who having Reason given him to judge of the
      different evidence and probabilities of Things, and to be sway'd accordingly;
      how *vain*, I say, *to expect Demonstration* and Certainty *in things not capable of*

it; and refuse Assent to very rational Propositions, and act contrary to very plain and clear Truths, because they cannot be made out so evident, as to surmount every least (I will not say Reason, but) pretence of doubting. He that in the ordinary Affairs of Life, would admit of nothing but plain Demonstration, would be sure of nothing, in the World, but of perishing quickly'.

61   *Ibid.*, IV.xi.9: 635.
62   *Ibid.*, IV.xi.9: 635–636.
63   Locke, *op. cit.*, IV.xi.12.
64   See, for example, Locke, *op. cit.*, IV.xi.12, IV.iii.27, and Locke's essay *Some Thoughts concerning Education* where he urges that, as we discover other spirits through revelation, children should be urged to read the Bible (1824 [1693]: 182–183).
65   *Ibid.*, IV.xv.2: 655.
66   *Ibid.*, IV.xvi.12: 665.
67   *Ibid.*, IV.xvi.12: 666.
68   *Ibid.*, IV.iii.6: 541–542.
69   See Locke, *op. cit.*, III.i.1.
70   *Ibid.*, IV.xi.3: 631.
71   See Chapter II, this volume, note 7.

V   BERKELEY AND KNOWLEDGE OF OTHER FINITE SPIRITS

1   Locke 1975, IV.iv. 3: 563.
2   Locke, *op. cit.*, IV.iv.4: 564.
3   Berkeley, *Three Dialogues between Hylas and Philonous* 1975 (1713): 131.
4   Berkeley, *A Treatise Concerning the Principles of Human Understanding* 1975 (1710): 65, introduction 3.
5   See Berkeley's *Three Dialogues*, the third dialogue, 233
6   Berkeley, Principle 29.
7   Bennett 1971: 219.
8   See, for example, Urmson 1982: 61; Luce 1934: 108–109; Parks 1972: 70; Hicks 1932: 147.
9   Berkeley, Principle 135.
10   Berkeley, Principle 136.
11   Berkeley, Principle 138.
12   See also *Three Dialogues Between Hylas and Philonous*, the Third Dialogue 232.
13   Berkeley, *Principles* 89.
14   Berkeley, *Three Dialogues*, the Third Dialogue 231.
15   Berkeley, *op. cit.*: 231.
16   Berkeley, Principle 140.
17   George Pitcher (1977) traces the interesting development of Berkeley's thinking on the idea of spirit through the Notebooks. Berkeley's Notebooks, the *Philosophical Commentaries*, can be found in *Berkeley: Philosophical Works* (1975 [1871]).
18   Bracken 1974: 137. Bracken also cites the work of the seventeenth century philosopher John Sergeant in connection with Berkeley's talk of 'notions'.

Sergeant discusses three aspects of notions: (i) the notion in the mind as identical with the object, (ii) the notion as meaning, and (iii) notions as real versus ideas as resemblances. See Bracken, Chapter 8.

19 Geach 1957: 108.
20 Berkeley, Principle 3.
21 Berkeley, Principle 8.
22 See Berkeley, *Three Dialogues*, the Third Dialogue 233.
23 Berkeley, *op. cit.*: 232.
24 Berkeley, *op. cit.*: 233. Cf. Principle 89: 'We comprehend our own existence by inward feeling and reflexion, and that of other spirits by reason.'
25 It is not quite right to say that ideas and spirits *alone* are the objects of human knowledge, for Berkeley also allows that we can have some notion, and hence knowledge, of relations. See, for example, Principle 89.
26 *Ibid.*
27 Cf. Berkeley, *Alcipron or the Minute Philosopher* 1901 [1732]: IV, 4 and 5.
28 *Ibid.*: IV.4.
29 *Ibid.*
30 *Ibid.*: IV.6.
31 Berkeley, *Three Dialogues*, the Third Dialogue 233.
32 See this chapter, note 8.
33 Bennett, *op. cit.*: 221.
34 Falkenstein 1990.
35 Berkeley, Principles 29.
36 Berkeley, Principle 30. Cf. Principle 146 and the *Alciphron* IV.
37 Kenneth Winkler suggests that, in Berkeley's time, scepticism about God's existence was far more likely than scepticism about one's fellow men. For this reason, Berkeley uses the reasons we have to believe in our fellow men to prove God's existence. See Winkler 1989: 285.
38 Berkeley, Principle 148.
39 Berkeley, Principle 147.
40 Berkeley, *Three Dialogues*, the Third Dialogue 236.
41 *Ibid.*, 237.
42 An analogical interpretation of Principle 140 is also suggested by Falkenstein, *op. cit.*
43 Berkeley, *Three Dialogues*, the Third Dialogue 247–8.
44 Reid 1969 [1785]: VI, V, 627. In fact, Reid claims that he can 'find no principle in Berkeley's system, which affords [him] even probable ground to conclude, that there are other intelligent beings like [him]self. . . .', II.x: 179.
45 Berkeley, *op. cit.* 232.
46 Berkeley, *Principles*, Introduction, 11.
47 Berkeley, *op. cit.* Introduction, 15.

VI THOMAS REID AND KNOWLEDGE OF OTHER INTELLIGENT BEINGS

1 See this chapter, 158–159.
2 Dan Robinson has brought to my attention the interesting fact that Reid insists (in debate with his friend and student Dugald Steward) that what he is

offering in his work is not a *system* but an *inquiry*. This may go hand and hand with another observation one could make about Reid's philosophy: that in his work he has a tendency to distance himself from the work of philosophers, referring to the work of his opponents as the work of *the philosophers*. See for example, *Essays*, II, ch. xxii, 309. See also Robinson 1989.

3   See Lehrer 1989: ch. 1.

4   See Kant 1950 [1783]: 7, where Kant writes, in opposition to those who would appeal to common-sense against the sceptic: 'But this appeal to common sense must be shown in action by well-considered and reasonable thoughts and words, not by appealing to it as an oracle when no rational justification for one's position can be advanced.'

5   See my 'Brief interlude: John Stuart Mill', this chapter, for a discussion of Mill's argument against Reid.

6   Reid, *Essays*: I ch. viii, 71.

7   *Ibid.*

8   *Ibid.*: 72.

9   *Ibid.*

10   See, for example, Reid, *An Inquiry into the Mind on the Principles of Common Sense* 1983 [1764]: ch. 2, sec. vi, 20.

11   Reid, *Essays*, II, ch. x, 179.

12   Lehrer traces the influence of Reid's ideas on the work of two major twentieth century American schools of philosophy, the New Realists and the Critical Realists. Lehrer also makes a case for Reid's indirect influence on both the Pragmatists and the work of Wittgenstein. Finally, Lehrer has argued for an influence of Reid's work on such twentieth century figures as G. E. Moore, H. H. Price, H. Sidgwick, R. Chisholm and D. Hamlyn. See Lehrer, 'Reid's Influence On Contemporary American And British Philosophy', in Barker and Beauchamp (eds) 1976; see also Lehrer, *op. cit.*: ch. 1.

13   Reid, *Essays*, the preface, xxxiii.

14   *Ibid.*: xxxv.

15   See Reid, *op. cit.*: I, ch. 1, 2. Reid does acknowledge that the first principles of philosophy are of a different nature than, say, mathematical principles. The evidence for the former is not the same as that for the latter. Furthermore, the first principles of philosophy are not necessary truths. Nevertheless, 'every man of common understanding readily assents to [the first principles of philosophy], and finds it absolutely necessary to conduct his actions and opinions by them, in the ordinary affairs of life', *Essays*, I, ch. ii, 32–33.

16   Reid, *op. cit.*: I, ch. ii, 31.

17   *Ibid.*: 33.

18   *Ibid.* Cf. also VI, ch. iv.

19   *Ibid.*: 33.

20   Reid, *op. cit.*: I, ch. iii, 41.

21   Reid, *op. cit.*: I, ch. iv, 50. See also Reid, *Inquiry*, ch. 7.

22   Reid, *op. cit.*: II, iv, 109.

23   Reid, *op. cit.*: II, ch. i, 75–76.

24   Reid, *op. cit.*: II, ch. i, 75.

25   Reid, *op. cit.*: II, ch. v, 111.

26 Reid, *op. cit.*: I, ch. i, 15.
27 Reid, *Inquiries*: ch. 1, sec. iii, 5.
28 Reid, *op. cit.*: II, ch. viii, 138.
29 Reid, *op. cit.*: II, ch. xx, 290.
30 Reid, *Inquiry*: ch. 6, sec. xx, 84–85.
31 David Hume 1978 [1740]: IV, vii, 269.
32 Reid, *Essays*: VII, ch. iv, 739.
33 Reid writes: 'Conceiving, imagining, apprehending, understanding, having a notion of a thing, are common words, used to express that operation of the understanding, which the logicians call *simple apprehension*'. *Essays*: IV, ch. i, 383.
34 Reid, *op. cit.*: II, ch. v, 111.
35 Reid, *op. cit.*: II, ch. xxii, 309.
36 *Ibid.*: 310.
37 *Ibid.*: 311.
38 Reid, *op. cit.*: II, ch. v, 115.
39 *Ibid.*: 118.
40 See, for example, Reid, *op. cit.*: II, ch. v, 118, and this chapter, note 23.
41 Reid, *op. cit.*: II, ch. xx, 292.
42 Reid, *op. cit.*: II, ch. xxii, 318.
43 Reid, *op. cit.*: II, ch. xxi, 305.
44 Reid, *op. cit.*: VI, ch. iv, 604.
45 Which he contrasts with the first principles of necessary truths. See this chapter, note 15.
46 It should be noted that the numbering of the principles in this chapter do not correspond to Reid's numbering.
47 Reid, *op. cit.*: I, ch. ii, 30.
48 *Ibid.*: 40–41.
49 Reid, *op. cit.*: VI, ch. v, 632.
50 *Ibid.*
51 Reid, *Inquiry*: ch. 1, sec. iv, 6–7.
52 See Reid, *op. cit.*: VI, ch. v, 635.
53 *Ibid.*: 633–634.
54 *Ibid.*: 634.
55 *Ibid.*: 635.
56 *Ibid.*: 634–635.
57 *Ibid.*: 626.
58 Reid claims that this is a point that Berkeley failed to appreciate. See *Essays*: VI, ch. v, 626.
59 *Ibid.*: 625–626.
60 *Ibid.*: 638.
61 *Ibid.*: 636. Cf. 638 where Reid writes that 'the operations of this sense is very analogous to that of the external senses'.
62 *Ibid.*: 636.
63 *Ibid.*
64 *Ibid.*: 637.
65 Reid, *Inquiry*: ch. 6, sec. xxiv, 90.
66 See Reid, *Essays*: VI, ch. v, 639.

67 Reid, *Inquiry*: ch. 4, sec. ii, 32.
68 In the *Inquiry* Reid suggests that artificial language is not simply founded on natural language, but that the two are intermingled. He writes: 'It is by natural signs chiefly that we give force and energy to language; and the less language has of them, it is the less expressive and persuasive', ch. 4, sec. ii, 34.
69 Reid, *op. cit.*: ch. 6, sec. xxiv, 94. And Reid continues: 'Speaking the truth is like using our natural food, which we would do from appetite, although it answered no end; but lying is like taking a physic, which is nauseous to the taste, and which no man takes but for some end which he cannot otherwise obtain'.
70 Reid, *Essays*: II, ch. x, 167.
71 *Ibid.*: 173.
72 Berkeley 1975 [1710]: Pt. I, 1.
73 Reid, *op. cit.*: II, ch. x, 179.
74 Reid, *op. cit.*: II, ch. x, 172.
75 What follows is only a very brief summary. For a fuller account see Chapter V, this volume.
76 Berkeley 1975 [1713]: 232.
77 Cf. Reid, *Essays*: II, ch. xi, 189.
78 Reid, *op. cit.*: I, ch. i, 27.
79 Reid, *op. cit.*: II, xi, 191.
80 Reid, *op. cit.*: II, ch. xvi, 249.
81 *Ibid.*
82 Reid, *op. cit.*: II, ch. xii, 200.
83 Reid, *op. cit.*: I, ch. viii, 71.
84 This is noticed by J. S. Mill when he writes, concerning the work of various philosophers: 'We have, in their opinion, the direct evidence of consciousness, only for the internal world. An external world is but an inference, which, according to most philosophers, is justified, or even, by our mental constitution, compelled: according to others, not justified' (*An Examination of Sir William Hamilton's Philosophy*: 138). Reid's position is the second described by Mill: the external world is something we are compelled to believe in by our mental constitution.
85 See Reid, *op. cit.*: V, ch. ii.
86 Reid, *op. cit.*: VI, ch. v, 637–638.
87 Mill, *A System of Logic* 1891: introduction 4.
88 Mill, *An Examination of Sir William Hamilton's Philosophy* 1872: 225.
89 Mill here appeals to Hamilton's 'principle of parcimony' which holds that we do not need to suppose an original principle of our nature to account for phenomena that admit of explanation from known causes. See *An Examination*: 232.
90 Mill, *An Examination*: 242. By the end of this chapter, however, Mill does notice a 'hindrance' to the application of his phenomenalism to mind. The problem, as Mill sees it, is this: The 'thread of consciousness' which composes the mind's phenomenal life consists of present sensations plus memories and expectations. Memories and expectations, however, go beyond the present sensation and cannot be adequately expressed without saying that the belief they include is 'that I formerly had, or that I myself,

and no other, shall hereafter have, the sensations remembered or expected'. Mill concludes that 'we are here faced with that final inexplicability'. See *An Examination*: 247–248.

91   *Ibid.*: 242.

92   *Ibid.*: 238–239, footnote *.

93   *Ibid.*: 243–244.

94   *Ibid.*: 245.

95   See, for example, Bilgrami 1992: 318. Norman Malcolm (1966a: 271) cites Mill's argument as 'representative' of the argument from analogy in his highly influential paper 'Knowledge of Other Minds'.

96   Mill, *An Examination*: 261.

97   See Mill, *op. cit.*: 260, footnote.

98   *Ibid.*

99   *Ibid.*

100   *Ibid.*: 259. Note Mill's 'exceptionally' here. Mill's point is that the case of other minds is importantly different from the case of the external world. There is, as Mill sees it, an argument to prove the existence of the former, but not the existence of the latter. I am, in effect, saying that Mill does not make good his introduction of this 'exceptionally'.

101   F. H. Bradley also rejects the argument from analogy to the existence of other minds on the grounds that 'we don't want inferred friends who are mere hypotheses to explain physical phenomena'. Bradley's remark is referred to by J. M. Urmson (1982: 61).

102   Mill, *An Examination*: 392.

103   The group's more immediate intellectual roots can be traced back to Auguste Comte and Ernst Mach.

104   Quoted by Friedrich Waismann in Foreword (1979 [1938]: xxvi).

105   Carnap, *The Logical Structure of the World* 1967: xvi.

106   See Carnap, *The Logical Structure*: secs. 18 and 20. Carnap says that he is taking the concepts of the physical and psychological in their 'customary sense', and he identifies cultural objects with those objects that belong to the domain of what he calls the 'cultural sciences'.

107   See *The Logical Structure*: sec. 58.

108   Carnap, *op. cit.*: sec. 64.

109   See *The Logical Structure*: sec. 140. Carnap accepts that ultimately there exists an identity between psychological processes and physical processes in the nervous system, and he allows that we might one day construct our system from this base. He also notes that this physical construction would, nonetheless, continue to be through the mediation of the body and so would not affect his basic point.

110   *Ibid.*

111   *Ibid.*: sec. 145.

112   *Ibid.*

113   Carnap, *Pseudoproblems in Philosophy* 1967: 335.

114   *Ibid.*: 336.

115   Schlick, 'Experience, cognition and metaphysics' 1979 [1926]: 99–100.

116   *Ibid.*: 100.

117   *Ibid.*: 102.

118 Schlick then says that this can be shown by the logical doctrine of implicit
     definitions. This is a way of arriving at concepts without content, without
     qualitative features. Schlick develops this doctrine in his *General Theory of
     Knowledge*.
119 *Ibid.*
120 *Ibid.*: 103.
121 Schlick, 'Meaning and verification' 1979 [1936a]: 473. Schlick here explic-
     itly refers Wittgenstein in connection with the phrase 'has no owner'.
     Schlick claims here to be 'closely following ideas expressed by Mr.
     Wittgenstein': 474. To see just how closely Schlick is here following
     Wittgenstein, see Chapter VIII, this volume.
122 *Ibid.*: 477.
123 *Ibid.*: 479.
124 Schlick, 'The Universe and the Human Mind' 1979 [1936b]: 507.
125 *Ibid.*: 505.
126 Waismann, *op. cit.*: xxv.

VII   WITTGENSTEIN AND LIVING WITH OTHERS

1   Wittgenstein, *Culture and Value* 1980b: 77.
2   Wittgenstein, *The Blue and Brown Books* 1958: 18.
3   McGuinness 1979: 182–183.
4   Cf. Wittgenstein, *Philosophical Investigations* 1968b: 90. Marie McGinn
    writes, 'Language is, for Wittgenstein, both the source of philosophical
    problems and the means to overcome them' (1997: 12).
5   Cf. *Philosophical Investigations* 108. This point has been emphasized by
    M. McGinn, both in her work on Wittgenstein and in conversation.
6   Wittgenstein, *Philosophical Remarks* 1975: I, 1. Cf. *Philosophical
    Investigations* 90.
7   F. Waismann's introduction to Schlick (1979: xxvi).
8   Wittgenstein, *Blue Book*: 18.
9   David Pears (1987: vol II, 296) has argued that it is the problem of other
    minds – and not that of the external world – that preoccupied Wittgenstein
    in the period 'in and around 1929'.
10 McGuinness, *Wittgenstein and the Vienna Circle* (1979): 49. In
    Philosophical Remarks 61 Wittgenstein writes that (ii) expresses a 'logical
    impossibility', This is one of the places where Wittgenstein's influence on
    Schlick is evident. See, Chapter VII, this volume.
11 *Philosophical Remarks* 58.
12 McGuinness, *op cit.*: 49.
13 *Ibid.*: 49–50. In a bracketed footnote Waismann adds the following
    elucidatory remark: 'If A has a toothache, he can say, "Now this tooth is
    hurting", and this is where verification comes to an end. But B would have
    to say, "A has toothache", and this proposition is not the end of verification.
    This is the point where the particular status of different propositions comes
    clearly to light.'
14 Cf. *Philosophical Remarks* 58: 'Only their application really differentiates
    languages; but if we disregard all this, all languages are equivalent. . . . I

cannot express the advantage of *my* language'. Cf. McGuinness, *Wittgenstein and the Vienna Circle*: 50. According to David Pears this identification of language's privileged status with the application of language allows Wittgenstein to represent factual language 'as a smooth, homogeneous surface without the vortices produced by other minds', *op. cit.*: vol. II, 299.

15 *Philosophical Remarks* 64.
16 Wittgenstein, *Philosophical Occasions* 1993: 97–99. Moore reports what Wittgenstein says here with a great deal of hesitancy. Moore claims that Wittgenstein spent a great deal of time on these topics and said that they were 'extraordinarily difficult'. Moore himself admits to being 'very much puzzled as to the meaning of much that he said' (97). I have not indicated the difficulties here, but simply extracted what I take to be one element of what Wittgenstein is saying here.
17 Wittgenstein, *Zettel* 1967: 87.
18 Pears, *op. cit.*: vol. I, 47. Pears takes the problem here to arise when Wittgenstein attempts to apply his account of the ego to sensations: the ego arguably can drop out of the picture, because it is as problematic intrasubjectively as intersubjectively; the same is not true of sensations.
19 Cf. *Philosophical Investigations* 261.
20 Wittgenstein, 'Notes for Lectures on "Private Experiences" and "Sense Data"' 1968a: 276.
21 *Ibid.*
22 *Ibid.*: 277, note 4.
23 *Ibid.*: 281.
24 *Ibid.*
25 *Blue Book*: 28.
26 *Ibid.*: 5.
27 Cf. *Philosophical Investigations* 7: 'I shall also call the whole, consisting of language and the actions into which it is woven, the "language-game".'
28 *Blue Book*: 17.
29 *Ibid.*: 46. Cf. 48.
30 *Ibid.*
31 'Note for Lectures': 286–287.
32 *Ibid.*: 293.
33 *Philosophical Investigations* Pt. II, p. 192. Cf. Wittgenstein's *Last Writings on the Philosophy of Psychology: The Inner and the Outer* 1992: 9.
34 *Last Writings*: vol. II, 9 and 10.
35 'Notes for Lectures': 295.
36 *Ibid.*: 287.
37 *Ibid.*: 312.
38 *Ibid.*: 286.
39 *Ibid.*: 302.
40 *Philosophical Investigations* 142.
41 *Ibid.*: 242. Cf. 241 and *Philosophical Investigations* Pt. II, p. 226 where Wittgenstein writes: 'Does it make sense to say that people generally agree in their judgement of colour? What would it be for them not to? – One man would say a flower was red which another called blue, and so on. – But what

right should we have to call these people's words "red" and "blue" *our* 'colour-words'?'

42 *Ibid.*: 455.
43 *Ibid.*: 539.
44 Wittgenstein, *Zettel*: 545. Cf. *Zettel* 541 and also Wittgenstein, *Remarks on the Philosophy of Psychology* 1980a: 151.
45 *Remarks on the Philosophy of Psychology*: vol. 1, 137.
46 Cf. *Philosophical Investigations* II, p. 223.
47 *Ibid.*: p. 227.
48 *Philosophical Investigations* 426.
49 *Ibid.*: 284.
50 *Ibid.*: 420.
51 Cf. *Philosophical Investigations* 381.
52 *Ibid.*: 384.
53 *Blue Book*: 17.
54 *Ibid.*: 27.
55 *Philosophical Investigations* 293.
56 Cf. Chapter IX, this volume.
57 *Philosophical Investigations* 26.
58 *Ibid.*: 31.
59 Cf. *Philosophical Investigations* 32.
60 *Ibid.*: 28.
61 Cf. *Philosophical Investigations* 257.
62 Cf. the discussion of the previous section.
63 *Philosophical Investigations* 71. Cf. *Philosophical Investigations* 88.
64 See *Philosophical Investigations* 258.
65 *Ibid.*
66 For a good discussion of Wittgenstein's argument here see Stroud 1983: 319–341.
67 *Philosophical Investigations* 261.
68 *Ibid.*: 415.

VIII THE CONCEPTUAL PROBLEM OF OTHER MINDS

1 Nagel 1986: 90 and McGinn 1979: 115. Another example of this coupling of radical scepticism with a form of realism can be found in Stroud 1984, especially 81–82.
2 In his review of Wittgenstein's *Philosophical Investigations*, Norman Malcolm distinguishes between two different arguments that may be found in Wittgenstein's work: the one, the private language argument, he labels 'an internal attack' on the possibility of a private language; the other he labels 'an external attack' on private language. The problem I am pressing in this chapter may be thought to be the second of these arguments, an external attack on private language. See Malcolm 1966b: 75.
3 See, for example, the pair of papers by C. Peacocke and C. McGinn under the title 'Consciousness and other minds' 1984: 97–137; T. Nagel, *op. cit.*: ch. II, especially sec. 3, and *The Possibility of Altruism* (1970); and S. Kripke (1982) *Wittgenstein on Rules and Private Language*, 'Postscript: Wittgenstein on other minds'. I discuss McGinn in this chapter, 226–230,

and Nagel in Chapter IX, below. Kripke's discussion of the conceptual problem of other minds has arguably been very influential in reviving this problem. (It is, for example, the jumping off point for McGinn's discussion of the issue.) However, although it informs the way I set up the problem, I don't discuss Kripke's interpretation of the conceptual problem as its main concern is with Wittgenstein exegesis.

4   Strawson 1959: 99, note 1.
5   Evans 1982: 75.
6   Cf. Chapter II, this volume, note 5.
7   McGinn 1984: 127.
8   *Ibid.*: 135–136.
9   Strawson, *op. cit.*: 99. Cf. 107 where Strawson writes: 'there is not in general one primary process of learning, or teaching oneself, an inner private meaning for [these] predicates . . . then another of learning to apply such predicates to others.'
10 We could say that, if we insist on giving priority to the first-person experience in the way that McGinn does, we are forced to accept that I may be under an illusion concerning the unity I *take* it my concept has. This is the mirror image of a point that is sometimes made against those who want to begin where I want to begin: by asserting the generality of the concept we run the risk of having to conclude that the first-person perspective is an illusion. Perhaps the latter point would seem less pressing once we see the way it can be turned.
11 Strawson 1966: 38. Cf. Strawson 1992, especially Chapters 1 and 2, and Strawson 1998.
12 See Strawson, *Individuals*: 9.
13 See Wittgenstein, *Philosophical Investigations* 116. See also this chapter, Strawson and descriptive metaphysics.
14 Cf., for example, Strawson, *Individuals*: 109. See also this chapter, Strawson and descriptive metaphysics.
15 Cf. G. Ryle (1949: 9) who writes: 'It is one thing to know how to apply . . . concepts, quite another to know how to correlate them with one another and with other concepts of other sorts. Many people can talk sense with concepts, but cannot talk sense about them.'
16 Davidson 1991: 155.
17 Davidson 1984b: 106.
18 Davidson admits this in his 'Reply to Anita Avramides' (1999: 154).
19 Strawson, *Individuals*: 99.
20 P. F. Strawson, 'Self, mind and body' (1974: 173).
21 Cf. Strawson, *Individuals*: 99, note 1.
22 Strawson, *Individuals*: 101–102.
23 In 'Self, mind and body', Strawson writes, 'The difference between the Cartesian and his opponent is a difference of view about the *relation* between the concept of a person on the one hand and the concept of a person's mind on the other. The anti-Cartesian holds that the concept of a person's mind has a secondary or dependent status. The fundamental concept, for him, is that of a human being, a man, a type of thing to which [both mental and physical] predicates . . . can be ascribed' (171).

24 In 'Self, mind and body' Strawson contrasts the Cartesian position with his own thus: 'For really [as far as the Cartesian is concerned] the history of a human being is not the history of one two-sided thing; it is the history of two one-sided things' (170).
25 Strawson, *Individuals*: 108.
26 *Ibid.*: 110.
27 *Ibid.*: 111.
28 *Ibid.*
29 *Ibid.*
30 *Ibid.*: 112.
31 *Ibid.*
32 D. Davidson, 'Three varieties of knowledge': 154.
33 Cf. Strawson when he writes: 'These remarks are not intended to suggest how the "problem of other minds" could be solved. . . . They are simply intended to help make it seem intelligible to us, at this stage in the history of the philosophy of this subject, that we have the conceptual scheme that we have' (*op. cit.*: 112)
34 See Davidson, 'First person authority': 106.
35 In his 'Reply to Anita Avramides' Davidson explains that he never set out to 'answer, refute or show empty' scepticism about other minds. What he does is provide a theory about beliefs and their contents which, if correct, has the result that scepticism cannot get started (155).
36 See Davidson 1984a.
37 See, for example, Davidson, 'Three varieties of knowledge': 155, and also Davidson 1996.
38 Davidson, 'Three varieties of knowledge': 155.
39 *Ibid.*: 154.
40 *Ibid.*: 155–156.
41 About the attitude of holding true Davidson writes, 'I call such attitudes **non-individuative**, for though they are psychological in nature, they do not bestow individual propositional contents on the attitudes'. Davidson, *op. cit.*: 158.
42 Together these two principles make up the principle that Davidson refers to as the principle of charity.
43 *Ibid.*
44 Cf., for example, Davidson 1990b: 77.
45 Davidson, 'Three varieties of knowledge': 159–160.
46 *Ibid.*: 164.
47 See Davidson 1997.
48 Davidson, 'Three varieties of knowledge': 160.
49 *Ibid.*
50 Traditionally philosophers have associated, as well as authority, indu-bitability and incorrigibility with first-person ascriptions of belief. Davidson rejects indubitability and incorrigibility, arguing that doubt and error are still possible here – although notably less than the doubt and error that is possible in connection with third-person ascriptions.
51 In 'First person authority' Davidson writes: 'The speaker, though he must bear many of these things in mind when he speaks [i.e. that the hearer

interprets on the basis of such clues as the speaker's actions, other utterances, and assumptions about the speaker such as background, general intelligence, and the like], since it is up to him to try to be understood, cannot wonder whether he generally means what he says' (110).

52 Notice that the 'explanation' offered by Davidson is not at all like the explanation considered – and rejected – by Wittgenstein (see Chapter VII, above). The explanation that Wittgenstein rejects makes reference to inner objects; the 'explanation' that Davidson proposes appeals only to the nature of interpretation.

53 Compare what Strawson writes in *Analysis and Metaphysics*: 'When we seek a reply to the question, What is it to believe something?, we seem impelled to turn to the concept of *action*' (75).

54 For more on the importance of the concept of action see Chapter 6 of Strawson's *Analysis and Metaphysics*: 'Classical empiricism: the inner and the outer. Action and society'.

55 See Stroud 1968, 1984, 1994 and 1999.

56 Cf. Strawson, *Individuals*: 106.

57 Davidson 1990a: 136.

58 *Ibid.*

59 B. Stroud, 'Kantian argument, conceptual capacities, and invulnerability': 140.

60 *Ibid.*

61 Cf. Strawson (1992: ch. 4, 53): 'In insisting that experience not only bridges the gap between Subject and Object, but also gives the concepts we use all their sense of content, we run the risk of the notion of objective reality being entirely engulfed or swallowed up in that of experience. Many idealisms and all phenomenalisms are the results of this engulfing; and the history of much of our epistemology, when one isn't sinking into (or wallowing in) this gulf, is one of struggle to get out of it, to show that various forms of scepticism about the Objective Reality are unwarranted. But it is better to avoid the gulf altogether.'

IX   THE CONCEPTUAL PROBLEM: ANOTHER APPROACH

1 Nagel 1986: 19–20.

2 Nagel, *op. cit.*: 71. Also, see Chapter VIII, this volume, the Introduction.

3 Nagel, *op. cit.*, especially Chapter V, section 1. I have transposed what Nagel has to say here about our relationship to the world to fit the case of other minds. Notice that when Nagel writes of a 'gap' here, this is not to be understood along the lines of the traditional substantial divide between mind and body. Nagel is not a Cartesian substantial dualist.

4 Nagel (1979a: 168).

5 Many of the points that Nagel makes here are reminiscent of Locke. Cf. Chapter IV, this volume.

6 Nagel, *op. cit.*: 170.

7 Nagel, *The View from Nowhere*: 95.

8 Nagel, 'What is it like to be a bat?': 170–171. Nagel's position here is this: Despite the fact that we cannot know what it is like, we cannot deny the

existence of there being something it *is* like to be a bat. Thus we have beliefs in the existence of minds in creatures like bats, although we cannot have sceptic immune knowledge that bats have minds. We can know what it is like to be another human being, or man, but this does not put us in any better position to have sceptic immune knowledge that other men have minds.

9   Nagel, *The View from Nowhere*: 95.
10 Nagel 1970: 103–104. Cf. Chapter VII, 190, this volume.
11 *Ibid.*: 106.
12 Nagel, *The View from Nowhere*: 24.
13 *Ibid.*: 20–21. Nagel here picks up a point from his earlier paper 'What is it like to be a bat?' where he introduces the idea of the imagination in connection with experience thus: 'It may be easier that I suppose to transcend inter-species barriers with the aid of the imagination. . . . The imagination is remarkably flexible. My point, however, is not that we cannot *know* what it is like to be a bat. I am not raising that epistemological problem. My point is rather that even to form a *conception* of what it is like to be a bat (and *a fortiori* to know what it is like to be a bat) one must take up the bat's point of view' (172, note 8).
14 Nagel here refers to Wittgenstein's work with approval. See *The View from Nowhere*: 20.
15 *Ibid.* Notice that Nagel takes this to be a consequence of *empiricist* assumptions. In the following section I argue that the problem arises even if, like Nagel, one eschews these assumptions.
16 Nagel, *The Possibility of Altruism*: 106.
17 See his *Other Minds* 1995.
18 *Ibid.*: 10. Notice a similar appeal to remembered and expected experience in what Nagel says in *The View from Nowhere*: 20–21, quoted above in the text.
19 Peacocke 1985: 20.
20 Peacocke, *op. cit.*: 21.
21 *Ibid.* Peacocke also writes that this condition 'seems to be a conceptual truth'.
22 Nagel, *The View from Nowhere*: 20.
23 *Ibid.*: 83
24 *Ibid.*: 84.
25 See C. Peacocke, 'Imagination, experience, and possibility', and also (1989).
26 Peacocke, 'Imagination, experience, and possibility': 33.
27 Nagel, *op. cit.*: 21.
28 In 'Panpsychism' he writes: 'We ascribe experience to animals on the basis of their behaviour, structure and circumstances, but we are not just ascribing to them behaviour, structure and circumstance. So what are we saying? The same kind of thing we say of people when we say that they have experiences, of course. But here the special relation between first-and third-person ascription us not available as an indication of the subjectivity of the mental. We are left with concepts that are anchored in their application to humans, and that apply to other creatures by a natural extension from their behavioural and contextual criteria that operate in the human case' (Nagel 1979b: 191).

29 Nagel, *The View from Nowhere*: 24. Cf. 'Panpsychism': 192, and 'What is it like to be a bat?': 167.
30 Nagel, *The View from Nowhere*: 23.
31 Nagel admits that he has nothing to say here, but thinks it sufficient to say that 'the generalization of the concept of experience beyond our capacity to apply it doesn't *contradict* the condition of application that it tries to transcend' (*The View from Nowhere*: 23). The problem is that Nagel offers us no understanding of our concept here so that we can satisfy ourselves that we have not contradicted the conditions of application.
32 See this chapter, note 1.
33 See this chapter, note 15.
34 Descartes 1985 [1647]: 303–304.
35 Cf. note 28, above.
36 See this chapter, note 29.
37 Armstrong 1968: 84.
38 McDowell 1994: 37. McDowell here acknowledges the influence of both P. F. Strawson and Gareth Evans.
39 *Ibid.*: 113.
40 Nagel, *op. cit.*: 68. Remember that the Cartesian framework, as I introduced it in Chapter I, is not dependent upon the acceptance of a mind–body dualism. The essential idea of this framework is the conceptual separation of the knowing subject and the known world.

X   REJECTING BEHAVIOUR

1 G. Strawson, *Mental Reality* 1994a: 222–223. Cf. Fodor who writes of the 'persistent bad habit of trying to run epistemic or semantic arguments for metaphysical conclusions' (1994b: 102).
2 Strawson, *op. cit.*: 34.
3 See Strawson, *op. cit.*: 98–99. See also Strawson 1994b, especially sections 3 and 4.
4 Strawson at one point refers approvingly to Nagel when the latter writes: 'Physicalism [or materialism] is a position we cannot understand because we do not at present have any conception of how it might be true'. Strawson, *op. cit.*: 47. The quotation is taken from Nagel, 'What is it like to be a bat': 176. Nagel and Strawson leave it open that one day we may be able to understand how all this is possible. In this respect their position here must be distinguished from one that holds that the question of how the physical can be or can cause the mental is not something we shall ever be able to understand. For an argument to that effect see McGinn 1989.
5 J. Searle, *The Rediscovery of Mind* 1992: 14.
6 In his review of *The Rediscovery of Mind*, Nagel (1993: 39) challenges Searle on this point. There is, claims Nagel, an important difference between the two cases: where it is possible to understand how a certain combination of molecules can be responsible for liquidity, we haven't the slightest idea how to begin to understand the way the brain can be responsible for consciousness. Here we see Nagel on the side of Strawson against Searle.
7 Searle, *op. cit.*: 13.

Notes

8 *Ibid.*: 20.
9 *Ibid.*: 21.
10 *Ibid.*: Chapter 3, I. Compare Strawson's story of an alien race called the Sirians (*vide* Strawson, *op. cit.*: Chapter 8, section 8.5; I explain and discuss the story of the Sirians on 282 below).
11 Searle, *op. cit.*: 69.
12 *Ibid.*: 73. We might note that Nagel, while he does make reference to behaviour in the identification of some minds, also makes reference to structure. See, Chapter IX, this volume, note 28.
13 Searle 1994b: 545.
14 Searle, *The Rediscovery of Mind*: 23.
15 This much, however, we *do* know: 'Any system capable of causing consciousness and other mental phenomena must have causal capacities to do it equivalent to the biological capacities of animal brains, both our own human brains and the brains of other kinds of animals. From the fact that brains do it causally, it is a trivial logical consequence that any other system capable of doing it causally, must have causal powers to do it equivalent to brains'. Searle 1994a: 214.
16 *Ibid.*: 76.
17 *Ibid.*: 75.
18 Ned Block has recently argued that even if we accept physicalism, it is not so easy as physicalists (and here we may include Searle) suggest to understand how *different* neurophysiological structures can realize consciousness. This problem – which Block calls the 'problem of other minds' – is, according to Block, the *really* hard problem of consciousness. See 'The Harder Problem of Consciousness', given as a talk at the Oxford Jowett Society, May 2000.
19 *Ibid.*: 77. For a good discussion of Searle's notion of the Background see Stroud 1991: 225–259. See also Searle's response to Stroud in the same volume.
20 Searle, 'Animal minds': 216.
21 Strawson, *Mental Reality*: 234. Strawson does not appear to distinguish between refuting scepticism and ignoring it. It is not at all clear that ignoring scepticism accords it too much force. Strawson's position is, nonetheless, clear: we must live with the sceptic. Cf. Nagel, McGinn and Stroud, Chapter VIII, note 1, above.
22 See Strawson, *op. cit.*: ch. 8, section 8.5. In 'The Experiential and the Non-experiential' Strawson writes that what is needed in order to be able to do this is 'personalized ostensive definition . . .: one says to each reader, "You know what it is like from your own case, as you burn your finger, listen to Beethoven, give birth, and so on"' (85, note 1).
23 *Ibid.*: 232. Cf. Bertrand Russell (1971: 130) when he writes: 'At any given moment, there are certain things of which a man is "aware", certain things which are "before his mind". . . . There is thus at any given moment a certain assemblage of objects to which I could, if I chose, give proper names.'
24 *Ibid.*: 234.
25 *Ibid.*: 77.
26 Searle, *The Rediscovery of Mind*: 76.

316

27 For a discussion of this Cartesian framework, see Chapter I, this volume.
28 Searle 1991: 237. See also Searle 1983: 154.
29 Strawson, *Mental Reality*: 317.
30 At least it is, according to Searle, an hypothesis if we consider our warrant for it. Cf. this chapter, note 20.
31 I include Searle here, despite what he says about the Background.
32 See *Mental Reality*, especially Chapter 11.
33 See Chapter VIII, note 31, this volume.
34 Strawson, *op. cit.*: 262.
35 Searle, *The Rediscovery of Mind*: 77. If, however, we look at an earlier account of the Background, we find Searle explaining it in what may be thought to be more solipsistic terms. He writes: 'The Background . . . is not a set of things nor a set of mysterious relations between ourselves and things, rather it is simply a set of skills, stances, preintentional assumptions and presuppositions, practices, and habits. And all of these, as far as we know, are realized in human brains and bodies' (*Intentionality*: 154). I take it that Searle is attempting to reconcile these two descriptions of the Background when he writes: 'A crucial step in understanding the Background is to see that one can be committed to the truth of a proposition without having any intentional state whatever with that proposition as content' (*The Rediscovery of Mind*: 185). Thus, I can be committed to the existence of other minds because my behaviour presupposes their existence even though I may have no belief about the existence of these others.
36 Searle, *The Rediscovery of Mind*: 66

Bibliography

Annas, J. and Barnes, J. (eds) (1985) *Modes of Scepticism: Ancient Texts and Modern Interpretations*, Cambridge: Cambridge University Press.

Armstrong, D. (1968) *A Materialist Theory of Mind*, London: Routledge & Kegan Paul.

Arnaud, A. (1990 [1683]) *Of True and False Ideas* (trans. S. Gaukroger), Manchester: Manchester University Press.

Augustine (1974) *De Trinitate*, in P. Schaff (ed.) *Nicene and Post-Nicene Fathers of the Christian Church*, vol. III, Grand Rapids: Eerdmans.

—— (1991) *Confessions* (trans. H. Chadwick, *St Augustine: Confessions*), Oxford: Oxford University Press.

Ayers, M. (1991) *Locke*, vol. I, Epistemology, London: Routledge.

Baker, G. and Morris, K. (1996) *Descartes' Dualism*, London: Routledge.

Barker, S. T. and Beauchamp, T. L. (eds) (1976) *Thomas Reid: Critical Interpretations*, Philadelphia, PA: Philosophical Monographs, 3.

Beanblossom, R. E. and Lehrer, K. (eds) (1983) *Thomas Reid: Inquiries and Essays*, Indianapolis: Hackett Publishing Company, Inc.

Bennett, J. (1971) *Locke, Berkeley, Hume: Central Themes*, Oxford: Clarendon Press.

Berkeley G. (1901 [1732]) *Alciphron or the Minute Philosopher*, in A. C. Fraser (ed.) *The Works of George Berkeley*, vol. II, Oxford: Clarendon Press.

—— (1975 [1710]) *A Treatise Concerning the Principles of Human Knowledge*, in M. R. Ayers (ed.) *The Philosophical Works*, London: Dent.

—— (1975 [1713]) *Three Dialogues between Hylas and Philonous*, in M. R. Ayers (ed.) *The Philosophical Works*, London: Dent.

—— (1975 [1871]) *Philosophical Commentaries*, in M. R. Ayers (ed.) *The Philosophical Works*, London: Dent.

Bilgrami, A. (1992) 'Other minds', in J. Dancy and E. Sosa (eds) *A Companion to Epistemology*, Oxford: Blackwell.

Block, N. (unpublished) 'The Harder Problem of Consciousness'.

Bracken, H. M. (1974) *Philosophers in Perspective*: Berkeley, London: Macmillan.

Burnyeat, M. (1982) 'Idealism and Greek philosophy: what Descartes saw and Berkeley missed', in *Idealism Past and Present*, G. Vesey (ed.), Royal Institute of Philosophy Lectures, vol. 13.

—— (1983) 'Can the skeptic live his skepticism?', in M. Burnyeat (ed.) *The*

Skeptical Tradition, Berkeley/Los Angeles/London: University of California Press.

—— (1997) 'Antipater and self-refutation', in *Assent and Argument, Studies in* Cicero's *Academic Books*, Proceedings of the 7th Symposium Hellenisticum, Utrecht, 21–25 August 1995. (B. Inwood and J. Mansfield (eds)), Brill.

Carnap, R. (1967) *The Logical Structure of the World (/) Pseudoproblems in Philosophy* (trans. R. A. George), London: Routledge & Kegan Paul.

Church, R. W. (1931) *A Study in the Philosophy of Malebranche*, London: Kennikat Press.

Cook, J. W. (1969) 'Human beings', in P. Winch (ed.) *Studies in the Philosophy of Wittgenstein*, London: Routledge & Kegan Paul.

Copleston, F. (1962) *A History of Philosophy*, vol. 2, Pt. I, New York: Image Books.

Cottingham, J. (1978) 'A brute to the brutes? Descartes' treatment of animals', *Philosophy* 3.

Couissin, P. (1983 [1929]) 'The stoicism of the New Academy', reprinted in *The Skeptical Tradition* (M. Burnyeat (ed.)), Berkeley/Los Angeles/London: University of California Press.

Dancy, J. (1987) *Berkeley: An Introduction*, Oxford: Basil Blackwell.

Davidson, D. (1984a) 'On the very idea of a conceptual scheme', in *Truth and Interpretation*, Oxford: Clarendon Press.

—— (1984b) 'First person authority', in *Dialectica*, 38(2–3).

—— (1990a) 'A coherence theory of truth and knowledge: afterthoughts: 1987', in A. Malachowski (ed.) *Reading Rorty*, Oxford: Basil Blackwell.

—— (1990b) 'Meaning, truth and evidence', in R. B. Barrett and R. F. Gibson (eds) *Perspectives on Quine*, Oxford: Basil Blackwell.

—— (1991) 'Three varieties of knowledge', in A. P. Griffiths (ed.) *A. J. Ayer: Memorial Essays*, Cambridge: Cambridge University Press.

—— (1996) 'Subjective, intersubjective, objective', in P. Coates and D. D. Hutto (eds) *Current Issues in Idealism*, Thoemmes Press.

—— (1997) 'Seeing through language', in J. Preston (ed.) *Thought and Language*, Royal Institute of Philosophy Supplement: 42, Cambridge: Cambridge University Press.

—— (1999) 'Reply to Anita Avramides', in U. M. Zeglen (ed.) *Davidson: Truth, Meaning and Knowledge*, London: Routledge.

Descartes, R. (1970 [1637]) *Discourse on Method* (trans. E. S. Haldane and G. R. T. Ross), in *The Philosophical Works of Descartes*, vol. I, Cambridge: Cambridge University Press.

—— (1976 [1648]) *Conversations with Burman* (trans. J. Cottingham), Oxford: Clarendon Press.

—— (1984 [1641a]) *Meditations on First Philosophy* (trans. J. Cottingham, R. Stoothhoff and D. Murdoch), in *The Philosophical Writings of Descartes*, vol. II, Cambridge: Cambridge University Press.

—— (1984 [1641b]) *Objections and Replies* (trans. J. Cottingham, R. Stoothhoff and D. Murdoch), in *The Philosophical Writings of Descartes*, vol. II, Cambridge: Cambridge University Press.

—— (1984 [1701]) *The Search for Truth* (trans. J. Cottingham, R. Stoothhoff and D. Murdoch), in *The Philosophical Writings of Descartes*, vol. II, Cambridge: Cambridge University Press.

—— (1985 [1637]) *Discourse on Method* (trans. J. Cottingham, R. Stoothhoff and D. Murdoch), in *The Philosophical Writings of Descartes*, vol. I, Cambridge: Cambridge University Press.

—— (1985 [1644]) *Principles of Philosophy* (trans. J. Cottingham, R. Stoothhoff and D. Murdoch), in *The Philosophical Writings of Descartes*, vol. I, Cambridge: Cambridge University Press.

—— (1985 [1647]) *Comments on a Certain Broadsheet* (trans. J. Cottingham, R. Stoothhoff and D. Murdoch), in *The Philosophical Writings of Descartes*, vol. I, Cambridge: Cambridge University Press.

—— (1985 [1664]) *Treatise on Man* (trans. J. Cottingham, R. Stoothhoff and D. Murdoch), in *The Philosophical Writings of Descartes*, vol. I, Cambridge: Cambridge University Press.

—— (1991) *Letters* (trans. J. Cottingham, R. Stoothhoff, D. Murdoch and A. Kenny), in *The Philosophical Writings of Descartes*, vol. III, Cambridge: Cambridge University Press.

Doney, W. (1967) 'Malebranche', *The Encyclopedia of Philosophy*, vol. 5, New York: Macmillan Publishing Co., Inc. and The Free Press.

Evans, G. (1982) *The Varieties of Reference* (J. McDowell (ed.)), Oxford: Clarendon Press.

Everson, S. (1991) 'The objective appearance of Pyrrhonism', in *Companions to Ancient Thought 2: Psychology* (S. Everson (ed.)), 121–148, Cambridge: Cambridge University Press.

Falkenstein, L. (1990) 'Berkeley and other minds', *History of Philosophy Quarterly*, 7(4), October.

Fodor, J. A. (1968) *Psychological Explanation: An Introduction to the Philosophy of Psychology*, New York: Random House.

—— (1994a) 'Fodor, J. A.', entry in S. Guttenplan (ed.) *A Companion to the Philosophy of Mind*, Blackwell's Companion to Philosophy Series, Oxford: Blackwell.

—— (1994b) *The Elm and the Expert: Mentalese and Its Semantics*, London: A Bradford Book, MIT Press.

Garber, D. (1986) '*In Semel Vitae*: the scientific background to Descartes' *Meditation*', in A. Rorty (ed.) *Essays on Descartes' Meditations*, Berkeley/Los Angeles/London: University of California Press.

Geach, P. (1957) *Mental Acts: Their Content and Their Objects*, London: Routledge & Kegan Paul.

Guttenplan, S. (ed.) (1994) *A Companion to the Philosophy of the Mind*, Oxford: Blackwell.

Hallie, P. P. (ed.) (1985) *Sextus Empiricus: Selections from the Major Writings on Scepticism, Man, & God* (trans. S. G. Etheridge), An Avatar Book, Hackett Publishing Co.

Hankinson, R. J. (1995) *The Sceptics*, The Arguments of the Philosophers Series, London: Routledge.

Henze, D. F. (1972) 'Descartes on other minds', *Studies in the Philosophy of Minds*, American Philosophical Quarterly Monograph Series, No. 6.

Hicks, D. (1932) *Berkeley*, London: Ernest Benn Limited.

Hume, D. (1975 [1748]) *An Enquiry concerning Human Understanding*, in *Enquiries concerning the Human Understanding and concerning the*

Principles of Morals (L. A. Selby-Bigge (ed.), third edition revised by P. H.
Nidditch), Oxford: Clarendon Press.

—— (1978 [1740]) *A Treatise of Human Nature* (L. A. Selby-Bigge (ed.), second
edition revised by P. H. Nidditch), Oxford: Clarendon Press.

Hyslop, A. (1995) *Other Minds*, Dordrecht/Boston/London: Kluwer Academic
Publishers.

Jessop, T. E. and Luce, A. A. (eds) (1948–57) *The Works of George Berkeley,
Bishop of Cloyne*, London.

Kant, I. (1950 [1783]) *Prolegomena to Any Future Metaphysics* (with an introduction by L. B. White), New York: Bobbs-Merrill.

Kripke, S. (1982) *Wittgenstein on Rules and Private Language*, Oxford: Basil
Blackwell.

Lehrer, T. (1989) *Thomas Reid*, London: Routledge.

Leibniz, G. W. (1981 [1765]) *New Essays on Human Understanding*, in *Leibniz:
New Essays on Human Understanding* (ed. and trans. P. Remnant and J.
Bennett), Cambridge: Cambridge University Press..

Locke, J. (1824 [1693]) *Some Thoughts concerning Education*, in *The Works of
John Locke*, vol. VIII, London: C. Baldwin, Printers.

—— (1824 [1706]) *An Examination of P. Malebranche's Opinion of seeing all
Things in God*, in *The Works of John Locke*, vol. VIII, London: C. Baldwin,
Printers.

—— (1975 [1689]) *An Essay concerning Human Understanding* (ed. P. H.
Nidditch), Oxford: Clarendon Press.

Luce, A. A. (1934) *Malebranche and Berkeley*, Oxford: Oxford University Press.

McCracken, C. J. (1983) *Malebranche and British Philosophy*, Oxford:
Clarendon Press.

McCulloch, G. (1995) *The Mind and Its World*, The Problems of Philosophy
Series, London: Routledge.

McDowell, J. (1986) 'Singular thought and the extent of inner space', in P. Petit
and J. McDowell (eds) *Subject, Thought, and Context*, Oxford: Clarendon
Press.

—— (1994) *Mind and World*, Cambridge, Massachusetts: Harvard University
Press.

McGinn, C. (1979) 'An *a priori* argument for realism', *Journal of Philosophy*,
LXXVI(3), March.

—— (1984) 'What is the problem of other minds?', *Aristotelian Society
Proceedings*, Supplementary vol. 58.

—— (1989) 'Can we solve the mind–body problem?', *Mind* 98.

McGinn, M. (unpublished) 'Pyrrhonism and the Cartesian Sceptic'.

—— (1997) *Wittgenstein and the Philosophical Investigations*, London:
Routledge.

McGuinness, B. (ed.) (1979) *Ludwig Wittgenstein and the Vienna Circle:
Conversations Recorded by Friedrich Waismann* (trans. J. Schulte and B.
McGuinness), Oxford: Basil Blackwell.

McNulty, T. M. (1970) 'Augustine's argument for the existence of other souls',
Modern Schoolmen, 48.

Malcolm, N. (1966a) 'Knowledge of other minds', in G. Pitcher (ed.) *Wittgenstein
the Philosophical Investigations*, London: Macmillan.

—— (1966b) 'Wittgenstein's *Philosophical Investigations*', in G. Pitcher (ed.) *Wittgenstein: Philosophical Investigations*, London: Macmillan.

Malebranche, N. (1980 [1688]) *Dialogues on Metaphysics and Religion* (trans. W. Doney), New York: Abaris Books.

—— (1997 [1674–1675]) *The Search After Truth* (translated and edited T. M. Lennon and P. J. Olscamp), Cambridge: Cambridge University Press.

Matthews, G. B. (1977) 'Consciousness and life', *Philosophy*, 52.

—— (1986) 'Descartes and the problem of other minds', in A. Rorty (ed.) *Essays on Descartes' Meditations*, Berkeley/Los Angeles/London: University of California Press.

—— (1992) *The Thought's Ego in Augustine and Descartes*, Ithaca and London: Cornell University Press.

Mill, J. S. (1872) *An Examination of Sir William Hamilton's Philosophy* (fourth edition), London: Longman, Green, Reader, and Dyer.

—— (1891) *A System of Logic*, London: Longmans, Green, and Co.

Montaigne, M. de (1987 [1576]) 'An apology for Raymond Sebond', in *The Complete Essays* (trans. M. A. Screech), Harmondsworth: Penguin Books.

Nadler, S. M. (1989) *Arnaud and the Cartesian philosophy of ideas*, Princeton: Princeton University Press.

—— (1992) *Malebranche and Ideas*, Oxford: Oxford University Press.

Nagel, T. (1970) *The Possibility of Altruism*, Princeton: Princeton University Press.

—— (1979a) 'What is it like to be a bat?', in *Mortal Questions*, Cambridge: Cambridge University Press.

—— (1979b) 'Panpsychism', in *Mortal Questions*, Cambridge: Cambridge University Press.

—— (1986) *The View From Nowhere*, Oxford: Oxford University Press.

—— (1993) 'Review of the *Rediscovery of Mind*', *The New York Review of Books*, 4 March.

Parks, D. (1972) *Complimentary Notions: A Critical Study of Berkeley's Theory of Concepts*, The Hague: Martinus Nijhoff.

Pears, D. (1987) *The False Prison: A Study of the Development of Wittgenstein's Philosophy*, vols I and II, Oxford: Clarendon Press.

Peacocke, C. (1985) 'Imagination, experience, and possibility: a Berkeleian view defended', in J. Foster and H. Robinson (eds) *Essays on Berkeley*, Oxford: Oxford University Press.

—— (1989) 'No resting place: a critical notice of *The View from Nowhere*, by Thomas Nagel', *The Philosophical Review*, XCVIII(1), January.

Peacocke, C. and McGinn, C. (1984) 'Consciousness and other minds', *Proceedings of the Aristotelian Society*, Supplementary vol. 58.

Pitcher, G. (1977) *Berkeley*, London: Routledge & Kegan Paul.

Plantinga, A. (1967) *God and Other Minds*, Ithaca and London: Cornell University Press.

Popkin, R. H. (1960) *The History of Scepticism from Erasmus to Descartes* (revised edition), The Netherlands: Royal VanGorcum Ltd.

Radner, D. (1978) *Malebranche: A Study of a Cartesian System*, The Netherlands: VanGorcum, Assen.

Reid, T. (1969 [1785]) *Essays on the Intellectual Powers of Man*, introduction by B. A. Brody, Cambridge, Massachusetts: MIT Press.

—— (1969 [1788]) *Essays on the Active Powers of Man*, B. Brody (ed.), Cambridge, Massachusetts: MIT Press.

—— (1983 [1764]) *An Inquiry into the Mind on the Principles of Common Sense*, in R. E. Beanblossom and K. Lehrer (eds) *Thomas Reid: Inquiry and Essays*, Indianapolis: Hackett Publishing Company, Inc.

Robinson, D. (1989) 'Thomas Reid's critique of Dugald Steward', *Journal of the History of Philosophy*, XXVII(3), July.

Russell, B. (1971) 'On the nature of acquaintance', in R. C. Marsh (ed.) *Logic and Knowledge: Essays 1901–1950*, New York: Capricorn Books.

Ryle, G. (1949) *The Concept of Mind*, Harmondsworth: Penguin Books.

Schlick, M. (1974 [1918]) *General Theory of Knowledge* (trans. A Blumberg), LaSalle, Illinois: Open Court.

—— (1979 [1926]) 'Experience, cognition and metaphysics', in *Moritz Schlick Philosophical Papers*, vol. II [1925–1936] (H. Mulder and B. F. B. van de Velde-Schlick (eds)), Dordrecht/Boston/London: D. Reidel Publishing Company.

—— (1979 [1936a]) 'Meaning and Verification', in *Moritz Schlick Philosophical Papers*, vol. II [1925–1936] (H. Mulder and B. F. B. van de Velde-Schlick (eds)), Dordrecht/Boston/London: D. Reidel Publishing Company.

—— (1979 [1936b]) 'The Universe and the Human Mind', in *Moritz Schlick Philosophical Papers*, vol. II [1925–1936] (H. Mulder and B. F. B. van de Velde-Schlick (eds)), Dordrecht/Boston/London: D. Reidel Publishing Company.

Searle, J. (1983) *Intentionality: An Essay in the Philosophy of Mind*, Cambridge: Cambridge University Press.

—— (1991) 'Reply to McDowell' and 'Reply to Stroud', in E. Lepore and R. Van Gulick (eds) *Searle and His Critics*, Oxford: Basil Blackwell.

—— (1992) *The Rediscovery of Mind*, London: A Bradford Book, MIT Press.

—— (1994a) 'Animal minds', in P. A. French, T. E. Uehling and H. K. Wettstein (eds) *Midwest Studies in Philosophy*, XIX, University of Notre Dame Press.

—— (1994b) 'J. R. Searle', entry in S. Guttenplan (ed.) *A Companion to the Philosophy of Mind*, Oxford: Blackwell.

Sextus Empiricus, *Outlines of Pyrrhonism*, partial translation in Annas and Barnes (1985) and Hallie (1985).

Sorabji, R. (1974) 'Body and soul in Aristotle', *Philosophy*, 49.

Strawson, G. (1994a) *Mental Reality*, London: A Bradford Book, MIT Press.

—— (1994b) 'The experiential and the non-experiential', in R. Warner and T. Szubka (eds) *The Mind–Body Problem*, Oxford: Blackwell.

Strawson, P. F. (1959) *Individuals: An Essay in Descriptive Metaphysics*, London: Methuen.

—— (1958) 'Review of Wittgenstein's *Philosophical Investigations*', in G. Pitcher (ed.) *Wittgenstein: The Philosophical Investigations*, London: Macmillan.

—— (1974) 'Self, mind and body', in *Freedom and Resentment and Other Essays*, London: Methuen.

—— (1992) *Analysis and Metaphysics*, Oxford: Oxford University Press.

—— (1998) 'Intellectual Autobiography', in L. E. Hahn (ed.) *The Philosophy of P. F. Strawson*, Chicago and LaSalle, Illinois: Open Court.

Bibliography

Striker, G. (1983) 'The Ten Tropes of Aenesidemus', in M. Burnyeat (ed.) *The Skeptical Tradition*, Berkeley/Los Angeles/London: University of California Press.

Stroud, B. (1968) 'Transcendental arguments', *Journal of Philosophy*, LXV(9), May.

—— (1983) 'Wittgenstein's philosophy of mind', in *Contemporary Philosophy. A new survey*, vol. 4: 319–341, Martinus Nijhoff Publishers.

—— (1984) *The Significance of Philosophical Scepticism*, Oxford: Clarendon Press.

—— (1991) 'The background of thought', in E. Lepore and R. Van Gulick (eds) *Searle and His Critics*, Oxford: Basil Blackwell.

—— (1994) 'Kantian argument, conceptual capacities, and invulnerability', in P. Parrini (ed.) *Kant and Contemporary Epistemology*, The Netherlands: Kluwer Academic Publishers.

—— (1999) 'The goal of transcendental arguments', in R. Stern (ed.) *Transcendental Arguments: problems and prospects*, Oxford: Clarendon Press.

Tsouna, V. (1998a) 'Remarks about other minds in Greek philosophy', *Phronesis* XLIII/3.

—— (1998b) *The Epistemology of the Cyrenaic School*, Cambridge: Cambridge University Press.

Urmson, J. (1982) *Berkeley*, Oxford: Oxford University Press.

Voss, S. (1994) 'Descartes: the end of anthropology', in J. Cottingham (ed.) *Reason, Will and Sensation: Studies in Descartes' Metaphysics*, Oxford: Clarendon Press.

Waismann, F. (1979 [1938]) Foreword, in H. Mulder and B. F. B. van de Velde-Schlick (eds) *Moritz Schlick Philosophical Papers*, vol. II [1925–1936], Dordrecht/Boston/London: D. Reidel Publishing Company.

Williams, B. (1978) *Descartes: The Project of Pure Enquiry*, Harmondsworth: Pelican Books.

—— (1981) 'The legacy of Greek philosophy', in I. Finley (ed.) *The Legacy of Greek Philosophy: A New Appraisal*, Oxford: Clarendon Press.

Williams, M. (1986) 'Descartes and the metaphysics of doubt', in A. Rorty (ed.) *Essays on Descartes' Meditations*, Berkeley/Los Angeles/London: University of California Press.

Winkler, H. P. (1989) *Berkeley: An Interpretation*, Oxford: Clarendon Press.

Wittgenstein, L. (1958) *The Blue and Brown Books*, New York: Harper Torchbooks.

—— (1961) *Tractatus Logico-Philosophicus* (trans. D. F. Pears and B. F. McGuinness), London: Routledge & Kegan Paul.

—— (1967) *Zettel* (trans. G. E. M. Anscombe), G. E. M. Anscombe and G. H. von Wright (eds), Oxford: Basil Blackwell.

—— (1968a) 'Notes for lectures on "Private Experience" and "Sense Data"', *Philosophical Review*, 77(3).

—— (1968b) *Philosophical Investigations* (trans. G. E. M. Anscombe), Oxford: Basil Blackwell.

—— (1975) *Philosophical Remarks* (trans. R. Hargreaves and R. White), R. Rhees (ed.), Oxford: Blackwell.

—— (1980a) *Remarks on the Philosophy of Psychology*, vol. I (trans. G. E. M. Anscombe), G. E. M. Anscombe and G. H. von Wright (eds), Oxford: Basil Blackwell.

—— (1980b) *Culture and Value* (trans. P. Winch), G. H. von Wright in collaboration with H. Nyman (eds), Oxford: Basil Blackwell.

—— (1992) *Last Writings on the Philosophy of Psychology: The Inner and the Outer*, vol. II (trans. C. G. Luckhardt and M. A. E. Ane), G. H. von Wright and H. Nyman (eds), Oxford: Basil Blackwell.

—— (1993) *Philosophical Occasions 1912–1915*, J. Klagge and A. Nordmann (eds), Indianapolis and Cambridge: Hackett Publishing Company.

Woolhouse, R. (1994) 'Locke's theory of knowledge', in V. Chappell (ed.) *The Cambridge Companion to Locke*, Cambridge: Cambridge University Press.

Index

Marquess of Newcastle 60, 61
material substance (matter) 10, 27,
    97, 120–3, 130–1, 159–60, 165
materialism 315 note 4, 316 note 18;
    agnostic materialism 276; in
    Berkeley 212; Lockean 132–3;
Matthews, G. 48, 49, 55, 295 notes 5
    and 14
memory 145, 150, 152, 258, 260, 314
    note 18
mendacity 192; *see also* deceit
Merleau-Ponty, M. xii
metaphysics 172, 177, 180, 187–9,
    231, 248, 315 note 1;
    metaphysically distinct 283;
    metaphysical foundation 64–5;
    metaphysical gap 34, 87, 111, 135,
    238, 252, 253, 255, 272, 284, 313
    note 61, 313 note 3; metaphysical
    underpinning 187; positive
    metaphysical results 251–3, 284
methodological solipsism 173, 177
Mill, J. S. 5–7, 11, 140, 164–72, 190,
    212, 306 note 90
modes 94
Molyneux's question 226–8
Moore, G. E. 185–6, 309 note 16
Morain, J. J. Dortous de 84
moral certainty 64–5, 67, 251, 292
    note 21
moral impossibility 67
More 60, 61, 66–7

Nagel, Thomas 17, 217, 254–73, 74,
    280, 285–6, 287
naturalism 179–80; *see also*
    biological naturalism
naturalized Cartesianism 276, 284
nature: of another mind 81–2, 211; of
    body 73, 76–8, 79; of mind 72–6,
    81–2, 118; our (human) nature
    154–7, 194–201, 213, 237–9,
    247–8, 253, 286
Newton, I. 142
non-deceiving God 65–6, 78
Norris, J. 299 note 45
notion 119–23, 134–5, 159–60

objective truths 34, versus subjective
    truths 34

occasionalism 129
O'Hanlon, H. F. 168, 170
opinion 10, 89–90, 105–10, 111, 212
opposing argument 22
ordinary life 1–2, 22, 24, 31, 37, 38,
    41, 104–5, 107–8, 211, 228–30,
    233–9, 280
ostensive definition 204–5

Peacocke, C. 260–1, 263
Pears, D. 186, 308 notes 9 and 14,
    309 note 18
perception 52–5, 62–4; in Arnaud
    85–7; in Berkeley 116; in Locke
    92–4 [internal perception
    (sensation) 92–3]; in Malebranche
    60, 69–71, 73, 77 [sensible
    perception 69; pure perception 69,
    72]; in Reid 147–8, 150–1, 160–2
person: our concept of a 233–9,
    247–8, 270, 311 note 23
phenomenological tradition xii, 291
    note 11
physicalism; *see* materialism
Pitcher, G. 302 note 17
Plantinga, A. 295 note 13
Popkin, R. 31–2, 33
positivist programme 177, 179
pre-Cartesian philosophy 13–15, 18,
    22–5, 55–7
pretence 192, 199
primary and secondary qualities 121
principle of coherence 242
principle of correspondence 242
principle of credulity 157
principle of veracity 157
private language argument 203–10,
    219
probability 107–10, 113, 125, 132–3,
    136, 139, 143, 170, 301 note 60
problem of unity 224–5, 228–30,
    252–3, 272, 274, 286, 287; *see also*
    univocity of meaning
pseudo problems 172
pseudo statements 175
psychological theory: Mill's 165–6,
    171–2
Pure Enquirer, Pure Enquiry 31, 41
pure perception 69–70, 72
Pyrrho of Elis 14, 23, 24